DEMOCRACY IN BOTSWANA

The Proceedings of a Symposium
held in Gaborone, 1 − 5 August 1988

Edited by
John Holm and Patrick Molutsi

THUTO KE THEBE

The Botswana Society
and the University of Botswana
Ohio University Press
Athens

Sponsored by
Friedrich Ebert Foundation
1989

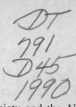

First published 1989

Ohio University Press
Scott Quadrangle
Athens, Ohio 45701

Cover illustration "The Kgotla"
Portion of a painting by Keemi Mosinyi.
The original work is in the collection of the National Museum, Monuments and Art Gallery, Gaborone.

Typeset in 9/11 pt Times Roman

Library of Congress CIP 89-16309

ISBN 0-8214-0943-3

CONTENTS

SECTION I
INTRODUCTION   1

1 Introduction by P.P. Molutsi and John D. Holm   1
1.1 The need for democracy   1
1.2 The democracy project and this symposium   2
1.3 The Botswana case   3
1.4 The future   4
1.5 Conclusion   7
    Endnotes   7

2 Welcoming remarks by Gobe Matenge   8

3 Welcoming remarks by Professor T. Tlou   9

4 Opening address by Hon. Mr P.S. Mmusi   11

5 Keynote speech: on democracy by Bernard Crick   13
5.1 Introduction   13
5.2 Democracy versus politics   13
5.3 Four usages of democracy   15
    The Greeks   15
    The Romans   16
    The French   16
    The Americans   17
    The present meanings   17
5.4 Three valid usages   18
5.5 Democracy as openness   19
5.6 Conclusion   21
    Endnotes   22
    Discussion   23

SECTION II
AFRICAN EXPERIENCES WITH DEMOCRACY   26

6 One-party rule in Tanzania and Uganda: how democratic?
   by Apolo Robin Nsibambi   26
6.1 Introduction   26
6.2 The rationale for a one-party system in Africa   26
6.3 One-party democracy in Tanzania   28
    Factors facilitating one-party democracy   28
    The problem of the mandate for one-party democracy in Tanzania 29

The problem of presidentialism in Tanzania   29
The problem of centralization of power and the one-party state   30
The problem of economic democracy and the one-party state   31
The failure of one-party democracy in Uganda   32
A one-party system without a mandate   33
The fall of Uganda's one-party system   33
Reestablishing civilian rule   34
6.4 Conclusion   35
    Endnotes   36

7 The experience of democracy in Senegal by Babcar Sine   **38**
7.1 Historical background   38
7.2 Senegal's new democracy   38
7.3 Conclusion   39
    Discussion   40

SECTION III
BOTSWANA'S HISTORICAL EXPERIENCE WITH DEMOCRACY   **42**

8 Tswana political tradition: how democratic? by L.D. Ngcongco   **42**
8.1 Introduction   42
8.2 The ward organization   43
8.3 Advisers to the chief   44
8.4 The kgotla meeting   45
8.5 Conclusion   47

9 Dikgotla, dikgosi and the protectorate administration
by P.T. Mgadla and A.C. Campbell   **48**
9.1 Introduction   48
9.2 The pre-colonial systems   48
9.3 Declaration of the protectorate: 1885-1891   49
9.4 Erosion of the powers of kgosi and kgotla: 1891-1920   50
9.5 The advent of advisory councils   52
9.6 The democratization of dikgosi   54
9.7 Conclusion   56
    Endnotes   56

10 The rights of minorities and subject peoples in Botswana: a historical
evaluation by K. Datta and A. Murray   **58**
10.1 Introduction   58
10.2 Commoners, foreigners and serfs   58
10.3 The concept of personal rights in Tswanadom   59
10.4 Economic rights   60
10.5 Political rights   64
10.6 Judicial rights   66

10.7	Social and cultural rights	68
10.8	Conclusion	68
	Endnotes	70
	Discussion	73

SECTION IV
CITIZEN PARTICIPATION IN DEMOCRATIC POLITICS   **75**

11 Do Batswana think and act as democrats? by Gloriah Somolekae   **75**
11.1	Introduction	75
11.2	Methodology	76
11.3	Knowledge of leadership	76
11.4	Knowledge of political issues	78
11.5	Attitudes towards political processes	79
	Elections	80
	Awareness of the differences between political parties	82
11.6	Commitment to the liberal democratic principles	84
	Multiparty competition	84
	Voting age	86
11.7	Conclusion	86
	Endnotes	86
	Discussion	87

SECTION V
THE SCHOOL SYSTEM AND DEMOCRACY   **89**

12 The school system: is it teaching democracy? by P.T. Ramatsui   **89**
12.1	Introduction	89
12.2	National commission on education	90
12.3	Implementing the commission's report	90
12.4	Conclusion	92
	Endnotes	92

13 The school system: shouldn't it be teaching democracy?
by G. Phoramo   **93**
13.1	Introduction	93
13.2	The theory of democracy	93
13.3	Education and democracy	94
13.4	Botswana's failure to educate for democracy	94
13.5	Toward a democratic school system for Botswana	95
13.6	Conclusion	97
	Endnotes	97
	Discussion	97

SECTION VI
CLASS, STATUS AND DEMOCRACY 99

14 The role a chief can play in Botswana's democracy
  by Chief Linchwe II 99
14.1 Introduction 99
14.2 The chief as moderator 99
14.3 The chief as a promoter of democracy 101
14.4 Conclusion 102

15 The ruling class and democracy in Botswana by P.P. Molutsi 103
15.1 Introduction 103
15.2 Historical background 104
15.3 The nature of the new ruling class 104
  Elected representatives 105
  Traditional authorities 106
  The bureaucracy 106
  The business and farming elites 106
  The expatriate community 107
  Political conflict with the ruling class 108
  The dominant position of the bureaucracy 108
  The chiefs 110
  The class orientation of government policy 111
15.4 Bureaucracy and democracy 113
15.5 The future 113
  Endnotes 114
  Discussion 115

SECTION VII
MEMBERS OF PARLIAMENT AND COUNCILLORS AS REPRESENTA-
TIVES OF THE PUBLIC 117

16 Problems of being an effective representative by the Hon. R. Sebego 117
16.1 Introduction 117
16.2 The job of being an elected representative 117
16.3 The problems of my constituency 119
16.4 Conclusion 120

17 Whose interests do Botswana's politicians represent?
  by P.P. Molutsi 120
17.1 Introduction 120
17.2 Social stratification in Botswana: an overview 121
17.3 Botswana's political elite: the first generation 122
  Occupation 122
  Politics 122
  Social status 123

17.4 The political elite in the post-colonial period   124
17.5 The changing character of the political elite   125
17.6 Who does this political elite represent?   126
17.7 Conclusion   129
      Endnotes   130
      Discussion   131

SECTION VIII
GROUPS POLITICS   **133**

18 Representation of cultural minorities in policy making
by Motsamai Keyecwe Mpho   **133**
18.1 Introduction   133
18.2 The true majority tribes   133
18.3 The tribal bias of the constitution   135
18.4 The power of the chiefs   136
18.5 Conclusion   137
      Endnotes   138

19 What should be the role of trade unions? by I. Mbonini   **139**
19.1 Introduction   139
19.2 A government policy for the workers   139
19.3 The role of labour in Botswana's democracy   140
19.4 Conclusion   141

SECTION IX
HOW EFFECTIVE ARE INTEREST GROUPS?   **142**

20 How effective are interest groups in representing their members?
by John D. Holm   **142**
20.1 Introduction   142
20.2 The climate of group politics   143
20.3 Linkages of organized groups to politics   145
20.4 Linkages of organized groups to the bureaucracy   147
      Interest group organization   148
      Full-time staff   149
      Leadership contacts   150
      Building alliances   150
      Public relations   151
      Summary   152
20.5 Conclusion   152
      Endnotes   152
      Discussion   154

SECTION X
POLITICAL RIGHTS   **156**

21 Group rights in Botswana by M.D. Mokama   **156**
21.1 Introduction   156
21.2 Group rights after independence   156
21.3 Gender rights   158
21.4 Conclusion   159
    Endnotes   159

22 The role of Botswana Police Force in democratic Botswana by the
Hon. P.H.K. Kedikilwe, MP   **160**
22.1 Introduction   160
22.2 The police as servants of the people   160
22.3 The police as enforcers of the law   161
22.4 Conclusion   162

23 Political rights in Botswana: regression or development?
by Athaliah Molokomme   **163**
23.1 Introduction   163
23.2 The right to citizenship   164
23.3 Freedom of assembly and association   165
23.4 Freedom of opinion and expression   167
23.5 Freedom of movement   170
23.6 Conclusion   172
    Endnotes   173
    Discussion   174

SECTION XI
ELECTIONS AND DEMOCRACY   **177**

24 Elections and democracy: how democratic is the process?
by L.E. Serema   **177**
24.1 Introduction   177
24.2 Supervisor of elections   177
24.3 The franchise   178
24.4 Qualification for election to the national assembly   179
24.5 Polling procedures   179
24.6 Conclusion   181

25 Election and democracy in Botswana by M.T. Motswagole   **182**
25.1 Introduction   182
25.2 The economic basis of bourgeois democracy   182
25.3 The electoral process in Botswana   183
    The electoral system   183
    The electoral constituencies   184
    Electoral procedures   185

Restrictions on voting rights   185
Restrictions on condidature   186
Campaign irregularities   186
Reporting election results   188
25.4 Conclusion   188
Endnotes   189

26 Elections and democracy in Botswana by John D. Holm   **189**
26.1 Introduction   189
26.2 Equality in voting   190
Malapportionment   190
Migrants   192
Registration   192
Voting age   193
Primaries   193
Possibilities for change   194
26.3 Freedom of political activity   195
Legal limits   195
Social discrimination   196
Financial limits   196
Possibilities for change   197
26.4 Elected representatives control policy making   197
Specially elected representatives   197
Civil service domination   198
Crossing the floor   198
Possibility of change   199
26.5 Conclusion   199
Endnotes   200
Discussion   201

SECTION XII
POLITICAL PARTIES   **203**

27 Political parties as facilitators of democracy in Botswana
by Rwendezi Nengwekhulu   **203**
27.1 Introduction   203
27.2 A brief history of political parties in Botswana   203
27.3 The two-party system and democracy in Botswana   205
27.4 The party organizations and democracy in Botswana   205
Political education   206
Training of political leadership   206
Class and gender discrimination   207
27.5 Conclusion   208
Endnotes   209
Discussion   209

SECTION XIII
THE KGOTLA AND FREEDOM SQUARE   **212**

28 The kgotla and the freedom square: one-way or two-way
   communication? by Kgosi Seepapitso IV   **212**
28.1 Introduction   212
28.2 Communication in freedom squares   213
28.3 Communication in the kgotla   214
28.4 Conclusion   215
     Endnotes   215

29 The kgotla and the freedom square: one-way or two-way
   communication? by Mogopodi H. Lekorwe   **216**
29.1 Introduction   216
29.2 The kgotla: its structure   217
29.3 The freedom square: its structure   220
29.4 Public perceptions of the kgotla and freedom square   224
     Political information   224
     Political influence   226
29.5 The kgotla and freedom square compared   227
29.6 Conclusion   228
     Endnotes   229
     Discussion   230

SECTION XIV
THE BUREAUCRACY   **231**

30 Civil service consultation: an examination of three cases
   by Seeiso D. Liphuko   **231**
30.1 Introduction   231
30.2 The consultation process   232
30.3 The self-help housing agency   232
30.4 TGLP consultation   233
30.5 The NCS consultation   235
30.6 Conclusion   236
     Endnotes   237

31 The bureaucracy and democracy in Botswana by Mpho G. Molomo 237
31.1 Introduction   237
31.2 The bureaucracy and the colonial state   238
31.3 Bureaucracy and participation in post-colonial Botswana   239
     TGLP   240
     SHHA   241
31.4 The Bureaucracy and elected officials   241
31.5 Conclusion   242
     Endnotes   242
     Discussion   243

SECTION XV
THE MEDIA   245

32 Government media as promoters of democracy: an examination
of three cases by L.M. Mpotokwane   245
32.1 Introduction   245
32.2 Government media as distributors of public opinion   245
32.3 Conclusion   247

33 The private press and democracy by Sandy Grant and Brian Egner 247
33.1 The legal background   247
33.2 The political background   247
33.3 Politicians versus journalists   248
33.4 Governmental press relations   249
33.5 The war mentality   250
33.6 The army and the press   250
33.7 Seeing justice done   251
33.8 Privately versus publicly owned media   252
33.9 Ownership, circulation and readership of the private press   252
33.10 Content of the papers   253
33.11 What has been achieved?   254
33.12 Could more have been achieved?   254
33.13 Costs and revenues of *The Daily News*   255
33.14 Costs and revenues of the private press   256
33.15 *The Daily News* versus the rest   256
33.16 Is this the government's media policy?   257
33.17 Is it all a sham?   257
33.18 The Botswana compromise   257
33.19 The proposed national press council   258
33.20 Legal support for the press   258
33.21 Training and logistical support   259
33.22 Financial assistance   259
33.23 Government support?   260
33.24 Conclusions and recommendations   260
      Endnotes   261
      Discussion   263

SECTION XVI
ROUNDTABLE OF OUTSIDE OBSERVERS   266

34 Democracy in Botswana: a Pan-African perspective
by Okwudiba Nnoli   266
34.1 Introduction   266
34.2 The meaning of democracy   267
34.3 The crisis of democracy in Africa: its causes   268

34.4 The future of democracy in Botswana   270
34.5 How to sustain the democratic condition of Botswana   272

35 On democracy and development in Botswana by Richard L. Sklar   **273**
35.1 Introduction   273
35.2 The danger of rent-seeking   273
35.3 Government accountability in Africa   276
35.4 Government accountability in Botswana   277
35.5 The intellectuals and marxism   277
35.6 Conclusion   278
     Endnotes   279

**36 Democracy in Botswana: an external assessment
by William Tordoff**   **280**
36.1 Introduction   280
36.2 Ideology and politics in Botswana   280
36.3 Botswana's democracy   281
36.4 The civil service: a new ruling class!   282
36.5 The future of democracy in Botswana   284
36.6 Some recommendations on democracy in local government   285
36.7 Conclusion   286
     Endnotes   287

37 Democracy in Botswana: an outsider's view by Bernhard Weimer   **289**
37.1 Introduction   289
37.2 On the meaning of democracy   289
37.3 The success of Botswana's democracy   289
37.4 Threats to Botswana's democracy   291
37.5 Some recommendations   292
37.6 Conclusion   292
     Discussion   293

**SECTION XVII
HOW CAN BOTSWANA IMPROVE ITS DEMOCRACY?**   **295**

A discussion of the symposium   **295**

SECTION I
INTRODUCTION

1 Introduction

P. P. Molutsi and John D. Holm

1.1 THE NEED FOR DEMOCRACY

Since the end of World War II, political analysts have written much about the causes, structures and consequences of different forms of government. At the core of this analysis has been a concern with the factors that give rise to fascism, totalitarianism, socialism and of course, democracy itself. Initially most analysis concerned the experience of Europe and North America. In the last decade, however, increasing interest has focused on the Third World.

At first most of the discussion of the Third World centred on Asia and Latin America, but in the last few years it has included Africa. Of particular importance has been the question of whether democracy can be established in Africa when these countries are also attempting to develop their economies and unite their ethnically diverse populations into cohesive nation states.[1]

Two considerations have been particularly important in directing our attention toward democracy in Africa. First, most of the liberal democracies inherited at the time of independence collapsed within a decade as they failed to maintain public order or a modicum of public support. They were followed by regimes which have turned out to be equally if not more ineffective, namely various versions of socialist and military rule. Some perceive the situation as so bad that the people are seeking ways to withdraw from the state.[2]

As a result, prominent commentators are pondering whether it might be better to return to some form of democracy as a means of bringing the state and the people more in contact with each other. Those who take this point of view, however, seek a different form of democracy than that established at independence. It would have to be modified to fit the realities of culture and economy in a given country and not be an attempt to mimic the parliamentary or presidential models of the industrialized West.

A second reason for turning to democracy comes from the economic realities of Africa. The socialist and military regimes which replaced the post-independence democracies have generally not had a good record in promoting economic development. Many have been outright disasters. The resulting economic stagnation and

1

deterioration of living conditions has been intricately related to the failure of political structures. The decline in living standards has turned many into political and economic refugees, and sometimes they have ended up as armed insurgents against existing governments.

These appalling conditions cannot be ignored. There is a need for political leaders to be kept in touch with the impact of their economic policies on their people, so that economic mistakes can be corrected before there is no option but wasteful military struggles. It is thus reasoned that a possible solution is to establish some form of democracy. Part of this search for viable democratic structures relevant to the Third World, and Africa in particular, must be an examination of those countries which have for a prolonged period of time been able to maintain one or more institutions of what Sklar refers to as 'accountability'.[3] The critical thing to be studied is not only the structures which have been created but also the processes by which these structures have been developed and modified, for in the end each country must develop its own institutions of democracy.

1.2 THE DEMOCRACY PROJECT AND THIS SYMPOSIUM

Most of the literature on democracy in the Third World which has emerged in recent years has emphasized a comparative approach. That is discussion focuses on the experience of a number of countries with particular forms of accountability such as elections or protection of political rights. On the basis of a series of comparisons a series of generalizations are deduced as to the particular conditions required for the existence of democratic structures.

While not contesting the value of this approach, we would contend that much more needs to be done in terms of studying individual cases in depth. The existing literature has little to say about such questions as: Is there any link institutionally, culturally or even ideologically between a country's traditional political system and the kinds of mechanisms of popular control which are employed? Are population size or ethnic homogeneity contributory factors to the rise and fall of democracy? Is it possible for economic planning processes to be rendered accountable to various interest groupings in a nation, including especially grass roots community organizations?

Pursuant to this necessity to have a better grasp of the factors accounting for the success and failure of democratic structures in Africa, nine faculty from different departments of the University of Botswana collaborated for over a year in a study of democracy in Botswana with Professor John Holm of Cleveland State University in the United States.

The Democracy Project, as it was called, started in July, 1987 and completed its initial field work in August, 1988 with a five day symposium on democracy. The symposium brought together members of the project faculty with various interested politicians, civil servants and journalists to discuss Botswana's experience with democracy since independence.

The idea of the symposium was twofold. The primary objective was to provoke a discussion among politicians and informed political observers on the successes and failures of Botswana's democracy. The researchers from the university provided a summary of some of the important facts and presented some analyses as to the extent of popular control which has been achieved. The various practitioners contributed personal statements with regard to their experience with particular democratic structures. Then both groups joined with the public in a general discussion of each topic.

We expected that the debate at the symposium would set in motion discussion about ways in which Botswana's democracy might be improved. Those of us on the Democracy Project were struck by the fact that while the Government of Botswana has for over two decades made impressive attempts to plan the development of the economy, almost nothing had been done to support similar thinking as to Botswana's polity. We hoped that the symposium would engage in at least some discussion of possible changes which might be made to entrench and improve democratic practice and that participants would leave with a desire to continue to think in this vein in the future. This volume is intended in part to serve as an encouragement to the people of Botswana as a whole to join in thinking about the future of democracy in their country.

Our hope was that the research of the Democracy Project staff and the discussion at the Symposium on Democracy in Botswana would also be of interest to politicians and political commentators in other parts of the continent who are interested in the development of democratic practices in their countries. If nothing else we thought that the discussion which is presented in this volume might both serve as an inspiration for others to talk about the development of democratic institutions and provide a model of some of the types of issues which could be discussed.

Both political and economic successes have made Botswana a showcase deserving serious attention from all quarters. However, too many praise songs, especially by outsiders, can lead to complacency on the part of the citizens and leaders of Botswana. This is not to say that praise should be withheld where it is appropriate. On the contrary, we understand that praise is a form of encouragement and that it is psychologically useful for more effort in the future.

Nevertheless, Batswana should understand that improvement of their government is much more important than receiving praise. There are many likely problems ahead. The litmus test of the success of Botswana's political system lies in building structure of accountability which insure that its leaders will be responsive to citizen concerns.

1.3 THE BOTSWANA CASE

Modern Botswana democracy currently rests on a fragile economic base. Economically the country is overwhelmingly dependent on the export of one product, diamonds. The income derived from this export has been rising for over 15 years but now appears to be stabilizing, thus meaning that government must begin planning in terms of a stable rather than increasing revenue. The agricultural sector on which most of people eke out a living still is not promising anything potentially different from the semi- subsistence output of the past. Meanwhile no dramatic new mineral developments are in the pipeline. The manufacturing industry, to which government has directed much investment over the last eight years, is growing at a snail's pace, if at all. In sum, there is little prospect of many more years of rapid economic growth. Yet, population numbers continue to climb at a high rate and unemployment, especially among the youth, has reached very high levels, which if not checked will alienate those who went to school on the expectation that they could obtain a job when they graduated.

The political context in which democracy is developing by no means assures that government will be able to deal with these economic problems. To be sure, there are certain factors which will help. For the most part Botswana is culturally homogeneous. The government and opposition leaders have a certain respect for each other. The courts have been able to resolve a few political disputes in a manner which has been generally impartial and acceptable to all sides. The elections themselves have been conducted, with a very few exceptions, in a most fair and open manner.

However, democracy is a complex form of government which calls for a certain amount of self-control and good judgement on the part of all participants. As if this were not enough, Botswana's powerful neighbour to the south is seeking to destabilize the region and cannot but be embarrassed by a multiracial democracy effectively coping with many of its problems of development. Unfortunately, Botswana must out of necessity deal with South Africa on a daily basis. It is therefore essential that the principles of Botswana's democracy be particularly well anchored in the hearts, minds and behaviour of its people.

1.4 THE FUTURE

The papers and discussion in this volume are encouraging about the chances for the continuation and development of Botswana's democracy, but they by no means reflect a complacent attitude. A whole series of issues of democratic development are raised which will be most difficult to resolve. Botswana's democracy is both succeeding and being challenged.

This duality of success and challenge is apparent from the very beginning of the symposium. Professor Crick's keynote speech emphasizes that the essence of democracy is openness, but that those in power are always looking for ways to limit public examination of their policies. The discussion which follows on African one-party systems illustrates this dilemma with respect to several states. Professors Nsibambi and Sine focus on the longing in Tanzania, Uganda, and Senegal to establish some form of popular control over government while each confronts incredible difficulties in moving toward this goal.

Next comes an examination Botswana's historical experience with democratic practice. Together the three papers reflect a combination of optimism and pessimism. Professor Ngcongco stresses the extent to which the traditional Tswana polity allowed for decentralization of decision making to the grass roots and forced the chief and his headmen to be accountable to their subjects. In contrast, Drs Murray and Datta see traditional Tswana politics as involving exclusion of minorities that has continued up to the present, particularly in regard to the Basarwa. Mgadla and Campbell take a more ambivalent position, pointing out that colonialism both reinforced the autocratic tradition of the chieftaincy and encouraged popular dissent against such forms of authority.

Ms Somolekae presents an overview of some public attitudes toward democracy derived from the Democracy Project's mass survey. On the one hand, she finds most of the population to be little informed of much besides the names of their councillors and members of parliament and lacking a clear commitment to democratic values. On the other hand, she shows that formal education is bringing a decided improvement in regard to both level of political knowledge and support for democratic procedures.

While both Messrs Ramatusi and Phoroano agree that the educational system must promote democracy, they disagreed on how much has thus far been accomplished. The former emphasizes that the Ministry of Education has done much to update its curriculum so that the students are instructed about the democratic aspects of government. Mr Phoroano on the other hand stresses that the process of education has remained in the authoritarian mould established during the colonial period with neither the students, their parents or the teachers having much say in the development of a new system.

The papers in the sections on social stratification and representation complement each other. Dr Molutsi's analysis of the ruling class in Botswana stresses the dominating role which top civil servants play in government policy making. In contrast, the other three papers suggest that this situation need not continue. Kgosi (chief) Linchwe shows that a chief can mobilize his people to change policies at the local level. Dr Molutsi himself points out that MPs are beginning to challenge the bureaucracy in policy terms. Assistant Minister Sebego emphasizes the need for the MP to mobilize his party and his constituency behind him if he is to have an impact on government officials.

The discussion of group participation in Botswana's politics focuses on both constraints and the potential for improvement. Mr Mpho contends that the eight dominant tribes have attempted to exclude the various minority tribes from having their own representation, particularly in the House of Chiefs, however, he pictures the minorities as becoming increasingly aware of the discrimination they suffer. Mr Mbonini complains of the controls which government imposes on trade unions in representing their members both politically and economically, but he emphasizes the readiness of the unions to speak for the workers. Dr Holm stresses that Tswana political culture has heretofore discouraged the participation of organized economic groups in politics but that formal education is fast reversing this attitude.

The papers on political rights generally indicate that the Botswana Constitution functions to constrain the state from infringing on the freedom of its citizens, however there is much debate between Attorney General Mokama and Ms Molokomme as to the state's primary responsibility. The Attorney General rejects the idea that the state should be responsible for group rights, whether these are defined in terms of gender or tribe. Ms Molokomme on the other hand sees a need for the state to make an effort to extend all rights of citizenship to women and to provide more protection for dissident groups in terms of freedom of speech and movement. Minister of Presidential Affairs Kedikilwe ends this section with a call for the Police to mobilize the public to participate in the law enforcement process.

The discussion of the role of elections in Botswana focuses on two separate concerns. On the one hand, Mr Serema points out that the elections are generally open and fairly administered. Mr Motswagole and Dr Holm, on the other hand, indicate that in various ways the rules favour certain groups and disadvantage others. While Dr Holm sees these problems as a natural part of the evolution of a democratic system, Mr Motswagole fears that a representative system may be unalterably biased toward the bourgeoisie.

In the next section on political parties, Mr Nengwekhulu reinforces Motswagole's concern with respect to the political parties. He contends that the present party leadership is not educating the public on how to use the parties to make government respond to their problems.

The problem of enhancing direct public influence over government is the primary concern of the two papers on the freedom square and the kgotla. Kgosi Seepapitso asserts that the freedom square cannot expand citizen control because it lacks the civility necessary for serious community discussion, but he sees the rules of the kgotla as facilitating a reasoned dialogue which leads to two-way communication, if the politicians will only listen. Mr Lekorwe finds both fora subject to substantial manipulation by political and government leaders, but that at least the freedom square does sometimes mobilize the people's concerns on national issues.

Mr Likphuko and Dr Molomo consider the extent to which the government bureaucracy responds to public opinion. The former believes it does respond through use of both external and internal consultation processes. Dr Molomo sees these processes as thus far doing little more than giving the appearance that government is listening.

The question of the proper role for government and private media in Botswana's democracy is a matter of considerable debate. Mr Mpotokwane perceives the government media as meeting most of the public's democratic needs by providing public affairs information and acting as a forum through which free speech can be exercised. Messrs. Grant and Egner contend that this role can only be performed effectively by the private media, which they perceive to be fulfilling its role intermittently because of government pressure and lack of funds.

Four foreign discussants weave the foregoing arguments into several broader perspectives. Professor Nnoli argues that until African countries develop an extensive market economy the basis for a sustained democracy does not exist, even in the case of Botswana. Professor Weimer perceives that Botswana must concentrate on increasing the openness described by Crick if democracy is to survive. Professor Tordoff thinks maintenance of democracy in Botswana requires the persistence of the economic redistribution policies of the central government and enhancement of the staff and powers of the local councils. Professor Sklar calls for Botswana to sustain and build forms of institutional accountability which will mandate that its leaders must answer to others for their conduct.

1.5 CONCLUSION

In sum all the various papers in this volume singly or in combination point to the developmental character of democracy in Botswana. Moreover, there is no consensus as to what should be done. The only solution is for those who are concerned about this development to continue to debate the problems and the solutions as the authors of the papers in this symposium do and as various members of the audience also do in the subsequent discussions. Slowly a consensus will emerge on particular courses of action.

A more positive note for the future is that more young and better educated people are showing increasing interest in politics. Also, the next election could well see close to twenty-five per cent of current members of parliament replaced by new faces, a number of them coming from the civil service and the private sector. These new recruits are likely to understand and be better defenders of democracy than their predecessors. However, they can only succeed if they are careful to build Botswana's democracy on the foundations of her past.

ENDNOTES

1   In the last few years four volumes have been published alone on democracy in Africa. They are Dov Ronen, ed., *Democracy and Pluralism in Africa* (Boulder, CO: Lynne Rienner Publishers, 1986); Fred M. Hayward, *Elections in Independent Africa* (Boulder, CO: Westview Press, 1987); Walter O. Oyugi, E. S. Atieno Odhiambo, Michael Chege and Afrifa K. Gitonga, *Democratic Theory and Practice in Africa* (Portsmouth: NH: Heinemann, 1988); and Larry Diamond, Juan J. Linz, and Seymour Martin Lipset, *Democracy in Developing Countries* vol, II (*Africa*) (Boulder, CO: Lynne Rienner Publishers, 1988).

2   See for instance, Goran Hyden, *Beyond Ujamaa in Tanzania: Underdevelopment and the Uncaptured Peasantry* (Los Angeles: University of California Press, 1980).

3   Richard Sklar, *Developmental Democracy*, a paper prepared for delivery at the 1985 Annual Meeting of the American Political Science Association, New Orleans Hilton, August 29 to September 1.

2 Welcoming remarks

Gobe Matenge, Chairman of the Botswana Society

This national conference is not convened at the request of the Botswana Government. It was not brought about as a result of any resolution of the National Assembly. No local political party has been involved in its organization; nor is it the brainchild of any well-meaning foreign foundation, interested in strengthening democracy on this continent.

This conference has two sponsors. They are both local entities. Neither is formally associated in any way with political institutions in this country. The two sponsors are the University of Botswana and the Botswana Society, both politically powerless, both non-partisan, both operating outside the formal democratic process.

It is entirely appropriate that these two indigenous institutions, the one created by law and the other voluntarily by a diverse group of socially concerned individuals who care about the future of this country, should take the initiative in promoting this symposium. By the very act of doing so, the university and the Botswana Society are enforcing one of the most fundamentally important preconditions for democracy namely, that there should be continuous public debate on issues of national importance, sponsored by non-political institutions, without fear of censure or recrimination.

Once the idea of holding such a symposium had been agreed upon, it was necessary to seek financial assistance to ensure that it could take place. This assistance came from Friederich Ebert Foundation. We are extremely grateful for it, because, without this very generous donation we could not have held the symposium at all. I should also mention that we have received help from the United Kingdom and the United States governments which have made possible the presence of some of our valued participants from overseas.

Democracy is not a function of any particular system of government. It does not depend on the existence of two or more established political parties. The kgotla tradition does not guarantee its survival. Democracy will live in Botswana only as long as freedom of public debate is cherished, as long as bodies like the university and the Botswana Society are free to promote such debate. We are not lobbying groups. We have no political ideology. Our sole objective in organizing this symposium is to provide a structured forum in which the role of democracy, its importance, its cultural roots, its future, and its prospects of survival can be discussed, openly and freely.

There is another sense in which it is wholly appropriate that the University of Botswana and the Botswana Society should co-sponsor this symposium. The university symbolizes the future. Its graduates and undergraduates hold in their hands the future of this country. Whether or not democracy and respect for human rights continue to be upheld in Botswana depends on them.

By contrast, the average age of members of the Botswana Society, myself included, must be close to forty-five. A number of us who belong to the society played some role in the development of the pre- and post-independence institutions through which democratic principles were entrenched throughout this society. We still cherish those principles. But our time is passing. We must join hands with the next generation to whom the mantle of leadership is now passing. The university and the Botswana Society share an interest in the future of freedom in this country. Democracy to both of us is synonymous with freedom.

Having said that, however, I feel that the association between the university and our society should become the forerunner of a similar close association between the university and public at large. The university as the apex of Botswana's cultural and educational institutions has an obligation to involve and enlighten the whole community. One way in which such an obligation can be discharged is by using the university's human and physical resources as a forum for public debate and discussion to the greatest practical extent in order that the university's unique position in the country can benefit an ever greater portion of the national community.

3 Welcoming remarks

Professor T. Tlou, Vice-Chancellor of University of Botswana

A few years ago, an interdisciplinary group of staff from the University of Botswana's Departments of History, Law, Sociology, Political and Administrative Studies teamed together with Professor John Holm of Cleveland State University in the United States of America to conceive of the idea of a project which came to be referred to as the *University of Botswana Democracy Project*. Together they drew up research proposals to give effect to their idea and attracted P65,000 from various donors. Their research effort was coordinated by Professor Holm, and the entire project was under the supervision of Professor Peter Takirambudde, the Dean of Social Sciences at the University of Botswana.

The Democracy Project is, in fact, the latest stage of a process that started with the study of the 1974 elections. That study set a tradition whereby the university studied every subsequent election. In contrast with these studies, the Democracy Project is more broadly based, encompassing, or shall I say attempting to encompass, a wide spectrum of what one might call the elements of democracy.

The Democracy Project stems from a firm belief that Botswana has a functioning democratic system worthy of study in all its aspects. Only by knowing the strengths and weakness of any political system can nations employ appropriate measures to further strengthen and to preserve the value of government to the people.

In carrying out their research members of the Democracy Project interviewed persons involved at various levels of Botswana politics. A general mass survey sampled 1 297 citizens. Various types of politicians and government officals were also interviewed, including 100 councillors, 60 civil servants and almost all the members of both houses of parliament. The historians collected oral histories on the evolution of the kgotla, the traiditional community meeting of the Tswana tribes, and the chieftaincy during the colonial period. Needless to say the members of the project also did extensive archival work. The Democracy Project concentrated their inquiries on the Kgatleng, Kweneng, Southern District and Gaborone. While other parts of the country are equally important, the project staff focused on these four areas because each in some respect was unique but representative of other areas as well.

Our faculty associated with the Democracy Project were eager to hold this symposium so that they might interact with the larger community regarding both the validity of their initial conclusions and some ideas they have on the further development and consolidation of democracy in Botswana. Because of limitations of time the analyses of project staff are necessarily condensed and some of the papers may give a more critical perspective than is the case with the overall views of the researchers. It was felt that it is more important to concentrate on the problems which exist rather than take too much time discussing Botswana's acknowledged successes as a democratic state.

Democracy Project staff are each entirely responsible for the analysis and conclusions in his or her paper. None claim that their conclusions provide the final word on this important subject. Rather they collectively invite this gathering to place their papers under your intellectual microscopes to identify the problems you see.

I want to express the University of Boswana's profound gratitude to the several donors who handsomely funded the Democracy Project: the Swedish International Development Agency, the Social Sciences Research Council of New York, the Human Rights Fund of the USA State Department, and Cleveland State University. Our university made its contribution through the efforts of its scholars and also gave support in kind. This was truly a joint effort, a brilliant testimony to the efficacy of collaborative research across national frontiers. May I also express the indebtedness of the Democracy Project to the many people in Botswana who freely gave of their time to be interviewed. Many of these persons are in this audience. *Le ka Moso bagaetsho!*

Last but not least I would like to pay special tribute to the Botswana Society which under the guidance of its very able chairman, Mr Gobe Matenge, agreed to organize this conference in collaboration with us. I must hasten to add that this is not the first, nor shall it be the last, time when the university will cooperate with the Botswana society on such intellectual ventures. We are extremely grateful to the society for the hand of friendship they continue to extend to us.

In closing let me quote from Alexis de Tocqueville, that brilliant French historian, political scientist and politician who in his seminar *Democracy in America* gave a perceptive comment on the concept of democracy which is still very relevant today.

It is our way of using "democracy" and "democratic" government that brings about the greatest confusion. Unless these words are clearly defined and their

10

definitions agreed upon, people will live in an inextricable confusion of ideas, much to the advantage of demagogues and despots.

Let us hope that at least some of the confusion where it exists will be removed by this symposium.

4 Opening address

His honourable Mr P. S. Mmusi, Vice-President of the Republic of Botswana and President of the Botswana Society

Mr Chairman, ladies and gentlemen. In my capacity as the President of the Botswana Society, I wish to extend a very warm welcome to all of you who have come to our 9th national symposium. I particularly greet those of you who have taken the time and trouble to come and contribute to the symposium from places outside Gaborone, from other parts of Botswana and from Africa, Europe and North America.

Our society has now been in existence for almost twenty years. We had our first national symposium in 1971 on rural development. Since then our symposia have ranged over other subjects of vital national interest — sustained production from semi-arid lands, the Okavango Delta, drought, settlement, education, research, culture and now democracy. In each case we have brought together the expertise and public participation to better understand present and past conditions and to generate informed discussion about future prospects.

For the next four days, we invite everyone to participate in the symposium by reading and listening to the contributions of our speakers, and by contributing freely to the discussion of ideas — in the best traditions of democracy based on open but well informed debate.

The subject of our symposium, democracy and the constitutionalism which sustains it, is a subject of concern throughout the world today. I am thinking of the debates over Perestroika in Socialist countries and the bi-centennial of England's so-called Glorious Revolution. I am also thinking of the return to some kind of democracy during the last dozen years in a number of countries - in Europe, Latin America, Asia, and Africa. Even apartheid has begun, though only begun, to crumble. Meanwhile there is no cause for complacency in more traditionally democratic societies, where civil liberties are potentially under threat by computers controlled by the state and large corporate interests.

All this you will no doubt bear in mind in the course of our symposium, while your main concern will be Botswana. You will no doubt ask if, how and why we are a democracy, as well as how we can sustain or improve the situation. I am sure the debate will cover many different definitions and alternative attributes of democra-

11

cy in Botswana over the next few days. I would simply ask you also to bare in mind what all this means for the everyday lives, health and happiness of Batswana in all parts of the country.

We are very much aware that democracy in any nation is a fragile flower, however deep its roots. It is a flower that has to be constantly nurtured to thrive and spread. The democratic achievements of any country, including Botswana, are limited by the level of development in general. The rights of free speech and participation in the political process are enhanced by improved literacy and general well being. That is why, if I may for a moment assume my role as Minister of Finance and Development Planning and Vice President of the Republic, my government is committed to development as well as democracy - as two faces of the same coin.

In essence, this symposium celebrates the coming of age of our democracy, since we achieved our independence a little more than 21 years ago. We flatter ourselves that we have now reached that stage of maturity where our democracy can be evaluated, criticized, challenged, dissected, and even denied by you.

Living as we do in southern Africa, we are under no delusion that our democracy is simply a natural and inevitable state. Democracy means choice. What democracy we have is because we have chosen a democratic path. We may well have drawn from two very different constitutional traditions in which democracy was inherent -- the Setswana tradition of consultation in kgotla and what is usually called the Westminster model. But we do not delude ourselves that either tradition, kgotla or Westminster, and similar traditions, all have autocratic tendencies which have to be fought against.

The price of democracy is constant vigilance, on the part of all individuals, to allow for choice of the people, by the people and for the people in our changing circumstances. In this country, as you are aware, we maintain a multiparty parliamentary system in which we think such vigilance is best realized. An opposition or oppositions keeps a government on its toes.

I would be defeating the purpose of this symposium to carry on speaking any longer — telling you what to say or think. Such are the potentials for autocracy over democracy even in this August gathering! It is therefore my pleasant duty to declare the proceedings of this symposium to be open and to wish you godspeed in our deliberations. May those deliberations be fruitful, and may they prove to be a trumpet call that will arouse the sleeping elements of democracy not only in this country but across our borders.

5 Keynote speech: on democracy

Bernard Crick

5.1 INTRODUCTION

We are gathered to consider the state of democracy in Botswana. You have asked me to discuss 'democracy' in general. But I must confess that I have come to learn not to preach. I know too little about Africa. I have only been to Africa once before, teaching a term at the University of Legon in Ghana just after the fall of Nkrumah at the time of the constitutional convention. I was then asked to give a public lecture on Parliamentary Democracy. I had just written a book on the reform of the British Parliament. It was a public lecture so important that the Vice Chancellor of the University, Alex Kwapong, was in the chair.

Rashly, I commented on the draft of the new constitution which was intended, as far as I could see, not to make good government possible so much as to make the return of Nkrumah impossible, even if a majority wanted him. The draft of the new constitution was full of clauses allowing the Lord Chief Justice (who was chairman of the convention) to declare laws unconstitutional, even the 'Bills authorizing expenditure introduced by private members' had to have a certificate from the Lord Chief Justice that they were constitutional. I asked rhetorically, 'who do they think the Lord Chief Justice is, God?' and from the back of the hall a loud merry Ghanaian student voice shouted, 'No, Alex's cousin'. My lecture was destroyed.

I will not make the same mistake again. My mother taught me as a proverb 'A little learning is a dangerous thing. Drink deep or taste not the Pierian spring . . .' All I will discuss is the concept and ideal of democracy; I must leave to others why it exists and in what form it works in Botswana.

I'm not unreservedly in favour of democracy. It depends what one means by it, and even then it may depend on how much is possible and what kind of circumstances. For instance, the great French political thinker of the nineteenth century, Alexis de Tocqueville, as well as his English friend John Stuart Mill, both warned against 'the tyranny of the majority': a majority can be as intolerant as a king, a tyrant or an oligarchy.

5.2 DEMOCRACY VERSUS POLITICS

I look at the definitions of types of democracy attached to our conference programme by Professor Holm. I note particularly the description of 'African democracy', that is consultation between tribal elders or headmen before decisions are made. This is certainly something very different from kingship, despotism or autocracy. But

13

personally I have difficulty recognizing mere consultation as democracy; but I see it as the essence of *politics*.

In traditional African society decisions, we are told, were made by debate between the elders, or more realistically between all those whose cooperation would be needed for a decision actually to be carried out. In my book *In Defense of Politics* I defined politics as the conciliation of differing interests, whether those interests are seen as values or material interests. I argued that all but the most small and primitive societies have differing interests and values, and that it is the mark of civilization to attempt to conciliate them by political institutions - like assemblies of elections, not to impose the will of any one group upon the others, by force or threat, even of a majority. I argued that if democracy is simply conceived as a majority power, it can threaten both individual and group rights.[1]

To my mind politics is prior to democracy both historically and logically. Long before the majority of members of any society were even consulted, some societies, always a minority, made their decisions by **open** and **public** debate among a ruling elite; others made their decisions privately and secretly in the name of a chief, king or emperor - even if often in fact after private discussion with councillors, great land owners and famous warriors. The distinction between public and private debate is of fundamental importance, whether or not the majority are allowed to join in that debate or even positively encouraged to do so. Some political regimes were more or less democratic, and some not democratic at all. Pericles, in his famous oration in Ancient Greece flatters his followers about how different Athenians were from the autocratic and militaristic Spartans:

> Let me say that our system of government does not copy the institutions of our neighbours. It is more the case of our being a model to others, than of our imitating anyone else. Our constitution is called a democracy because power is in the hands not of a minority but of the whole people. When it is a question of settling private disputes, everyone is equal before the law; when it is a question of putting one person before another in positions of public responsibility, what counts is not membership of a particular class, but the actual ability which the man possesses. No one, so long as he has it in him to be of service to the state, is kept in political obscurity because of poverty.
>
> Here each individual is interested not only in his own affairs but in the affairs of the state as well: even those who are mostly occupied with their own business are extremely well-informed on general politics - this is a peculiarity of ours: we do not say that a man who takes no interest in politics is a man who minds his own business: we say that he has no business here at all. We Athenians, in our own persons, take our decisions on policy or submit them to proper discussions: for we do not think that there is an incompatibility between words and deeds; the worst thing is to rush into action before the consequences have been properly debated.[2]

Historians believe that at the most he can have been addressing some forty to fifty thousand citizens among a population of probably ninety to a hundred thou-

14

sand males of whom about a quarter were slaves; and excluding entirely, of course, women. Modern historians also speak of Pericles himself as a tyrant or else a demagogue - a stirrer and user of the masses, not someone prone to sharing power or even to being answered back effectively: he was a man who in his oratory articulated the democratic ideal superbly and for the ages, but who did not always practise what he preached. 'In what was nominally a democracy,' said Thucydides, 'power was really in the hands of the first citizen.'[3]

'Democracy' is a relative term. In my little book *In Defense of Politics* I had a chapter titled, 'In Defense of Politics Against Democracy'. I was rude enough to say that 'democracy' can sometimes be too promiscuous to make a good friend. She is everyone's mistress, and yet somehow retains her magic even when a lover sees that her favours are being shared by so many others. However she behaves, she has such a good name. Egypt under Nasser called itself officially, that is the Constitution, 'Presidential Democracy'. Pakistan is still a 'Basic Democracy'. Sukarno's Indonesia was, of course, a 'Guided Democracy'. General Franco called Spain 'Organic Democracy'. General Stroessner in Paraguay spoke frankly of 'Selective Democracy'. Trujillo grandly designated his tyranny in Dominica 'neo-democracy'. Castro, following East European practice, calls his Cuba, 'A Peoples' Democracy'. Ayattolah Houmani speaks of 'Islamic Fundamental Democracy', and my country and your country are doubtless 'true' or 'real democracies'.[4]

5.3 FOUR USAGES OF DEMOCRACY

Democracy has no one true meaning. But the term is not meaningless, however much it is exploited. It has different meanings, but historically only a limited number are of real importance. We can only sensibly use it in some established tradition of usage. Historically there have been four broad usages. So the first thing is to examine these traditions. We should draw distinctions before we attempt any synthesis, for synthesis attempted prematurely is apt to be mere empty platitude.

The Greeks

The first broad usage is found in the Ancient Greeks, in Plato's attack on democracy and in Aristotle's highly qualified defence: democracy is simply *demos* (the mob, the many) *kracia* (rule). Plato attacked democracy as being the rule of the many, the poor and the ignorant over - what should be, he thought - the rule of the few as the wise and the disinterested. His fundamental distinction was between knowledge and opinion: democracy is thus the rule of mere opinion.

Aristotle tempered this view of his own teacher severely. A democratic constitution was to him also the rule of the many, usually the poor; but he pointed out that an aristocratic (*aristoi* meaning wisdom) constitution was seldom, in practice, the rule of the wise, but more often rule by the rich (plutocracy). To Aristotle a democratic constitution was a lesser evil than a plutocratic or a corrupt aristocratic one, but

15

the best form of government was not unqualified democracy. Rather it was a blending of the democratic principle of consent with the aristocratic principles of experience, skill and wisdom. All are fit to choose, he argued, but not all are fit to serve in public office. So democracy to Aristotle was a necessary element in just and stable government, but it was not an unqualified good. The democratic fallacy, he said, is to believe 'that because men are equal in some thing, they are equal in all'. The whole ship's company must decide the purpose and general direction of a voyage, but few are competent to navigate.

The Romans

The second usage is found in the Ancient Romans, in Machiavelli's great *Discourses* of the sixteenth century and in the seventeenth century English and Dutch republicans: that good government was mixed government, just as in Aristotle's theories, but that the democratic popular element, when it did not run out of control, actually gave **greater power** to a state. The argument was as much military as moral. The moral argument is more famous: that both Roman paganism and Protestantism shared a view of man as an active individual, a maker and shaper of things, not a patient and passive acceptor of the existing order of society. Life was at its best when acting as a citizen.

In the familiar literature of these times, rather than in the great works of political philosophy, the military factor was greatly stressed: that states with many free citizens in them were in a better position to expand (said the Romans and Machiavelli) or to defend themselves (said the English and Dutch) than states which either depended on unskilled peasant hordes, with little interest, morale or loyalty to motivate them in defending their masters, or on expensive and shifty mercenaries. From this military perspective, a democratic element gives power to the modern state. Disraeli argued in like manner: if the skilled manual worker could be brought into the franchise, Britain (and the Conservative Party) would be stronger. The Italian Communist Gramsci argued that the skilled industrial worker is the key to modern power.

In this framework, the 'people' or *populus* never, in fact, meant everyone: 'the people' were limited to those who were fit to be citizens, usually judged by possession of arms, property and education. The pre-industrial states were not 'democratic' in a full modern sense, but were nevertheless states in which the numbers of citizens were too large to be managed simply by king and court. Parliaments and assemblies flourished in these 'republics' or more often, limited monarchies. Democratic institutions have had their origins more often in the divisions of oligarchies than in mass movements.

The French

The third usage arises from the events of the French Revolution and is found in the arguments of Jean Jacques Rousseau: that every man, irrespective of property or education, had a right to make his will felt in matters of state. It is argued that

16

'the people' have been oppressed and they must and will act together, through popular leaders who govern in the interests of the people, even if not - revolutionary times seldom allow - with perfect legality or procedural consistency. Here democracy means, quite simply, the rule of the people - and the destruction of the enemies of the people! The idea of freedom and liberty is also prized, but is seen as something distinct: democracy is popular power, and until it has been used to sweep away the last vestiges of oppression, liberty and freedom for all cannot flourish.

Napoleon was as democratic as the Jacobins in the sense that he was a popular figure. 'The politics of the future,' he once said, 'will be the art of stirring the masses'. He could fight and nearly defeat all Europe because he could trust his own common people with arms, whereas the autocrats could only conscript cautiously and selectively.

Until Napoleon unintentionally stirred up a Russian and a German nationalism, 'the people' were the last persons whom Russian emperors or Prussian kings wanted to give arms to. Napoleon was the first to be able to introduce universal conscription - an institution only possible amid democracy and nationalism. Now, this tradition of democracy simply means popular power, that modern states depend on the active support of their population whereas old autocracies throve on passive obedience or indifference ('Kings may come and Kings may go, but we go on for ever'). This revolutionary tradition is historically just as authentic as the liberal view of democracy. But those democratic regimes which have proved the most stable are those who experienced liberty before arrival of a mass franchise.

The Americans

The fourth usage is found in the American Constitution, in many new constitutions in Europe in the nineteenth century, and in the writings of John Stuart Mill and Alexis de Tocqueville: that all can and should participate at the very least in the franchise, but must respect the liberty of each to choose to do what he will so long as the action does not clearly and directly hurt the equal opportunities for choice of his fellows. This usage entails a combination of democracy and liberty. It is two things, not one, as is now so often confused.

Both Tocqueville and Mill, writing after the French Revolution, saw the danger of a new kind of tyranny, 'the tyranny of the majority'. It was a danger to be overcome in terms of educating the people, not of shutting them out from political life, and in having legal restraints on the power of both governments and popular assemblies.[5]

Present meanings

What is today most ordinarily meant by 'democracy' in the Western world is a fusion or confusion of the idea of the power of the people with the idea of individual liberties and rights. The two should be combined; but they are distinct ideas. There can be and have been intolerant democracies, and there can be and have been reasonably tolerant autocracies. But the distinction must be understood and drawn. Personally I do not find it very helpful to describe the system of government of my own country (even if she is the 'Mother of Parliaments') as a democracy: certainly there is a strong democratic element in it, but I think no government as such - such as we need governments **both** to advance collective needs and to defend each of us against others - is fully democratic or can be fully democratic. If it is more democratic to make important decisions by popular referenda then one must either say that democracy is unworkable, or that the concept can never meaningfully be used, without a host of qualifications, to describe a whole system or a whole society. A régime can be more or less democratic, but it is impossible for any régime to be fully democratic: numbers are too great and decisions are too complicated, sometimes simply too pressing, for everyone to participate.

In fact, the description of my country as a democracy is no older than World War I. Before the war, the Conservative Party warned against becoming any more democratic, the radicals and the Labour Party wanted it to be more democratic, and the main Liberal leadership thought that things were about right, at least when Mr Asquith and his friends were in power; but nobody in their senses called the country as a whole a democracy.

Americans have more commonly used the term, but even there it long retained a partisan flavour: 'democracy' conveyed the belief of some sections of the Democratic Party in popular power, but other Democrats and most Republicans preferred to describe their country as a 'Republic' - for that term seemed to connote the old ideas of checks and balances, constitutional restraints, in other words, of mixed government. It was only during the propaganda and rhetoric of World War I that the habit grew of talking about 'the defence of democracy'. No wonder a few sceptics felt that they had better achieve it first.

5.4 THREE VALID USAGES

I face the practical problem of what to teach by teaching that there are three equally valid usages of democracy in the modern world. 'Our own', the conflation of liberty and democracy in 'liberal democracy', is one. Then there is the old-style Communist use of democracy, not hypocritical at all, pointing to their belief that their system is one of class rule, the rule of the working class (which is the Greek and Jacobinical sense of majority rule). And, thirdly, a variant on that, the belief so common in the Third World that a régime is democratic, quite simply, if it is ruled by people of its own nation and not by aliens - a view that seems odd in European history where we are quite used to tyrants of our kin and kind, but is much more plausible amid the first and second generation of decolonization. That is why so many military dictators elsewhere in Africa can call themselves 'democratic' without visibly blushing.

None of these views of democracy is inherently correct. They are all simply different types of democratic government. None of them are autocracies in disguise; each of them needs citizens, an active people, not simply passive subjects. The term is at least precise enough to say that some claims of governments in the modern world to be democratic are nonsense in any possible sense, say Haiti and Paraguay. Only Arab trucial sheikdoms are honest, medieval or brutal enough not even to make the legitimating claim at all. They simply practise, they would say, 'good government'.

Suppose, however, we should discuss the questions: which of these forms of democracy has the most personal liberty, provides the most economic and social equality, allows the most criticism of the government, even of the régime, and appears to make and administer law the most fairly? These are - and this is my whole point - important but different questions.

5.5 DEMOCRACY AS OPENNESS

If one wishes to use the term democracy as a universal value rather than as an historical description of some particular and fortunate régimes, then one should at least consider that **communication** and **publicity** may well be as important as participation and personal decision making. The limits on direct participation are severe, but governments are also restrained by the fact that they cannot ever keep their major policies and acts fully secret. It is certainly not enough to teach the origins of democracy in America, Britain or elsewhere, simply in terms of the growth of the franchise, or even of the extension or the possible extension of democracy into industry, welfare and education - 'social democracy'. It must also be taught in terms of communication and publicity: that historically people have had to struggle even to know **what** the law was, even to get absolute rulers to abide by their own rules, to cease being arbitrary - 'With written laws the humblest in the state is sure of equal justice with the great (Euripides)'. Then followed a struggle to know **how** laws were made and to ensure that they were made in a regular and properly discussed manner - the growth of the powers of parliaments and assemblies in the eighteenth and nineteenth centuries; and of the right to publicize and report their proceedings. And, finally, people begin to ask for more consistent information on **why** decisions are made - committees inquire into the sources of advice that governments receive, not simply whether they bring them into law in proper form. The powers and effectiveness of the press and of broadcasting media are now-a-days an essential part of the complicated equation of 'true democracy' and 'good government'.

But does one really need to use the term 'democracy' as a value-judgement at all? This may seem absurd, almost blasphemous. But if it is a value, it is not one value but rather a joining together, for different purposes in different places and hence in different proportions, of the values of equality, liberty, justice, participation and openness. Politicians must lump them all together rhetorically, but students of politics and good journalists must be more discriminating and look at each concept separately.

When used as a descriptive term, democracy would point to the fact that nearly all modern governments are democratic, in the basic sense established by the French Revolution: they depend as never before on the active support of their inhabitants

- whether that support is freely given or created by the exclusion of real alternatives and by deliberate indoctrination. No state can defend itself or industrialize unless it is popular with its people - whoever it thinks its people are.

Rome was not built in a day. None of us must hope for too much too quickly. If we cannot get a fully participative mass democracy at once, there is no need to abandon the ideal. We must think in terms of stages. The idea of democracy as mass participation is attractive in principle but is unknown as yet in practice. If false ideals and impossible time-scales are set, the result is disillusionment and cynicism, both among rulers and ruled. To my mind, after national self-government, the first priority is **open government.** Governments should be tolerant of criticism, individual or organized, and should only maintain secrecy in the narrowest possible area of the safety of the state (not just their own belief in what constitutes the national interest, so often the party interest) and in those financial operations of government from which people might profit by advanced knowledge. The test of a free government is that its operations can be accurately described by journalists, scholars or rival politicians and published without its efficiency being harmed. Open government helps, not hinders, the efficiency of governments. If governments censor the press and repress any opposition, they end up losing touch with reality and believing their own evasions and lies.

Always remember that a government with the power of the people behind it, that is able to mobilize the masses, is very much stronger, for good or ill, than old-fashioned autocracies which did not need 'for their more limited purposes' the positive support of the masses; so, on the whole, they let sleeping dogs lie. Parliaments are as much devices for mobilizing consent as they are for representing people and restraining government. If we are talking about good government and a just society, the idea of majoritarian democracy always needs qualifying with ideas of liberty and of openness.

We have a great deal of fine rhetoric in all our national traditions about popular participation. But we are only at the beginning of seeing democracy as communication: the maximization of a free flow of information. And the argument for this is not simply one of democratic or human rights, and I do believe strongly that we all have a right to know and a right to speak out; but it is also an argument for efficiency. The famous liberal philosophers and economists in Europe in the 18th and 19th centuries who systematically criticized autocratic government, did so not just in the name of human rights or because it was arbitrary; constantly they pointed to the inefficiency of arbitrary government. Policies of autocratic and secretive governments inevitably lack criticism and lose touch with reality. The leaders of the Soviet Union themselves have discovered this, and the demand for *glasnost* and *peristroika* show that economic enterprise and development are inseparable from political liberties and debate.

In the 1930s in Europe a powerful myth grew up that the totalitarian régimes, whether Nazi or Communist, were highly efficient; and that the liberal democracies paid a price in terms of efficiency for their freedom. But the economic history of the Second World War suggests otherwise. The two great democracies were able to achieve a greater mobilization of their economies for the purpose of war than either Germany or Russia. The reasons were basically very simple: people trusted each other and so long as the general purpose was clear, local commanders and factory managers could exercise initiatives without waiting for central commands. And central commands in secretive autocracies are not always as central as they seem: rival bureaucracies may struggle for power and actually impede the effective use of power. The lack of free and open debate in autocracies makes any devolution of power difficult in circumstances where power to be effective needs devolving.

Let me give you an interesting example that was once of some importance to the world. On 6th of June 1944 the German General Rommel correctly realized that the Allied invasion of Normandy was the real thing and not a feint and a bluff to conceal the main assault elsewhere. But Hitler thought it was a bluff and would not let Rommel commit three armoured divisions correctly situated. It took him three days to change his mind, two days too late. If Rommel had acted on his own, he might have destroyed the Allied invasion on the beaches, but if he had acted on his own and succeeded he would have shown up his leader and his demotion or death would only have been slower than the quicker treatment had he acted on his own and failed. Most British or American commanders, used to exercising their judgement, would have seized the chance, if they were good generals, and become national heroes if they had succeeded, or the governor general of a small colonial island if they had failed. Punishments in democracies must not be so severe as to frighten subordinates from acting for the common good: that is another aspect of the conditions for an open and a free society, and of its advantages - what Aristotle called, as a pre-condition for citizenship, 'mutual trust'.

It seems to me both from theory and experience that the attempts of the South African government to prevent public criticism of government, reporting of sensitive events and discussion of basic issues in the news media, will, quite apart from the narrowness of the franchise, inevitably weaken if not destroy its own sense of reality. If one could imagine a rational friend of such a regime or at least one hopeful for a peaceful transition, this friend should advise that such methods are foolish for their own ends, are 'cures' that exasperate the disease not contain it. One should counsel any country trying to develop or even come to terms with popular democracy to use its secondary educational system not just to inculcate knowledge but to give an experience of discussion, debate and criticism - the origin of citizenship.

It is equally foolish to say that democracy must be 'one person one vote', or that granting the vote to all is the only way to achieve real democracy. This is to limit arbitrarily and almost certainly dangerously the range of **political** negotiation, or to confuse a rationally and morally desireable outcome through time with the politics and tactics of a process at various points of time. 'Small steps' are not base compromises if they each point upwards.[6]

5.6 CONCLUSION

Thus I argue that the maximization of communication and openness is both the prior objective for good government over maximization of participation, and something more easily realizable. As participation increases, the example of established openness and public criticism will influence the new citizens. If, on the other hand, a newly franchised electorate are simply mobilized for votes by rival leaders, habits of tolerance and mutual respect may never grow. Openness, in other words, is a precondition for any democracy that respects liberty. And, of course, we should be speaking not just of the participation of individual electors organized by political parties, but also of the role in public debate that should be openly played by pressure groups of all kinds, be they churches, trade unions, educational bodies, tribal allegiances or industrial and commercial interests. Advanced democracies, it seems to me, are inevitably pluralistic democracies. Highly organized pressure groups are fully compatible with democracy so long as they have to operate openly in a public arena, not behind closed doors. Group organization is not the enemy of democracy, it can be a part of it, or at least a stage along the way.

May I end by quoting a constitutional lawyer in my own country (which has its own problems in this respect) demanding less secrecy in government - a Professor David Williams. What he says is specific but the principles are, I believe, general:

> In short, it is desirable that as far as possible the workings of the central government should either be subject to publicity or subject to some form of independent scrutiny. Sweeping assertions of executive secrecy ought not to be tolerated in a democratic country. The responsibility for ensuring that they should not be tolerated rests in varying degrees with Parliament, the courts of law, the Press (and other media of communication) and the central government itself. The country as a whole needs to be aware of accepting too easily the basic assumptions of executive secrecy. The public interest has many facets, and it would be deplorable if the assessment of the public interest were to become the exclusive province of the executive itself. Secrecy and security have to be balanced against the legitimate demands of an informed public opinion which is, when all is said and done the essential element in a country which claims to be democratic.[7]

Good governments have nothing to hide. Democratic regimes thrive on and strengthen themselves by means of openness and public debate.

ENDNOTES

1   Crick, B. *In Defence of Politics* 2nd. ed. (London: Penguin, 1982).
2   Thucydides, *The Peloponnesian War* trans. Rex Warner (London: Penguin, 1954), pp. 117-19.
3   Ibid., p. 135.
4   Adapted from the last chapter of Finer, S.E. *The Man on Horseback: the Role of the Military in Politics* (London: Pall Mall, 1962).
5   What many people want to mean by 'democracy', i.e., a majoritarianism compatible with individual liberties, is better expressed by scholars as 'constitu-

tionalism'; but that word, unlike 'democracy', is not one that 'warms the blood like wine'. See Friedrich, C.J. *Constitutional Government and Democracy* 4th. ed. (Waltham, Mass.: Blaisdell, 1968). This traditional doctrine, for which Friedrich acknowledges his debt to McIlwain, C.H. *Constitutionalism and the Changing World* (1939) and *Constitutionalism, Ancient and Modern* (1940), needs reconsidering by modern political scientists and synthesising with the best of the modern 'systems' approaches to comparative government. Both intellectually and politically there is beginning of a revival of 'constitutionalism' against **excesses** of 'realism'. Crick, B. *Basic Forms of Government: a Sketch and a Model* (London: Macmillan, 1963) was a sketchy and overly speculative probe in that direction.

6   In Northern Ireland, for instance, the 'democratic' demand for 'one man one vote' is part of the problem not a solution.

7   Williams, D. *Not in the Public Interest* (London: Hutchinson, 1955), p. 216.

DISCUSSION

Professor Nsibambi of Makerere University began the discussion by saying that Professor Crick's paper did not address the issue of the development of democracy in Africa. For instance, does economic growth require a form of political stability that democracy cannot provide? Crick agreed that he did not talk about Africa or any other unique path to democracy. He, however, did not see that democracy precludes political stability. Indeed, Crick felt that all systems of government can only be effective and last if they make some effort to maintain the openness which is the essence of democracy. When, however, stability becomes paramount, its realization will probably be inconsistent with openness, e.g. with freedom of speech and press. The problem in autocratic systems is that without openness they loose contact with reality.

Professor Tordoff of the University of Manchester thought that Crick's ideas had much relevance to the African experience with democracy. First, a constitution cannot by itself guarantee democracy in a country; it has to reflect the experience of a people. The first Ghanaian constitution was drawn up by lawyers and had no relevance to the people. The general public forgot this constitution as soon as the coup came in 1966. Second, there is much myth making about traditional African forms of democracy. In so far as such forms of democracy did exist, they are for the most part not useful for today's nation states. Third, it is important to understand that in Europe political freedom came before the inclusion of the masses in politics. In Africa, in contrast both came at the same time, thus putting more strain on political leaders.

Professor Sklar of the University of California at Los Angeles stated that the essence of democracy is accountability of government to the rest of society. There is no perfect democracy. In all societies there are fragments of accountability. We examine the experience of specific countries like Botswana to learn about new forms of democracy which can be helpful to those seeking accountability in other societies. Crick thought accountability and openness were the same thing. It means 'don't hide things from us (the public)'.

Professor Nnoli from the University of Nigeria at Nsukka had a problem with Crick's discussion in that Nnoli sees democracy as a process by which citizens demand and obtain control over their governments. Crick said that the form democracy takes will vary with the specific conditions, but common to all is the idea of openness. It is an idea which even 'gangster' dictatorships use to justify themselves. He sees the Soviet Union today as becoming more open and thus more democratic. It is possible that some one-party states will be more open in terms of the interplay of ideas than in a supposed multi-party state.

The Honourable Tlhomelang, Member of Parliament from Kanye, commented that the failure of democracy in the Third World comes from too much concern to follow the Western model of democracy. He thought this may explain why democracy is more often present at the local level in Third World countries. The forms of openness employed are traditional and thus understandable to the people. At the national level, the concern is with foreign systems of democracy which are not compatible with the local culture.

Mayor Rantao of Gaborone felt that Crick ignored the economic context of democracy. The capitalist system leads to rule by the those with money, regardless of whether all citizens have the right to vote. This is what happens in capitalist USA where only millionaires become president. Also, Rantao said that pluralism is not the same as democracy. It only means that the elites rule. Democracy requires perpetual involvement of the people in government decisions. Thus, this conference is pluralistic in that the elite are involved, but it is not democratic in the sense that the workers and peasants are not participating.

Crick agreed that in the West democratic systems tended to emerge after the industrial revolution, but this does not need to happen. Some governments, regardless of their economic situation, are more open than others. As to the matter of the masses being involved in decision making, he felt that this definition of democracy was 'too romantic'. There is always leadership in politics. The critical question for the democrat is the extent to which these leaders are open to the ideas from others in society. There must be freedom of movement, freedom of speech, freedom of press, among other things.

Professor Sharma from the University of Botswana asked how open a political system must be to be considered democratic. Is it democratic if there is freedom of press but the reality is that the press is underdeveloped? There may be several parties, but the opposition parties are too weak to challenge the ruling party.

Dr Weimer from West Germany suggested that Crick's view of democracy means that life itself must be valued for the realization of democracy. It also requires that all aspects of communication are important including not only communication with other humans but with God and nature. Crick agreed, saying that governments in societies where there was a low life expectancy for some parts of the public, as in South Africa, the system cannot be considered democratic.

Mr Mpho, leader of the Botswana Independent Party, thought Crick was saying that democracy was different for black and white peoples, that there was a different set of rights for each. Mr Mpho rejected this idea. He felt that democracy could only be practised by a government which respected itself and others in society.

Mr Mongwa from Francistown observed that many countries call themselves democracies but the government involves only rule by the few, while the masses are kept ignorant. This is the case in Botswana and South Africa. Crick responded that he was not justifying elite rule; nevertheless the fact is that democratic developments are promoted by elites and not by the people as a whole. It takes time and involves increasing pluralism and group negotiation in society. He would expect this to happen in South Africa, rather than expecting the immediate recognition of the moral rights of a majority. Ultimately, however, stable democracy involves the idea of fraternity, that is seeing others as brothers.

Mr Nielson, a businessman from Gaborone, suggested that democracy requires the development of capitalism first. Where there is socialism, there is party dictatorship. The people must become self-reliant and that means all persons must be involved in economic production. Welfare is inhuman. Crick responded that historically democracy came before capitalism. He also did not think that governments can wait for the markets to produce goods required to feed and cloth the entire population. While state industries rarely work well, generally the state must step in and redistribute wealth through taxation. Otherwise the economic injustice resulting will breed revolution.

Professor Ngcongco of the University of Botswana said that our definition of democracy must emphasize government 'for' the people, that is that government should be run in the interests of all the people and not just the rich or an elite. Crick said he agreed but that the problem was in determining the substance of these interests. It cannot be done by the government. The people must be emancipated. Politicians are great self-deceivers who believe they know the interests of the people simply because they are elected. There must be many channels of communication or feedback, including elected politicians, consultants, and public opinion polls.

SECTION II
AFRICAN EXPERIENCES WITH DEMOCRACY

6 One-party rule in Tanzania and Uganda: how democratic?

Apolo Robin Nsibambi

6.1 INTRODUCTION

In the process of examining the experience of Tanzania and Uganda with the one-party system, two arguments will be developed. First, the realization of one-party democracy requires exemplary, tolerant and committed leadership, most ideally in situation of relative cultural homogeneity. Second, societies such as Uganda which are highly pluralistic are unlikely to be governed democratically using a one-party system.

This paper is divided into three parts. The first provides a general discussion of the theory of the one-party state. The latter two examine the experience of first Tanzania and then Uganda. Since democracy has been adequately defined in previous chapters, it is not necessary to repeat the definition here. However, important elements of this concept include political accountability; free and effective participation in the political process; a reasonable degree of accessibility to scarce resources; freedom of life, liberty, security, conscience, expression, assembly and association; and freedom from deprivation of property without compensation. It is also essential to have effective political institutions for resolution of political and economic conflicts.

6.2 THE RATIONALE FOR A ONE-PARTY SYSTEM IN AFRICA

Julius Nyerere, the former President of Tanzania, has been among the most articulate defenders of the one-party system. He advances four basic arguments. All have major weaknesses, though to this point they still carry considerable weight with many African politicians and intellectuals.

The first is that a two-party system is justified only when the parties are divided over some fundamental issues. Otherwise, the political conflict is nothing more than factionalism.[1] In Nyerere's mind a single party system overcomes factionalism and promotes national unity. However, he never tell us what issues qualify as fundamental. Thus we are left not knowing when a two-party system can be justified in Africa.

Nyerere's second point is that as long as there are no irreconcilable groups in society, it is not efficient to have political discussions constrained by party 'lines'. With no contesting parties, people can debate the issues and not worry about possible conflicting interests of their parties. The problem is that it is difficult to find societies where there are no groups which do not regard their positions as being irreconcilable. In addition, the extent to which conflicts become intractable depends on how the different positions of affected groups are handled by the political leaders.

Nyerere's third rationale for a single-party system is that Africa is in a state of crisis and all the talented people in society must devote their energies to solving this crisis. A one-party system helps this consolidation process in that talented people are not divided along party lines. While this reasoning is plausible, the reality is that politicians, who are less gifted than the civil servants, tend to use the single-party system to establish their power over talented civil servants. Thus the one-party system does not necessarily ensure that talent is used in the interests of the nation.

Nyerere's final argument is that the single-party system reflects the basic consensus of African society.[2] In his view, the traditional African society was not divided among classes and thus decisions were arrived at through a consensus of the people as a whole. This argument ignores the fact that there has always been some sort of class differentiation in African societies and that sometimes the so-called consensus was achieved by the rulers imposing their will on the masses who lacked political skills.

Underlying this argument for the one-party system is a belief that political stability is critical to economic development. Huntington and Nelson are two academics who have been particularly articulate with regard to defending this perspective.[3] They hold that political elites in developing countries are inevitably drawn to authoritarian solutions to promote economic development and stability. The assumption is that technocratic elites need power in order to make authoritative professional decisions and to initiate effective economic policies. It is further argued that if the masses are not substantially restrained, they will make more demands on the political system than it is capable of handing. The result will be paralysis, not only politically but in terms of decisions required for development. Thus, the only solution is autocracy.

A number of analysts hold that in fact the situation is the reverse.[4] They argue that citizen participation facilitates economic development in that participation, economic equality, and government subsidies which result generate support from the masses and thus the political system enjoys affection and political stability. From this perspective there is no necessary zero-sum relationship between participation and growth. To be sure, the actual rate of growth may be slower.

The assumption of this paper is that this alternative perspective has much relevance to Africa, given the experiences of Tanzania and Uganda to which we will now turn.

27

6.3 ONE-PARTY DEMOCRACY IN TANZANIA

The experience of Tanzania has clearly demonstrated that it is possible to realise democracy in a one-party system. It has held fair, competitive and regular elections in 1965, 1970, 1975 and 1980. Independent observers have confirmed that they have been democratic.[5]

There are some deviations, however. During the 1980 elections Mwakawago, Minister of Labour and Manpower Development, lost, even though the government gave him open support. While he made no attempt to rig elections, President Nyerere did use his constitutional power to nominate Mr Mwakawago as a member of parliament and to reappoint the defeated minister to another cabinet post.[6] At the very least, the whole idea of electoral democracy is nullified when a rejected candidate is subsequently appointed to the legislature and continues as a cabinet minister.

Tanzanian elections are competitive because the electorate chooses between two or more candidates. When President Nyerere proposed competitive elections in 1963, some members of the then Tanganyika African National Union (TANU), which became Chama Cha Mapinduzi (CCM), did not like the proposal because they feared they might be replaced or that anti-party groups would attain power.[7] There was substantial support for competitive elections within the party. This derived from the fact that TANU already had such internal democratic practices as election of leaders by the rank and file and the prevalence of free and frank discussions. In addition, many of those occupying middle-level leadership roles in the party welcomed a system which would facilitate their upward political mobility.

A high percentage of the registered voters have persistently gone to the polls during the four elections which have taken place since Tanzania acquired political independence. Empirical studies have shown that 85% of the Dar-es-Salaam sample voted and 70% and 88% of the two sets of rural interviewees cast their ballot.[8] This high turnout during elections suggests that people are reasonably mobilized and that they have acquired some sense of civic competence. It is important to note that even some long established democracies like the USA have consistently had a lower turnout in this century than that achieved in Tanzania. It would appear that there is more motivation on the part of the citizens to vote in this one-party system where there is internal competition than in the USA's two-party system.

Factors facilitating one-party democracy

The following factors have facilitated this democratic process. First, Tanzania enjoys a high degree of cultural homogeneity. Almost all of the 120 tribes are classified as Bantu. The Nilotic and Nilo-Hamitic groups are in very small numbers. Second, unlike Uganda and Kenya, the capital is not situated in the area of the heartland tribe, thus giving this tribe disproportionate power. Third, Kiswahili, the national language, is widely spoken and unlike English, it is not a language of the educated. Thus it bridges the gap between the elite and the masses. Fourth, Nyerere, the founding father, has been tolerant, exemplary and a consummate builder of political institutions to resolve political conflict. Indeed, he resigned from being president in order to strengthen TANU. He has used the Preventive Detention Act sparingly. As Mudoola has argued, 'Unlike other African political systems, the Tanzanian leadership demonstrated a concern with building political structures for purposes of fulfilling desired political goals'.[9]

The problem of the mandate for one-party democracy in Tanzania

If a one party-system is to be established, a clear electoral mandate should exist and should be reaffirmed periodically. For the most part, no such mandate has existed in the case of African one-party states such as Ghana and Uganda. In Tanzania, TANU had such a mandate. It won all the National Assembly seats except one in the election which preceded independence. As Goulbourne aptly observes, '. . . although other political parties appeared between 1954 when TANU was founded and 1965 when the Republic became, dejure, . . . TANU . . . was really the only viable party in Tanganyika.'[10]

Since the mandate for a one-party state cannot be considered permanent, it can only be democratic if citizens are free to call for a return to a competitive system. This turned out not to be the case in Tanzania. Mr M Chogga, a member of parliament from Iringa South, was expelled from the party by the National Executive for requesting government to establish a multiparty state. If there is only one party in the country and a member is expelled from it, where is he expected to practise his political belief?[11] We should also remember that being expelled from the party means that one cannot hold a public office.

The problem of presidentialism in Tanzania

The one-party system tends to lead to presidentialism. In the case of Tanzania, Nyerere was able to stay in power from 1962 to 1985. According to Goulbourne, presidentialism involves 'the centralisation of state power in the hands of President' who is 'supposed to represent the people as a whole in nearly all matters relating to the country.'[12] Effectively the President privatises all political power in his hands. This means that presidents can loot the state treasury with impunity for their own use and reward their personal supporters whenever they see fit.[13] No effective challenge can be mounted to rule by the president since he controls overwhelming force and elections provide at best a chance for the voter to choose to retain the president or turn him out. Such a system thus results in abrogating the power of the citizens to determine their leader in any effective sense.

We are happy to note that Tanzania has limited the tenure of office of the president to two, five year terms. When Nyerere voluntarily stepped out of presidency, he joined a list of very few African presidents who institutionalized the process of handing over the 'sweet' of political power voluntarily. His abdication of power has not been complete in that he stayed on as chairman of the party. His reasons for so doing are the external threats Tanzania faces from such sources as the International Monetary Fund (IMF) and South Africa, and the instability of the union between Zanzibar and the mainland because of externally inspired separatists. It is also possible that Nyerere's 'henchmen' felt insecure if he went into political oblivion.

It was wrong for Nyerere to retain the chairmanship of the party in that it is effectively the supreme organ of the state. By so doing, he has made it almost impossible for Tanzanians to excercise their democratic right to reject those of Nyerere's policies which have failed. To reject these policies decisively would almost certainly be equated with 'disowning' the Baba Ya Taifa, the Father of the Nation.

Yet, pursuing long term interests of the state must entail disowning decisively some of his policies which were wrong. Another experienced person should have been asked to be the chairman of the party. The process of democratization entails recognizing that no man is indispensable.

The problem of centralization of power and the one-party state

The main problem in Tanzania in terms of democracy has been preventing the centralization of power. This centralization has not led to the abridgement of political rights. The freedoms of assembly, association, speech, and press have been observed for the most part. There is also freedom from arbitrary arrest and imprisonment.

The problem has rather been that citizens cannot play a role in decision making through local government or voluntary associations. Democratic forces are not completely overwhelmed in that of late there has been pressure to turn some power back to such structures.

Tanzania has gone through a number of phases of granting power to local governments and then taking this power back.[14] In 1963 councils were placed under the control of field-based central government officials who controlled their finances among other things. Also, a Unified Local Government Service Commission was created which appointed, promoted, transformed and disciplined local employees. This commission was inimical to the interests of local autonomy, since councillors could now no longer hire and fire their staff without consulting the commission in Dar-es-Salaam.[15] In 1965 there was further centralization in that the chairman of TANU in a district was automatically also chairman of the district council, a measure which increased the control of TANU in the districts. Then in 1972 local authorities were abolished, which created a situation of complete dependency for grass-roots organizations on higher levels of government.[16] Subsequently the process has been reversed with the reactivation of local authorities.

Another aspect of centralization was that most important interest groups have come under the party's control, including trade unions, youth, women, co-operatives and educational organizations. The party approves the rules and procedures of these groups, endorses candidates who stand for election to office, and supervises the elections themselves.[17]

Shivji has argued that the bargaining power of trade unions has been frozen. A government commission approves all wage increases, thus limiting collective bargaining. Strikes are effectively illegal. Given the fact that the commission has refused to let wages rise with inflation, the overall consequence has been a decline in real wages for the workers.[18] The result has been a wave of industrial unrest in which the power of management was weakened as workers locked managers out of their offices. In effect, government has had to pay a cost in terms of weak industrial discipline.

The situation is equally serious with respect to cooperatives. The primary produce cooperatives were abolished in 1976. The peasants' interests were hurt immensely.[19] These cooperatives had distributed farm inputs and marketed farm produce even before independence. Nyerere declared that although marketing cooperatives were socialist, they were serving capitalism in that agricultural production was in the hands of private producers.[20]

For each major cash crop, the government established parastatal crop authorities which were given the sole right to purchase and export the produce involved. All became corrupt and inefficient. By 1982, not a single crop authority had its accounts audited for at least five years.[21] Part of the agricultural crisis which forced Tanzania to import food was the failure of these centralized marketing structures to produce income for peasants. By 1984 the government reversed its policy and cooperative unions were restored. The party does, however, control their leadership and procedures.

Still other centralizing policies could be mentioned. One that was particularly unpopular was the forced villagization drive which was carried out in the face of massive peasant opposition. On 21st December 1971, Wilbert Kleruu, the TANU Regional Secretary for Iringa and Regional Commissioner, was assassinated by a well-to-do peasant opposed to the politics of the Ujamaa Villages.[22] Again as in the case of other forms of centralization, this process has been halted.

The problem of economic democracy and the one-party state

When Nyerere launched his one-party state, it was possible to pursue the socialist goal of economic equality because the middle class was very small. He did not have a major middle class challenge either within the society or the party. At least initially, the government achieved a measure of success in reducing the gap between the elite and the masses. The country has, for example, attained a high degree of literacy through universal primary education, and there was some equalization of income.

Nyerere's success was far from complete. The nationalization programme failed to prevent the penetration of foreign capital. The nation remains dependent on foreign aid. The economy displays the same features of distortion as other peripheral

31

capitalist states, with a heavy dependence on cash crops and with industrialization geared to processing and import substitution rather than capital goods. Most important, the gap between the rich and the poor peasants is growing.[23]

These developments may give rise to the necessity of having a multiparty system. Fully fledged capitalists may wish to organize their own party. At the other end of the spectrum, the radicals who prefer a more purified form of socialism, may find the government party to compromised for their liking.[24] In other words, new socio-political forces which have emerged may not be contained in a one-party system. In these circumstances government can only retain a democratic one-party system if it renews its mandate through an election.

The failure of one-party democracy in Uganda

Uganda has a highly plural society. There are thirty ethnic groups which are divided into four major cultural groupings — the Bantu, Nilo-Hamitic, Nilotic and Sudanic peoples. These groups lack a common language. English, the official language, is not widely understood except among the educated. Historically, Uganda was also divided between the kingdoms and republican areas until 1967 when Obote used force to abolish monarchy. Still more rivalry comes from the religious differences among the Catholics, Protestants and Muslims.[25] There are substantial disparities in economic development as the North is much less developed than the South. The heartland tribe, the Baganda, has enjoyed both geographical centrality and more autonomy than other tribes.[26]

For a while after independence, all these various conflicts seemed to be balanced in a semi-federal constitution allowing for multiparty competition. No single party was able to master an overall majority. Initially, the Uganda Peoples Congress (UPC) decided to make an alliance with Buganda's traditional Kabaka Yekka (King alone) Party to form a national government. The Democratic Party (DP) became the opposition party.[27]

From 1962 to 1966, the weak Central Government led by Obote had to contend with a robust sub-political system in the form of the Kingdom of Buganda. In 1964 things began to change when the UPC picked up sufficient defections from KY and DP to gain an overall electoral majority. Nevertheless, until 1966 Uganda enjoyed unprecedented freedom of speech, association, litigation, press and freedom from arbitrary arrest and imprisonment without the due process of law. The basic reason for this was that central government's power was counter balanced by strong local governments.

In 1966, Obote abrogated the constitution when his leadership was challenged both from within and outside his party. Henceforth, his rule depended largely on the army which was predominantly recruited from the northern and eastern parts of Uganda. Federalism and monarchy were abolished in the process.[28]

A one-party system without a mandate

In 1969 when an attempt was made on Obote's life, he banned all other political parties except the ruling UPC. Innocent people were falsely implicated as Obote became suspicious of everyone surrounding him. The party machinery collapsed.

Obote by no means had a mandate to establish a one-party system. Rather the change was part of the establishment of an increasingly autocratic regime. Previously, he placed Buganda under a state of emergency in 1966 which lasted until Obote's overthrow in 1971; he used the Detention Act to detain political opponents including a former Secretary General of the UPC and a number of ministers; he abolished the 1962 constitution in 1967, a move which caused a constitutional and a military confrontation between the Central Government and the Buganda Government; and he never renewed his political mandate by holding fresh elections when they were due in 1967.

The fall of Uganda's one-party system

Obote's one-party system did not fail simply for lack of a mandate. It also lacked any long term agreement about the rules and institutions for resolving political conflict. When Obote abolished the independence constitution, he abolished a document which had been arrived at after a great deal of political bargaining. Henceforth, Uganda was ruled by a minority group which depended on the use of force to sustain itself. The quasi-federal constitution had taken into account the plural nature of Uganda's society and given each segment a share in decision making at either the national or local level or both. With no constitution, the determinant of who should rule became the naked force of the army, whose loyalty Obote at first obtained. In addition, Obote intimidated the population through the General Service, a political intelligence organization under Obote's cousin Akena Adoko. It was not answerable to parliament. Finally, there was a police para-military section, the Special Force, which specialized in terrorizing Obote's opponents.[29]

The UPC's only function was to give a semblance of popular participation to the decisions taken by Obote and significant sections of the army and police.[30]

The army compounded the situation in that could not serve as an intermediary between the various contending forces. It was ill-disciplined, unpatriotic, and increasingly violent in its dealings with the local population.[31]

Obote and his followers could not provide the exemplary, committed and liberal leadership that was necessary to sustain some form of civilian rule. From 1961 to 1964, Obote appeared to be a leader of reconciliation. Subsequent events proved that this was a tactical move on the part of Obote and that he was not committed to constitutionalism.[32] He made no effort to move toward a new structure of civil rule. Obote ceased being exemplary and a builder of political institutions. He did not even make an attempt to gain some form of mandate when elections were due in 1967 until his overthrow in 1971. Indeed, even when he came back into office after Amin's rule, he continued to identify with the groups which want to rule Uganda by force, hardly the behaviour of founding father committed to leading his country to democracy.

When Obote was overthrown by Amin in 1971 there was no pretence of flirting with democracy. For purposes of our discussion, we must skip this period.

Reestablishing civilian rule

Following the overthrow of Amin's government in 1979, 28 groups met at Moshi in Tanzania where they formed the Uganda National Liberation Front. Political parties were disallowed to operate until constitutional government returned. Professor Y. Lule was elected Chairman of an 11 man Executive Council of the Front. A National Consultative Council, (NCC) composed of one member of each group associated with the front, was formed to provide direction. During this period, there was a revival of a remarkably vigorous Uganda press.[33]

The front collapsed before it could negotiate a new constitutional consensus. A considerable amount of time was bound to be required given the fact that all the complex divisions remained from the Obote period.[34] Under these circumstances, any faction which wished to control the other, depended on the military support of Tanzania, a neighbouring country which had substantially contributed to the overthrow of Amin. When, for example, one faction challenged Lule's government and asserted the supremacy of the NCC over the government, 'Tanzania's refusal to support Lule, rather than recognition of the council's claim to supremacy, actually forced Lule out of office'.[35] The government in effect lacked the necessary military power to enforce its decisions.

The situation could only have been saved had the various political parties been willing to agree to an umbrella organization which could have contained the various factions which held objectives which were fundamentally different. There were radicals who sought to create a socialist state while the capitalists sought to restore a free enterprise system.

The Front was overthrown, and a Military Council led by Mr Paulo Muwanga was established. It organized elections which were rigged in favour of UPC in 1980. Mujaju correctly observes that even when the multiparty system was revived in 1980, the DP and UPC did not attempt to arrive at a consensus to rule Uganda. Worse still, each party had a capacity to paralyse the system without having absolute capacity to neutralize each other.[36] Under these circumstances, the country could not practise democratic principles because it lacked stability and primary consensus.

The result was the launching of a guerrilla war which was most effectively carried on by the National Resistance Army (NRA) under the leadership of Yoweri Museveni. The NRA enjoyed popular support in the countryside which had been brutalized by Obote's ill-disciplined and ruthless army.

In January 1986, the NRM took over power and it established Resistance Councils to which all people who are eighteen years and over belong. Meanwhile, political parties have been suspended. The National Resistance Movement (NRM) has, however, made an attempt to bring the various groups within society into its government coalition. It has ably restored an ordered society in most parts of the country. Where unrest remains Museveni is creatively using political negotiation with military muscle. The NRM government for the first time since independence is providing Uganda with exemplary leadership.

The movement is more accommodative of political divergence than a one-party system which restricts membership to the people who accept its basic principles. However, the movement faces the problem of giving a clear thrust to the implementation of its basic policies. Currently, the High Command and the Political Organ appear to play a key role in determining the major issues. The High Command consists of top leaders of the army while the Political Organ consists of the thirty eight founders of the movement who went to the bush in order to wage a guerrilla war against the dictatorial regime of Obote.

The existence of dissidents in the North and North East tends to give the army a significant role. This is so because as the army confronts the dissidents who have support from some external powers, the demands of the army acquire special importance. The resolution of the conflict in the two areas should enhance the realization of civilian efficacy.

The challenges of the expanded National Resistance Council, (the national legislature) is to ensure that this political organ which enjoys political legitimacy, becomes the centre of making major political and economic decisions.

6.4 CONCLUSION

The Tanzanian example establishes that with some limitations democracy can be practised under one-party rule. There are no competing parties or alternative programmes. It is possible however to build institutions which resolve social conflict, particularly if an exemplary, liberal and committed leadership exists to facilitate this institution building. More could be done if the tenure in office of political officials was limited.

The Ugandan case shows that a one-party system is not likely to be established if a highly plural society exists and there is an absence of a top leadership committed to building and maintaining a set of constitutional arrangements which can contain the inevitable and intense conflict which occurs.

We must remember that external factors and efficient allocation of resources affect the viability and character of democracy in the one-party system. When the Tanzanian economy was ailing, the government was forced to make an agreement with the IMF which required the rejection of socialist policies. In so doing, the very basis of the party's mandate to rule through a one-party system was brought into question.

Ultimately, African one-party states cannot insist on their right to rule because they provide stability. They must seek the appropriate structures which will maximize the realisation of public opinion through representative groups and elected officials.

ENDNOTES

1   Nyerere, J. K. *Freedom and Unity: A Selection from Writings and Speeches, 1952-65.* (Nairobi: Oxford University Press, 1967) p. 196.

2   Tordoff, W. *Government and Politics in Africa* (London: The Macmillan Press Ltd., 1984) p. 103.

3   Huntington, S. P. and Nelson J. M., *No Easy Choice: Political Parties in Developing Countries* (Cambridge: Harvard University Press, 1976) pp. 17-29.

4   Kabashima, 'Supportive Participation With Economic Growth: The Case of Japan', *World Politics*, Vol. XXXVI, No. 3, April, 1984, pp. 309-338; Huntington, S. P. and Nelson, J. M. *No Easy Choice, pp. 17-29.*

5   *See, for example, Cliffe, L. (ed.) One Party Democracy: The 1965 Tanzania General Elections* Vol. I. (Nairobi: East African Publishing House, 1967).

6   He became Minister of Industry.

7   Cliffe, L. 'The Impact of the Elections', in his *One Party Democracy*, p. 91. See also Hermet, G. et al., *Elections Without Choice* (London: The Macmillan Press Ltd., 1978).

8   Prewitt, K. and Hyden, G. 'Voters Look at the Elections', in Cliffe, L. (ed.), *One Party Democracy*, p. 68. See also Hyden, G. 'The Role of Symbols in the Tanzania Elections of 1965', *Mawazo*, Vol. 1 (June 1967), pp. 41-48. Hyden suggests that symbols served as a means to make the choice more meaningful in those areas and among those people who had little or no knowledge about the actual candidates.

9   Mudoola, D. 'The Pathology of Institution Building – The Tanzanian Case', in Kiros, F. G. ed., *Challenging Rural Poverty* (Trenton, New Jersey: Africa World Press, 1985) p. 119.

10 Goulbourne, H. 'The Role of the Political Party in Tanzania Since the Arusha Declaration', in his *Politics and State in the Third World* (London: The Macmillan Press Ltd., 1983) p. 204.

11 Thoden Van Velzen, H. U. E. and Sterkenburg, J. J. 'The Party Supreme' in Cliffe, *One Party Democracy*, p. 263.

12 Goulbourne, H. 'The State, Development and the Need for Participatory Democracy in Africa' *Social Science Research Review*, Vol. II, No. I, (January 1986) p. 7.

13 Four details on this phenomenon, read Apolo Nsibambi, 'Corruption in Uganda, 1971-1986,' *UFAHAMU*, Vol. XV, No. 3, (Winter 1986/8,7).

14 For details read Mutahaba, G. R. 'Organization for Development: Tanzania's Search for Appropriate Local Level Organization Forms', in Kiros, *Rural Poverty*, pp. 127-145.

15 Ibid., p. 136.

16 Ibid., p. 141.

17 Tordoff, W. *Government and Politics*, p. 107.

18 Shivji, I. G. 'Working Class Struggles and Organization in Tanzania, 1939-1975', *Mawazo*, Vol. 5, No. 2 (December 1983) p. 19.

19 For details read Maghimbi, S. 'The Co-operative Movement and the Crisis

in the Rural Economy of Tanzania' a paper presented to the Second Triennial Congress of OSSREA, held at Eldoret, Kenya, 28-31 July 1986.

20   Nyerere, J. K. 'Socialism and Rural Development' (1967) in Nyerere, J. K. *Ujamaa, Essays on Socialism* (London: Oxford University Press, 1973) p. 116.

21   The World Bank, *Report No. 4052 − TA: Tanzania Agricultural Sector Report* (Washington, D.C., August 1983) p. 71.

22   For details read Martin, D. 'The 1975 Tanzanian Elections: The Disturbing 6%', in Hermet, G. *Elections Without Choice*, pp. 119-120.

23   Shivji, I. G. *Class Struggles in Tanzania* (Dar-es-Salaam: Tanzania Publishing House, 1975).

24   On the emergence of these groups within the Party, see Hartmann, J. 'The Debate on the Two Socialisms in Tanzania, 1962-1982', a paper presented at the OSSREA Second Triennial Congress held at Eldoret, 28-31 July 1986. On the debate concerning the IMF, read Campbell, H. 'The IMF Debate and the Politics of Demobilisation in Tanzania' *Social Science Research Review*, Vol. II, No. 2 (June 1986).

25   For details, read Welbourn, B. F. *Religion and Politics in Uganda, 1952-1962* (Nairobi: E.A.P.H., 1965).

26   For the latest account on Uganda, read Hansen, H. B. and Twaddle, M. (eds.) *Uganda Now: Between Decay and Development* (London: James Currey, 1988); Apolo Nsibambi, 'Solving Uganda's Food Problem', in Hansen and Twaddle (eds.) Ibid., pp. 135-158; and Kasfir, N. 'Cultural Sub-Nationalism in Uganda' in Olorunsola, V. A. (ed.), *The Politics of Cultural Sub-Nationalism in Africa* (New York: Doubleday & Company Inc. 1972.).

27   For details on the political parties, read Mujaju, A. B. *Consensus and the Party System in Uganda*, Political Science Monograph Series No. 1 (Kampala: Orbitas Publishers (U) Ltd., 1986). The DP was identified as a party for Catholics while UPC was regarded as a party for Protestants.

28   Read Nsibambi, A. 'Some Reflections on the Uganda Independence Constitution of 1962', *The Uganda Journal*, Vol. 39 (1980).

29   Willets, P. 'The Politics of Uganda as a One-Party State', *African Affairs*, Vol. 74, No. 296 (July 1975) p. 288.

30   Mudoola, D. 'Political Transitions Since Idi Amin: A Study in Political Pathology' in Hansen, H. B. and Twaddle, M. (eds.) *Uganda Now*, p. 287.

31   Kabwegyere, T. 'The Politics of State Destruction in Uganda Since 1962: Lessons for the Future', in Wiebe, P. D. and Dodge, C. P. (eds.), *Beyond Crisis: Development Issues in Uganda* (Kampala: MISR and Crossroads Press, 1987) pp. 17-18.

32   Mudoola, D. 'The Problems of Institution Buildings: The Uganda Case', in Wiebe and Dodge (eds.), *Beyond Crisis*, p. 56.

33   Gertzel, C. 'Uganda After Amin: The Continuing Search for Leadership and Control', *African Affairs* (October 1980) p. 474.

34   Ibid., p. 462.

35   Ibid., p. 472.

36   Mujaju, *Consensus*, p. 16.

7 The experience of democracy in Senegal

Babcar Sine

7.1 HISTORICAL BACKGROUND

In Francophone Africa, Senegal stands out as an exemplar for its democratic system. The reason for this is the country's long experience with democratic politics. Indeed, representative government in Senegal goes back as far as any country in Africa. The existence and development of a political life was conducted by several parties which organized the representation of the country in the French Parliament under colonial rule, and which represented the country in different assemblies and colonial institutions as well. The first African Member of the French Parliament was the Senegalese Blaise Diague in 1914. He later became a minister in different French governments including that of Clemenceau in 1917.

After World War II Leopold Senghor and Lamine Gueye were Senegal's representatives to the French National Assembly. There were also three Senegalese senators in the Council of the Republic. All these elected officials had full rights of participation in the legislative process right up to independence in 1960, even though Senegal was still a colony. Effectively Senegal was a part of France when it came to elections.

After independence multiparty politics in Senegal underwent a crisis which resulted in various limitations on political competition. All the parties belonging to the legal opposition disappeared and Senegal became in fact a one-party state. Within the ruling party, the Union Progressiste Senegalais (UPS), considerable political competition remained. Moreover, during this entire one-party period, there was general freedom of debate and very limited abridgement of the other political freedoms.

Beginning in 1974, Senghor encouraged a move toward limited pluralism. Political representation was at first limited to four parties which were to represent four distinct ideological perspectives: conservatism, socialism, social democracy, and marxism. In 1978, the UPS which was the socialist party won 81.7 per cent of the vote with the social democratic party taking most of the rest. Thus for the first time since independence, Senegal had an official opposition party in the assembly.

7.2 SENEGAL'S NEW DEMOCRACY

When Abdou Diouf replaced Senghor as President in 1981, Senegal's pluralism further expanded. The limit on the number of parties was annulled and their number grew quickly. Today there are 17 political parties representing all kinds of ideologies. Besides the socialist UPS which commands four-fifths of the vote, there are four marxist parties, two trotskyist parties, one conservative party, and one social democratic party.

Both majority rule and proportional representation are used in selecting members of the assembly. Half the seats are allocated to single member districts where the candidate must obtain a majority to win. The other half are distributed in proportion to the number of votes a given party receives. The proportional representation system is designed to allow certain opposition parties to be represented in the assembly even though they cannot win a majority in any one district. At the last elections, however, only two parties were able to gain seats. The President of the Republic is chosen by direct vote of the people.

The liberty of the press is total. There are thus journals of various opinion in existence, some of which speak for the opposition parties. In addition there is the government press. There is no prior censorship on the private press. The only remedy is to seek a judgement in court after publication. Since the courts are relatively independent from the government, this means that there is little restraint on the press.

Access to the government media of television and radio is assured for all political parties. These media cover the various events of all the political parties including press conferences, round table conferences, and rallies. During electoral campaigns, the opposition has equal time on radio and television with the ruling party. To be sure, the most important point of debate between the government and opposition parties is the demand of the latter for more time on both the state media.

President Diouf has also considerably expanded the autonomy of various organized groups from the state. The exercise of trade union power including the right to strike is guaranteed in the constitution. Four major trade unions have emerged. The main workers' trade union, the National Workers Confederation of Senegal is affiliated to the government party in the name of the principle of 'responsible participation.' It is no longer 'integrated' with the ruling party. The new principle allows the union to adhere to governmental policies while it also retains its organizational autonomy and is able to be represented in the assembly according to well defined quotas. The result of the principle of responsible participation is that it allows the effective organization of participation and the permanent control of government management by the majority of organized workers.

7.3 CONCLUSION

Senegalese democracy is characterized by the strength of feeling of the partisan opposition. Ideological and political struggles collide with personal ambitions. The main problem is to find a national political consensus as to the direction our society is to go. There cannot be democracy without differences of opinion or opposition parties. At the same time this struggle must be based on some agreement on the general types of objectives which are to be sought, as is the case in the great democracies of Great Britain, France, and the United States of America. If our democracy can solve the problem of consensus, it will have taken a great step towards its consolidation.

The current party system also fails to represent all the various groups which exist in the nation. This diversity includes youth groups, elites both urban and rural, cooperatives of producers and consumers, and many others. All these sectoral groups have aspirations and needs. There is a need to find ways to make sure they can participate in articulating and solving their problems.

To sum up, Senegalese democracy with all its strengths and weaknesses is functioning and consolidating itself, despite the crises which result from too rapid change in the economy and society.

DISCUSSION

Mr Mothobi (attorney) began by asking if anything could be done about the apathy of the masses, deriving from their ignorance and unconcern with their rights. Professor Nsibambi said that certainly the level of education is low in Africa. More important, the problem is that the people have found out that they cannot influence events in African countries. Compounding the situation is the fact that governments in Africa do not communicate with their people.

Professor Wallace (University of Birmingham) asked if the structural adjustments required by the World Bank and the IMF were helping or undermining the chances of democracy in Africa. Professor Sine responded that these programmes clearly went against the popular will. Nsibambi contended that the politically unpopular policies of the World Bank and the IMF have made African governments more authoritarian and resulted in coups and unrest. He admitted that many governments like to blame these international organizations because top officials do not want to take responsibility for their country's economic plight.

Professor Rubadiri (University of Botswana) asked if the founding fathers in Africa had not become autocrats, while portraying themselves as philosopher kings. He also wondered whether Sine had not presented too glowing a picture of the situation in Senegal. Nsibambi said that the real problem in African states is the development of a consensus as to the values which govern politics. At present different tribes often have very different values. Sine said that the government in Senegal did have a crisis after the last elections, but on the whole democracy has assured stability.

Professor Tordoff (University of Manchester) remarked that the one-party system can provide an umbrella under which a variety of social groups cooperate. This has happened successfully in such countries as Tanzania and Zambia. The problem in Tanzania was that Nyerere stayed in power too long. The result was that policies he had initiated could not be questioned even though they did not work. Nyerere also brought so much power into the office of the president that it was difficult to allow technicians to handle technical problems. All issues thus became political. Nsibambi generally agreed with Tordoff's comments. He thought President Kaunda had been more effective as a president, even though he has stayed in power for many years, because he was accommodative to many points of view. The Honourable Tlhomelang (member of parliament) asserted that Botswana is a multiparty democracy because Batswana are accommodative of other people's ideas. Nsibambi said that he thought Botswana was a democracy because there was more cultural homogeneity than in most African states, and there had been continuous economic growth. He also felt that Seretse Khama's leadership had helped in that the former president was tolerant of political opposition. He wondered what would happen when economic hard times come.

Mr Jean-Luc Balans (Director CREDU, Harare) stated that the stability of Senegal depended very much on clientelism and power of the Muslim Brotherhood. In Both Senegal and the Ivory Coast he thought the success of the founding leader arose from his ability to distribute wealth through political networks. He felt that there was not much democracy in Senegal's past. There was little in French colonialism, and after independence, Senegal was virtually a one-party state for its first twelve or thirteen years. Sine rejected the idea that clientelism was important in Senegal. He thought that the Ivory Coast was very different from Senegal in one respect. Houphouet-Boigny has refused to step down or designate a successor whereas Senghor has done so. Also, a system of political rights has developed which is founded on the cultural system of the country. Nsibambi noted that the governments of the former French colonies still rely on French military forces to keep themselves in power while the British do not intervene at this level.

Mr Mpho (President of the Botswana Independence Party) asked how elections were conducted in one-party states. Nsibambi said that there was a screening of candidates by the party in most cases. The voters tended to make their choice on their perception of the record of the candidates and the way in which the candidates presented themselves.

Ms Makgema said that she thought the speakers had avoided the question of why Botswana was different from other African countries. Nsibambi said that neither he nor Sine could make statements since they had not studied Botswana extensively. There were, however, a few things which seemed obvious. The fact that Botswana was much more culturally homogenous than other African countries made communication easier and thus enhanced the possibility of democracy. The presence of a destabilizing neighbour in the form of South Africa served to encourage national unity. And, Botswana's economic success makes the prevailing system of government popular. In other African countries, like Tanzania, one-party rule came about because of a mandate from the people. Such an overwhelming majority voted for the winning party that the opposition was too weak to play an effective role. In closing the session, the chairman, the Honourable A. H. Mogwe, remarked that he hoped more comparisons with other African countries would be possible by the end of the symposium. He also noted that in contrast to Tanzania, the people in Botswana had always shown support at elections for a multiparty system.

SECTION III

BOTSWANA'S HISTORICAL EXPERIENCE WITH DEMOCRACY

8 Tswana political tradition: how democratic?

L. D. Ngcongco

8.1 INTRODUCTION

Many Batswana believe that pre-colonial Tswana political tradition, particularly relative to the kgotla, was democratic and thus provided a historical basis for the liberal democracy which has emerged. This paper examines various aspects of the traditional polity to assess the extent to which this claim can be said to be valid. The data for this analysis come from interviews Dr Mgadla and I conducted during 1987 and 1988 in the Kgatleng, Ngwaketse and Kweneng with elders who have regularly participated in their ward and tribal kgotlas. My assumption is that the pictures our interviewees had in their minds about traditional politics reflect the essential elements of Tswana tradition shaping the thinking of those presently active in public affairs.

The democratic heritage of traditional government certainly centres on the kgotla and its role in policy making. However, other aspects of this experience must be considered as well. Two are particularly important: the decentralization of governance in the Tswana polity in the form of ward organization, and the institutionalization of various adviser roles in the decision making processes associated with the chieftaincy. This paper will begin with these latter two concerns and then conclude with an examination of the role of the kgotla in establishing a tradition of direct democracy in Botswana.

8.2 THE WARD ORGANIZATION

By custom every Motswana has always been a member of a specific morafe and associated with a particular ward. Even strangers joining a morafe were formally affiliated to a ward. Wards were of varying sizes. Some could be very small, comprising a few dozen families and amounting to less than 100 people. Others were very large with over 1000 members. A few were so large that the ward constituted a village by itself. The average size would normally be between 300 and 600 individuals. A ward was made up of a number of family-groups or households. While it was possible for most of the families to be related to the headman or ward-head, it also happened that completely strange family groups would be placed under a particular headman. A good example is the Monare ward in Kanye.

Originally this ward was founded in the eighteenth century for Mosina, son of Kgosi Moleta. But in the 1909 the headman of this ward, one Selerio, was transferred to Mokgamane by Kgosi Bathoen I to take charge of this boarder settlement. The reason was to enhance the chief's control of the area. Selerio's brother, Mokgabisi, remained in charge of the section of the ward at Kanye. At Mokgomane, Selerio found families of Barolong, Batlhware and Bakgalagadi who were incorporated into his ward. In 1912 Selerio asked Kgosi Seepapitso II to give him more 'people' as he was alone with his family 'among the foreigners'. Five men were sent to join him: two brothers from the Mabe ward, two from the Kgatleng ward and one from the Molele ward. The descendants of those men continue to be a part of the Manare ward. The Ngwaketse members of this ward live partly at Kanye and partly at Mokgomane and Kokong. The Batlhware, Barolong and Masetedi members all live at Kokong.

New wards were also established when a kgosi sought to create a niche for members of his family, usually brothers or sons. Consequently, some ward-heads belong by birth to the ruling line in the morafe. Sometimes the kgosi wished to attach servants to the house of the some of his wives. Households would then be selected from already existing wards and placed under the authority of a leader under conditions that could ensure that the families concerned and their descendants became hereditary retainers to the particular households of the kgosi's wives. It was usual to set up such a ward formally when the eldest son of a particular wife of the kgosi was ready to be installed as headman.

To a considerable extent, governance of the Tswana tribes took place in the wards. The wardhead was not elected by the inhabitants over which he presided. He was appointed by the chief. Once appointed the office became hereditary in his family. The headman did not act alone, but in consultation with the adult male members of his ward assembled at their ward kgotla.

The wardhead had specific powers and duties. He was responsible to the kgosi either through his kgosana (where this applied) or directly to the kgosi for developments in the ward. He was also the communication channel between his own people and the kgosi and vice-versa.

The members of a ward tended to function as group in deciding on affairs only affecting the village. Among other things, as will be noted latter, they constituted a court which handled all matters relating to the violation of law and custom. Members of the same ward also assisted each other in times of need. In the tribal regiments, members of each ward constituted a subunit led by the most senior members. The cumulative effect was substantial -- a bond of fellowship existed in which fellow wardsmen were described as *ba ga etsho* (the people of my home).

In sum, Tswana political tradition emphasizes the devolution of governing authority to local political units. Traditionally this was the ward; in the modern state it is the district.

8.3 ADVISERS TO THE CHIEF

Each ward had its own public meeting place called the kgotla. It was near the headman's residence and the ward's cattle enclosure. It was not a building, but a simple wind break of stout poles. At the centre was a hearth round whose fire the men of the ward gathered almost daily in the early mornings and late in the afternoons. Attendance tended to be most substantial at the kgotla of the tribal chief. The most regular were the basimane ba kgosi (literally the chief's boys), basimane sebeso (the fire fighters) or other similar groups of retainers who acted as advisers to the chief.

Asked why Batswana appear to spend an inordinate amount of their time at the kgotla, respondents stated that they wanted to reetsa melao (to hear or listen to the promulgation of laws). While it is correct that the kgosi did promulgate new 'laws' at kgotla, he also used that forum generally to advise or admonish his followers as well as to impart information to them.

The Basimane ba kgosi said they felt a duty to be at the kgotla in order to assist their master with the wide range of responsibilities discharged daily at kgotla. Particularly important was to be available for informal consultation on any matter the chief might be considering. This constant consultation was very important in lessening the risk of personal absolutism on the part of the chief. There were no rigid provisions, written or otherwise, that compelled the kgosi to consult with basimane and other courtiers. But convention in favour of such consultation was strong. It was accordingly difficult for a kgosi to ignore the courtiers at the royal kgotla.

One informant illustrated this with an example of one kgosi who regularly attended social gatherings into the early morning hours. As a result, the kgosi slept late and neglected his duties. Finally some senior advisers woke the chief one morning and compelled him to come to kgotla to see his subject waiting for him to perform his duties. The elders are supposed to have asked the kgosi to choose between being kgosi and continuing his nocturnal entertainment.

This incident serves to demonstrate that Batswana did not regard the authority of the kgosi as absolute. It was always qualified by what his people wanted. This will of the people was, as in this instance, often represented by a group of elders who took it upon themselves to speak for the tribe as a whole. They were not elected spokesmen, but they nevertheless spoke on behalf of the people and in the interest of the people to control unreasonable or irresponsible behaviour by their kgosi. They comprised some of the kgosi's uncles and brothers (boo-rrangwanaa-kgosi and boo-monnaa-kgosi), reinforced by a number of hand-picked persons selected by the kgosi himself from non-royal elders. Together these men constituted the lekoko of the kgosi or his bagakolodi (special advisers).

Another forum used by the kgosi to reduce the semblance of autocratic rule and to broaden the base of his decisions was an advisory council consisting of the headmen of various wards. This body could force the kgosi to consider opinions of people from all geographic areas of the tribe and not just those living in the chief's town. Nothing obliged the kgosi to summon the council of headmen if he himself did not see the need. In practice, chiefs appear to have made use of this device to assess the people's reaction to most innovations they were contemplating or as a mode of communication on new policies. The view of many informants was that these were excellent occasions for the headman to speak frankly to their leader. Usually, if there were any strong views against a particular policy, these were candidly articulated at the headmen's council since it was not considered good etiquette for them to disagree strongly with the kgosi in public.

8.4 THE KGOTLA MEETING

A gathering of the 'nation' or the morafe is called a kgotla meeting. In the past, all adult males who had undergone initiation were expected to attend. The kgosi called such meetings. They always took place in his kgotla and were usually held in the morning before sunrise. All those eligible to attend were expected to do so. It appears little compulsion was used. The headmen were definitely required to be present. All the chief's other advisers also had to attend. In Ngwaketse and Kgatleng, at least, a particular functionary of the chief would check to see that there were at least some elders from each of the tribe's wards at the meeting. In Ngwaketse the chief's police were usually stationed at the exits to the village. They would turn back people who were leaving in their wagons for their fields and urge them to attend the meeting first.

In the kgotla, the kgosi sat in front surrounded by his senior relatives arranged according to their rank in the hierarchy of the morafe. Immediately in front of the chief sat Batswana from different parts of the morafe according to their wards. When the praise singer had praised the kgosi, the latter would introduce the main business of the day. Invariably this would comprise issues on which he had consulted his advisers.

Many elders stated that the agenda for the kgotla meeting was the responsibility of the kgosi. As one informant put it, 'We go to the kgotla and listen to what will be presented there. It is seldom that one goes there already aware of the issues to be discussed.' Others noted that ordinary members in the morafe could place items on the chief's agenda by so requesting in the ward kgotlas. Their wardheads then took the proposal to the kgosi.

When the kgosi had introduced an item for discussion, it was customary for senior members of the morafe, dikgosana or the principle assistants of the kgosi (Dintona) to open the discussion. Headmen would follow and then any member of the morafe could stand up and make his contribution to the debate. Theoretically all males had unrestricted right of speech at the kgotla. The dictum mmualebe o bua la gagwe or mahoko a kgotla a mantle otlhe meant that no one could be debarred from voicing his opinion, no matter how unpopular.

Practice was somewhat different. Elders interviewed in Kweneng stated that Bakgalagadi were not as a rule expected to speak at a kgotla, even though they were free to attend like any other Motswana. As with children in the home, they were to be seen and not heard.

Bangwaketse gave conflicting information on this point, but the majority described a situation that approximated that outlined by Bakwena. They also mentioned that the Bakgalagadi sat behind Bakwena. The explanation given was that by nature the Mokgalagadi was timid or bashful and thus found it difficult to stand up and speak at such a gathering. Some Bangwaketse informants boldly stated that Bakgalagadi were children and that their over-lords were the ones who could and did speak for them.

One very frank Mongwaketse elder recollected an incident that he himself had witnessed. A Mokgalagadi who attempted to speak at a particular kgotla meeting was rudely pulled down by Bangwaketse who said: Nna hatshe o tla re tlholela (Lit: sit down, you will be spying on us.) He concluded that the general treatment accorded to the Mokgalagadi by the Bangwaketse contributed to his inferiority complex.

Tswana societies like other African societies, just did not consider public affairs a domain for women. Women were treated like children. Thus, they did not participate in kgotla as a rule.

With the exception of these restrictions in terms of ethnicity and gender on free participation, the Tswana kgotla as a public assembly operated in a fairly democratic fashion. The government involved the people and more particularly it was for the people. The mode of selection of leaders apart, the system operated in such a way that it checked and restrained the powers of the leaders. It prevented autocracy. The leaders were thus forced to a very large extent to rule in the interest of the people. It was not a replication of Greek or American democracy; it was a peculiarly Tswana form of democracy.

Besides being a place for community discussion, the kgotla functioned as a judicial court in which the community as a whole could participate in the process of adjudication. The emphasis in kgotla justice was not on the employment of specialists to interpret the intricacies of the law but on an open discussion of the facts and public agreement as to appropriate remedies. Also in contrast to Western justice, the rights of the individual were not as important as those of the community.

Every ward had its own court presided over by the headman. Trials normally started at this level, where the parties were heard by fellow members of the community. Appeals proceeded to the court of a chief's representative and then to the chief's kgotla. At all levels, the proceeding was open to any member of the community to participate, including even cross examination of any of the parties to the dispute. There was no escape through technicalities. This was particularly true in the case of stock theft in that everyone knew the true owner of the cattle in dispute.

In a very real sense Batswana males had civic duties not unlike the citizens of Greek democracies. They attended communal assemblies where they debated issues. They attended courts where they were expected to speak their opinion as to the merits of a particular case. The emphasis, however, was on the leader consulting with the public in the case of Tswana democracy. Even the young were sometimes consulted for the Batswana believed that botlhale ba phala botswa phalaneng (the wisdom of the impala cow comes from the little impala).

The Tswana family played a very important role in preparing its members for their civic responsibilities. The family emphasized the importance of kinship and the loyalty of all in the family to the elders. At a very early age the young learned to recognize the existence of a definite pecking order, not only in the family but also in the society at large.

An elder in Kanye stated that the head of a Tswana household was not a despot in his family. When there was a serious issue he consulted his wife or wives and their elder children. He then took the matter, if unsolved, to a meeting of his brothers and uncles in the same kgotla. From there the matter might go to the kgotla of the ward. If still unsolved it would go to the chief's kgotla.

The age regiments also played a crucial role in teaching Batswana the virtues of obedience, royalty, respect for seniors and a sense of responsibility. The result was that Batswana had a special quality of humility which enabled them to give allegiance readily to whosoever was in authority. This humility kept the people of a morafe from engaging in prolonged disputes which could unnessarily split the community.

8.5 CONCLUSION

This essay has sought to stress the democratic character of the traditional Tswana polity. Through the ward structure decision making on local issues was handled by the headman in consultation with his people. Each ward thus had considerable autonomy. The chiefs of the Tswana tribes consulted their various advisers who were available in kgotla on a regular basis. The result was a government with a certain openness. On important issues the nation was brought to the chief's kgotla where all males at least could express their opinions. The whole idea of public debate is consequently recognized as an important part of policy making. Finally, the kgotla also operated as a court in which the community was given the right to participate in determining the facts of a case and to advise their wardhead on the appropriate decision.

At a very minimum, this whole structure taught the people the necessity of observing and participating in their own governance. The problem of the post-independence government is to maintain this tradition.

9 Dikgotla, dikgosi and the protectorate administration

P.T. Mgadla and A.C. Campbell

9.1 INTRODUCTION

A striking aspect of contemporary government in Botswana has been its ability to communicate with the people through the kgotla and dikgosi. To understand the existence of this phenomenon, we must explore the evolution of these two institutions during the colonial period. This paper argues that the positions of the kgotla and dikgosi both weakened and strengthened during protectorate administration times.

The kgotla weakened because it lost some of its democratic customs in the 1920s since less consultation occurred between the morafe on the one hand, and dikgosi and the administration on the other. Dikgosi during this period lost some of their judicial and legislative powers which they had hitherto enjoyed. Further, their right to allocate land, in so far as concessions to foreigners was concerned was restricted. Most important, the protectorate administration reserved the right to approve and depose dikgosi, thereby undermining the customary and hereditary system of *bogosi* where this was done by a group of tribal elders.

The strengthening of the kgotla and dikgosi lay partly in the fact that the protectorate administration turned to both as critical for reaching the people and introducing its various policies. But the dikgosi further enhanced their power by opposing certain innovations of the colonial central government which they saw as interfering with 'tribal' society and administration. The compromise was often to increase the role of the kgotla in the decision making of the morafe.

The overall effect was a transformation of the dikgosi and the kgotla from institutions of tribal rule into ones which constrained the emerging central government in the name of the people. This change laid the basis for the integration of the old tribal states with the new nation state of Botswana. However, before discussing these developments, the baseline of the pre-colonial structure must be briefly outlined.

9.2 THE PRE-COLONIAL SYSTEMS

The kgotla has existed from time immemorial. It is the central feature of Tswana life. All initiated men were expected to attend and had the right to air their views without fear of reprimand.[1] The kgotla was a forum for national deliberations. In it, the kgosi promulgated all Tswana laws. To it the people came to adjudicate all civil disputes and criminal cases.

The kgosi was a hereditary ruler by primogeniture. He held all powers of government. He presided in kgotla, where after lengthy discussion, in which all could participate, the kgosi had the right to make the final decision on all matters.[2] He held the overall right to allocate land, summon regimental labour and settle legal appeals from subordinate kgotlas. In short he exercised sovereign power.

In his administration, the kgosi was assisted by the basimane ba kgosi, people of high social standing often related to the royal house, who headed the various wards or divisions of the morafe or nation. In important discussions, their opinions were sought and carried considerable weight.[3] Generally, decisions were seen as a consensus of opinion expressed through the kgosi. In practice dikgosi sometimes tried to enforce their own unpopular decisions which might be gradually accepted or ignored.

The extent of democracy in this system of government depended on the interaction of the various ruling groups. Where the kgosi and his relatives were weak, the kgotla was sometimes overawed by rich commoners. Where a relative was stronger than the kgosi, the latter often became the surrogate. When a kgosi was overbearing and autocratic, his behaviour could split the nation with many people living under one of his relatives. A kgosi who acted according to custom and in the interests of the group as a whole retained allegiance and respect. He allowed the kgotla to become a mechanism for popular control. A kgosi who did not, often had little actual power, and politics degenerated into oligarchy.

None of the above should be taken to mean that all adults participated in the governance issues. It was only a core element consisting of males who were members of the dominant Tswana group who participated in kgotla. Other Tswana peoples such as Bakaa or subservient groups, including invariably Bakgalagadi and Basarwa had no right to voice an opinion or take part in any important discussions. Women were also excluded regardless of their ethnicity.

9.3 DECLARATION OF THE PROTECTORATE: 1885-1891

From 1885 when the country was declared a 'protectorate' to about 1919, the position of the British administration was in theory one of non-interference in local administration. Its concern lay largely in protecting the land from external forces, particularly the Boers in the Transvaal, Mzilikazi in Zimbabwe, and the Germans in Namibia. A dispatch to the first Assistant Commissioner of the Bechuanaland protectorate reflects this point. He was

> . . . not to interfere with the native administration: The chiefs are understood not to be desirous of parting with their rights of sovereignty nor are Her Majesty's Government by any means anxious to assume the responsibilities of it.[4]

There were a few matters, however, that could not be left to the traditional system. The British moved to establish an administration within the protectorate to control the country's European residents. They established a superior court system to deal with cases among Europeans, and between Africans and Europeans.[5] They also took control of issues involving trade, hunting by foreigners and concessions. Effectively, from 1885 the European administration based on Cape laws worked alongside African Administration based on Tswana tradition.[6]

This system came to be known in British circles as 'parallel rule' and the Tswana part was often termed 'indirect rule'. It meant that the kgotla retained its democratic traditions, continuing to implement Tswana law and custom, and dikgosi enjoyed relative autonomy concerning the affairs of their own people.

9.4 EROSION OF THE POWERS OF KGOSI AND KGOTLA: 1891-1920

Gradually, the protectorate administration began to impose its own policies and dikgosi came to oppose those which they considered conflicted with their laws and customs. During this period, however, the administration used dikgosi to implement most of the innovations it wished to make. The result was that for the most part the administration made only minor changes and did not make any serious attempt to intervene in dikgosi's relation to the kgotla.

In 1891, six years after the declaration of the protectorate, the British administration promulgated an Order in Council authorizing the high commissioner for the protectorate, the British crown's representative in Cape Town, to 'legislate for Bechuanaland by proclamation'. The order further specified that in so doing, 'he shall respect native law and custom'.[7] The order empowered the high commissioner on the advice of administration officials, to suspend, fine and depose uncooperative or troublesome dikgosi and to draw boundaries between the various Tswana nations.

Some dikgosi contested the granting of these new powers to the high commissioner. Sebele for instance openly disagreed that the colonial administration could grant hunting and trading licences to foreigners. For the most part the Bakwena kgosi ignored the directives of the colonial administration, characterizing them as interference with the laws of his people. In one instance the administration fined him ten heads of cattle for disobeying its orders.[8] The situation became so bad that there was some talk among colonial officials of deposing Sebele in favour of his brother, Kgari, but they eventually concluded that the former had more support. This would indicate that although the administration in theory asserted it had certain powers over dikgosi, the pre-colonial system was continuing to function in fact because of political viability.

There were a few instances where the British did exercise their new authority. One occurred in 1893 when the Batawana were divided on the rule of their kgosi, Sekgoma Letsholathebe. He was aggressively rejecting the administration's laws and the position of Christian missionaries. The Resident Commissioner, Sir Ralph Williams, after a kgotla meeting at Tsau, deposed the kgosi in favour of Mathiba Moremi.[9]

Sometimes the administration backed the people and the kgosi against undesirable elements. In Raditladi's disagreement with Kgosi Khama III, the administration supported Khama's move to banish Raditladi from Ngwato as a divisive element. In 1898, the administration supported Kgosi Khama III following his quarrel with his son, Sekgoma Khama. The latter was banished to Nata although later allowed to return to Bamangwato land.

Together the four incidents just mentioned suggest that the administration supported dikgosi's powers so long as they were not in conflict with its policies. Even if the kgosi did challenge colonial policy, the administration was hesitant to remove the chief unless there was clear support in the kgotla for such a decision.

Around the turn of the century the British began to seek more than occasional interventions in the rule of the Batswana dikgosi. They began a process which has continued to this day of incorporation of dikgosi into central government structures. The first major step in this regard was the rendering of dikgosi the collectors of the hut tax which was intended to fund the administration of the protectorate. Instead of receiving tributes from their own people, dikgosi henceforth only received ten per cent of their collections. This change clearly antagonized the people and the dikgosi because they saw no reason for supporting the new administration financially and often did not have the money to pay.

The colonial government also took certain powers from the chief. By about 1910, the kgosi could no longer grant mining concessions without the express permission and approval of the secretary of state nor make practical agreements with neighbouring states without administration approval. Cases of murder and those involving Europeans were transferred to the jurisdiction of European courts.[10] All these changes were a reduction in popular control in that the colonial government was not forced to defend its policies in kgotla before the people.

Sometimes the administration limited its efforts for change to persuasion. At the request of the missionaries, it called on dikgosi and their people to limit participation in bogwera (initiation) to children whose parents approved of the practice. Some groups agreed, but others continued with the tradition, despite the administration's and the missionaries' attempt to halt it. This indicates not only the strength of the custom, but also the fact that the administration did not feel at this stage that it could introduce changes in custom without kgotla approval.

From time to time the administration restricted the dikgosi because of popular demand. The classic instance was the Native Labour Proclamation of 1907 which made it illegal for dikgosi to bind themselves by contract for the provision of labour.[11] Dikgosi were trying to raise money for development, as well as the required taxes, by sending youth to South African mines. The population did not support this practice and asked the administration to act on their behalf to stop dikgosi from sending their people to the mines against their will. In this respect, dikgosi's powers were curtailed, and the people's welfare enhanced.

The protectorate administration also gave ordinary people the opportunity to complain against individual dikgosi. In 1916, for example, Sechele II was forced to accept three councillors to help him rule the people because the people recognized his administrative inefficiency. In this instance the common people were able to complain directly to the administration about their kgosi.

Recognizing popular opposition, and trying to appease dikgosi, the administration sometimes involved the latter in some decision making rather than simply imposing rules over their heads. In 1893, for example, the high commissioner asked dikgosi to help in the protection of big game including elephant, giraffe and eland. In 1913 Khama was asked to prohibit the sale of cattle to traders without his written authority. In this way, dikgosi gained authority even though they were implementing laws suggested by the administration.

The relationship of the administration and dikgosi took still another turn in 1919 when the law was changed to allow appeals from dikgotla to the magistrate. Both kgosi and the magistrate sat together in court to hear such appeals. Thus, power was taken from dikgosi, at the same time the administration recognized the need for traditional authorities to participate in such decision making processes. However, overall the fact remained that the kgosi and his councillors no longer had the power to make the ultimate decision.

The period up to 1920 was one in which the kgotla's powers of control over dikgosi generally remained unfettered except for a few policy questions which were turned over to the protectorate administration. The chiefs on the other hand were facing the first stages of the incorporation into the central government structure of the territory. In addition, the administration was taking some of their powers for itself. However, for the most part, dikgosi remained unfettered and the administration sought to work through them.

9.5 THE ADVENT OF ADVISORY COUNCILS

The establishment of the Native Advisory Council in 1920 was the start of a major change in policy making in Botswana. After this date, the central government began increasingly to take for itself the authority to initiate social change. The task of the Native Advisory Council was to legitimize this new locus of power by debating, approving and in some cases possibly modifying administration proposals. The European Advisory Council was launched the following year to do the same for the settler community.

The Native Advisory Council consisted of dikgosi and councillors who were chosen in kgotla. It lacked any sense of popular representation in that the 'elected' councillors were chosen by chiefs without adequate consultation with their people in kgotla.

The resident commissioner based in Mafeking acted on behalf of the high commissioner, meeting dikgosi and presiding over council sessions. Initially the council agenda was prepared by the administration, but gradually dikgosi were also allowed to submit their own matters for inclusion.[12] The council's original purpose was to discuss affairs on a national rather than at a regional level. A principle concern of the council was to decide on the allocation of funds for developments such as education, animal health, and new boreholes. This was the first major move towards development planning on a national scale.

Not all dikgosi attended council. Khama refused to attend, giving old age as an excuse; but the truth lay in his belief that the council reduced dikgosi's powers while itself having no legislative force.

Deliberation and resolutions made at council were rarely, if ever, discussed in dikgotla prior to the meetings. Once resolutions had been approved by the resident commissioner and dikgosi, the latter announced them in dikgotla and the public had little say in deliberating over them, contrary to the customary democratic practice of dikgotla.[13] Thus the introduction of new policies on hunting, initiation and the sale of cattle were discussed in the council and only announced at the kgotla. The kgotla continued to be the main forum for discussions among the morafe, but the issues increasingly were ones relating to instituting administration policies rather than the substance of these policies.

The European Advisory Council tended to work for balkanization of Botswana. It called for the protectorate administration to have Bechuanaland incorporated either into South Africa or Southern Rhodesia (now Zimbabwe) or to be divided between them.[14] This pressure and Britain's wish to rid itself of responsibilities for the protectorate made the issue of incorporation a constant concern to those Batswana who were politically aware. The position of dikgosi was probably strengthened as a result since they argued strongly against incorporation and in the end the administration listened to their united voice. Kgosi Bathoen II and Tshekedi Khama were particularly vociferous about the issue, convincing the British about the strong opposition of Batswana to becoming part of the Union of South Africa.

Even with the Native Advisory Council in existence, the administration sometimes passed laws which were unfavourable to dikgosi. In 1926 and 1927 for example, the administration passed laws removing civil marriages and *boloi* (witchcraft) from dikgosi's jurisdiction.[15] Both these actions were taken at the behest of the missionaries. Dikgosi protested vehemently at council, arguing that the powers they hitherto held were being eroded by the administration's expanded jurisdiction on these matters customarily dealt with at the kgotla. For its part the administration saw its role in council as a means for perpetuating mutual relations between itself and traditional authorities, the more so since these authorities were able to discuss traditional and national laws at such council meetings. The officers of the administration, including district commissioners and resident magistrates, were appointed without any consultation with the Native Advisory Council, let alone there being any discussion with dikgosi and the morafe concerned. If there had been some degree of consultation, no matter how minimal, the theory of 'parallel rule' or indirect rule would have made more sense to Botswana. As it was, some officers barely understood Tswana law and custom, yet had authority over dikgosi and their institutions. The more progressive members of the Native Advisory Council became concerned about the lack of development of any sort of Batswana controlled and run territorial administration. Thus Tshekedi Khama remarked:

> . . . after sixty-five years of British rule, the British government has so far not appointed African people to fill responsible posts in the administration of the country.[16]

In sum, the advent of the Native Advisory Council began a process of transferring policy making powers from the dikgotla to the central government. The council itself exercised little of this power itself, rather serving as a forum in which the protectorate administration could demonstrate that it had consulted the people. In some cases the Council's advice was rejected. It did, however, provide a united voice of the dikgosi against incorporation into either South Africa or Rhodesia. The kgotla remained a place for community discussion only in so far as issues related to implementation of policy were brought to it.

9.6 THE DEMOCRATIZATION OF DIKGOSI

In the 1930s a new generation of dikgosi began to come to power. Often educated at missionary colleges, they challenged the authority of the administration over a series of issues related to bogosi.[17] In particular they asserted positions as custodians of Tswana bogosi and rejected the idea that the administration could interfere in these matters. The administration's response was the introduction of a set of proclamations in 1934-5 to regulate the activities of dikgosi, who were allegedly abusing their powers.

The administration contended the changes involved would make local government more democratic by reducing dikgosi's powers and rending the kgotla a legal entity.[18] These laws would have given the administration total power of policy making and would have left dikgosi to implement them without taking any real part in their formulation. The people, through the kgotla, would no longer have had any part at all in decision making. The proclamations also gave the High Commissioner power to recognize dikgosi, meaning that unrecognized dikgosi received no official backing. Additional important changes were: provision of a mechanism whereby the administration could regulate and modify traditional practice by the introduction of British procedural laws; provision of formal establishment of local councils designed to advise dikgosi on the affairs of their people; powers vested in the district commissioners to 'introduce a form of bureaucratic administration to the Tribal Authority by providing a salaried clerical staff'; and the introduction of 'a British financial system designed for the creation of local treasuries in each district and the appointment of the financial staff to each Tribal Authority'.[19]

The initial reaction of the two leading chiefs, Tshekedi Khama and Bathoen II was to contest the proclamations in the courts. Dikgosi argued that the Order in Council of 1891 left powers of traditional authorities unaltered, even though successive resident commissioners had tried to erode them. The proclamations were thus a violation of the 1891 Order and a serious undermining of democratic institutions. They also contended that the proclamations set up senior and junior local tribunals to try cases which was contrary to Tswana law and custom.

They saw the institution of magistrate courts above the kgotla as limiting the latter's authority to try cases.[20] The public would now attend the magistrate's court instead of the kgotla, which not only denigrated the democratic institution of the kgotla but was a departure from traditional practice. The proclamations forbade traditional authorities from imposing any levy without approval of the administration and, according to dikgosi, our forefathers made levies without even seeking advice or approval of the resident commissioner. Besides, they argued, there never existed any official communication about the draft proclamations and as dikgosi put it, 'we should have been consulted before they were formed'.[21]

Such were dikgosi's grievances which led to their court action against the high commissioner. Dikgosi lost the legal battle, the conclusion of the court being: 'His Majesty has unfettered and unlimited power to legislate for the government and administration of justice among the native tribes of Bechuanaland Protectorate'.[22]

The author of these laws, the Resistent Commissioner, Sir Charles Rey, departed in 1938. The new Resident Commissioner, Arden Clarke, decided to cooperate with dikgosi in revising the proclamations to the extent that could be accepted by dikgosi. The result was an enhancement of the power of the kgotla. The revised proclamations provided that dikgosi could make laws with 'the agreement' of the kgotla. The tribal treasuries established to control collection and expenditure of taxes, were operated by a finance committee appointed by the kgosi. Although dikgosi lost their ten per cent from taxes, they now received a fixed salary.[23]

The major effect of the proclamations appears to have been a strengthening of dikgotla because both dikgosi and the administration eventually compromised by recognising the existence of the kgotla as a means of instituting policy and as a way of rallying support from the people for government policies. This was a reversal of the trend which had begun in the twenties. The administration, while saying it recognized the need to consult dikgotla before implementing its policies, in practice was relying more and more on dikgosi and ignoring the general population. Dikgosi themselves had gone along with the administration, in failing to bring their people into policy discussions.

The experience of fighting the proclamations may have strengthen dikgosi's powers as well since they boldly challenged the administration in a bid to maintain traditional democratic principles in their societies. As a result they gained in popularity. The administration for its part became directly aware of the strength of the kgotla and its power in bringing about popular acceptance of government policies.

The idea of working through the kgotla and kgosi was further recognized by the proclamations of 1943.[24] The drafting committee established in 1941 consisted of Tshekedi Khama, M. Seboni, Bogatsu Pilane, Sebopiwa Molema, Dr S. Molema and an equal number of government officers. The high commissioner announced that the new proclamations, based on the findings of the committee, would replace the controversial 1934 proclamations, which had caused so much unhappiness among Batswana.

The new proclamations among other provisions brought back some of the powers of dikgosi. Although the high commissioner could still appoint and depose dikgosi, he was required first to consult with the kgotla. The result was that the kgotla once again assumed a prominent role among Batswana, with the kgosi consulting with it rather than tribal elders. In 1954, the African Administration Proclamation went further and provided that dikgosi had legislative and executive authority as long as they exercised it with the consent of the kgotla.[25]

Clearly, the post-war policy of the administration was development of a more representative forum of government based on the institution of bogosi. However, by the mid-fifties this policy was overtaken by constitutional developments at the national level. By 1956, it was patently obvious that British rule was ending and that steps must be taken to form the basis of the internal government which would lead the country to independence. In 1951 a Joint Advisory Council had been formed consisting of both Africans and Europeans. In 1959 this council advised that a new constitution be established with a legislative council. The council came into existence the following year. The new Legislative Council in its turn led to the general elections of 1965 and the formation of a national government.

Once the new government was in power after 1965, the powers of dikgosi and the function of dikgotla diminished as dikgosi became advisers to the parliamentary government and administrators of the local court system. The remainder of their powers over land, education, water, and matimela cattle were transferred to the newly formed district councils and land boards.[26]

9.7 CONCLUSION

From 1885 to 1965, the position of dikgotla and dikgosi by and large remained relatively democratic but was considerably affected by change of administration. Between 1885 and 1920, both kgotla and kgosi remained relatively autonomous. Then for a time the administration sought to make policy with the advice of the chiefs. Dikgotla appeared to be in a process of decline, but after 1934 they were brought back into the policy process as dikgosi sought to maintain their powers in the face of the central government's attempt to create a territorial administration. This preservation of the dikgotla as part of the policy making process at the local level probably helped to insure their persistence into the post-colonial period.

Dikgosi's relation to the dikgotla has been changed dramatically. In pre-colonial period, they looked to dikgotla as a place where they gave the public a chance to voice their opinions but not to make the final decisions on policy questions. Such decisions were the purview of dikgosi. Now the situation is becoming reversed. Dikgosi seek to enhance the role of the kgotla so that they can prevent further encroachments on their authority by the central government. They preserve their influence, now largely symbolic, by calling for consultation with the still revered kgotla. They legislate by the same means.

Oral data gathered in the three villages; Kanye, Molepolole and Mochudi indicate that the people see the dikgosi as a dying institution since 1966. 'People do not attend the kgotla as before because there is no obligation,' remarked one informant. 'Kgosi is now a civil servant receiving instructions mainly from the government,'[27] he added. Yet another asserted 'the kgotla has changed most drastically, so have the powers of dikgosi because all the laws affecting kgosi are made by government whereas before, the kgosi made the laws in consultation with his people.'[28]

ENDNOTES

1 Interview with Difatlhwe Seame, Tlokeng ward, Mochudi, 16 June 1988.
2 Interview with K. Kooagile, Maunatlala ward, Lelwelakgosi, Molepolole, 5

October 1987. Also see Schapera, I. 'Kingship and Politics in Tswana History', *Journal of Royal Antropological Institute* 93, 2 (1963) pp. 160-169.

3   Interview with S. O. Pilane, Kgosing ward, Mochudi, 12 February 1988; and D. Masimega, Tshosa ward, Molepolole, 18 November 1987.

4   Quoted from Schapera, I. *Tribal Innovators: Tswana Chiefs and Social Change: 1795-1940* (New York: Athlone Press, 1970) p. 51.

5   Ibid.; see also Tlou, T. and Campbell, A. *History of Botswana* (Gaborone: Macmillan Botswana, 1984) p. 177.

6   Ibid.

7   Schapera, I. *Tribal Innovators*, p. 51.

8   Tlou, and Campbell, *History of Botswana*, p. 178.

9   Ibid.

10   Schapera, I. 'The Political Annals of the Tswana Tribe: Minutes of the Ngwaketse Public Assemblies 1910-1917' Communication from the school of African Studies, University of Cape Town, 1974 p. 7.

11   Schapera, I. *Tribal Innovators*, p. 53.

12   Interview with Masimega, November 1987.

13   Ibid.

14   Stevens, R. *Botswana, Lesotho and Swaziland: The Former High Commission Territories of Southern Africa* (New York: Praeger, 1967).

15   Schapera, I. *Tribal Innovators*, p. 53.

16   Khama. T. 'Developing Representative Government in a Changing Africa: Problems of a Political Advancement in Backward in African World' (1965) p. 13.

17   Simmon, G. 'Survival of Chieftainancy in Botswana', in *Journal of African Affairs*, Vol. 72 (1973) p. 179.

18   Simmon, G. 'Survival of Chieftainancy in Botswana', p. 180.

19   Picard, L. A. *Politics and Rural Development in Southern Africa: Evolution of Modern Botswana Politics* (London: Rex Collings, 1985) p. 12.

20   Minutes of the Special Court of Bechuanaland Protectorate held in Lobatse, 1936, p. 47.

21   Ibid., p. 195.

22   Quoted from Parson, J. *Botswana: Liberal Democracy and the Labour Reserve in Southern Africa.* (London: Westview Press, 1984) p. 22.

23   Ibid.

24   Tlou, and Campbell, *History of Botswana*, p. 186.

25   Odell, M. J. 'Local Government Tradition and Modern Roles of the Traditional Kgotla', in Picard. *Modern Botswana*, p. 66.

26   Ibid.

27   Anonymous, Madimetse ward, Mochudi, 5 May 1988.

28   Interview with Mparuele, Ntloedibe ward, Molepolole, 12 July 1987.

10 The rights of minorities and subject peoples in Botswana: a historical evaluation

K. Datta and A. Murray

10.1 INTRODUCTION

This paper focuses on the rights accorded to non-Tswana groups incorporated into Tswana states voluntarily or by conquest. These subject peoples, or minority groups as they are nowadays termed, often outnumbered their Tswana overlords. Even today, the 'minority tribes' are in fact in the majority in the Central District and Ngamiland. Yet it has been true of both traditional and modern Tswanadom[1] that ethnic conflict has been largely avoided. This paper suggests that the reason for this absence of conflict has been the openness of Tswanadom, its capacity to absorb and adapt outside influences without losing its own identity in the process.

Some minority groups were never accorded the same rights or privileges as those of Tswana origin, but most of these minorities had the opportunity of being granted the same rights and privileges over time. There was exploitation and political domination, but the injustice was hardly ever perceived to be so great as to justify or fuel rebellion.

This paper begins with a discussion of the status structure of historical Tswanadom and the theory of human rights accorded therein. Then consideration is given to the specific political, economic, social and cultural rights which existed in practice for minority groups. Finally the changes in the condition of minority groups since independence are examined.

10.2 COMMONERS, FOREIGNERS AND SERFS

In Tswanadom during the pre-colonial and colonial eras, social status derived from cultural or kinship proximity to the kgosi and his relatives, the dikgosana. There were three broad classes of subjects in descending order of status: commoners, foreigners and serfs.[2] Commoners were non-royal members of the Tswana nuclear group as well as those immigrant or conquered groups who had proved themselves loyal subjects of the kgosi.

Foreigners were immigrants or conquered groups who had not yet attained the status of commoners or who had no wish to meld their identity with that of the dominant Tswana group. As Schapera points out, the rights initially granted foreigners by their Tswana overlords varied 'according to their mode of absorption, their organization and numbers, and their culture'.[3] Important too was the physical distance of the settlers from the Tswana capital.

A group of foreigners who were absorbed voluntarily, had a tradition of centralized leadership, were of a size sufficient to maintain a corporate identity, lived far from the capital, and whose culture could meld easily with that of the Tswana were likely to be granted more rights and privileges and to attain more quickly full rights of citizenship as commoners. A people who had been absorbed by conquest, were acephalous and lacked a corporate identity, lived close to the capital, and were alien in language and culture to their new masters would be forced into the class of serfs and would be exploited for the benefit of the other classes. The result was that subject peoples could be commoners (e.g. the Babirwa, Bakaa, and Bakhurutshe), foreigners (e.g. the Ovaherero, and Kalanga), or serfs (e.g. the Basarwa and Bakgalagadi).

Over time some subject groups moved from one status to another. The Bayei, for example, at different periods, were treated as serfs, foreigners and commoners by the Batawana. To complicate matters even further, within a particular subject group there could be serfs, foreigners and commoners, although usually one type predominated at any one time. At the turn of the century, among the Bayei, those who lived close to the capital tended to have a master-serf relationship with the Batawana. Those resident at the periphery of the state were likely to be treated as foreigners. Many Bayei seemed to be accepting their lower status in that they would refer to themselves as Makuba ('useless people'), the Batawana term for the Bayei.

Because the spectrum of subject groups' rights is so broad, we propose to focus on those subject groups found at the 'least rights' end of the spectrum. These groups often shared a common characteristic: cultural distance from Tswanadom.[4] As one authority states, 'It is apparently only when incorporated peoples differ appreciably from those of the nuclear stock in language and culture, and above all race, that they are relegated to a position of marked social inferiority and economic exploitation'.[5] Not surprisingly, among some of these subject groups (the Kalanga and the Bayei for example) serious challenges to the legitimacy of Tswanadom arose during the colonial period. And it is also the plight of one of these subject groups (the Basarwa) that today represents the most serious challenge to Botswana's claim to be a liberal democracy.

10.3 THE CONCEPT OF PERSONAL RIGHTS IN TSWANADOM

Jack Donnelly has argued that 'the idea of human rights, as that term is normally understood – namely as rights/titles/claims held by all individuals simply because they are human beings – is foreign to traditional African society and political culture'.[6] Human rights, he suggests, can only be held by an individual; since their source is human nature, they are also universal. Rights in 'traditional' societies, contends Donnelly, are usually held by communities, not individuals; their source is membership in a particular community.[7]

In Tswanadom this generalization appears to hold true: rights were accorded those who were members of the morafe, and membership in the morafe was defined by membership in a kgotla or ward, the basic administrative unit of Tswanadom. Those who were not ward members, for example most if not all Basarwa, were treated as serfs, as persons without rights. Thus the rights we shall be talking about — economic, political, cultural and judicial — are primarily communal rights.

This concept of rights has not gone unchallenged however. The penetration of capitalism since the nineteenth century has brought with it notions of individual property rights in land and capital. And the ideology of nationalism has undermined the legitimacy of communal politics with the notion that all Batswana are citizens of one nation, Botswana, and owe their primary loyalty to this nation.

The conflict which has arisen between the old concept of morafe citizenship and this new definition is a recurrent theme of the paper. Nowhere is it more striking than in the present plight of the Basarwa, a people denied rights to land because they are not members of a morafe, yet who are being removed from land they have occupied for centuries because it has been commercialized for the use of the private citizens of Botswana.

10.4 ECONOMIC RIGHTS

Schapera states that 'every member of a tribe enjoys certain rights and privileges in common with his fellow tribesmen. He is entitled to land on which to erect his home, to plough and to graze his cattle, and to all other facilities for earning a livelihood . . .'[8] In theory, and usually in practice, members of subject groups recognized as being members of the morafe had the same economic rights as any other Mongwato, Mokwena or Motawana. They had access to land and water, absolute property rights, control over their own labour, and were usually subject to the same restrictions concerning movement and settlement. They paid the same taxes and, subsequent to the late nineteenth century, paid no tribute to the Tswana kgosi.

Some subject groups such as the Ovaherero, which were incorporated into Tswanadom impoverished and propertyless, have prospered in the twentieth century, taking advantage of a system of cattle-lending (mafisa), a form of cattle-feudalism, to eventually rival their Tswana overlords in numbers and quality of cattle herded. Under the mafisa system, in return for herding a patron's cattle, the client is entitled not only to the use of the cattle but usually also to appropriate one or more of the offspring each year.

Parsons argues that throughout much of southern Africa mafisa has been the most important basis of state organization.[9] By lending-out cattle obtained by conquest to commoners, nineteenth century Tswana dikgosi created a client class which, like the feudal lords of Europe, promised loyalty and service in return for use of their cattle. These vassals or servants (batlhanka) became basimane ba kgosi (literally the chief's boys), and also performed administrative functions as overseers, or later district governors.

The mafisa system was used in much the same way to incorporate foreigners into the economic life of the morafe, and it has continued to be the most important means of access to cattle and cattle accumulation for the poor. Solway's study of one

Bakgalagadi group in the western Kweneng shows how by means of mafisa, cattle ownership in Bakgalagadi households 'has grown from a small percentage at the beginning of the century to over 90 per cent by the late 1970s'.[10]

Not all subject groups have been allowed to profit from the mafisa system. Some have been denied the right to own cattle, or more commonly, denied access to land and water. They have been forced to become serfs, rather than clients of the cattle owners. The Basarwa in particular, and to a lesser extent the Bayei, the Bakgalagadi and the Batswapong, have been the victims of a form of hereditary serfdom called *bolata* by the Bangwato and *botlhanka* by the Batawana.

Tlou suggests that in Ngamiland serfdom evolved out of a system of voluntary clientship: 'It seems plausible that, having been dispossessed of their property by the Batawana, some Bayei, Bakalagadi, and a few Basarwa attached themselves as clients to wealthy Batawana in order to secure a livelihood. As time passed, what began as voluntary service turned into a hereditary one, imposed and perpetuated by the more powerful Batawana'.[11] Miers and Crowder paint a similar picture in the Central District: 'What began as a relationship between Bangwato pastoralists and traders and their Basarwa hunting partners and pastoral clients changed into a servile relationship wherein the Basarwa served first the Ngwato state and later became the private property of Ngwato pastoralists'.[12]

It has been suggested that the transformation of clients into serfs was the result of the 'dramatic expansion of the hunting economy' after the arrival of white traders in the second half of the nineteenth century.[13] When the Tswana elites began to invest their profits in expanding their cattle herds, they looked to the Basarwa to supply their increased labour requirements. Tlou too emphasizes the importance of botlhanka as a 'dependable and easily exploitable labour force'.[14]

Schapera, however, sees serfdom as a product of the process of state-formation: 'the Kgalagadi, Sarwa, Koba (Bayei), Tswapong, or other vassal peoples living in any district were the serfs of the overseer who was entitled to appropriate whatever property they acquired'.[15] Both Schapera and Solway view the arrival of European traders as bringing about the decline of serfdom, not its reinforcement, since their presence allowed the serfs to develop independent trading relationships and thereby forced the Tswana masters to treat their serfs as clients if they wished to obtain goods for trade.

It is certainly true that there was legal reform of property relations in some Tswana states during the last decades of the nineteenth century. Sebele of the Bakwena and Bathoen I of the Bangwaketse gave their serfs the right to hold property, thus, in theory at least, greatly weakening the institution of bolata/botlhanka. Khama III of the Bangwato went even further in efforts to free his malata. In his words, 'these tribes became in the first instance so apprehensive of the declaration granting them property rights that at last I had to ask European traders to travel among them and sell goods'.[16]

Despite the declarations of dikgosi, serfdom actually increased its hold over certain subject groups, in particular the Bayei and Basarwa, during the first half of the twentieth century. Whatever the origins of serfdom, its usefulness to Batswana cattle owners ensured longevity. This was reflected in the Tagart Commission report of 1931. The commission, which was inquiring into the conditions of the Basarwa, reported that many were still treated as serfs. They were unable to dispose freely of their labour, enjoyed limited property rights, had no control over land, and were liable to be transferred as property on the death of their master.

Representatives of the Bayei in Maun presented a petition to the district commissioner in 1948. The character of their demands reflects the persistence of serfdom. One requested the abolition of the practice whereby a Motawana master claimed the property, and sometimes the children of, his Moyei serf on the latter's death. Another demanded 'full rights to the use of land for purposes of grazing and ploughing'.[17]

The key factor which maintained, or reintroduced, restrictions on the economic rights of Bayei and Basarwa does appear to have been the labour requirements of the booming pastoral economies of Ngamiland and Gammangwato.[18] Parsons suggests that evidence presented before the Tagart Commission shows that 'market conditions had intensified the use of serf labour while the serfs themselves increasingly attempted to flee such oppression by becoming labour migrants'.[19] Paradoxically, it was through the operation of 'market conditions' that the British hoped to banish serfdom from the protectorate.

During the 1930s, partly because of external pressure from organizations such as the League of Nations, and partly because Resident Commissioner Charles Rey saw the Basarwa issue as a stick with which to beat Tshekedi Khama, the colonial administration ceased to ignore the plight of the serfs and took what it believed was the final action to abolish bolata/botlhanka. Proclamation No.14 of 1936 required that all 'native labourers' should be paid for their labour, either in cash or in kind, that they should be free to choose their employer, and that they could terminate their employment with one month's notice. According to Miers and Crowder, 'the British believed they had broken the back of the problem and that in time the economic and social position of the Basarwa would improve as more of them entered the wage-labuor force and acquired stock of their own or took to farming'.[20]

It was not only the Basarwa who were going to be thus liberated. In 1938 the district commissioner for Ngamiland predicted that the opportunities provided by migrant labour would 'act as a strong influence to emancipate the subservient tribes of Makuba (Bayei) and Mambukushu who when they have been to the mines and have seen the outside world and have earned a little money will not submit so readily to the arrogant demands of the Batawana proper'.[21]

In Ngamiland incomes from migrant labour did have a significant impact on the region's economy. The Witwatersrand Native Labour Association had been given permission to establish a depot in Maun in 1937. By 1950 over 4 000 labourers were sent to the mines via the Maun depot each year. Although most of these were from Angola, those who did come from Ngamiland received a total of £81 743 in deferred pay in 1950, and according to the district commissioner 'a large proportion of it was spent in the district'.[22]

While some income went for consumer goods, most was spent on cattle by men who had owned few or no cattle before. Some Bayei, although primarily fishers and agriculturists, attempted to build up cattle herds of their own after the rinderpest epademic of 1896 had rid large parts of the delta of tsetse-fly. This aspiration had been blocked for most Bayei by a lack of cash and by the institution of botlhanka. Work in the mines now provided that cash.

The ruling Batawana were very hostile to these efforts on the part of their subject peoples, particularly since available grazing land was shrinking as the tsetse-fly returned during the 1920s and 1930s. They restricted access of Bayei to grazing land and sought, unsuccessfully, to prevent the Bayei accumulating more cattle.[23] If the Bayei sought redress in kgotla, the Regent Pulane Moremi herself admitted that 'in cases where a Motawana and a Moyei are involved the Moyei does not stand a chance'.[24] The result of this frustration of Bayei economic aspirations by the ruling Batawana was the emergence of Bayei separatism which is a part of Ngambiland politics to this day.

While the opportunities offered by migrant labour to the Bayei may have helped in their emancipation, the same cannot be said of the Basarwa. Unlike the Bayei, who had a measure of economic independence based upon their agricultural and fishing activities, the Basarwa were almost totally dependent upon their Tswana masters. Cultural traditions too were a handicap: 'Basarwa who wished to accumulate stock or grow crops faced social pressure to share food and possessions, which discouraged their efforts'.[25] Even those who did manage to build up a small herd found that without wards of their own and access to dikgotla they were denied access to land and water. Miers and Crowder argue that 'despite the expenditure of time and effort, and the considerable publicity given to the question in the 1930s, the great majority of the Basarwa in the reserve (Central District) were worse off when the colonial period came to an end three decades later'.[26]

The Basarwa apart, Solway has argued from her Kweneng study that as the capitalist concept of ownership gradually replaces communal property rights, the significance of ethnicity and kinship as economic determinants is reduced and subsumed under class. She comments, 'Whereas in the recent past ethnic and/or kinship affiliations may have determined a household's ability to gain access to mafisa cattle for ploughing or to water for livestock, these ties, while certainly still important, no longer provide the same security'.[27] The trend towards privatization, both of land (TGLP) and of cattle (the decline in importance of mafisa) has limited access to pastoral resources. She foresees the growing polarization of society 'with a capitalist class which owns a disproportionate share of the means of production and an increasingly large poor class which has few prospects for direct participation in agro-pastoral production'.[28]

To summarize the forgoing discussion, the economic rights of subject peoples in Tswanadom were largely determined by the extent to which they were regarded as legitimate members of the political community. Those peoples who had their own wards, dikgotla and headmen, thereby had access to land and water and could also thus protect their property rights. Those subject peoples who did not have these institutions were not members of the morafe, were usually deprived of access to land and water, and did not have absolute property rights. Whether one became a client or a serf depended on proximity to the Tswana elite in terms of culture, economy and geography.

Over time most subject groups did become fully incorporated into the morafe. The institution of mafisa appears to have played a central role in this process of incorporation since it provided subject groups with access to pastoral resources. The major exceptions to this rule have been the Basarwa, and to a lesser extent, the Bayei. In recent decades, though the process originated during the era of Khama III, the growth of the capitalist concept of ownership, particularly of land and cattle, has reduced, but not eliminated the significance of ethnicity as a determinant of economic status. To be sure, the Basarwa have not been able to take advantage of this process since, as Hitchcock points out, from the government's perspective 'because the Sarwa are not tribesmen and because they are nomadic hunter-gatherers, they do not have land rights'.[29]

10.5 POLITICAL RIGHTS

In theory, access to the kgotla system guaranteed freedom of speech, as well as judicial rights and a degree of political participation in the administration of the morafe. In practice, scant respect was often accorded members of 'low status' subject peoples (such as the Bayei, Kalanga and Bakgalagadi) who attempted to voice complaints and grievances. They were often bullied and ridiculed by their 'betters'. Nor was there in fact 'freedom of speech' for members of these groups. During a kgotla held in Maun in 1948, a Moyei was fined £5 for affirming the continued existence of botlhanka status (he had said that 'Bayei are still made to carry burdens').[30]

Those of the lowest status, the Basarwa, were excluded from the kgotla system altogether. In theory the reforms of Khama III ended this exclusion, but in reality it still continues. Hitchcock found in his interviews conducted in the Western Sandveld of the Central District during the late 1970s 'that a large proportion of the people in the region are still outside the traditional political structure'.[31]

Participation in central government by subject peoples in Tswanadom, as for every member of the morafe, was limited by the custom that 'the government of the tribe is ultimately concentrated in the hands of the Chief'.[32] Participation in central government was therefore determined by whether or not one could advise the kgosi, and in general, although the kgosi could take advice from whomsoever he wished, the inner council of the morafe was usually constituted by dikgosana.

In 1948 when a section of the Bayei petitioned the Regent of the Batawana, Pulane Moremi, for the right to have representatives at every level of administrative affairs, she replied that 'it was a long standing custom that if there is any important matter affecting the tribe, it is first discussed by members of the Royal family only, as a preliminary step. I do not intend to break away from this custom and the Bayei cannot expect to claim something that is even refused to Batawana who are not of royal blood'.[33]

The degree of participation of subject groups in local government, that is the extent to which they were allowed to rule themselves, ranged from semi-autonomy to complete subjection. The most important variable was culture. According to

Schapera, 'Immigrants of Sotho (and especially Tswana) stock were normally granted the same political and other rights as "true" tribesmen'.[34] He goes on to cite the example of the Khurutshe under Rauwe, who settled in Gammangwato in 1913, and were allowed to build their own village and retain Rauwe as their leader, with the proviso that they had to observe Khama's laws. Subject groups such as the Bayei and Kalanga, however, received very different treatment. When the Kalanga were incorporated into the Bangwato state during the nineteenth century, they were placed under the authority of Bangwato overseers.

Khama introduced an element of self-government after 1896 when he allowed the hereditary rulers of bafaladi groups to re-assume control. Tshekedi Khama, however, later rejected this idea. The latter's re-introduction of direct rule sparked the rebellions of the Bakanswazwi and the Babirwa of Malema.[35]

The Bayei of Ngamiland once conquered were placed under the authority of overseers, re-named Chief's Representatives during the 1930s. The Bayei did not have kgotlas of their own until after 1948, and they struggled in vain until the office was abolished in the 1950s to have a Moyei appointed as a Chief's Representative.

From the 1930s onwards, the British made efforts to 'democratize' local government in Tswanadom by the establishment of representative councils. These councils were supposed to give more political rights to subject peoples. Their ultimate objective, however, was the integration of the various peoples of the territory into one homogeneous group.

The councils failed to function at all effectively until the early 1960s, partly because of the opposition of the dikgosi, but also because of the opposition of subject groups. Among the more resistent were the Bayei who did not wish to lose their identity in the Tswana 'melting pot'. As mentioned above, Bayei 'separatists' continued to fight up to and even beyond independence for communal political rights.

The nationalist politicians of the 1960s had the same goal as the British officials. For them local councils were the foundation of a new Western-style democracy which did not recognize the legitimacy of communal rights. Demands by an ethnic group to rule themselves by their own law and customs were now labelled 'tribalist'.

Finally, a word must be said about the political right of freedom of movement. Under Tswana law, all subjects had limited freedom of movement. Commoners could move freely within the tribal reserve, but crossing into the areas of neighbouring states or settling somewhere other than one's ward was possible only with the chief's permission. Khama III, for example, appointed a guard at each of the four railway stations in Gammangwato in order to prevent the unauthorized departure of women by train to South Africa.[36] Generally, subject communities lived where their Tswana overlords told them to live, and if they refused, force was used without a great deal of discretion to persuade them to move. In 1920 the Babirwa of Malema were evicted from the Tuli Block by Khama III at the instigation of the British South Africa Company and the colonial administration. Their houses were burnt and they were forcibly taken to Bobonong.[37]

Subject peoples were not only expected to live in a certain area but also to live in a certain way: in Tswana-type villages or towns. Khama III began the process of concentrating scattered subject communities into more easily administered and controlled villages, Bobonong was such a village. During the 1930s the process of 'villagization', as termed by colonial officials, received British approval. From their perspective it was a means of increasing the efficiency of tax collection.

There was resistance. The Ovaherero in Ngamiland were successful in their battle with the Batawana kgosi Moremi III. They convinced the British that, being nomadic pastoralists, 'it was impracticable to model Damara (Ovaherero) settlements on the Setswana model'.[38] The Ovaherero in Gammangwato were faced with a more formidable foe. Tshekedi Khama boasted that 'the Damaras in Banwato (sic) country have permanent villages at Mahalapye and Mabeleapodi . . . because the Chief enforces the principle of administration upon all members of his tribe irrespective of clan'.[39] However, the effectiveness of this policy of villagization can be judged by the fact that it is still being advocated by the BDP government.[40]

In short, the political rights of subject groups in traditional Tswanadom were recognized more in theory than in practice. The main area where subject peoples were given freedom was in the sphere of local government. In the post-colonial era, the only political rights recognized are those of the individual Motswana.

10.6 JUDICIAL RIGHTS

Judicial rights in traditional Tswanadom, as with political rights, were based upon access to the kgotla. Without access to the kgotla, and usually this was granted only to commoners, there simply was no justice. The kgotla served as the court of every Tswana community, from the ward to the morafe. The 'commoner' subjects, such as the Bakaa, Babirwa or Kalanga, or even the Bakgalagadi in areas too remote to be under effective control of their patrons, had their own ward kgotla, often chaired by their own hereditary headmen. Minor social conflicts could thus be resolved on the basis of the specific laws and customs of a given community. Appeal from the ward courts to the court of the kgosi was possible in all cases.

By the beginning of the twentieth century the growing practice of appointment of regional overseers/representatives created a new hierarchy in the judicial system. All appeals to the court of the dikgosi had to pass through the representative's court. The judgments of the lower courts could be quashed or revised by the higher courts. The extent to which the laws and customs of the parties to the dispute were considered by the appellant courts probably depended upon the degree of subservience of the appellant's community as well as the character of the court itself. There are reports that Khama III ascertained the name of a community before judging cases on appeal.[41]

But in cases of serious conflict between subject peoples and their rulers, the formers' right to defend themselves was determined by the latter. During the early 1920s, the Babirwa chief Malema hired a South African lawyer to fight for the Babirwa's right to live where they wished - in the Tuli Block. The colonial administration denied them the right to do so. The otherwise liberal Khama III had argued that by allowing his subjects to sue him, the administration was transgressing his 1895 agreement with the British Queen.[42] Similarly in a Serowe kgotla meeting, called in 1927 to discuss the Bahurutshe trouble in Tonota caused by their joining the Anglican Church, it would seem that one Mohurutshe was allowed to speak only one sentence.[43]

Under the Native Tribunals Proclamation No.75 of 1935, all courts of the dikgosi and their representatives were designated as senior tribunals. The remaining courts were labelled junior courts. Regulations for both levels of courts were created, but in practice the pure logistics of having hundreds of ward courts work according to prescribed composition and procedure defeated the purpose.

Only a few important village headmen and district governors were given their own 'junior tribunals' which ranged from eight among the Batawana to fifteen among the Bakwena. Although unrecognized, the ward courts continued to function very much as they had done prior to 1934, though they had no power to impose punishments or enforce their decisions. The main result of this proclamation was the creation of a new intermediate grade of court in the form of junior tribunals which removed one step further the possibility of appeal to the kgosi's, senior court.

Despite all these courts and theoretical rights of appeal, few cases involving subject peoples were brought to the senior courts. Schapera found only fourteen out of the 107 internal disputes in the eight Tswana states between 1750 and 1945 explicitly involved a subject community.[44]

Before 1900, serfs were denied the right to seek justice. In the words of Hindness and Hurst, a molata was a contradictory being as 'he was a human subject but a legal non-subject'.[45] Since their legal status was that of human property of their masters, serfs were not allowed wards or headmen of their own. They thus had no rights of action against their master for any wrong inflicted upon them, not even of the seduction of their women or the alienation of their families to the master's house to perform various domestic chores.[46] A serf could probably marry any other serf but in practice it was not done without the permission of their masters if the parties belonged to different masters.

Serfs were often changing hands as rewards or fines, and although they had no freedom to change their masters, the latter could force them to move anywhere. In the 1890s, Khama took away the matimela cattle and Basarwa serfs from his rebellious son Sekgoma before allowing him to leave the chiefdom. Similarly, Sekgoma confiscated the serfs and cattle of those of his followers who decided to return to Khama. One of the points of conflict between Simon Ratshosa and the Tshekedi Khama was the return of serfs given to his wife by Khama III.[47]

Schapera hints that Bangwato masters sometimes sold Basarwa children to Boers and other Europeans.[48] Instances of bodily harm being inflicted on the serfs are too numerous to be documented here, but it is interesting to note that Simon Ratshosa, who in 1926 was so vocal in his criticism of how the Basarwa were being mistreated and enslaved by the Bangwato had himself been fined £60 in a Serowe court for killing a Mosarwa.[49] In the sphere of judicial rights then, as in the spheres of political and economic rights, most commoners, whether Tswana or non-Tswana, were treated alike: they were allowed autonomy to practise their own law and custom. It was only at the level of the morafe that Tswana judicial custom and practice assumed primacy. In the case of serfs, however, they were denied access to Tswana justice almost without exception.

10.7 SOCIAL AND CULTURAL RIGHTS

In social and cultural terms all subject communities were considered inferior to their Tswana rulers, but none more so than the serfs and those communities who were culturally and socially distinct from the Batswana. Intermarriage with these groups, according to Schapera, was considered 'disgusting' by the Batswana. Among the Bangwato, the Kalanga and Bakgalagadi were referred to as *dikgokong* (wildebeest). In 1920 Khama was forced to arrange for the marriage of two of his leading commoners' daughters to two Kalanga headmen in order to 'destroy the old prejudice'.[50] The extreme quality of this prejudice, at least among some, is best reflected in a case cited by Wylie in which a MoNgwato cattle owner thrashed one of his Basarwa serfs to death for deserting his cattle and stealing a cow. In his own words he had 'never beaten dogs like I beat those Masarwa and never would'.[51]

The social and cultural rights of other subject communities were as respected, or as limited, as those of the Batswana themselves. For example, during the first part of the century, the dikgosi of the Bangwato, Bangwaketse, Bakwena and Bakgatla had abolished the initiation ceremonies. Some subject communities rebelled against this prohibition. It was one of the root causes of the revolt of the Bakgatla of Moshupa under Gobuamang against Bathoen II during the early 1930s. For the most part, however, Batswana rulers allowed their subject peoples to continue their own cultural traditions.

The other exception to this rule of non-interference was in the area of religious freedom. During the twentieth century, the London Missionary Society (LMS) became effectively the state church among the Bangwato and the Bangwaketse. Dikgosi of these morafe used the LMS to bolster not only the moral but also the material and political base of their power. The same role was played by the Dutch Reformed Missionary Church in the Kgatleng. When some of their subjects joined a church other than the 'established' church, such an act was regarded as political rebellion. For example, the Bakgatla kgosi Molefi banned the Zion Christian Church from the Kgatleng and persecuted its members, including his mother, although the members had helped him regain his chieftainship in 1945.[52] And when Mothowagae Motlogelwa established in independent church in Kanye, he was eventually exiled, without his followers, by Seepapitso to Lekgolobotlo near Gamalete.[53] The Khurutshe of Chief Rauwe were allowed to settle in Tonota by Khama III in 1913 only after they had agreed not to bring Anglican Church with them. Tshekedi Khama sent a regiment to punish the offenders in 1927 after they continued to practise Anglicanism. When the colonial administration failed to back the Bangwato in their religious persecution of Rauwe's people, at least one Mongwato questioned whether the British 'were placing Servants above us to lead us'.[54]

10.8 CONCLUSION

Since independence 'subject groups' have, in theory, ceased to exist. There are only Batswana, each with the same political, economic and judicial rights. The government labels demands for special or different treatment made on behalf of 'minority groups' as 'tribalist' (for example, the Kalanga demands on behalf of Ikalanga). In practice little has changed as far as the rights of subject peoples are concerned. This is particularly true of the Basarwa.

The political rights of the Basarwa have been handicapped by their lack of Tswana-type headmen and the absence of dikgotla. Without these institutions their wants and needs are not communicated to government, nor indeed are government's decisions communicated to the Basarwa. Two years after the launching of the Tribal Grazing Land Policy (TGLP), it was discovered that only 8 per cent of the population of the Western Sandveld, mostly Basarwa, had ever heard of it. The countrywide process of consultation carried out through radio programmes and kgotla meetings did not reach those people who were to be most (adversely) affected by the policy.

Economically, more Basarwa have grown more dependant on their employers since independence. What land rights they had have been under threat from land reform, wildlife conservation strategies, and the expansion of the cattle economy. The privatization of land under TGLP has been launched primarily in areas occupied by the Basarwa, i.e. the Central, Kgalagadi and Ghanzi districts. TGLP has in effect turned many Basarwa into squatters on the land of their ancestors.[55]

There are also pressures from conservation interests. Central Kalahari Game Reserve residents have recently been told (June 1988) that they must resettle outside the reserve, and plans to create new Wildlife Management Areas (WMA) will impose restrictions on permanent settlement in another fourteen per cent of the country. Hitchcock estimates that if the land set aside for commercial ranching areas, national parks and game reserves, and the proposed WMAs is added together, forty-one per cent of Botswana's land area will be 'off limits to remote area dwellers for subsistence procurement and production purposes'.[56] Also important is the fact that increasing numbers of boreholes and cattle, as well as growing human pressure near boreholes have depleted plant and game resources and thus undermined the hunting-gathering economy of the Basarwa who still depend very largely on veld products for food and shelter. Because they do not have access to water resources and grazing land, Basarwa cannot keep the few cattle they do acquire.

No compensation is available for this appropriation of the Basarwa's various means of subsistence. The conditions of farm labour, which many Basarwa take up to earn some income, remain exploitative and apparently unchanged since independence. Cash wages, if paid at all, are low and irregular.[57] Education could help the Basarwa, but despite the professed aim of the state to spread development, the Basarwa have been left largely outside the educational network. Hitchcock found that in the Western Sandveld only 1 per cent of the Basarwa were literate and one-third of them did not speak Setswana.[58]

Access to justice is another avenue of advancement blocked. Without dikgotla of their own they are at the mercy of the dikgotla of their employers/masters. Although complaints about late and underpayment of wages were heard in 94 per cent of the locations visited by Hitchcock in the Western Sandveld, only 11 people had taken their cases to the kgotla, and only two of these were actually heard.[59]

With their claims to land, veld products, game, cattle, and water sources all under threat, a very low degree of literacy, poor understanding of the modern system of government, and even greater dependence on their Tswana employers in practically every sphere of life, the Basarwa are more unequal than any ethnic group and the most exploited of all.

Government policy vis-a-vis the Basarwa has been fairly predictable: villagization. Efforts have been made through the Remote Area Development Programme to 're-group' the Basarwa into Tswana-type villages where they can be provided with water and social services, taught Setswana, and gradually transformed from mobile foragers into solid, pastoralist Tswana yeomen. Thus far the policy has been unsuccessful, primarily because the settlements have not been allocated sufficient resources, particularly good arable and grazing land, to make them viable in the long-term.[60]

To a large extent the grievances of the Basarwa have been voiced not by the Basarwa themselves but by self-appointed spokesmen from Europe and North America. Other minority groups have voiced their own discontent with the government's policy vis-a-vis minority rights. Bayei and Kalanga leaders, for example, are currently pressuring the government that their chiefs should be constitutionally included in the House of Chiefs as is now the case with the eight principle Tswana 'tribes'.[61] The language issue is another popular grievance: some minority groups would like to have the option of having their children educated in their own language. Most of these grievances are at least at present largely symbolic. This may change if and when economic growth slows to the extent that government has to make hard choices about the allocation of resources.

This paper has suggested that during the pre-colonial and colonial eras, rights were granted or not granted to subject peoples according to the degree of political, cultural and economic similarity between the subject people and the Tswana masters. In this way Tswana elites rewarded assimilation and punished separatism. By means of the institution of bogosi and later the manipulation and identification of the idea of the nation with Tswana culture, Tswana cultural hegemony has triumphed in Botswana, and this perhaps helps to explain the success of its liberal democracy. It is not just a rhetorical flourish when at election time politicians declare 'we are all Batswana now'. However one group, the Basarwa remains outside Tswana cultural hegemony and perhaps for that reason has still been denied basic political and economic rights. They are still not regarded as legitimate members of the morafe, even though the morafe has now been redefined to include all who are citizens of Botswana.

ENDNOTES

1   A term used by Neil Parsons to describe those states where Tswana culture was hegemonic.
2   Among the Bangwato, commoners were called batlhanka (literally 'servants') whereas among the Batawana the serfs were called batlhanka. Similarly the

Bakgatla use the term badintlha (literally 'outsiders') for their commoners, the same term used by the Batawana for their foreigners (the Bangwato use bafaladi (literally 'refugees'). This apparent terminological confusion is a reflection of the fluid overlapping quality of these classes.

3   Schapera, I. *Government and Politics in Tribal Societies*, (London: Watts, 1956) p. 198.
4   The Bakgalagadi and the Batswapong are the obvious exceptions to this 'rule'.
5   Schapera, I. *Government and Politics* . . ., p. 198.
6   Ibid., p. 268.
7   Donnelly, J. *The Concept of Human Rights*, (London: Croon Helm, 1985) pp. 80-87.
8   Schapera, I. *A Handbook of Tswana Law and Custom* (London: Frank Cass, 1955) p. 123.
9   Personal communication, April 11, 1988.
10 Solway, J. S. *Commercialisation and Social Differentiation in a Kalahara Village*, Botswana (Ph.D. thesis, University of Toronto, 1987) p. 294.
11 Tlou, T. *A History of Ngamiland 1750 to 1906: The Formation of an Afrian State* (Gaborone: Macmillan Botswana, 1985) p. 55.
12 Miers, S. and Crowder, M. 'The Politics of Slavery in Bechuanaland: Power Struggles and the Plight of the Basarwa in the Bamangwato Reserve, 1926-2940', Unpublished paper, pp. 1-2.
13 Ibid., p. 4.
14 Tlou, T. *A History of Ngamiland 1750 to 1906: The Formation of an African State* p. 56.
15 Schapera, I. *Native Land Tenure in the Bechuanaland Protectorate* (Cape Town: Lovedale Press, 1943) p. 260.
16 Parsons, N. 'The Economic History of Khama's Country in Botswana, 1844-1930', in *The Roots of Rural Poverty in Central and Southern Africa*, edited by Robin Palmer and Neil Parsons (Berkeley: University of California Press, 1977) p. 133.
17 Bayei Petition, April 1948, BNA S.285/3/1.
18 The cattle population of the Protectorate increased from 139 000 in 1904-5 to 495 000 in 1921-22 and 1 400 000 in 1934 (Figures from Hubbard, p. 250). In 1923 the richest headmen in Ngamiland, Mogalakwe Nabeng, owned 20 000 cattle. (BNA S. 285/3).
19 Parsons, *Khama's Country*, p. 135.
20 Miers and Crowder, p. 38.
21 *Handing Over Notes, Ngamiland and Chobe District*, BNA DCMA 5/15.
22 *Annual Report for 1950, Ngamiland and Chobe District*, BNA DCMA 5/15.
23 The Regent of the Batawana, Pulane Moremi, was sympathetic to the plight of the Bayei. She condemned the 'cattle kings (who) advocate the selling of breeding stock so that the poor Bayei may sell all theirs and then become the servants of the wealthy Batawana', Regent to Resident Commissioner, 12 June 1951, BNA S.285/3/2.
24 Ibid. A similar situation prevailed in the Central District during the 1920s and

1930s: 'Ngwato cattle owners were using cases brought to the dikgotla and other legal means to systematically deprive Basarwa of stock and to dispossess those who still had any control over land and, most crucial, over sources of water' (Miers and Crowder, p. 40).

25   Miers and Crowder, p. 38.

26   Ibid., p. 40.

27   Solway, p. 366.

28   Ibid., p. 368.

29   Hitchcock, R. K. 'Tradition, Social Justice and Land Reform in Central Botswana' in *Land Reform in the Making: Tradition, Public Policy and Ideology in Botswana*, edited by Richard P. Werbner (London: School of Oriental and African Studies, 1982) p. 22.

30   District Commissioner, Maun, to Government Secretary, Mafeking, 14 September 1948, BNA S. 285/3/1.

31   Hitchcock, R. K. *Kalahari Cattle Posts: A Regional Study of Hunter-Fatherers, Pastoralists, and Agriculturists in the Western Sandveld Region, Central District, Botswana* (Gaborone: Government Printers, 1978) p. 122.

32   Schapera, I. *Law and Custom*, p. 53.

33   Judgment by Regent Pulane Moremi concerning a petition by the Mayei, BNA S.285/3/1.

34   Schapera, I. *Tribal Innovators: Tswana Chiefs and Social Change, 1795-1940* (London: Athlone Press, 1970) p. 87.

35   See Jeff Ramsay, 'Resistance from subordinate groups: Babirwa of Malema, BaKgatla Mmahanaana and BaKalanga Nswazwi' in Fred Morton and Jeff Ramsay eds., *The Birth of Botswana: A History of the Bechuanaland Protectorate from 1910 to 1966* (Gaborone: Longman Botswana: 1987).

36   Schapera, I. *Tribal Innovators*, p. 84.

37   See Morton and Ramsay, pp. 64-81.

38   Minutes of meeting to settle the Damara troubles, 10 December 1940, Serowe, BNA S.214/1/2.

39   Tshekdi Khama, 'The Batawana-Damara Trouble', dated 21 September 1940, BNA S.214/1/2.

40   The Vice President and Minister of Finance and Development Planning, Mr Peter Mmusi, called for such villagization on his recent tour of Ghanzi District (*Daily News*, May 20 1988).

41   Schapera, I. *Tribal Innovators*, p. 88.

42   Khama III to High Commissioner, 21 August 1922, cited in Q.N. Parsons, *Khama III, the Bamangwato and the British with special reference to 1895-1923*, (Unpublished Ph.D. thesis, Edinburgh University, 1973) p. 397.

43   Wylie, D. *'The Centre Cannot Hold': The Decline of the Ngwato Chieftainship 1925-50* (Unpublished Ph.D. thesis, Yale University, 1984) p. 254.

44   Schapera, I. 'Kinship and Politics in Tswana History' *Journal of Royal Anthropological Institute* 93, 2, (1963) pp. 159-173.

45   Hindness, B. and Hurst, P. Q. *Pre-Capitalist Modes of Production* (London: Routledge and Kegan Paul, 1977) pp. 112-113.

46 Schapera, I. *Law and Custom*, pp. 250-251.
47 BNA S.43/7. Various documents in this file provide information on 'Slavery and slave trade among the Batawana and Bamangwato, 1911-28'.
48 Schapera, I. *Tribal Innovators*, p. 89.
49 See BNA S.43/7 for Ratschosa's pamphlet 'Disclosing some of the serious facts for the first time to Administration of the Bechuanaland Protectorate. How the Masarwa became slaves and why the Chief's word is law'. Details of Ratshosa's killing of a Mosarwa are also in this file, document no. 37.
50 Schapera, I. *Tribal Innovators*, pp. 87-88.
51 High Court Case No. 8 of 1931 in BNA cited in Wylie, p. 143.
52 Philip Monnatsie 'The Growth and Spread of Religious Sects in Kgatleng: the case of the Zion Christian Church 1933-77', BA dissertation, University of Botswana, 1980.
53 Morton and Ramsay, p. 18.
54 Otsile Moseweu, speaking at a kgotla meeting held at Serowe on 7 January 1927, cited in Wylie, p. 254.
55 Bob Hitchcock estimates that almost 21 000 people were residents of commercial ranching areas in the 1980s. Figure quoted in his speech 'The Future of Remote Area Development in Botswana', a seminar paper given at the National Institute of Research, July 1988.
56 Ibid., p. 11.
57 Hitchcock discovered that over 10 per cent of the farm bands in the Western Sandveld were not paid anything at all for their labour. Of those who were paid cash, the average wage was one fifth of the recommended minimum wage (*Kalahari Cattle Posts*, p. 314, p. 319).
58 Ibid., p. 366.
59 Ibid., p. 368.
60 Hitchcock suggests that a much more imaginative approach is needed by Government to these settlements, one that involves a radical break with the past. Instead of trying to turn the Basarwa into Tswana yeomen with a primarily pastoralist base, their economic systems should be diversified as much as possible making use of game harvesting, utilization of wild products, beekeeping, poultry schemes, woodcrafts, etc.
61 See Mr Mpho's essay in this volume for further discussion of this subject.

DISCUSSION

Mr D. Kwele (Leader BPU) said pre-colonial democracy was limited to so-called major tribes. Minorities were denied freedom of speech in the kgotla. He agreed with Datta and Murray that in the pre-colonial times minorities were discriminated against.

Commenting on the Mgadla and Campbell paper, he further said, it was nonsensical to talk of democracy during colonialism. He said there was no such thing, as colonialism by its nature is anti-democracy.

In the post-colonial era he said the ruling party is dominating and abusing the institution of kgotla.

Prof. Crick (Edinburgh University) felt Mr Kwele's restriction of the definition of democracy to participation was limiting. He felt that the papers did not say much on the efficiency of the kgotla as a political institution.

Mr Morake (Minister of Education) said democracy must exist within propriety. He agreed that past, present and future democracy were and will never be perfect. For example, women in the past were excluded from kgotla discussions for unconvincing reasons. He felt we should take the best elements of the past and integrate them with what is good today.

Mr M. Mpho (Leader, BIP) agreeing with Mr Kwele's comments quoted an instance in 1944 when his own father was shouted down when he tried to speak in a kgotla debate in Maun.

Dr N. Parsons (Botswana Society) said that in the 1940s the British colonial government used minorities to weaken strong chiefs in the name of democracy. He said the colonial administration demanded introduction of more representative tribal councils to undermine chiefly power.

Dr P. Molutsi (Sociology, University of Botswana) expressed concern that from the three historical papers there does not seem to be a link between traditional political system and modern democratic institutions. He said the fact that there was some consultation does not demonstrate existence of democracy, otherwise we will be forcing the link and romaticising the past.

Mr Molomo was worried that instead of discussing democracy as a political system participants were degenerating into tribal and political differences. He felt the concentration should be on the constitution.

Mr Magang (MP) said everybody has a right by the constitution to be a leader in modern Botswana, contrary to claims by representatives of minority groups.

Mr Giddie (BNF) asked the question: For whom does democracy exist in modern Botswana? He answered that it was the ruling class.

Reacting to questions and comments Mr A. Campbell said consultation can be both a good and a dangerous exploitative tool.

Dr Murray (History, University of Botswana) said Basarwa were not consulted about the Tribal Grazing Land Policy of 1975. He also said when Bayei in 1948 asked for a chief of their own, they phrased it in Tswana objectives and perspectives.

Dr Datta (Historian, Democracy Project) said what the constitution says may not always be found in practice. To access democracy it is necessary to ask people their experience on issues of rights to land, water, etc.

Professor L. Ngcongco (History, University of Botswana) disagreed with Molutsi's assertions that there appears to be no link between past and present democracy. Tswana society was not an ideal type of democracy but was open and accepting to different viewpoints.

The Chairman, Professor T. Tlou (Vice Chancellor, University of Botswana) in conclusion said there are a number of important traditional institutions and aspects of tradition which will be useful to adapt to the present.

SECTION IV

CITIZEN PARTICIPATION IN DEMOCRATIC POLITICS

11 Do Batswana think and act as democrats?

Gloriah Somolekae

11.1 INTRODUCTION

Botswana has functioned as a liberal democracy since 1965. A number of analysts have acknowledged this fact.[1] The country has many features of a liberal democratic system such as freedom to run for office, freedom of press, rule by elected representatives, secret ballot and equality of franchise. These procedures were not found in the traditional Tswana political system. The rulers, namely chiefs, acquired office through ascription. They did not have to compete in elections.

This should not, however, be misunderstood to mean that traditional Tswana political system was not democratic. What is perhaps true and worth taking note of, is the fact that liberal democracy and traditional Tswana democracy are two very different systems of government. In spite of this fact, it appears that the liberal democratic system, (which is just over twenty years old), is being built on and continues to find its support and continuity in the foundations of the traditional political system.

This essay explores the extent to which Batswana have come to accept the new democratic way of life. In particular, we examine, firstly, the extent to which Batswana are informed about the various democratic structures and what goes on within them; secondly, the people's attitudes toward representative structures such as parliament and village committees relative to the traditional chieftaincy system; and, thirdly, the public's commitment to some basic democratic values.

Throughout this paper a major concern will be the impact of basic social and economic factors on the involvement of Batswana within the new democratic structures. Two hypotheses are considered. First there is the idea that various aspects of modernization of society promote participation in and acceptance of democratic institutions in a developing country like Botswana. The specific modernization variables considered are education, urbanization, and participation in political parties and organized groups.

The second hypothesis is that the most important defining characteristics of traditional Tswana political existence, namely age and sex, continues to govern who participates in the modern system, even at the grass roots level. Specifically, older males will be the most likely to be active in the new political arena created by democratic politics.[2]

11.2 METHODOLOGY

The data analyzed in this study come from a mass survey conducted by the Democracy Project in August and September of 1987. The survey was conducted in four areas of the country: Kgatleng, Kweneng, Ngwaketse, and Gaborone. Respondents were selected from census enumeration areas chosen on a random basis, with a quota of persons to be selected from each enumeration area. The survey questionnaire was written in Setswana. A total of 1297 respondents were interviewed. We have checked basic census socio-economic profiles for the four areas, and they correspond fairly closely with the distributions of the sample we obtained.

11.3 KNOWLEDGE OF LEADERSHIP

One of the key features of a liberal democratic system is that there should be popular control of leaders through elections. According to Mayo,[3] it is the prospect of an election which 'keeps governments under popular control and sensitive to public opinion'. The implication here is that voters, or those eligible to vote, know who their leaders are. This is because they would either have voted for or against their representative previously or they should be preparing to make a decision on this person in the future.

We tried to find out whether people knew who their leaders were by asking them the names of their member of parliament (MP) and their councillor. The MPs are the most well known (71.9%), while councillors ran a poor second (only 58%). The mayor or the council chairperson is relatively unknown (27.2%).

The fact that even the MPs are only known by a little over two-thirds of the population in their areas is distressing. One possible reason is that during elections some people simply cast their votes for a particular party and not necessarily for individuals.

But what accounts for the fact that MP's are far better known than councillors and council chairpersons? It is important to note that a council chairman or mayor is not chosen by the electorate directly. He or she is chosen by the councillors, and thus the people are not directly involved. This lack of knowledge, however, says something about the public's general awareness of council activities. If people followed council's decisions, they would likely know who the head of the council was as much as their representative.

Another fact that could account for the fact that MPs are much more known compared to councillors is that MPs are more politically active. They call more meetings than councillors do. Most of the MPs we interviewed informed us that as many as half of their councillors called few if any meetings. The recently introduced radio programme where MPs repeat some of their remarks in parliament may also give the MPs added publicity.

Level of education is very important in determining our respondents knowledge of MPs and the mayor or council chairperson. For those who have had no formal education, only 58 per cent knew the name of their MP while for the college educated this figure was 93 per cent. In the case of the mayor or council chairperson, the spread was even greater: 11 per cent to 75 per cent. On the other hand, education has no effect on knowledge of the councilor. This is shown in Table 1.

Political activists, that is those who take part in any one or all of the activities of political parties, such as singing in the party choir or raising money for the party, have a greater awareness of who their representatives are as is indicated in Table 2. Most interesting is that political activism makes the most difference as far as councilors are concerned. Twenty-five per cent more activists know their councilor than non-activists.

Table 1: Impact of education on political knowledge

Level of education	Members of parliament	Councillors	Council chair/ mayor
None	58,2%	56,2%	11,1%
Less than Standard 7	78,9%	69,3%	22,9%
Standard 7	77,6%	65,3%	35,5%
Secondary less than O'levels	88,9%	65,1%	56,1%
O'levels	89,7%	63,0%	67,6%
Post-secondary	93,8%	62,3%	75,0%

Table 2: Political knowledge of political activists

	Member of parliament	Councillor	Council chair/ mayor
Political activists	85,1%	84,4%	41,3%
Non-activists	71,2%	59,4%	27,5%

One of the key features of democracy is the existence of organized groups seeking to influence governmental decisions. Ball considers them to be part of the political process and notes that 'they attempt to enforce or change the decisions of governmental policy, but do not wish, as pressure groups, to become the government'.[4] We expected to find some relationship between membership in groups and awareness of political leadership. This is because a group is assumed by many theorists to be an effective way for individuals to obtain information on politics. The local representatives, (i.e. the MP and councilor) who respondents were asked to name are supposed to be an immediate link between a respondent's group or association and the entire political machinery.

Table 3 confirms the existence of a group membership effect on political knowledge. The table gives responses of three categories of people. The first belongs to those active in more than two groups. The second category is for those who belong to two groups only; the last for those in just one or no group at all. In every case, those who are active in two or more groups are much better informed than the less active members of the community.

Table 3: Impact of group membership on political knowledge

	Member of parliament	Councillor	Council chair/ mayor
More than two	81,6%	75,4%	41,3%
Two	75,4%	59,7%	24,8%
None or one	66,4%	53,5%	23,2%

The relationship between membership in groups and knowledge of representative suggests that groups are quite effective in giving their members some political education. It is also quite possible though that those who are more politically aware tend to participate in group activity.

It should be noted that only group and party activism seem to be associated with knowledge of the councilor whereas education has no effect. This would seem to indicate that knowledge of the councillor is a function of face-to-face interactions in the community. This seems reasonable given the fact that councillors receive little attention in the mass media whereas MPs, the Mayor of Gaborone and the council chairmen are often featured.

The two variables of age and sex had a very minimal impact on knowledge of the three political actors we have been considering.

11.4 KNOWLEDGE OF POLITICAL ISSUES

Botswana has followed a Westminster model of parliamentary democracy since independence in 1966. Parliament as the supreme legislative body makes the laws of the country. One expects therefore that whatever happens in this institution will be of interest to the average citizen.

At the local level, councils are charged with several functions for the immediate development of their areas. Though much is still controlled by the central government, councils are policy making bodies at the local level. Their deliberations and activities do affect, in one way or another, those among whom they are operating.

In our survey people appear not to follow what takes place in both councils and parliament. Respondents were asked to name an issue before parliament and/or council in the past few years. Only 24,1% were able to name one. The relationship between whether a respondent named an issue before council or parliament and his level of education is shown in Table 4. It is clear that for all education groups (excluding post-secondary), the percentage of people who named an issue is generally low. For those with no education at all, the problem of ignorance is most pronounced. Only 17,4% named an issue and the figures for the other educational categories are also not that impressive. It is only the post-secondary group that has a sizeable proportion that is aware of an issue before either council or parliament. This strongly suggests that the interest in politics for the average citizen is significantly increased with some education and then again as a result of attending post-secondary institutions.

Table 4: Impact of education in issue awareness

	Named one issue
None	17,4%
Less than Standard 7	29,5%
Standard 7	27,6%
Secondary less than O'levels	30,4%
O'levels	15,6%
Post-secondary	40,6%

Again political activists and those who participate in two or more groups are significantly more likely to know about issues before council or parliament. In both cases the figure is 35 per cent. This is not great, but it does indicate a good core of informed people are participating in politics. The large group which cannot name an issue substantiates the complaint of some political activists that many of those who are active in community politics have little issue awareness.

Neither age nor gender affects issue awareness. Thus as we have already indicated above, information on democratic politics is not affected by traditional stimuli for participation. It would appear that the two systems of politics are not related as far as feeling an obligation to be informed is concerned.

11.5 ATTITUDES TOWARDS POLITICAL PROCESSES

For elections to be effective they must be perceived by citizens firstly as a meaningful way of making a choice as to political leaders and secondly, involving a choice of some sort as to the direction of government policy. In this section, we look at our respondent's perceptions with regard to both these concerns.

Elections

The right to vote, is one of the most essential ingredients of a liberal democratic system. Outlining the purpose of elections in a democracy, Mayo[5] wrote:

> from the point of view of the individual voter, elections are the means by which he takes his share in political power by voting for the representative of his choice.

At the level of the community as a whole

> elections . . . bring the decision-makers under popular control, a control that is ever present in the minds of the representatives because any part of their behaviour in office (or in case of aspiring candidates, out of office) may affect their chances at the next elections.

The victory of candidates is also

> an authorization of representatives to make decisions to govern within the broad drift of a policy platform, if there is one, subject to the sanction of the next election. The election result invests representative and decision with legitimacy.

Elections in other words perform a very fundamental role in a democratic system. The question is whether the public is willing to accept that this is the process by which their leaders should be selected. We asked our respondents whether they favoured election of their leaders over the chieftaincy method, that is when chiefs inherited their role, at least ideally, from their fathers. In our sample the majority (63,9%) favoured the electoral system. Only 26,4% preferred to go back to chieftainship system.

Education plays a big role in commitment to elections. Among those with a post-secondary education, 95% are for elections. On the other hand, among those with no education there is little more than a majority in favour (56,5%) of the new system. Table 5 presents the complete results. The other social mobilization variables of party and group activity have no effect.

Commitment to the new system, however, is not simply a cognitive effect. Age is also important. As Table 6 indicates, particularly among those 65 and over there is a strong tendency to support the chieftaincy. That does not seem surprising since this age group was close to 40 at the time of independence. Even among those between 52 and 65, that is those who were in their late 20s or 30s at the time of independence, two-fifths still prefer the chieftaincy. Such a generation effect clearly indicates that time is on the side of democracy in Botswana in terms of increasing popular acceptance.

Table 5: Impact of education on preferred form of government

Education	Election system	Chieftaincy system
None	56,5%	43,5%
Less than Standard 7	70,8%	29,2%
Standard 7	77,1%	22,9%
Secondary less than		
O'levels	85,8%	14,2%
Secondary	94,6%	5,4%
Post-secondary	95,2%	4,8%

Table 6: Impact of age on preferred form of government

Age (yrs)	Election system	Chieftainship system
21 − 29	83,2%	16,9%
30 − 39	74,0%	26,0%
40 − 52	70,1%	29,0%
53 − 64	60,9%	39,1%
65+	46,4%	53,6%

We also asked our respondents whether they thought MPs and councillors were better problem solvers than various other actors in the political system. We thought this would give us some idea as to whether they thought their leaders selected through elections where doing a better job than other possible types of leaders. The results are in Table 7. Clearly, the people prefer their elected representative over either the chiefs or the civil servants. It would appear that the new system as a method of selection is not only preferred but people like the results in terms of solving community problems.

Table 7: The best community problem solver

	Percentage
Local councillor	35,5
Member of parliament	20,6
Chief of headman	17,2
Civil servant	6,2
None of the above	7,9
Don't know/No response	12,6

Awareness of the differences between political parties

Democracy implies that people have a choice and that they exercise it. Of critical importance here is the fact that there has to be competition between candidates and parties for office. Of equal significance is the fact that the various parties and candidates compete on the basis of policy differences, thus providing the voters with a choice. Mayo[6] regards this competition as the litmus paper test which proves that formal conditions of democracy are working within a country: the parties should not only provide a variety of policy choices, but the electorate should be aware of such choices or policy differences.

No one can dispute the fact that Botswana offers this choice of parties. There are six political parties in Botswana, namely, the Botswana Democratic Party (BDP), the Botswana National Front (BNF), Botswana Independence Party (BIP), Botswana Peoples Party (BPP), Botswana Progressive Union (BPU) and the Botswana Liberal Party (BLP). The key question is: Are all these parties different? Do they offer any policy choice that the electorate can identify? So far, several scholars on Botswana have argued convincingly that the various political parties in this country do not necessarily mean that the Botswana electorate has policy choices when voting.[7] In fact, recently, political observers have pointed to the frequent crossing of the floor between the two major parties (BDP and BNF) as a clear indication of the fact that even the active members of the parties, namely elected officials, perceive no major differences between the two parties. Our respondents were asked to state the major differences between the BDP and each of the three major opposition parties, i.e. the BNF, BPP and the BIP. Responses obtained were classified as follows;

(a) General like/dislike statements (e.g. a party was 'helpful', 'good' and the like).
(b) Power and party competition (e.g. 'BDP is ruling party'; 'BNF provides an alternative').
(c) Group benefits (e.g. a party helps a particular group such as farmers or poor).
(d) Issues (e.g. employment, unemployment, drought relief, free schools).
(e) Ideology (e.g. socialism, capitalism).
(f) South Africa (reference made to stand on South Africa).

The results for our respondents are presented in Table 8.

Table 8: Perceived differences between the BDP and the BNF

Type of response	Percentage
General like/dislike	11,4%
Power party competition	14,3%
Group benefit	1,7%
Issues	2,3%
Ideology	1,7%
South Africa	0,1%
No difference/Plus no answer	68,5%

Two-thirds of our respondents (68,5%) said they did not know a difference between the two major parties – BNF and BDP. The figure for those who do not know is very high. In fact since these are the two major parties in the areas we surveyed, one would have expected that at least the differences between them would be known. Needless to say our respondents do much worse for the other opposition parties in relation to the BDP.

The table also shows that apart from general like/dislike reasons or party competition for political office, there were really no clear-cut and concrete differences identified. Note that only 6% of the population are thinking in terms of issues or group benefits. This situation, however, is not peculiar to Botswana. Ball states:

> . . . from research carried out mainly from Britain and the United States we make the following generalisation: the policy issues have little or no effect on how the elector uses his vote and that voters inherit loyalties from their families, usually based on such factors as social class.[8]

Education does play a role in determining whether or not voters are aware of differences between political parties. Table 9 shows that the biggest proportion of people who do not know the difference between the two parties is in the category of respondents with no education (76,9%), while the smallest proportion of those who do not know the difference is from the respondents with post-secondary education (53,8%).

Table 9: Impact of education on knowing difference between BDP and BNF

None	23,1%
Less than 7 years	42,9%
Standard 7	41,6%
Secondary lower than O'levels	42,9%
O'levels	35,1%
Post-secondary	46,2%

Education is not the only mobilization factor affecting whether people are aware of a difference between the two major parties. Remote area dwellers are the least aware of the differences between the BNF and the BDP, with 27% mentioning some dimension. Besides lack of education, poor access to the mass media or lack of contact with councillors and council staff may make a difference.

Some differences are also evident with regard to group participation. In the case of those belonging to more than two groups, 46% knew the difference between the BDP and the BNF. On the other hand, among those in one or no group, only 27 per cent could name one. Party activists are even more knowledgeable. More than half (58,8%) said they knew the difference while non-activists averaged 31%. Again, group involvement, particularly in the parties leads people to be able to put some meaning, even if only at the like and dislike level, to the activity of parties.

But if the difference between these two major political parties are not known by

83

over two-thirds of the public, why do voters support particular parties? Table 10 gives a breakdown of responses. It shows that close to a third (28,8%) support the particular parties for no clear reason at all (note that some of these may have concealed their reasons). Almost the same proportion (27,6%) gave general like and dislike reasons. Personal factors such as the particular party is supported by family members, a certain ethnic group, chief or generally the community accounted for another 10%.

Still there are slightly over one-fifth who do articulate some issue or ideological reason. While at first glance this might seem very low, the fact of the matter is that in the advanced industrial countries such lack of information about political parties is not usual, particularly when the parties do not present clear differences on policy.[9]

Table 10: Reasons for supporting a particular party

Reason	Percentage
No reason	28,8%
General like/dislike	27,6%
Personality	10,9%
Power-party competition	10,3%
Issue reasons	21,0%

11.6 COMMITMENT TO THE LIBERAL DEMOCRATIC PRINCIPLES

The long term survival of the liberal democratic system in Botswana depends on, among other things, the extent to which Batswana are committed to the basic principles which are involved in its operation. While bearing in mind that the system is still new and in the process of being institutionalized, we assess in this section the extent to which Batswana are committed to two such principles, specifically preference for the multiparty system over a one-party system, and allowing members of the traditionally discriminated against groups such as the youth and minorities to participate on an equal basis in discussions of community issues.

Multiparty competition

Close to half (47%) of our respondents considered the multiparty system as the best system. The second largest category (30,9%) are in favour of a one-party system. Only 5,7% favoured a no-party system, while 13,5% said they did not know which was the best option. The fact that such a significant percentage is in favour of a multiparty system indicates considerable public support. To be sure, one can also say that as of yet a majority do not support the multiparty system, preferring a one- or no-party system or failing to have an opinion. This seems particularly surprising since the leaders of all political parties almost without exception have spoken consistently in support of the multiparty system. It seems probable that half the public for one reason or another does not like the combative quality of the party struggle in Botswana.

Table 11 shows that there is a direct relationship between preference for a multiparty system and level of education. Only among the uneducated or those with less than seven years of education is there a majority against the multiparty system. Likewise support for the one-party system falls off as the years of formal education increase, with only 11,7% of those with 12 years of schooling making this choice. This may be due to the fact that those with no education or very little are less aware of what is happening around them in other developing countries. They are probably not aware of the full implications of a one-party type of arrangement. It is also likely that the educated are much more open to propaganda from the written media about the supposed advantages of the multiparty system.

It is worth noting (see Table 11) that the greatest percentage of people who do not know which form of government is best (23,7%) is from the category with no education at all. This is not surprising because party politics is quite radically different from the traditional system. The uneducated may take longer before they understand the benefits involved.

Table 11: The impact of education on best party system

Education	One party	Multiparty	No party	Don't know
None	34,3%	35,3%	6,1%	39,35%
Less than Standard 7	39,3%	41,3%	9,7%	9,7%
Standard 7	36,4%	51,1%	4,0%	8,5%
Secondary less than O'levels	24,1%	66,9%	4,5%	4,5%
O'levels	11,7%	84,4%	–	3,9%
Post-secondary	7,7%	89,2%	1,5%	1,5%

To test our respondents' commitment to multiparty politics, we asked them if they thought a communist party should be allowed to compete in elections. Most (61,4%) opted out of answering the question because they said they did not know what communism meant. Of the remaining group only slightly more than a quarter agreed that a communist party should participate. It would thus appear that multiparty democracy for those who know about communism, or at least think they do, is not a system in which they are willing to allow such radical parties as the communists.

Voting age

Mayo rightly observes that the history of the franchise in the recent times has been one of widening the class of people who can vote.[10] Such groups as non-property holders, minority races, and women have first been excluded and then included. The normative belief is that all adult citizens should vote unless there is a clearly justifiable reason for their exclusion.

In line with keeping to this ideal, many Western countries have lowered their voting age to 18. In Botswana the minimum age is still twenty-one. The majority (57,5%) in our sample support this higher limit. The usual reason given is that youth below 21 are not sufficiently mature. Only 28,8% wants to include these young people, while 13,6% did not state any preference.

Whatever reasons there are for keeping the voting age at 21, fears have been voiced especially by supporters of the ruling party that if the age is lowered, the BNF would increase its votes because many of the people who find it attractive are the young. Evidence from the mass survey shows that such fears are not without any basis. Over 60% of the BNF supporters are under 40 years of age. The figure for BDP supporters belonging to the same age group is 41%. One would expect that the proportions in the 18 to 20 group might be even higher for the BNF.

11.7 CONCLUSION

The attainment of an ideal democratic system is always a goal to be worked towards. This analysis indicates that the ideal is something that is most easy for those who have had more formal education to realize in terms of being informed and to support with regard to their values. In addition, those who participate in groups and party activities also develop information about and a commitment to democratic politics. Thus we can say acceptance of and involvement in democratic politics is definitely a consequence of the social mobilization which comes with modernization of society. Our first hypothesis is thus confirmed.

For the most part the two systems of politics, the chieftaincy and elections, seem to have little overlap. Those who are older and males may feel obliged to take part in the politics of the traditional system but they do not show any greater involvement in the politics of elections than the rest of the population. Thus our second hypothesis does not seem to be born out.

The results of the foregoing analysis indicate the need for all involved in mobilization and education to sensitize people to the realities and values that are involved in a democratic system. The structures alone without working on the cultivation of complementary attitudes to support them are not likely to be able to strengthen and sustain our still fragile democracy in the public mind.

ENDNOTES

1   Holm, J. D. 'Botswana: A Paternalistic Democracy', in Diamond, L. Linz, J. J. and Lipset, S. M. eds., *Democracy in Developing Countries*, vol 2 (*Afri-*

ca) (Boulder, CO: Lynne Rienner, 1988); Polhemus, J.H. 'Botswana Votes! Parties and Election in an African Democracy', *Journal of Modern African Studies*, 21 no. 3 (1983); and Parson, J. *Liberal Democracy and the Labour Reserve in Botswana* (Boulder CO: Westview Press, 1984).

2   See Holm, J. D. *Dimensions of Mass Involvement in Botswana Politics: A Test of Alternative Theories* (Beverley Hills CA: Sage, 1974; and Almond, G. A. and Verba, S. *The Civic Culture* (Boston: Little, Brown & Co., 1965).

3   Mayo, H. B. *An Introduction to Democratic Theory* (Oxford: Oxford University Press, Inc. 1960) p. 78.

4   Ball, A. L. *Modern Politics and Government* (London: The Macmillan Press Ltd, London, 1971) p. 100.

5   Mayo, *Democratic Theory*, p. 73.

6   Ibid.

7   See Holm, 'A Paternalistic Democracy', and Wiseman, J. A. 'Multi-partism in Africa: The Case of Botswana', *African Affairs*, vol 76, no. 302 (1979).

8   *Modern Politics*, p. 128.

9   Converse, P. E. 'The Nature of Belief Systems in Mass Publics', in Luttberg, N. R. ed., *Public Opinion and Public Policy* (Homewood, Ill.: Dorsey Press, 1974).

10 Ibid.

DISCUSSION

Mr D. Magang (MP, BDP) commended the paper as well researched and reflecting what he also hears as he moves around. He agreed that many people are agreeable to women participating in politics, although not many thought women could be successful as national leaders.

Pointing to the shortcomings of the paper, Mr Magang said, Botswana's democratic behaviour pre-dated independence in 1965. He said it was therefore superficial to assess democratic behaviour from 1965. He said while it is true that the public was ignorant of a number of issues relating to their representatives and modern democratic institutions, this was partly because of the absence of an effective media. Even then, he said, public political ignorance was not peculiar to Botswana. It was a common feature of democracies such as Great Britain and the United States.

He also argued that the paper should have evaluated party manifestos in order to understand why people voted for certain candidates and not others. In manifestoes, he claimed, one finds concrete promises such as provision of roads, schools, and water which attract people. Finally Mr Magang felt the paper demanded too much from the respondents, even on unknown concepts such as communism.

Mr Tlhomelang (MP, BNF) also praised the paper and said the question of whether Batswana acted democratically was relevant and important. He noted that Batswana still vote for individual leaders and not policies, contrary to Mr Magang's claim.

In terms of public understanding of political issues he said urban people were a lot clearer compared to those in rural areas. He called on the ruling party to take the lead in educating the public on modern political institutions.

Professor Tordoff (University of Birmingham) questioned the methodology of the study and felt that concepts and issues asked appeared too complex for an ordinary person to understand. He said it was important to know that the manner in which questions are asked can predetermine the response.

Mr Rantao (Mayor, Gaborone) wanted to know what percentage of the sample preferred lowering the voting age. He agreed that the public was ignorant and alleged that this was a result of both lack of information and misinformation by some bourgeois politicians who told the people that their poverty was God's curse on them because they have sinned.

Ms A. Molokomme (Law, University of Botswana) felt participants were talking at cross-purposes due to lack of a common definition of democracy. She wondered whether a set of definitions sent to paper authors should not have been given to participants as well.

She said women were often incorrectly bracketed together with minority groups whereas they were a majority. She said not many people are genuine about encouraging women's participation in politics.

Professor Nsibambi (Makerere University) wanted to know how the sample of the study was selected. He also pointed out that the paper should have discussed availability of economic resources and how these encouraged democracy.

Mr P. Sethantsho (BNF) refuted the suggestion that independent candidates were ineffective and the phenomenon was on the decline. He said when he stood as an independent candidate in 1984 he got enough votes to retain his deposit.

Dr B. Weimer (Research Institute for International Affairs, Germany) praised the paper but noted a contradiction in saying the people did not know the issues on the one hand and on the other saying modern leaders and institutions were able to address and solve their problems.

Mr K. Moesi (BDC) wanted to know whether the electioneering exercise was legitimate or whether it was a legitimizing tool. He also wanted to know the different perceptions of rural and urban people on the person of the president.

Replying to comments Mrs Somolekae said her paper was meant to discuss attitudes and behaviour towards modern institutions only. She said there were other papers dealing with some of the questions raised and she felt it would be inappropriate to respond.

On the question of the methodology of the mass survey she said she is aware of the limitations of a survey of this nature and will cover the methodology in the final draft. She felt it was not necessary to dwell on these in a symposium of this nature. She however assured the conference that the survey was conducted in the most professional way possible.

SECTION V
THE SCHOOL SYSTEM AND DEMOCRACY

12 The school system: is it teaching democracy?

P. T. Ramatsui

12.1 INTRODUCTION

Man's preoccupation with the social dimensions of education continues to be a subject of intense debate. Most citizens want the schools to play an important role in teaching our children norms and values critical to the peaceful functioning of society. There must be a contextual framework within which the educational system functions. Normally the national government defines what aspects of the cultural context are to be promoted by the educational system. A country's general aims of education thus have political significance. Government's policies will specify the major goals and intentions of education as well as the overall framework of the educational system. Of course it is normally the task of the professionals, like curriculum developers, to work out the practical details of school life and the content to be addressed in the various subject-areas. The decisions of these professionals must, however, support the broad educational aims and guidelines reflected in government policy.

Examples can be given of general education aims in national policy documents that are handed down to curriculum developers to design the overall curriculum. For example, a handbook on Curriculum Evaluation produced by the International Institute for Educational Planning refers to a study that was carried out in Malaysia to determine the role of education in society.[1] The study identified the following general aims for the country's school system: a) promotion of a common Malayan culture, b) provision of equal opportunities for free primary education, c) increasing the relevance of school experiences to national identity, d) inculcation of norms of good citizenship, and e) teaching high standards of moral and social behaviour.

All national governments are almost certain to seek similar objectives in their countries. In some cases, these aims of education are accorded such importance that they are incorporated in written constitutions, as for instance is the case in Japan. Julius Nyerere's book, *Education for Self Reliance*,[2] stresses that such goals for education are essential in Africa.

89

12.2 NATIONAL COMMISSION ON EDUCATION

Coming nearer home and to the context of this symposium, it should be recalled that the Botswana Government convened a National Commission on Education in 1975 to review the entire education system and recommend strategies for improvement. The Botswana National Commission on Education presented its findings and recommendations in the report *Education for Kagisano*,[3] and it is this report that has guided the Botswana Government in the formulation of the current National Policy on Education that was approved by the National Assembly in August 1977.[4]

The commission attached particular significance to democracy as an overriding principle which should be promoted in the school system. It adopted the view that democracy implies a voice for all the people in their future, not only in political elections but also in the community's social and economic affairs. In its report the National Commission on Education made the following comments and observations on education and democracy.

If democracy is to work, then people must have sufficient *information* to make wise decisions, and their decisions must be respected.

In education, as many *decisions* as possible must be left to the community. At a minimum, this means that the people must have a direct voice through local school committees, parent-teacher associations and elected councilors in the way their schools are run.

Teachers and other educational professionals must be consulted about changes in their conditions of service and participate in the work of syllabus change and curriculum reform.

The *curriculum* should include teaching about democratic institutions and the way each works, including some opportunities for practical experience through visits to kgotla, council or Parliament.

Pupils, because of their relative immaturity, can be given only a limited voice in any important decisions affecting the school community, but should be encouraged to manage their own affairs to the greatest possible degree and to participate in the running of the school. They should be given every possible opportunity to exercise choices in groups and individually. In particular they should obtain information about opportunities for further study, training and careers.

12.3 IMPLEMENTING THE COMMISSION'S REPORT

Since the recommendations of the National Commission on Education are policy, we have been working to determine their practical implications for curriculum and other aspects of school programmes. Our challenge is to transform our schools and colleges into effective training grounds for the youth to learn about democratic practices and gain experience in self government. Thus far we have done a number of important things, but it is abundantly clear that more remains to be done.

One step the Ministry of Education has taken is to revise the curriculum for the Nine Year Basic Education Programme.[5] Perhaps, it might be appropriate for the purposes of this discussion to isolate those aims of the new Nine Year Curriculum that were developed to provide students with some exposure to basic elements of politics, which of course incorporate aspects of democracy. Four of the general aims of the revised programme have been deliberately framed to address the political, economic and social obligations of students as citizens and future leaders. These are:

a)   Knowledge and understanding of Setswana culture and traditions.

b)   Understanding and fulfilment of political, economic and social obligations in the local community, the nation, Africa and the world.

c)   Development of a sound moral code compatible with the ethics and traditions of Botswana.

d)   Development of respect for others and ability to liaise and work co-operatively with them.

The above stated aims at the combination of Botswana's traditions pertaining to democracy with the institutions of government we inherited at independence. It should also be noted that our intention is not to establish an overt political indoctrination programme for students but rather to render the political and social ideas of our youth congruent with the context within which our national government operates.

At a more specific and subject-area level, the general aims of the Nine Year Programme that have just been referred to are to become operational through the Social Studies curriculum. Social Studies as a subject in the curriculum was only introduced in the primary schools in 1981. This development was as a result of implementation of the recommendations of the National Commission on Education Report.

At the junior secondary level, Social Studies was only introduced at the beginning of 1986.[6] The main rationale behind the introduction of Social Studies (to replace Geography and History which were formerly offered as separate courses in the curriculum) was that it presents an appropriate avenue through which key issues and concepts of national development and government practices can be addressed.

Going through the current draft Junior Secondary Social Studies Syllabus, it is evident that the nature of the Botswana system of democratic government is presented in detail to the students. They are expected to know the structure and duties of of the three branches of government (i.e. the executive, the judiciary and the legislature), the system of checks and balances which results, the character and operation of the multi-party system, the ways in which civil and human rights and freedoms are guaranteed, the operation of the justice system, and the duties and responsibilities of citizenship. Our syllabus also seeks to develop informed citizens who can effectively perform their role as voters. Students are thus expected to identify the main developmental issues facing Botswana as well as the most serious social problems facing Botswana and other Africa countries. They should be able to compare Botswana's situation with that elsewhere.

Currently the ministry is developing detailed instructional modules that would present the content and teaching/learning approaches to be used by teachers at the junior secondary schools. Of course, it is well known that the final test of any curriculum programme, no matter how best designed and validated, finally lies with its practicability and actual use in the teaching situation. Questions might be asked as to whether our teachers and the general community in Botswana are sufficiently informed to provide our children with the necessary orientation to issues involved in our way of government and its associated practices. Do we know enough to ensure that our students adequately understand the cardinal attributes of the kgotla system, including such ideas as tolerance of views of all social groups in society and equal participation of the members of the community along side their leaders?

Another issue that needs emphasis is that even in a democratic system of government consultation must eventually lead to the making of decisions. Consultation as a process cannot be open-ended and lead to no decisions being taken. Government must provide firm leadership and direction.

It is also important to impress upon our students that once decisions are taken they are binding on everyone, including those that might disagree with the outcome. This is especially important for the implementation of those decisions that end up becoming laws and national programmes of the country.

12.4 CONCLUSION

It should be reiterated that democracy involves giving each mature person a voice in the running of society's affairs and the chance to participate directly or through representatives in decisions affecting his life. As the commission report correctly pointed out, democracy will only work if people have sufficient information to make wise decisions, and, of course, their decisions must be respected. This I believe is already provided for in our education system and government policy guidelines. Our curriculum includes teaching about democratic institutions and the way they work, and it incorporates practical experience of democratic institutions through visits to the kgotla, council and parliament.

Hopefully, the education system we are building will instil in Batswana children a respect for democratic values. Of course, having stated this, it must be conceded that students at different levels of the education system are bound to exhibit varying levels of maturity, and it is only fair to expect that they would be accorded a limited voice in some aspects of decision making.

ENDNOTES

1   Levy, A. et al., *Handbook of Curriculum Evaluation* (Paris: International Institute for Educational Planning, UNESCO, 1977).
2   Nyerere, J. *Education for Self Reliance* (Dar-es-Salaam: Government Printer, 1967).
3   National Commission on Education, *Education for Kagisano* (Gaborone: Government Printer, 1977).

4 Government of Botswana, *National Policy on Education (Government Paper No. 1 of 1977* (Gaborone: Government Printer, 1977).
5 Ministry of Education, *Aims of the Nine Year Curriculum* (Gaborone: Government Printer, 1986).
6 Ministry of Education, *Junior Secondary Social Studies Syllabus* (Gaborone: Government Printer, 1987).

13 The school system: shouldn't it be teaching democracy?

G. Phorano

13.1 INTRODUCTION

My thesis is that all aspects of the school system from administration to instruction and sports must both operate in a democratic fashion and promote democracy in society as a whole. We cannot just teach the principles of democracy as exercises in instruction. In the discussion that follows four topics will be considered: the theory of democracy, the role of the schools in a democracy, the failure of Botswana's schools to educate for democracy, and the outlines for a democratic educational system for our country.

13.2 THE THEORY OF DEMOCRACY

Democracy entails the overall participation of the majority of the people in decision making, i.e. in discussion and solution of problems, in planning and controlling production. Democracy can only be meaningful if the majority of the toiling people dominate the production process and participate in the direction of the economy. Within the school, democracy entails raising the level of pupils participation and their complete integration within the school structures.

In the wider community the school should serve the people who produce the material base for the people's welfare. It should be the people's resource and it must move towards them by helping in agricultural production, acquisition of literacy, non-formal education and the gathering of oral history. Democracy becomes a reality 'when a school begins to move from being an elitist, reactionary and hierarchical

93

institution to a base for the sons and daughters of peasants and workers to take power and to learn and to liye democratically, and to equip themselves with the scientific knowledge necessary to lead their country into the future and end hunger, naked-ness, ignorance, disease and exploitation'.[1]

13.3 EDUCATION AND DEMOCRACY

Education is the passage of societal experiences and knowledge to the new genera-tion. As Castle and Wustenberg say, 'Education is . . . the planned and systematic shaping of consciousness'.[2] It involves both maintenance and development of so-ciety's economic and social structures, values and culture. In a democracy educa-tion should be an instrument for social transformation that extends the enjoyment of the fruits of life to those who are oppressed and exploited.

To do this education must move away from narrow specialization and must fight for a high level of scientific, political and cultural education for everybody. Values such as individualism, profit seeking, competitiveness and belief in the superiority of mental work over manual work should be discouraged for they do not enhance democracy. Meaningful education should aim at producing fully developed human beings; that is, people who are capable not only of doing productive work, but also of controlling production and running society. This does not mean that specializa-tion can be completely avoided, but rather that everybody must possess sufficient knowledge and capabilities to be able to learn any occupation as needed. This is necessary since education is a living part of the totality of social structure, with a dialectical relationship to the mode of production, distribution and material products, as well as to social consciousness.

The government's programme of *Education for Kagisano* evidences a definite commitment to such a programme of education. It states that 'Democracy in educa-tion involves giving each mature person a voice in the running of affairs and the chance to participate directly or through representatives, in decisions affecting his life'.[3] Education for Kagisano at least implies that as many decisions as possible should be left to those closely affected by them; i.e. community and parents, profes-sional workers in education and pupils. This means that the above groups must have a direct voice in the way their schools are run. *Education for Kagisano* goes further to say that teachers must be consulted about changes in their conditions of service, given the opportunity to participate in the work of syllabus change and curriculum reform. The programme even recommends that teacher unions be strengthened.

13.4 BOTSWANA'S FAILURE TO EDUCATE FOR DEMOCRACY

The education system in Botswana reflects the political economic and social struc-ture developed during the colonial past. The schools teach the virtues of a free en-terprise society which is hierarchically structured. Educators prepare their pupils for different roles in this system, selecting some for privilege and rejecting others.[4] Our schools make it almost impossible for all those who enter to succeed, while

94

at the same time holding up education itself as the only legitimate channel for evaluating worth and certifying quality for advancement. Those who cannot succeed are considered failures rather than the system.

The very structure of education in Botswana rejects the idea of democracy. There is a ladder of seniority which is uncompromising. The principal is at the top, followed by the deputy principal, the assistant principal, the senior teachers, and then the ordinary teachers. One can tell this hierarchy from the position and size of offices. The authoritarian nature of our schools is reflected in the person of the teacher who enforces discipline with a stick, whose teaching is dominated by the lecture method. Desks in classes are regimentally arranged with the teacher in front reflecting his dominant and authoritarian role and the passivity of the pupils. The teacher even supervises evening studies and entertainment.

The schools also impose a hierarchy among the students. There are prefects, monitors and senior students. The administration still appoints prefects. As a result their peers see them as tools whose allegiance is to superior authorities and not as representatives of students.

In the end children learn how authority works in schools and the wider society; they learn that they are expected to conform to the dictates of the rulers, no matter how irrational the commands are. If they do not conform, they experience the high cost of punishment.

Our education system from a democratic perspective also is lacking in its content. It specializes in verbalization, abstraction and theory. Practical activities, in so far as they are incorporated in the curriculum, are artificial, separate, limited and divorced from the realities of life. Teaching students skills which will earn them an income is seen as a low priority.

Regimentation leading to social isolation pervades all aspects of school life. The division of the school into offices, staff rooms, laboratories and classrooms prevents a lot of useful and free communication between students and teachers. There is no common room in which teachers and students could work and exchange experiences on a more equal basis. The school day is divided into periods, each separated by bell ringing from the beginning to the end. Students must be punctual for teachers to push the syllabus so that when ministry inspectors come they find that everything is done correctly and in the correct order. Knowledge is divided up into separate subjects. It is fragmented. Students do not have a complete picture of what they are learning.

13.5 TOWARD A DEMOCRATIC SCHOOL SYSTEM FOR BOTSWANA

To be democratic, the school system must reject all social and economic structures which are exploitative and promote the establishment of new ones reflecting the interests of the masses. It will mould a new person who loves his country and respects his teachers and other students.

Schools should create a unity necessary for collective organization and planning that will serve as a base for all activity, whether in the classroom or not. Students and teachers should learn from each other. Exchange of experiences from all levels should be encouraged. There should be regular discussions among all in the school about the victories and weaknesses registered in the course of work so that necessary lessons for collective progress can be learned. The collectivization of management integrates the masses into power. Whenever possible, administration of schools should be actually entrusted to the students. The headmaster/principal should make his decisions in conjunction with a representative body including all sections of the school.

A school which teaches democracy should have work groups of students so as to be imbue them with a collective spirit. Pupils should select their leaders in class councils which will in turn elect those who will be in the higher echelons of administration dealing with such issues as: a) pedagogy, b) administration and finance, c) health, d) production, and e) sports and cultural activities. Teachers and workers should participate fully in all facets of the life of the school. Students should be encouraged to reason out problems and help each other without looking to the teachers. Students should participate in campaigns dealing with vaccination, literacy, census or even make posters about South African destabilization of Botswana.

It is only through such a system of governance that our young people can learn to assume responsibility and develop their creative initiative. It is also the means whereby we as citizens learn to develop new relations of mutual respect, assistance and confidence. The criticism and self-criticism involved in such a form of administration teaches those involved to recognize their errors and those of others. 'The spirit of criticism and self-criticism must be carried into all aspects of school life for the constant improvement of the school and the raising of the awareness of all its participants'.[5]

The older people in our society have much to teach us. Hence 'in the establishing of teaching and educational centres the rich experiences of our people and our national values must be synthesized. These constitute our personality and enrich the scientific and cultural heritage of humanity.'[6] To take advantage of this resource regular meetings should be held with parents of our students. They should be involved in the life of the school. They have much to teach regardless of the extent of their formal education. By such involvement parents will also come to understand transformations taking place in the school. Parents can be involved in various ways. Peasant parents can help in production; bank workers in administration; builders and carpenters in repairs; sports enthusiasts in training our footballers and athletics.

To achieve this transformation, much will have to change. There must be a new teacher, in the words of a great African revolutionary 'a teacher must behave like a doctor who before approaching the patient in the operating theatre, disinfects and sterilises himself so as not to infect the patient'.[7] Through meetings, discussions and self-criticism teachers can eliminate old ideas and tastes so as to acquire a new consciousness to pass it to the new generation. There is also need to write new textbooks reflecting the people's democracy.

13.6 CONCLUSION

To entrench democracy in our schools we must consult all students in all corners of Botswana together with their communities so that the changes which take place come through a democratic process. There is need to establish an education charter that would outline student demands and present a view of a viable alternative to our present system of education.

Our education system should embody democratic practices if we are working for democracy. We cannot say that our aim is democracy and then act in authoritarian ways. We must do more than talk about principles like 'justice' and 'fairness' and 'equality'. We have to look carefully at what this means in practice in schools.

ENDNOTES

1 Searle, C. *We're Building the New School*. (London: Zed Press, 1981) p. 1.
2 Castle, S. and Wusternberg, W. *The Education for the Future* (London: Pluto Press, 1979) p. 1.
3 *National Commission on Education for Kagisano* (Gaborone: Government Printers, 1977) p. 25.
4 See *Mmegi wa Dikgang* Vol. 5 No. 11, 26th March, 1988.
5 Searle, C. *We're Building the New School*, p. 101.
6 Ibid., p. 22.
7 Saul, J. S. ed., *A Difficult Road: The Transition to Socialism in Mozambique* (New York: Monthly Review Press, 1985) p. 165.

DISCUSSION

Mr Morake (Minister of Education) said the problem in the presentation, especially of Mr Phorano's paper, was that of definition of democracy. He said democracy should not mean the same thing as lack of authority in school. He said in all countries the education system is not perfect.

Mr P. van Rensburg (Foundation for Education for Production) said he believed learning is a total social process and therefore what happens at school should be linked with what is happening in the rest of the society. He felt Botswana is not doing enough to educate for democracy as what is learned is not matched by practice. He said although the school is not the only institution which should identify job creation opportunities, children must learn to create their own jobs.

Mr P. Rantao (Mayor, Gaborone) said the first condition for democracy is equality but our educational system encourages inequality.

Professor Nnoli (Nsukka University, Nigeria) argued that democracy is best taught if pupils are told about nationalist struggles against colonialism and the subsequent failures of the post-colonial state in Africa.

Dr Weimer (Research Institute for International Politics, Germany) said the definition of education so far used in the presentation suggested stuffing knowledge into a student's mind. He said the original meaning of education was to 'let grow'. He felt treating education as technical matter will retard democracy.

Professor Crick (Edinburgh University) said suggestions that the school can transform society were incorrect as empirical studies all over the world show that on the contrary the school tends to reflect what takes place in the wider society and not to change it.

Mr T. Joina (University of Botswana, Student) complained to the organizers of the conference that students were not invited. He said this was not a good sign of democracy. He argued that students should be allowed more participation and representation in schools than is currently the practice. The youth, he said should also be allowed to vote.

Ms M. Makgema (National Assembly staff) noted that no mention had been made of pre-school and post-secondary level education and wondered why, as these were important aspects of child development and life learning.

Mr Tlhomelang (MP, BNF) complained of English medium schools promoted inequality and reduced opportunities for democracy.

Summing up Mr Ramatsui said the school was trying its best to be democratic, but there were always problems of misunderstanding. Mr Phorano concluded that Botswana's education system was elitist and theoretical.

SECTION VI
CLASS, STATUS AND DEMOCRACY

14 The role a chief can play in Botswana's democracy

Chief Linchwe II

14.1 INTRODUCTION

Democracy may be defined in several ways. It is not only a matter of theory or philosophy but a way of life. It is the latter that makes a difference for the average citizen for it involves a *modus vivendi* or an arrangement for the peaceful coexistence of people in a society. It entails a covenant between the ruled and the rulers to create within the community mutual respect for all citizens and a collective responsibility for everybody's political and material survival.

From this perspective democracy requires the full participation of every individual in the running of the affairs of the community. There cannot be collective responsibility without collective involvement. Where full participation is physically impossible, it is done vicariously through delegation and mandating of representatives. Hence we have a representative parliamentary system of democracy.

14.2 THE CHIEF AS MODERATOR

The primary responsibility of the chief in Botswana's democracy is to be a moderator for his people. In so doing he serves as a social engineer who provides leadership as the community decides whether to modify, develop or abolish certain organizations or practices. For instance, take my case. Bogwera, the initiation of young people into the Kgatla tribe, was abolished without full consultation, and perhaps even arbitrarily, by my Christianized great-grandfather Linchwe I. I concluded that the matter should be put before the tribe in order for them to take responsibility for the decision. After much discussion, we agreed that the initiation school should be revived. Of course, a few mavericks remained opposed, but the fact that the majority of the Bakgatla support it is evidenced by the scores of families who voluntarily bring their children to the schools every time we have them. This year, almost one thousand young men graduated from our school.

Another example of where chiefs have served as moderators promoting the realization of our Tswana democracy involves the attendance of women and children at kgotla. In our tradition, only men who had been circumcised could attend kgotla meetings. Since independence, however, our government has encouraged participatory democracy at the community level.

As a result the chiefs have brought about what I choose to call 'the liberalization of the kgotla'. Everybody now is expected to attend kgotla meetings. We especially encourage women and children to attend. Moreover, women are no longer treated as minors; they take part in the decisions as equals with men. If there are still places where women hesitate to attend kgotla meetings, it is the duty of the chief to encourage them to do so.

The chief must be concerned that all aspects of the operation of the kgotla are democratic. There is sometimes a tendency for the chief, his uncles and government officials to publicize their pet policies and programmes while the tribe provides a passive, receptive and helpless audience. The tribe must ask questions and make suggestions as to how government plans can best be implemented. The chief must also encourage government to bring important issues before the tribe to test their acceptability. The chief also has a duty as moderator of the kgotla to keep himself fully informed on important matters of government policy and guide the people into understanding the implications of a given proposal for them and the country as a whole.

A good example of the important role we chiefs have played in this regard has been with the implementation of the Tribal Grazing Land Policy (TGLP). Because of extensive consultation with the people in kgotla, TGLP was implemented only in those parts of Botswana where land was available. Had it not been for the kgotla process, TGLP would have caused great political discontent in those districts where land was already scarce.

The most important role of the chief as a moderator of democratic processes concerns the protection of fundamental human rights. These rights are the very foundation of any effective democracy. Most important are the rights of association, assembly, speech, and life, liberty and pursuit of happiness. The chief in the exercise of his functions as an administrative and judicial officer cannot escape having to touch on these fundamental principles. For instance, in pronouncing judgment in a theft case, he has to indicate that the accused has violated a principle of living together by unlawfully dispossessing a rightful owner of his property. In prohibiting late night singing, he stresses the need for one's freedom or exercise of a fundamental right not to encroach on other citizens' rights. His subjects must know that their rights to exercise their fundamental freedoms do not entitle them to interfere with or even impede other citizen's desire to exercise their own freedoms. This is important and must be grasped by all citizens if there is to be peaceful coexistence. The chief must stress the need for restraint, accommodation and tolerance to his people. Peace is nothing more than the balance between these rights and selfish pursuits or interests.

The need for the chief to promote this respect for the rights of others was particularly apparent in the recent consultations at dikgotla, conducted by the Ministry of Commerce and Industry regarding the future of discos. Many disgusted parents and adults think that the solution to the problem of juvenile degeneration is the closure of bars, bottle stores and liquor restaurants or the prohibition of the sale of liquor at discos. My immediate reaction to this response is that the advocates of these austere measures have completely forgotten the law-abiding youth whose freedoms would be unjustly curtailed by such measures. This would not be democratic. Can we sacrifice democratic principles in order to solve social problems? Is it democratic fanaticism to say that democratic principles should under no circumstances ever be sacrificed? This is a philosophical issue which can be debated for a long time. The chief must all the time be alert that the freedoms of some of his subjects are not violated by those who think only of their own survival.

Among the chief's subjects are bafaladi (immigrants) who very often suffer discrimination by so-called true-citizens. The community must understand that legally there can be no second-class citizens who are not entitled to some of the rights enjoyed by first-class citizens. It is the chief's duty to protect these bafaladi against unscrupulous exploitation of their timidity because they feel that their acceptance and incorporation into the society was a favour which can be withdrawn any time. They have to be accepted fully and in their turn must strive to be assimilated. The chief as the moderator of the community must protect not only the interests of his tribe as a whole but also the interests of minorities, the children and all those who are incapable of protecting themselves against social and political predators.

14.3 THE CHIEF AS A PROMOTER OF DEMOCRACY

With all these responsibilities the chief cannot escape being a democrat himself and a promoter of democratic development within the community. He has to see to it that economic growth does not thwart such change. Political maturity will be reached when a reasonably democratic society has been established. This means that all members of society enjoy their fundamental freedoms without hindrance by either the state or some members of the same society. I am aware that this is only a dream because a perfectly democratic society has only existed in philosophers' theories – perhaps in our minds too. But I must stress that while we cannot reach the ideal, there will be hope for peaceful coexistence if we constantly strive to maintain and sustain a democratic society.

We as chiefs must be particularly concerned to promote democratic practice in the kgotla. Much remains to be done. At present the agenda in most dikgotla is determined by the chief or those government organs having a message to deliver to the people in a non-political manner. Perhaps it is time for individual tribesmen to bring forward issues for discussion at an impending kgotla so as to avoid suppression of individual subjects or issues on the grounds of irrelevance.

Another innovation we should consider is taking notes of kgotla discussions and recording of the decisions taken. If such minutes were then distributed, the people could be informed about what was discussed and decided at a previous kgotla. The circulation of this information would stimulate the community, both those who attended and those who did not, to follow up on issues. This might also help to instruct tribesmen on orderly debate and remind them that the kgotla is the place where they can freely express themselves. Attendance would improve, and participation would increase as citizens would not function only as receptacles of messages but would also regard the kgotla as a forum where issues of general interest could be discussed and thrashed out to everybody's benefit.

The kgotla, therefore, has a big potential as a small parliament in terms of its status and also as a big parliament in terms of the magnitude of the participation there. It can be more than parliament also in that we need not be bound by partisan affiliation when we discuss issues in kgotla. The tribe can discuss the problems of the community fully and find solutions that are best for the community rather than making partisan advantage the primary concern of the discussion, as often seems to be the case in parliament.

This potential can develop, however, only if the chief promotes such dialogue in the kgotla. Perhaps one of the reasons why there is relatively permanent stability in Botswana is the fact that, while there is multiparty democracy in our country, even members of political parties still rally behind the chiefs, divest themselves of party affiliations when they are at kgotla meetings and see the kgotla as an effective institution for resolving issues that extend beyond political barriers. I do not think that many important community issues can be effectively resolved in parliament, at freedom squares, or in government offices.

14.4 CONCLUSION

In other parts of Africa where there is only a little of this participatory type of democracy, there is sharp disagreement, no restraint, no tolerance, no accommodation, and the result is civil strife and internecine fighting. In Botswana the people still rally more behind the chief than behind the politician. The chiefs are thus vital in building democracy in this country. They can moderate the conflict that comes with economic development and social change.

In the kgotla they must ensure that the people can speak freely about what they want. They can also ensure that the rights of minorities are protected. The chiefs should therefore not be looked at as retrogrades who should be pushed aside. Rather Botswana needs to build a political structure in which the Westminster type of government and our traditional government coexist for the preservation and development of our unique form of democracy.

The chiefs have a big task before them, particularly because many whom they lead are not so enlightened to appreciate these issues. We must not give up. After all the purpose of life is to struggle and our success is measured by our distance from the goal.

15 The ruling class and democracy in Botswana

P. P. Molutsi

15.1 INTRODUCTION

This essay begins from the obvious but often underplayed reality that all modern governments are run by only a section of the whole population. It is this section which makes and/or influences government policy and decisions that we shall here call the ruling class. The ruling class need not necessarily be homogeneous. It also normally changes over time through the process of social mobility, as some old members drop out and new ones are recruited. At any one moment one or more sections of the ruling class dominate others. The dominant sections are not only ruling but governing as well. They are the ones directly involved with the day-to-day decision making of government.

Suffice to say, forms of government are distinguished from one another by the method the ruling class uses to maintain its power. For example, in a dictatorship the one or a few persons dominate the rest of the population using primarily but not exclusively force and coercion. In a chieftaincy or monarchy, the chief or the king and his class use mainly tradition to sustain their right to rule over the rest of the population. In a democracy, the ruling class derives legitimacy by following clearly established norms such as holding competitive elections at regular intervals, allowing for one-adult-one-vote, protecting basic human rights and private property (in the case of liberal democracy).[1]

At independence in 1966 the new leaders of Botswana chose a liberal democracy as the country's system of government. The basic principles of this system, namely regular competitive elections, multiparty system, universal adult suffrage, freedoms of press, association, speech, and protection of life and property, have all been enshrined in the constitution which has undergone minimal changes. Many will also agree that the majority of these democratic principles have so far also been realized in practice.[2]

This essay attempts to understand and explain Botswana's ruling class through its system of government. We will try to analyse factors underlying the apparent success of Botswana's liberal democracy. We proceed from the premise that Botswana's democracy is initiated and sustained by a specific ruling class. Our task therefore, is to identify and examine this class and its components.

15.2 HISTORICAL BACKGROUND

An analysis of any post-colonial society cannot fail to make reference its pre-colonial and colonial antecedents. Thus an understanding of the evolution of the modern ruling class in Botswana makes more sense if placed against the background of British colonialism in Bechuanaland (technically called a protectorate). Colonialism in Bechuanaland was characterized by gross neglect which meant that there was almost no social, political and economic development of this territory.[3]

Following the declaration of the protectorate over Bechuanaland in 1885, the territory was perceived in London as little more than a barren desert which protected the road to Rhodesia. The approach to governance was to keep the formal presence of colonial officers to a minimum, allowing the traditional leaders to rule their communities much as before the protectorate. This system was later given the more lofty title of 'indirect rule'. The result was almost no institutional development necessary for self-government. Not only was there no functioning legislative assembly until the year before independence but no secondary schools were started until the sixties.

Thus in Bechuanaland, unlike in most other African countries, Britain left no army, no strong bureaucracy, and a weakling middle class. This situation created a critical technical and political vacuum at independence. The Tswana educated elite was so small that it ended up collaborating with the colonial state, the chiefs and European settlers to form the new ruling class at independence. This was the only option the educated Batswana had given their numbers.

Two other factors both related to Botswana's colonial experience further acted as constraints on the ruling class. One was the existence of some powerful chiefs who had been part of the colonial state and wanted to either inherit the new state or be actively involved in its government. At a local level they posed a serious threat to the legitimacy of the new state. The new political elite had therefore to present and prove itself as a new type of government, a better and more democratic one than the chiefs. This, as elsewhere in Africa was not an easy task to achieve.[4]

The second problem facing the new political elite at independence was coping with the economically indispensable but politically unacceptable racist regimes in South Africa, Southern Rhodesian and to a limited extent in Angola and Mozambique. While acknowledging the economic superiority of these states and the resulting dependence of Botswana, the country's ruling class chose a multiracial ideology compatible with democracy as the cornerstone of the new society and as a defence against racist encroachment.

15.3 THE NATURE OF THE NEW RULING CLASS

Botswana's ruling class closely resembles those of other developing countries. It combines elements of traditional leadership, former white settlers and a preponderance of Western educated groups who either became politicians or public and private sector senior officers at independence.

My other paper in this volume details the background of this class. However, put briefly the new ruling class was formed out of individuals who either because of their early access to education, their connections with traditional leaders or their role as white settlers during the colonial period participated in the Joint Advisory Council, the Legislative Council and consequently in the political and administrative institutions of the post-colonial state.

Today this class consists of five major subsections including, **elected representatives**, i.e. members of parliament, councillors and village development committee members; the **traditional rulers** – the chiefs and headmen; the **bureaucracy** – senior officers in the public, parastatal and private sectors; the **business** elite; and leading **livestock** and **crop farmers**.

These divisions are made for purely analytical purposes. It is acknowledged for example, that a senior civil servant, here called a bureaucrat, can at the same time be a businessman and a leading farmer. Or a politician can and is usually both a leading farmer and a small businessman. However, the perceptions and influence each category exacts on policy differs depending upon the section to which the individual sees himself/herself as professionally belonging.

The discussion of how each sub-section influences policy decisions follows later. For the moment an elaboration of the specific context of the components of this class will suffice.

Elected representatives

This section of the ruling class consists of members of parliament and councillors. The former are members of the National Assembly which is the supreme legislative body of the country. There are thirty-eight of them at the moment (thirty-four elected and four specially elected by the elected members). The Attorney General and the Speaker of the House are ex-officio members of the assembly. Members of the National Assembly are elected every five years from single-member districts in which the winner prevails over other candidates by a plurality.

Councillors are elected concurrently with MPs. There are an average of six within every MPs constituency. They are supposed to be policy makers at a local level. Also at this level there are nominated members, though they are selected by the Minister of Local Government and Lands and not their peers as is the case in parliament.

Below the councillors are a myriad of representatives elected to the grass roots committees for development, health, schools, and safety. In addition, there are appointed and elected members of district land boards which allocate tribal land for various purposes including housing, crop production and grazing. All these various community officials are not supposed to be political but in various ways they associate with and mobilize support for the elected officials.

Traditional authorities

As noted earlier, the colonial government retained and strengthened the traditional system of authority. At independence these authorities sought to be actively involved in the law making body of the post-colonial state. The various political leaders as well as the British themselves resisted, and the chiefs ended up being stripped of much of their formal powers, e.g. land allocation and administration of schools, and only function now as advisers to the National Assembly through their membership in the House of Chiefs. The chiefs' and their headmen do retain considerable respect of the people. As a result in many areas, they are able to informally influence many activities that appear to be under community control. In addition, in some cases chiefs or headmen are an important influence on the outcome of elections.

The more active chiefs like Linchwe of the Bakgatla and Seepapitso of the Bangwaketse are able to have an important impact on the decisions of local councils. After a number of years of battling Linchwe, the council in the Kgatleng pretty much looks to him for direction, even to the point of accepting his suggestions on who should be chairman of council. The traditional leadership is therefore in varying degrees part of the ruling class, both because of its local influence on development policy and because of its participation at a national level.

The bureaucracy

This is a large and heterogeneous group of Western educated people who by virtue of high levels of education occupy important positions in government ministries. They include the professional cadres of planners, administrators, engineers, medics, academics, teachers, members of both the army and the police force.[5] They also include senior level council employees.[6] Outside the local and central government sectors, the bureaucracy include directors of private and parastatal companies such as Debswana, Botswana Telecoms, BP Botswana, and the Botswana Meat Commission.

From the above it is clear, as Liphuko in this volume notes, that bureaucracy is not a homogeneous entity. It is a complex hierarchical organization susceptible to all types of internal and external pressures and conflict. Molomo's paper in this volume discusses how the government bureaucracy operates. Our task here is to show how the government bureaucracy influences policy and thus functions as part of the ruling class.

The business and farming elites

Two other groups operating in both the rural and urban areas of the country seem to have substantive input on policy and government decision making processes in Botswana. These are the business and farming communities. They are both organized or in the process of organizing into associations. Although Holm in this volume correctly notes that most organized groups are ineffective, farmers (both leading crop and livestock) have an advantage in intervening on policy questions because most politicians, chiefs and even some bureaucrats are also farmers. Adding to the farmers political leverage are two other factors: the shortfall in domestic food production relative to local demand and the important role of beef exports in the national economy (about 20% of the total exports in the 1980s). The result is that farmers have not only enjoyed substantial grants, subsidies and soft loans but they have on two occasions, 1984 and 1988, had part of their debts with the parastatal National Development Bank written off by government.[7]

The business community has also been getting better organized especially in the 1980s. The growth of local business interests beyond the traditional general dealers, butchers, and bottle stores into manufacturing, construction and real estate, all in the late 1970s and early 1980s, have put pressure on government for favourable financial assistance policies and tax regimes. Policies limiting foreign investment to certain types of businesses such as chain stores, and hotels, as well as the famous Financial Assistance Policy (FAP) all came in the wake of the growing concern by the local business community.

The expatriate community

One group that influences much government decision making in Botswana but which is difficult to categorize is a small but very influential expatriate community. The technical backwardness of the Batswana in the context of a rapidly growing economy has made the country highly reliant on foreign technical support for many years.

In addition, the regional geo-political threat to Botswana's democratic experiment has attracted international support that has been critical to its development and sustenance. Material support came in the form of aid for a myriad of development projects. For example, the Accelerated Rural Development Programme (ARDP) of 1973/74 which provided water, schools, clinics, health posts and gravel roads to many villages was over seventy per cent supported by foreign governments.[8] There have also been soft loans given by, among others, the World Bank (IAD) and the IMF.

Stevens, (1981) notes that:

> The diversification of aid sources and the increase in the total amount available did place a burden on the administrative machinery of government . . . Virtually all . . . provided Botswana with large amounts of technical assistance, in the form of consultants, advisers and executive personnel holding established posts at the technical or administrative level.[9]

Given the weak political institutions, the expatriate personnel who played the role of techno-bureaucrats in government invariably found themselves in key decision-making positions.[10] It can be argued therefore that a large number of expatriates have become part of Botswana's ruling class in the post colonial era.

Political conflict within the ruling class

Earlier we mentioned that five groups are part of the domestic ruling class in Botswana: the politicians, the chiefs, the bureaucracy, businessmen and the leading farmers. To understand Botswana politics it is important to understand the relative role of each in relation to the others. The thesis here is that the bureaucracy is dominant.

The dominant position of the bureaucracy

In a democracy, decision-making is supposed to be made by elected representatives, that is the politicians. Because representatives are voted into power on the basis of their policies, the voters must have the opportunity to vote them out on the basis of the failure of their policies. The rest of the state institutions namely the army, the bureaucracy and the legal institutions are supposed to advise and carry out policies and decisions made by elected representatives.

This is a theory of democracy not always born out in practice. Very often non-elected officers make decisions for the politicians.[11] This is very much the case in Botswana. Those who gained elected office at independence lacked the education and experience to rule, and this encouraged non-elected state officials to take over the policy initiation and deliberation roles for themselves. At best, politicians were left with a veto responsibility.

The political leadership has generally remained weak and relatively uninformed. The average number of years of formal education for councillors in the Democracy Project's recent survey was 8.4 and 11.3 for members of parliament. In contrast, permanent secretaries had in most cases attended college, and many had earned advanced degrees. The situation was even worse before younger and better educated MPs were brought into parliament after the last two elections.

Generally, politicians are less informed on national and international issues than top civil servants who travel a lot and generally work in a cosmopolitan environment provided by expatriate officers. Asked what newspapers they read on regular basis, most councillors said none. A few read the government's *Daily News*, even then not on regular basis. A substantial number of councillors were barely literate. They admitted that they did not understand most of council position papers written in English.

Confirming the problem of semi-literacy among councillors and their inability to be articulate on matters of policy during council debates, sixty per cent of council civil servants said that most councillors did not understand position papers and that as a result debates were often dominated by better educated, nominated councillors (Nominated had an average of 10.8 years of formal education). They pointed out that most nominated councillors who are retired civil servants are more understanding and easier to work with. Given this situation, council officials and central government extension personnel said that if they wanted certain decisions endorsed by the council they simply approached and gained the support of nominated councillors to obtain the necessary vote. Many council officers and civil servants alleged that their job was made more difficult by 'ill-informed politicians' who very often misrepresented government policy or literally told the people to reject them. In spite of several years in parliament (the average number of years is 11.7), most members of parliament do not read much more than the local newspapers, except for South African Sunday papers. More important, however, MPs in spite of their better education than councillors have rarely initiated policy. Very few reported that they made a motion in the past three years of the present parliament. Where motions are raised they are generally concerned with issues of implementation rather than policy. Most MPs, like councillors, spend most of their time complaining about lack of a school, clinic, post office, water or road in their constituencies.

Very few MPs have made an attempt to study in any detail important issues such unemployment, agricultural productivity, population growth and industrial policy. Because of their pre-occupation with the policy implementation, both the councillors and MPs often find themselves in conflict with the civil servants. Thus it is common during debates in parliament and the freedom square to listen to an MP or councillor criticizing nurses, teachers, agricultural demonstrators or community development officers. That is, instead of supervising for example, council officers, elected politicians wait for them to make mistakes which they then criticize at various public meetings.

This is not to imply that the civil servants take up their policy making role unwillingly. They believe they should make policy both at the national and local levels. Many senior civil servants interviewed alleged that if policy making was left to the politicians there would be chaos. They claimed that elected officials were naive and parochial in their demands. Some civil servants even mentioned that they found it easy to use their sophistication derived from formal schooling to intimidate elected officials, particularly councillors. In their view, however, this was justified by their expertise and wider view on national interests.

Asked to explain why councils are centrally so controlled, senior civil servants categorically said councillors were not educated or informed enough to make intelligible decisions. They claimed some councillors like chiefs have in the past abused their power and misappropriated public funds. These bureaucratic officers who hardly ever visit districts, rather sending their juniors when necessary, saw nothing wrong in making local councils overly dependent on the central government (see Table 1). They further admitted that the policy of decentralization will take very long to be realized. Thus while councillors and MPs form a part of the ruling class and do endorse policy decisions, in practice they have little control over policy.

After the 1984 elections a number of politicians began to show greater determination to challenge the civil servants. Attending the National Council of the ruling party during this study, it became clear to us that ministers are under great pressure from the party's rank and file to control civil servants. Ministers were strongly criticized for failing to implement past party resolutions demanding curtailment of civil servants' power. The latter have been accused of misleading politicians and making decisions which will lead to the downfall of the present government.[12]

Table 1: Sources of revenue for district councils

Council Name	Area (km²)	Population (1986 est.)	Recurrent estimates (Pula) 1986-1987			Development Expenditure 1979-1984
			Income	Expenditure	Deficit	(Pula)
	(1)	(2)	(3)	(4)		(5)
Central	142 669	346 371	2 345 200	12 335 820	9 990 620	14 518 000
Ghanzi	117 910	22 149	513 900	2 716 670	2 202 770	2 290 000
Kgalagadi	110 100	28 931	377 650	3 124 240	2 746 590	2 331 000
Kgatleng	7 600	49 545	485 210	2 730 890	2 245 680	2 453 000
Kweneng	38 120	138 757	914 900	4 866 300	3 951 400	5 618 000
North East	5 323	42 032	334 120	2 444 610	2 110 490	1 966 000
North West	130 087	86 225	641 360	4 231 520	3 590 160	6 375 000
South East	1 492	37 185	390 370	1 894 910	1 504 540	1 367 000
Southern	26 876	135 848	640 770	5 114 200	4 473 430	6 031 000
	580 177	905 034	6 643 480	39 459 160	32 518 680	42 931 000

Adapted from: William Tordoff, *Local Administration and Development in Bot-swana*. Unpublished paper presented at the Centre for African Studies, University of Edinburgh, UK, 15-16 Dec. 1988, p. 11.

Also leading to increased interest in policy making, particularly by the leaders of the ruling party, is the fact that a growing number of the leadership are former civil servants who retired early to join politics. This new group has already created much anxiety among civil servants because on the basis of their background they feel confident to suggest lines of policy which need to be formulated. They also know how to motivate civil servants because of their previous experience in the bureaucracy.

The chiefs

The chiefs seem to be declining in significance in the policy process since independence. The House of Chiefs has not yet made any major policy proposal since independence. Asked to summarize their achievements in terms of promoting change in their tribal areas, many (the average number of years as chief was 14.8) said they had done nothing. A few changed the way headmen were appointed. Instead of taking the first born son of the previous headman, they have tried to select their subordinates on bias of 'merit'. Whether in fact this new criterion is actually being employed seems doubtful in that many observers reported that effectively the chiefs in question were using merit as a guise under which to appoint their friends as headmen.

Overall the government has clearly established in the public mind that the chiefs are a subordinate part of the ruling coalition. Nevertheless, like councillors and members of parliament, chiefs still command respect and enjoy legitimacy among their followers. Many of our respondents in the Democracy Project's mass survey reported that they approach both politicians and chiefs when they have problems. They also said that both these were often helpful in solving their problems. Thus in so far as they control the population at the local level, chiefs constitute part of the national ruling class.

The class orientation of government policy

Our analysis to this point has emphasized the dominant role of the top bureaucrats in Botswana's government policy making. The question remains: To what end are they making policy? Previous studies[13] have tended to argue that the prime concern of government policy is to serve the livestock owners, mainly because the majority of the politicians and senior civil servants are farmers. These studies assume that either top officers of government are subject to direction from cattle owning politicians in making policy or that the civil servants themselves have a similar interest in promoting the development of the cattle sector. There is thus in one way or the other a coalition of interests between politicians and bureaucrats to serve the cattle sector.[14]

The Democracy Project elite survey showed on the contrary that the top echelons of the bureaucracy not only make policy but make policies which generally promote interests other than those of the political elite. The principal decision-making section of the bureaucracy appears to have rejected the cultural trap of investing in cattle and increasingly preferred to support more urban-oriented policies intended to protect, support and encourage local business outside agriculture and retailing. The Financial Assistance Policy is a classic example. This type of investment requires skills and information on management and market situations. It therefore necessarily requires better educated and better informed people. There are not many such locals outside government bureaucracy. Consequently, top civil servants have demanded and gained permission to hold business investment outside farming.[15]

Following this important decision by government top civil servants and private company local directors have formed themselves into real state companies. Our survey found that 70% of permanent secretaries did not own cattle, or at least they did not perceive of cattle post their family owned as having any investment potential. Instead most of these civil servants held shares in private companies and parastatals such as Botswana Development Corporation (BDC), Sechaba Investment Trust and Sefalana, and commercial banks. Some were also engaged in commercial poultry and horticultural production.

Another aspect of policy making that reflects the increasing influence of these top civil servants in policy making relates to the rapid rise in their salaries which has taken place of late. Until 1986 the politicians fought to prevent a the gap between the income of permanent secretaries and the lower rungs of the industrial class from widening in aggregate terms. Different salaries commissions chaired by ministers emphasized equity not only among government employees but between them and the rural poor as well.

In the late 1970s the top civil servants demanded higher percentage increases for themselves, claiming that compressed salary notches were a disincentive to junior officers who did not find the need to work hard for promotion. Consequently the 1986 Salaries Review Commission (chaired by Mr Gasennelwe, Manager of the National Development Bank) called for and cabinet approved a 'de-compressed' salary structure.

The next year the Directorate of Personnel announced the results of its decade-long job evaluation study. The core of the recommendations was a proposal to base salary awards on the amount of supervision for which a civil servant was responsible in terms of decisions made and personnel involved. Those who headed a department or a section were the ones who would benefit the most. Thus the upper level of the civil service received a second improvement in their income relative to that provided for their subordinates.

The most important instrument of control on policy used by the senior civil servants over the politicians and everyone else is the National Development Plan. Theoretically, all sections of society are supposed to contribute in the formulation of the Development Plan. In practice, however, this as a technical document is drafted by experts better informed on the vast array of interacting variables. The result is that non-experts make little or no contribution to this policy blueprint. It is here that many politicians who usually endorse the plan without much understanding of some of the policy implications feel shut out. On the other hand bureaucrats feel safe if they can say they are only implementing what has been developed by the people and approved in parliament by their leaders. Once the new plan is approved, politicians' proposals not in the plan are turned aside on the grounds that only emergency measures can be adopted until the next plan is formulated.

The question that arises is: Why do the civil servants develop policies like the Tribal Grazing Land Policy and the Accelerated Rainfed Arable Programme which benefit the farmers? Two points explain these policies which favoured the livestock and arable industry. First, there is the colonial legacy. The colonial government established the livestock industry as the central element of the territory's economy. Decisions on extensive water development, reform of grazing land and better management methods were made in the late 1960s with the idea that government would promote the cattle sector as main focus of economic development. Eventually the resulting income could be used to help balance the government's budget, which at the time was funded by Great Britain. Subsequently, these decision have been implemented largely by expatriate dominated parts of bureaucracy which are interested in promoting their continued presence in the country. In any case, as long as the mineral industry was still less developed and providing relatively small revenue returns during most of the seventies, there was no good reason to object to livestock policies such as TGLP, especially as they purported to redress environmental degradation.

Secondly, there is no doubt that both the lower sections of the bureaucracy, the politicians and the majority of rural population still perceive cattle ownership and crop production as the most secure forms of investment. Policies which favour agriculture are thus likely to be popular at a local level.

15.4 BUREAUCRACY AND DEMOCRACY

Botswana's bureaucratically dominated ruling class, although so far successful in maintaining a liberal democratic system, has sought to limit the effectiveness of popular control. Two methods have been particularly useful. One comes from the expatriate and foreign aid community. Manifestly the various aid organizations encourage democracy in Botswana, but the reality is that most aid projects support numerous consultants who propose policies which government is then induced to adopt because of offers of foreign funding. In the process neither the Botswana government nor the foreign aid organizations take much time to find out the priorities of local communities, let alone the politicians. The latter in fact are easily written off as self-serving rather than representing their communities. For the most part, the outside consultants are invited to Botswana by top level civil servants. No one seems to notice that their terms of reference are to carry out research on potential developments which will serve the interests of the bureaucracy.

The recent controversial Job Evaluation is one such policy. Since the late 1970s senior civil servants have advanced 'responsibility' as an ideology justifying wide differences in remuneration. This ideology basically pushed the other contending ideology of social justice aside. Today the wide gap between the Permanent Secretary to the President and an industrial worker is acceptable on account of different responsibilities. The reports which justify this change are all written by outside consultants who are very little concerned with the value implications for society at large. One can go on pointing to other consultancies involving expatriates such as those on land tenure and economic opportunities which have enabled civil servants to engage in private business other than farming.

Another important tool the civil service is increasingly using against popular control is the kgotla itself. Since 1965 elected politicians have been addressing kgotlas as a means of mobilizing popular support in their areas to try to direct a particular ministry toward projects they prefer or they think their people desire. However, in recent years the kgotla is becoming more of a battle ground between the politicians and the bureaucracy. The top civil servants make sure that their juniors are at these meetings to defend their decisions. Moreover, these same juniors are often encouraged to hold kgotlas on their own to mobilize community support for civil service developed policies and thus place the politicians who might object on the defensive.

15.5 THE FUTURE

Botswana's ruling elite has yet to be tried. Those who won political power have not yet been seriously challenged by opposition parties. It remains to be seen whether the BDP will step down when it loses an election. The prosperous economy has permitted a flow of resources to all segments of the population, thus increasing the legitimacy of the BDP's rule as well as promoting relative unity within the ruling class. When these conditions change, it is not at all clear what will happen.

As far as maintaining a low level of class conflict, the dramatic increases in mineral revenues thus far and their transfer to other sectors of the economy by government have been of particular importance. The BDP has been able to undertake petty welfare programmes in the areas of education (education is free from primary school to university), health and agriculture. The dominant bureaucratic class has also been able to meet many of the demands of the politically potent cattle and businesses elites, thus rendering them relatively lethargic as far as challenging the prevailing structure of influence.

In addition, the democratic system itself has attracted diverse material and technical support to Botswana over the years. This help has gone a long way in improving the present government's legitimacy across the population. To be sure, this aid has also allowed the bureaucratic class to expand and justify its development programmes.

The liberal democratic ideology is also closely associated with the free market economic system in Botswana and has attracted multinational corporations into the country. These corporations have provided much of the capital and skills that have fueled the rapid development of the minerals sector.

In effect, economic development makes democracy possible and democracy renders foreign aid and capital willing to continue to play their roles in keeping development going. When this cycle stops, we are likely to see how entrenched democratic controls on the bureaucratic class have become.

ENDNOTES

1 Mayo, H. B. *An Introduction to Democratic Theory* (New York: Oxford University Press, 1960) p. 70.

2 Except for a few individual cases where one or two people have been declared prohibited immigrants, Botswana has an excellent record of human rights. To date there has been no case of political imprisonment.

3 Sir Seretse Khama, 'Botswana: Developing Democracy in Southern Africa,' Address by His Excellence the President of the Republic of Botswana at the Dag Hammerskjold Centre, Uppsala, Sweden, 11th November, 1970.

4 Markovitz, I. *Power and Class in Africa* (Englewood Cliffs, NJ: Prentice-Hall, 1977).

5 The army is however small and not very open perhaps because of regional security problems. It is thus not too clear how it relates to the central bureaucracy.

6 There are of course common misunderstandings between those at central level with those at the periphery.

7   See Government Paper on 'Drought Recovery Measures,' April 1988.
8   Colcough, C. and McCarthy, S. *The Political Economy of Botswana: A Study of Growth and Distribution* (Oxford: Oxford University Press, 1980).
9   In Harvey, C. (ed.), *Papers on the Economy of Botswana*, (London: Heinemann Educational Books, Ltd., 1981) pp. 168-172.
10 See Colclough and McCarthy, *The Political Economy of Botswana*.
11 Alavi, H. 'The State in Post Colonial Societies,' *New Left Review*, No. 74 (July/August 1972).
12 Personal interviews with some BDP politicians.
13 Parson, J. 'Cattle, Class and the State in Rural Botswana' *Journal of Southern African Studies*, vol. 7, no. 2 (April 1977); and L. Picard, 'Bureaucrats, Cattle and the Public Policy: Land Tenure Change in Botswana,' *Comparative Political Systems* vol 13, no. 3 (October, 1980).
14 This idea of a coalition is particularly explicit in R. Hitchcock, *Kalahari Cattle Posts: A Regional Study of Hunter-Gathers, Pastoralists and Agriculturalists in the Western Sandveld Region, Central District, Botswana* (Gaborone: Government Printer, 1978).
15 See for example the *Presidential Commission on Economic Opportunities* (Gaborone: Government Printer, 1982).

DISCUSSION

Mr Butale (Minister of Works and Communication) started the discussion by agreeing with Chief Linchwe that the Chief is an agent of change and in so doing must be democratic and adapt to change rather than being an idol of tradition.

Turning to Molutsi's paper the Minister said the paper was wrong to emphasise literacy as a factor determining who is a member of the ruling class. He said illiterate farmers were part of this class. He disagreed with Molutsi's claim that one section of the ruling class, namely the state bureaucracy, has emerged hegemonic and dominant in matters of policy in Botswana. He said, as can be read in the BDP manifestoes, the relations between politicians and the bureaucracy are like that of a husband and wife. They complement one another. He said the allegations that the bureaucracy used the 'plan' — National Development Plan (NDP) — to close out uninitiated politicians from determining policy made no sense. If the politicians were allowed to interfere with the Plan, "we could have politicians disrupting projects as they pleased". He said that Botswana runs a planned economy and politicians must come in at a specified time. That is it.

Mr B. Egner (Economic Consultancies) said chief Linchwe's paper was a short and lucid account of the potential of the chieftaincy in a democratic society. He said the paper was talking about the ideal and not practice. There are according to Egner contradictions in the fact that the chief is a law-maker and law-giver. Chiefs he said made unwritten laws even when Parliament is supposed to be the supreme law-making body. He blamed delays in women's participation in politics to conservatism of most chiefs and said the kgotla after all is not a participatory but consultative institution.

Turning to Molutsi's paper Egner said it was not clear to him what constitutes the ruling class and how the author came to the categories that he described in the paper. He said in some cases it may appear intuition rather than evidence was the source. He said the concept of elite needed to be defined. Mr Egner was not clear why the paper omitted academics as part of the ruling class, as they had the most education.

Furthermore Egner said politicians and bureaucrats are half-time business people. They are generally small and unsuccessful farmers. He said contrary to Molusti's claims the real farmers have nothing to do with politics. Rather they are busy managing their enterprises.

The important point of the paper is its exploration of the myth of an alliance between civil servants and politicians. The paper shows a rift developing in the ruling class.

Professor Nsibambi asked why the army has been omitted from the ruling class. He also wanted to know the role played by the personality of Seretse Khama. He said that two other factors should be considered in the stability of the ruling class in Botswana: First the chief plays a bridging role between tradition and modernity. Second the presence of South Africa is a factor promoting alliances between different sections of the ruling class and foreign elites. Finally he said the widely spoken Tswana language was a horizontal homogenizing factor in Botswana.

Mr Mayane (BDP) wanted to know whether the civil service was democratic. He also wanted Chief Linchwe to comment on claims that he was an absolutist.

Ms L. Molema (University of Botswana) wanted to know how the bureaucracy rewarded and punished?

The Honorable Kedikilwe said that job evaluation came from senior civil servants who were concerned that permanent secretaries had a lot of power on matters of promotions, grading, etc and that job evaluation was intended to give other officers a say by sitting in promotion and grading panels.

Professor Nnoli (Nsukka University, Nigeria) wanted to know the social basis of the ruling class.

Responding to comments Chief Linchwe said chiefs do not make laws but the House of Chiefs makes recommendations to parliament. On his turn Molutsi said some of the criticisms were fair and will be taken into consideration when revising the paper. He said both Ministers Kedikilwe and Butale seem to agree with him that the bureaucracy was the dominant policy maker in Botswana. He disagreed with Egner that politicians are not leading farmers at the same time and said if need be he could give a long list of them. On the role of academics he said although they potentially belong to the ruling class, in actual fact they have very little influence on policy making, especially local academics.

SECTION VII

MEMBERS OF PARLIAMENT AND COUNCILLORS AS REPRESENTATIVES OF THE PUBLIC

16 Problems of being an effective representative

The honourable R. Sebego

16.1 INTRODUCTION

This essay briefly addresses two considerations. First, I will point out the various aspects of being a representative I have come to appreciate since becoming a member of parliament. My basic message is that we as representatives act as intermediaries between the government, the people and our party. Second, I identify the basic problems of my constituency and the extent to which government has responded to the situation.

16.2 THE JOB OF BEING AN ELECTED REPRESENTATIVE

To be an effective representative a politician must fully understand his party's political philosophy, principles and policies. This is important especially in a multiparty system so that he does not appear to run with the hare and hunt with the hounds, thereby jeopardizing the credibility of his party as well as his loyalty to the party. The party expects a representative to sell its ideas. This means he must persuade his constituents to support the party's policies to ensure that they derive benefits from such policies.

A representative must not just sell the party's ideas. He must also be a good listener.

117

He has to get the views of the constituents and articulate them to government. In talking with his constituents about their expectations, it is the duty of an elected official to make sure these expectations are translated into realistic demands. He has to reconcile constituent needs with government priorities. In addition, he must be aware of the problems which government policies create for his people. Thus while urbanization must continue, he should address the problems of crime which arise within the context of rapid social change. Whenever the representative is listening to his people he must make sure that articulate groups do not distract him from the genuine needs of the silent majority in the constituency.

Politics requires give and take. Hence, the representative not only speaks for his constituency but also supports other elected colleagues so that they will back him on what he considers important. In so doing he will find there are three judges: the party, the government and the people. Only by attending to the concerns of each of three groups will desired policies be transformed into tangible results.

There is no blueprint for effective representation. Adaptability to ever changing situations is the key to success. A representative has to have qualities such as honesty and admit the existence of constraints. He has to balance his pessimism with optimism in order to act and achieve whatever is possible.

The problems of constituents are of real life. Minor incidents and events can change attitudes. A representative must attend to these very personal needs or he will quickly become unpopular. On the other hand too much involvement in the lives of constituents can also inflame local controversies. Thus it is important for a representative to be alert to the mood of the constituents without being carried away.

It cannot be overemphasized that in rural Botswana physical presence of a representative in dikgotla, freedom squares and many other forms of community meetings like those of village development committees and parent-teachers associations is very important. In the absence of other means of communication, such as newspapers and television, there is no other way to stay in contact with public opinion. A representative thus must divide his time between official meetings and exchanging ideas with constituents. It is an enormous task to make his presence felt throughout his constituency, particularly when he must visit many small villages spread out over a large territory. It leaves very little time for personal hobbies and friends.

In developing countries there is a very large gap between the standard of living of a representative and those he speaks for. He must watch that he does not allow this gap to separate him from average citizens. They will quickly come to consider him no longer as one of them. The representative's ambitions must always be tempered with modesty.

Balancing all these considerations is not easy. Struggling to obtain it however is required for continued election. In addition, the representative must be a leader who initiates new ideas and speaks out on the issues of the day without fear or favour. In short, he must not only seek to coordinate the party, the government and the people, but also think and speak for the needs of the nation as a whole.

16.3 THE PROBLEMS OF MY CONSTITUENCY

My constituency is more complex than most. It includes an urban center, Lobatse, and the most important cash crop area in the country, Barolong Farms. Each has a unique set of problems, so I will address each briefly. My expectation is that this will provide a grass-roots perspective on the kinds of problems a representative in Botswana must attempt to solve.

Despite the fact that Lobatse, like Francistown, is one of the oldest towns in Botswana, it has not grown like other towns due to the fact that there are no new industries. If the Botswana Meat Commission and Sefalana were to close for one reason or another, Lobatse would become a ghost town overnight. There is soaring unemployment, especially among the youth. The population growth rate far exceeds the job opportunities. The result is all the social problems which such economic stagnation creates.

No development can take place until Lobatse's shortage of land for industrial, commercial and residential housing is addressed. The problem of squatters in the town has always been a representative's nightmare. This land shortage results from the fact that the city is surrounded by hills on which it is difficult to build and that the Southern and Southeast districts control land outside the city. If we are to begin development in the area, land must be made available. SHHA has helped to alleviate the squatter issue and the shortage of land for development will be greatly reduced when the Government's Accelerated Land and Housing Programme is implemented. Lobatse has been allocated an enormous amount of P53.3 million.

As a rural area Barolong Farms has different problems. All households depend mainly on crop production for their survival. They also keep a few cattle and some smallstock. Barolong Farms is the main crop producing area in Botswana. In the six year drought which just ended, the area was most hard-hit. Farmers were impoverished. Many even went broke and were liquidated by banks (especially the National Development Bank). Compounding this economic disaster is the fact that the area is increasingly short of grazing land for their livestock. Government should consider buying adjacent private farms for the tribe, as it did in other districts.

Adding to the effects of the drought is the absence in Barolong Farms of many basic elements of social and economic infrastructure which the government is responsible to provide. Roads are very poor and dangerous for peoples lives. The council has not been maintaining its roads for many years. Other services also make economic recovery difficult if not impossible. The telephone system is almost non-existent. Electricity is available in only a few places. Probably most serious is the acute shortage of secondary schools in the area. Despite the fact that there are almost twenty primary schools in Barolong, there is only one newly opened Community Junior Secondary School which presently admits only about 200 students to Form I per year. Things should improve somewhat in that three more junior secondary schools are in the pipeline.

16.4 CONCLUSION

In confronting the conflicts and problems mentioned above a representative constantly faces criticisms from all sides. The criticisms do not always come from members of the other parties but also from one's own party, especially if you hit very hard at the front benchers. Some label the active MP as radical and controversial. Even worse such a representative is accused of supporting opposition parties. In these circumstances a representative should draw strength from his own convictions on the issue under discussion. Any response must be in a calm and respectful way, just as he should do when taking credit for a successful and popular parliamentary motion.

17 Whose interests do Botswana's politicians represent?

P. P. Molutsi

17.1 INTRODUCTION

Liberal democracy revolves around the concept of representation. Those elected win in part because they promise to speak effectively for and adequately represent interests and views of individuals and groups that are their supporters.[1] Of course it is always understood that representatives are more than delegates.[2] Representatives have to use their judgement to determine their stand on a number of issues and in the process they find themselves contradicting established positions of those they represent. To continue to win a mandate to represent a particular constituency, however, a representative must take positions in legislative deliberations which are somewhat consistent with prevailing constituency opinion.

A basic question is how can a representative effectively speak for his people? Political theory, particularly of a Marxian grounding, specifies common social background with a constituency as the first requirement for effective representation. Those whose social background closely resembles that of their constituents are better placed to know and effectively articulate the interests involved. Following this axiom electorates everywhere, but particularly in Africa, often insist on a representative who is their 'child', their 'tribesman' or their legitimate chief.

Although most representatives may come from the same ethnic group and belong to the same religious denomination as their constituents, very often they come from privileged cultural groups and classes in society.[3] In many African countries such representatives rather than making some pretence of representing their electorate have tended to pursue their own individual interests or those of their social class. They have shamelessly manipulated state institutions, engaged in myriad forms of corruption and resorted to gross patronage politics to win votes. The result is that most Third World politicians have failed to represent the interests of those who elected them to office.[4]

This essay examines the extent to which Botswana politicians fit in this pattern. The first section looks at who, in terms of occupation, educational attainment, and social status, became the leading politicians of the new state at independence? Suffice to say our hypothesis suggests that these individuals were generally persons of privilege from their respective communities.

Secondly, this analysis aims at identifying the changes that have taken place within the country's political elite over the years by comparing the new recruits with their predecessors in terms of occupation, educational levels and social status. The main finding is that although changes have been moderate, overall the new generation of politicians is better educated, has worked as trained professionals and is more articulate than the previous one.

Finally, this paper addresses the central question of who do these relatively privileged politicians represent? The argument made is that a number of factors in Botswana have worked to create a state which is relatively autonomous from the status and class structure. Thus while the political elite consists of a prosperous, capitalist class, it also provides a series of welfare programmes for the poorer segments of the population.

This analysis is based on historical sources dating back to the 1920s and 1930s, the data from our year-long survey of the country's political elites, and a Radio Botswana programme called *Botshelo jwa motho* or *Autobiographies*. The latter has over the past few years traced the social backgrounds of the leading figures in Botswana's political and social life. It has been particularly comprehensive in unearthing details of educational training, pre-political activities and general family background of Botswana's leaders.

17.2 SOCIAL STRATIFICATION IN BOTSWANA: AN OVERVIEW

Botswana's social structure like that of many societies manifests different forms of inequality and stratification based on class, status and ethnicity. This inequality has been an important variable determining participation by individuals and groups in local and national politics. The traditional and caste- like stratification of Tswana society[5] remains an important lever for political participation, particularly at the council level. Many minority groups such as Bakgalagadi, Kalanga and the most lowly rated Basarwa have found it almost impossible to stand as candidates for either council or semi-political village development committees where the Tswana groups are dominant, such as in the villages of Kanye, Molepolole or Serowe. Not only are the Basarwa of lowest social status, but also their hunter-gatherer economy puts them at the bottom of Botswana's class structure.

The same cannot be said about other minorities amongst whom are found the country's leading cattle owners and commercial farmers.[6] In the latter case status or rather ethnic status, not class, is more critical as a factor working against their political candidature.

At the national level the situation becomes more complex. Not only traditional status and ethnicity but class, that is, wealth, occupation and educational attainment have combined in an intricate manner to determine who stands and succeeds as a candidate for a parliamentary seat.

17.3 BOTSWANA'S POLITICAL ELITE: THE FIRST GENERATION

Most of the first generation of politicians were educated outside Botswana, mainly in South Africa. A few went to school in Southern Rhodesia. For most, formal education terminated with O' levels. They attended school in the forties and the fifties, but principally in the earlier decade. The handful who proceeded beyond the O'levels, then known as 'Matric', went to the famous African colleges in South Africa such as Tigerkloof and Lovedale. An even smaller number went to college in Britain, the United States or Western Europe.[7]

Occupation

Most of the early elites first were employed in the late 1940s or the early 1950s as court clerks, junior newspaper reporters, teachers or government civil servants. Like many young Batswana men they also engaged in agriculture. A few took up modern farming and rose through the pupil farmer scheme in the 1950s, earning themselves popularity and new status as master farmers. Several stayed on in South Africa as workers and, like those at college during this time, had their formative political ideas shaped by South African nationalist politics and the rise of Malan's apartheid regime to power in 1948.

Politics

Many of this elite were drawn to politics by their education which made them a politically conscious group. Some were selected by the chiefs to work within the tribal administration (e.g Ngwako in the Central District and Kgabo in Kweneng). Others because of their political awareness tended to see the chiefs as autocratic rulers who had to be opposed (e.g. Masire in Kanye, Ratshosa in Serowe). Some were favourites of the colonial administration which recruited or encouraged them to join politics (e.g the late Seretse Khama on his return from England). Whatever the reason they came into politics, most later participated in the African Advisory Council, the Legislative Council and ultimately in the post-independence national politics. Those who developed their political interest from their South African experience, i.e resistance to white rule, had a hard time becoming part of the main stream national politics in Botswana in that the issues were not the same.

Social status

The first generation of political elites were predominantly young men (with very few women) of different ethnic origins. Some enjoyed traditional royal status, but the majority came from prominent families in their communities. Their families had attained prominence because of early contact with and acceptance of Christianity and western education (e.g the Mogwes in Kanye, Molemas in Barolong Farms, the Ratshosas in Serowe) or had been among the first to establish trading businesses (e.g Molomos in Mochudi).

Reports of the colonial administration in the 1950s and 1960s as well as independent writers show that these few elites represented something of a new middle class.[8] They held different values from the mass of the population and the traditional leaders. Conflicts with the chiefs were an increasing political reality.

This new elite used their privileged educational status to move up the social ladder. They could do this because there were so few educated people in the country. Munger succinctly observed that:

> With the exception of the elite numbering under 1 000 one can compare the Bechuanaland people with a potentially fertile but dry field . . . what will happen when water in the form of education, irrigates the field, is impossible to assess.[9]

Writing at the same time Jack Halpern commented on the scarcity of the educated Batswana as follows:

> Educationally Batswana are probably more backward than any other people in Africa who have been under British rule.[10]

To have 7 to 9 years of education at this time was a privilege which the vast majority of Batswana did not enjoy. Thus this group saw itself and was seen as having a right to rule when nationalist politics began in the 1960s.

Some members of this group were not only educated and wealthy, but also directly related to the royalty of their ethnic groups. Royal Batswana as elsewhere in the colonies were among the earlier recipients of western education. By the 1930s for example chiefs like Bathoen II of Bangwaketse, Tshekedi Khama of Bangwato and Molefi Kgafela of Bakgatla represented the first generation of educated chiefs in the country.[11] Some chiefs had actually been in the same schools with many of the non-royals discussed above. A number are still in power and participate in the House of Chiefs which forms part of the modern government.

A few royals like the late Seretse Khama, Gaefalale Sebeso, and Englishman Kgabo because of their more tenuous links with chiefly rule decided to reject the chieftaincy for party politics. The result was that first generation of modern political elites in Botswana sometimes appeared more anti-chief than anti-colonial.

A small but important element of the first generation of politicians came from the European settlers. They were leading members of either the European Advisory Council or the Legislative Council. They usually had substantial investments in the commercial cattle sector or large trading organizations (e.g. James Haskins, Jr. and Phillip Morgan). There were other Europeans who had served in influential positions in the colonial administration, such as Russell England and Phillip Steinkamp, and who remained in politically sensitive roles after independence.

In summary, the first generation of Botswana's post-colonial politicians were very much privileged relative to the rest of the population. They were better educated, wealthier, of higher ethnic and royal status, and some enjoyed the then privileged European identity.

17.4 THE POLITICAL ELITE IN THE POST-COLONIAL PERIOD

Class, status and gender have remained important factors in determining access to elected representative roles in Botswana's democracy. Most who stand as members of Parliament or as councillors are people with some form of status in their communities. Such status is usually obtained from high levels of education and/or substantial property holdings (e.g. a large herd of cattle, a ranch, a tractor, a restaurant, or a general dealership). Table 1 reports on the broad occupational categories of the councillors interviewed in the Democracy Project survey of elites.

Table 1: Occupation of councilors

	Frequency	Percentage
Nothing	21	23.9
Farmer	34	38.66
Business*	33	37.5
(shops & bars)		
Total	88	100

*Some in business are also farmers.

Several things should be noted about councillor occupations. Except for those who do not have a job, all are involved in the private sector and work on farms or in businesses of one kind or another. With a few exceptions, these individuals own the enterprise which is their place of employment. Only a few are wage or salary workers. Thus most councilors are private entrepreneurs of one type or another. Previous studies such as those by Camoroff on the Barolong and Hitchcock on the Central District have established that such groups in the rural areas constitute an economically privileged class.[12] Samboma, Lipton and Colclough and McCarthy indicate the same is true for the entire country.[13] In sum, councilors are clearly people of high social and political status.[14]

Members of cabinet have a somewhat different occupational structure. Among the 14 ministers interviewed, 11 said they were farmers, one said he was doing nothing apart from being a minister, and two others said they were businessmen. Prior to coming to parliament, three of the ministers had been civil servants and one worked as a tribal administrator. Another four had worked in the private sector, though most had not owned their own business. If anything, the ministers tend to represent the old type of status, which emerged at the end of the colonial period, with the predominant group being farmers who are engaged in cattle raising of one type or the other.

Among the 19 MPs not in cabinet, the occupational distribution is similar to that of councillors. Apart from the two who do not have an occupation besides being an MP, nine are businessmen with a number having some cattle interests, and eight concentrate on farming. Four of the MPs were civil servants before joining politics.

In sum, elected representatives have continued occupationally to be persons of high social status. The ministers, however, come largely from the farming sector while the lower rungs of the political class, the non-cabinet MPs and the councillors, contain a rising number of businessmen who may also own cattle. It would appear that the political class is becoming less dependent on cattle holding and more focused on commercial activities.

Gender also remains an important factor with regard to entry into Botswana's politics. To be male increases the candidate's chances of being selected by his/her party and his/her chances for winning the election (e.g over 40% of our mass survey respondents expressed reservations on women in leadership positions). Gender inequality is clearly reflected in membership of parliament. Out of the 14 cases interviewed among cabinet members, 13 were males. For the ordinary members of parliament there were 18 males out of the 19. Asked whether some measures should be taken to facilitate female participation in politics, over 80% of cabinet ministers and members of parliament said that nothing needed to be done. They alleged in one way or another that conditions already existed that give women an equal chance with men in politics.

17.5 THE CHANGING CHARACTER OF THE POLITICAL ELITE

The political system like a biological organism survives by reproducing itself. Botswana's political elite — chiefs, councillors and members of parliament — has been changing over the years. The change has not been rapid. For example in our survey we found that the average number of years in parliament was 11.7. For the chiefs it was 14.8. Councillors had the highest rate of turnover, at 6.3 years.

In the case of both parliament and councils the new recruits tend to be younger and better educated than their predecessors. The new generation of the political elite therefore appears more equipped to participate in policy initiation rather than leaving it largely to the senior civil servants as has been the case. Indeed, if the few cases reported to us during the Democracy Project interviews are anything to go by, the next decade will witness a definite maturation of Botswana's politicians in the sense that they will give much more substantive direction to civil servants on policy questions. The new generation of politicians have a better idea of how the civil service bureaucracy works and are determined to reform the civil service so that it takes direction from politicians.

17.6 WHO DOES THIS POLITICAL ELITE REPRESENT?

The analysis of Botswana's political elite shows them to be people of privilege and influence in their respective communities. Their status as royals, highly educated persons, successful farmers, prominent businessmen or retired public officers are important in their election as councillors or members of parliament. The question then arises as to whether such privileged persons can represent a broader set of interests than their own. Can they serve the entire electorate?

A number of previous studies have alleged that in Botswana a class of commercial farmers rules and that the civil servants formulate policy to benefit this elite.[15] Policies on livestock, arable agriculture, income tax and land tenure system are according to Hudson, Lipton and Hitchcock[16] more in favour of the country's leading cattle and arable farmers. Among these are found chiefs, councillors and members of parliament.[17] Urban policies on housing, industrial development, wages and salaries have also benefited the politicians and the upper echelons of the bureaucracy.

Without denying that important government policies benefit the rich and influential sections of society, our analysis starts from the theoretical premise that in a capitalist system the state may well enjoy varying degrees of autonomy from dominant economic interests. In Botswana, the state is not *sui generis* an instrument of local shopkeepers and cattle owners. Instead it is capable because of its relative autonomy from the major classes in society of concurrently advancing accumulation programmes in favour of the propertied classes on the one hand and welfare programmes for the poorer masses on the other. The latter especially is important if the state is to establish itself as legitimate for the entire population.

In an era in which masses have a concern for economic as well as political democracy, it is important that those who claim to be democratic are seen to address basic problems of mass poverty. Many capitalist states, even those in Third World societies, are increasingly finding it obligatory to provide some limited welfare benefits for the absolute poor as part of their political programmes. This concern for poverty on the part of political leaders has meant that the critical policy issue is not whether the poor should be assisted but to what extent government should be responsible.

The state in Botswana has been successful in formulating and implementing welfare policies and programmes for the masses since independence. Elections have been an important factor in this process. Despite their privileged social and class position, political representatives regularly consult their constituents and seek to respond to their concerns, or at least appear to be so doing. This constituency influence has been reinforced by pressures from foreign aid organizations, which tend to demand a certain measure of social justice. The consequences have been significant. The government is engaged in a number of programmes which are specifically designed to provide substantial economic opportunity for those in conditions of poverty.

As noted in my other paper in this volume, the development of democracy in Botswana has been influenced by several internal and external factors. Among the internal factors is the need for the new form of government to be fundamentally different from and more effective than chiefly rule. This is the only way modern representatives can gain support and challenge the locally popular chiefs as rulers of a modern society. In the Democracy Project interviews it was apparent that many people consult their chiefs on political issues along with councillors and MPs. Our respondents also reported that in most cases these different authorities were able to solve their problems. In other words competition with the chieftaincy for local leadership is not over yet, and politicians still face problems of credibility and legitimacy relative to the ever present chiefs.

The effectiveness of political representatives is often assessed by the regularity with which they consult their constituents. In our survey, almost all councillors reported holding at least four or five meetings in their wards over the course of a year. Some held many more. The general pattern is to hold a kgotla meeting before a council meeting. At the meeting, the councillor calls for community complaints and demands. Then the councillor attends the council meeting and asks for action, often in the form of one or more motions or questions. At his next community meeting the councillor reports back on the progress he made with his council colleagues and the council staff as to his community's concerns. A councilor who aggressively pursues community interests is almost certain to obtain reelection.

Members of parliament engage in a similar process. In most cases they tour their constituency at least four times a year. These trips last from one to two weeks, and there can be as many as twenty different kgotlas addressed in the course of a tour. The MPs also receive briefings in each village on the tour from the resident councillor and members of various community committees including those for health, education, and development. The result is that the MPs are in constant touch with their constituents.

The MPs look upon themselves as supervisors of the councillors as well. It is not unusual for constituents to report to the MP when they feel their councillor is not doing his job, such as not holding meetings or not taking the community's concerns to council. MPs tend to follow up on such complaints because they fear that their own election chances could be adversely affected if the community becomes upset with a councillor of the same party. During the Democracy Project elite survey a number of councillors expressed the fear that some MPs acted on hearsay and that their positions as councillors were threatened by false reports given to the MP by malicious constituents wanting to become councillors themselves. The result of all this is that most councillors feel under some pressure to be active and responsive to the demands and wishes of their constituents. To be sure, there are a good number who are insensitive to even these pressures.

Apart from competition with the chiefs and the pressure to constantly consult with local communities in their kgotlas, elected representatives have to face the possibility of competition from opposition parties. In the seventies many constituencies were without any serious opposition party organization. However, in the last decade opposition parties have gained strength and in a number of constituencies their challenge is taken seriously by the ruling party. The Botswana National Front (BNF) has a strong organization in almost all urban constituencies. In the last several years, the BNF has launched an effort in the rural areas to rally so-called subject tribes to its side. A particularly intense effort has taken place in Bakalagadi areas like the Western Kweneng. If the BNF could form an election coalition with the Botswana Progressive Union, it could place severe pressure on the BDP in the Kalanga areas in the Central District near Francistown.

Not all political competition is inter-party in nature. Beginning with the 1984 election, the two major parties, the BDP and the BNF, instituted primary elections which allow party members to caste a preference vote regarding who is to be the party's candidate in a given ward or constituency. Many representatives have found this threatening as they are often challenged by several sometimes strong candidates.

A number of BDP councillors were not renominated in 1984 because they failed to win their primary. While no MPs have been removed, several came very close to losing in the BDP primaries. Recently the BNF MP in Gaborone North survived an attempt by some leaders of the party to oust him by winning a constituency primary. In our view primaries have become an important factor in heightening the awareness of politicians of their constituents.

These forms of political competition have led the BDP to introduce a series of new programmes. Among others are free secondary education (1988), Accelerated Rainfed Agricultural Programme (1985) and Drought Relief (1982-1988). In a recent session of parliament a motion calling for a social security programme for senior citizens was debated and passed by the BDP. This important legislation will go a long way in helping senior citizens who are poor.

It is hard to believe that all these favourable policies have been developed out of political benevolence. The ruling party sees a need to meet the BNF challenge at the grass roots level. The Democracy Project mass survey provided some evidence that the BDP has been very successful in this regard. For instance, the single most important reason given by respondents in policy terms for being a member of the BDP was the Drought Relief Programme. Through this project, where many people are fed, subsidized, employed and assisted in so many ways, the ruling party has successfully resisted political inroads into its popularity, especially in the rural areas.

Recently the ruling party has made a major effort to counter its declining popularity in the cities by launching a housing development programme which will erect several thousand new housing units before the next election. Quite rightly the party leaders perceive that anger over the urban housing shortage is a major source of the BNF's strength. For the same reason, the BDP government has been inclined to overlook non-payment of the Self Help Housing Agency (SHHA) rates and loans in the cities when the persons involved do not have sufficient income.

Botswana's growing social welfare programmes are not simply the result of political competition introduced by democratic structures. Both economic prosperity and foreign influence provide necessary but not sufficient preconditions promoting equity and social justice. The prosperous economy has provided the funds which made possible not only more jobs but the large sums of money that are allocated by the government for education, drought relief programmes, Remote Area Dwellers' Assistance, and the feeding scheme in clinics and schools. The function of political competition has been to ensure that these resources were not put to alternative choices which would have had less beneficial social welfare consequences.

Also important, many rural development programmes have been sponsored by foreign governments and non-governmental organizations. The ARDP of 1973/76 is one example where countries like Sweden contributed substantial sums of money for construction of clinics, schools, roads and development of drinking water. SHHA in the country's towns is yet another example. In this case Canada, among others, donated large sums of money for its development. The food which is currently distributed in clinics and fed to school children has for many years come from the United States and United Nations agencies.

In brief a combination of foreign assistance and available revenue from government has helped to channel the competition fostered by the democratic system into programmes which benefit the rest of the population.

17.7 CONCLUSION

Botswana' political elite has come from a position of social privilege and economic influence. This was the case at independence and it remains so to date. In spite of this background, these elected representatives have not followed the path of many African political elites who seem to pursue relentlessly their selfish interests at excessive cost to the rest of the population. While economic prosperity and generous foreign aid have played a role, inter- and intra-party competition have put pressure on Botswana's political elites to allocate at least some of the national wealth to the poorer segments of the population. Competition within and between parties is likely to intensify in the next few years. Thus a continuation of the same growth with equity approach should be possible.

This competition, as long as it is healthy, augurs well for democracy in Botswana. With increasing education and economic specialization of the population, the character of the contact between the elites and the masses will change. It will become necessary for the next generation of politicians to become more effective at reaching out to the public, not only during campaigns but also in terms of disseminating information and addressing issues during the intervening periods. If this adaption does not take place, there is no guarantee that the political elite will continue to expand its role in representing the mass of the population.

ENDNOTES

1   See Ball, A. R. *Modern Politics and Government* (London: Macmillan Publishers, 1971) pp. 121-128.

2   Ibid, pp. 121-128.

3   Markovitz, I. *Power and Class in Africa* (Englewood Cliffs, N.J.: Prentice Hall, 1977) pp. 247-260.

4   See Sandbrook, R. *The Politics of Basic Needs: Urban Aspects of Assaulting Poverty in Africa* (London: Heinemann Education Books Ltd., 1982) p. 183.

5   See Ngcongco L. in this volume.

6   Almagor, U. 'Pastoral Identity and Reluctance to Change: The Mbanderu of Ngamiland,' in *Land Reform in the Making: Tradition, Public Policy and Ideology in Botswana,* ed. by Werbner, R. P. (London: Rex Collings Ltd., 1982); Molusti, P. *Social Stratification and Inequality: Issue in Development* (Oxford University: PH.D Thesis, 1986), Chapter 4.

7   Interview with Chief Linchwe, April 1988, in Mochudi and Edwin S. Munger, *Bechuanaland: Pan-African Outpost or Bantu Homeland?* (London: Oxford University Press, 1965).

8   See among others Young, B. A. *Bechuanaland* (London: HMS Stationery Office, 1966) p. 93.

9   Munger, *Bechuanaland,* p. 5.

10 Halpern, J. *South Africa's Hostages: Basutoland, Bechuanaland and Swaziland* (Harmondsworth: Penguin, 1965) p. 308.

11 See Parsons, N. 'The Idea of Democracy and the Emergence of an Educated Elite in Botswana, 1931-1960,' A paper presented at Centre for African Studies, University of Edinburgh. UK, 15-16 December, 1988, pp. 5-6.

12 Comaroff, J. L. *The Structure of Agricultural Transformation in Barolong* (Gaborone: Govt. Printer, 1977); Hitchcock, R. *Kalahari Cattle Posts* (Gaborone: Government Printer, 1980).

13 Colclough, C. and McCarthy *The Political Economy of Botswana: A Study of Growth and Distribution* (Oxford: Oxford University Press, 1980); Lipton, M. *Botswana: Employment and Labour Use* (Gaborone: Government Printer, 1978); Samboma, L. M. *Survey of the Freedom Farms of Botswana* (Gaborone: Government Printer, 1980).

14 See for instance Wanatabe, B. and Muller, W. 'A Poverty Profile in Rural Botswana' *World Development,* Vol. 12, No. 2, 1984.

15 See for instance studies by Cliffe, G. K. T. and Morsoom, R. 'Rural Class Formation and Ecological Collapse in Botswana' *Review of Aflrican Political Economy,* No. 15/16/79; Picard, L. 'Bureaucrats, Cattle and Public Policy: Land Tenure Changes in Botswana,' *Comparative Political Studies,* 13, 3 (October 1980) pp. 313-356; Picard, L. *The Politics of Development in Botswana* (L. Rienner: Boulder, CO, 1987); and Parson, J. 'Cattle, Class and the State; in Rural Botswana,' in *Journal of Southern African Studies,* 7, 2 (April 1981) pp. 236-255; Werbner, R. (ed), *Land Reform.*

16   Harvey, C. ed., *Papers on the Economy of Botswana* (London: Heinnemann Educational Books, 1981); Lipton, *Employment and Labour*; and Hitchcock, *Kalahari Cattle Posts*.
17   Sandbrook, R. *The Politics of Basic Needs*, pp. 77-98.

DISCUSSION

Mr Rantao (Mayor - Gaborone) set off the discussion by agreeing with the general outline of the social origin of Botswana's political class. He however felt that the different sections of the political class can best be described as the comprador, bureaucratic bourgeoisie, and cattle barons. He said these sections set the policy agenda in government and indirectly in the private and parastatal sectors.

On Mr Sebego's presentation, the Gaborone mayor felt it did not address problems involved adequately. This is because:

a)   The paper limited its analysis to the author's own constituency - Lobatse/Barolong; and

b)   It did not address problems of being a representative of the opposition.

He said as a mayor of a recently elected opposition council he and his party colleagues were facing insurmountable problems of sabotage from the central government.

As the second discussant, Mr Setshogo said he was worried by the suggestion, or what appeared to be a suggestion, that the way Botswana's leadership emerged was somewhat sinistrous. He said these individuals had worked hard from the grassroots to climb to a leadership position. He asked Molutsi to reconcile his claims that in the final analysis the leadership advanced first its group interests before those of the masses with the fact that the government has adopted policies for low income groups, such as Arable Lands Development Programme (ALDEP) and the Self-Help Housing Agency (SHHA).

Mr M. Wallace (University of Birmingham) felt the opposition in Botswana instead of complaining about frustrations from central government should credit the latter for even permitting an opposition council to run the capital city.

Supporting Molutsi's presentation, Mr Mayane (BDP) said it is true a number of rural development programmes, for example NG32 (Remote Area Dwellers' Assistance) have been largely financed from external sources. He said it is high time government financed these programmes herself. He said government should do more to reduce inequality in Botswana.

Mr Tlhomelang said he expected Dr Molutsi to clearly distinguish between the old (1965/66) politicians and the new ones who have replaced them. He said the paper has not done justice to these two different groups. On representation he said problems differ from rural to urban areas.

Professor R. Sklar (University of California, Los Angels) said Molutsi's paper using class analysis presented a pessimistic picture and the current paper which dropped the class approach appeared more optimistic and somewhat contradictory. He also wanted Molutsi to say more about how the elite reproduced itself.

131

Both Mr Modise (BPP) and Mr Mogome (BPP) reiterated problems of opposition representatives. They also asked if the resources are available to the poor in Botswana, how then do we explain growing unemployment?

In the concluding remarks, Dr Molutsi said his is a preliminary sociological description of Botswana's political elite. There was no reason or intention to be sinister as suggested by Mr Setshogo. He said by talking about the requirements of legitimacy his paper was able to explain how government was able to initiate policies such as ALDEP, SHHA, and RADS. He also said relative economic prosperity did not mean that everybody has benefited, hence unemployment.

Speaking for Mr Sebego, Mr Magang responded to comments by saying he tried to address problems of representation as they relate to both MPs and councillors, irrespective of parties.

SECTION VIII
GROUPS POLITICS

18 Representation of cultural minorities in policy making

Motsamai Keyecwe Mpho

18.1 INTRODUCTION

Democracy appears to exist in Botswana because the majority of the people belonging to the so-called 'minority' tribes have remained peaceful and patient about their oppression. Democracy requires that every person is equal. It is impossible, however, to realize this end when as in this country some tribes are said to be the 'main' or 'senior' ones and the others are called 'subject' or 'subordinate'. There can be no first, second, third and fourth class citizens, rather all should be of one class, that of first class citizens.

With all the sincerity of a patriotic and peaceful politician and a citizen of Botswana, I request that the Botswana Democratic Party government take steps immediately to change this situation. The first step should be to amend sections 77 and 78 of the Constitution so that all tribes are entitled to have their chief in the House of Chiefs.

18.2 THE TRUE MAJORITY TRIBES

In Botswana those called the minority tribes are really the peaceful majority tribes of Botswana. They include such 'subordinate' or 'subject' tribes as the Bayei, Hambukushu, Basarwa, Babirwa, Bakalanga, Bakgalagadi, and Basubiya. The government since independence has tried to hide the fact that the eight Tswana tribes are in fact a minority. If we go back to the 1946 census, the reality of the population size of the various tribes is made clear. For instance, the population distribution of Bamangwato and Ngamiland[1] was as follows in 1946:

Bamangwato reserve

Group	Population
Bakalanga	22 777
Bamangwato	20 159
Batswapong	11 237
Babirwa	9 636
San	9 567
Bakhurutshe	5 441
Bakgalagadi	3 963
Batalaote	3 538
Bakaa	3 055
Bapedi	2 572
Baphaleng	2 409
OvaHerero	1 013
Balozi	1 006
Bakwena	892
Baseleka	889
Banajwa	844
Bayei	724
Total	99 742

Ngamiland

Group	Population
Bayei	13 261
Batawana	7 543
OvaHerero	5 798
Hambukushu	5 286
San	3 703
Bakgalagadi	1 918
Total	37 509

These figures tell quite a different story than the BDP government would have us believe. The total number of Bamangwato in the Ngwato reserve was only 20 159 in 1946 whereas the so-called minorities numbered 79 583. In other words, almost 80 per cent of the population at this time belonged to minority groups. In Ngamiland, the percentages are the same with only 20 per cent belonging to the Batawana tribe.

It should also be noted that in both territories, the ruling Tswana group, the Bamangwato and the Batawana respectively, were not even the most numerous tribe within the area they ruled. Thus in Bamangwato, the Bakalanga had a population of over two thousand more than the dominant Bamangwato group. In Ngamiland, the Bayei were close to double their Batawana overlords in population. There is no reason to believe that the situation is not the same today. Those who are from the so called major tribes are actually in the minority.

The government of Botswana insists on covering up this picture. Thus, after twenty-two years of independence, a government publication, *Botswana: A Review of Commerce and Industry* states 'The **main** tribal group is the **Tswana**; other important tribal groups are the Kalanga, the Yei, the Mbukushu, the Subiya, the Herero, the Kgalagadi, the Lala and the Bushmen. *Tswana make up more than half the population*'.[2]

This is making fiction into truth. The Tswana are not more than half of the population. The BDP government has effectively neglected to recognize such tribes as the Batswapong, the Babirwa, the Bakhurutshe, the Batalaote, the Bakaa, the Bapedi, the Baphaleng, the Balozi, the Baseleka, and the Banajwa. It is only by such neglect that the statement that 'Tswana make up more than half the population' can appear to be correct. All the tribes not mentioned in the above government statement were enumerated in the 1946 census as living in the Ngwato territory. Now they do not exist.

Also part of the myth of the Tswana majority in Botswana is the idea that the subject tribes joined the eight dominant tribes on a voluntary basis. Chief Tshekedi Khama said this openly in 1957:

> The inhabitants of the Protectorate consist mainly of Bantu tribes of which eight are 'independent' tribes . . .There are a number of subordinate tribes. These have either voluntarily surrendered their independence to a stronger tribe or have been forced to submit . . .[3]

The truth is that no tribes ever voluntarily surrendered their independence. They were all forced to submit to the eight main war-mongering tribes, now constitutionally entrenched.

As long as the government continues to regard some tribes of Botswana as the 'main' tribal groups and others as important tribal groups, and the remaining tribal groups, I suppose, as nothing; then words like 'democracy, unity, self-reliance, development' are meaningless.

18.3 THE TRIBAL BIAS OF THE CONSTITUTION

The composition of House of Chiefs is spelled out in sections 77 and 78 of the constitution. It grants to the chiefs of the eight major Tswana tribes, i.e. the Bakgatla, Bakwena, Bamalete, Bamangwato, Bangwaketse, Barolong, Batawana, and Batlokwa — the right to sit in the House of Chiefs by virtue of their office. The rest of the tribes in the country, even though they constitute a majority of the population, are given four seats which are to be elected from the various sub-chiefs. In other words, the Constitution of Botswana calls for the supremacy, of the eight major tribes, the 'used-to-be war-mongers', and a permanent minority status for the ever peaceful majority tribes.

Sections 77 and 78 are undemocratic and discriminatory. They sow seeds of discontent among the eight supposed main tribes and the uncounted peaceful majority or subject tribes of Botswana. Even after twenty-two years of political independence, the government has given no indication that it is willing to consider changing this undemocratic situation.

Given this legalization of the seniority of eight tribes of Botswana, how can cultural minorities have fair representation in the policy making process of Botswana? I belong to one of the remaining uncounted tribes. How can my master who does not speak or understand my language be expected to represent my culture? No member of one tribe can correctly and faithfully or truly respect another's culture, especially if one tribe regards itself as superior. Effectively, these two sections in the constitution encourage members of the supposed majority tribes to continue to regard themselves as superior or masters over the remaining uncounted peaceful tribes of Botswana.

A person is defined by his or her culture. That is, culture determines how he or she behaves towards his or her family, community and nation. One's culture is found in one's language, art and music, food, clothes, and one's interests in life generally. Culture is a pointer to the past history of any society. It is the footprint by which men can trace the past life of society and compare it with the present through the use of language, art and music, property and land. It is highly hypocritical, at least for a true politician, to say that cultural minorities, which means tribes, are being properly represented in this country if only certain forms of culture are granted recognition in the constitution. Those who are not of the approved culture are effectively denied their right to be human.

The only way this situation will be improved is if all tribes in this country are represented by their chiefs in the House of Chiefs. Section 78 must read that such persons as perform the function of chief for 'any' tribe in Botswana shall be ex-officio members of the House of Chiefs. This would be a constitutional guarantee that all tribes are equal. In addition, by awakening the political consciousness of the so-called subject tribes and raising their level of political understanding, they would come to understand that they are born free human beings who are free to develop their mental talents and to make their own decisions without fear of being victimized by the supposed superior tribes.

18.4 THE POWER OF THE CHIEFS

Schapera said of the chief in the past that he 'was the ultimate authority and recognised nobody above him?' This authority was extremely broad. According to Schapera, the chief was 'at once ruler, judge, maker and guardian of the law, repository of wealth, dispenser of gifts, leader in war, priest and magician of the people'.[4]

I know the advocates of the mind poisoning policy of tribal seniority would like us to believe that the chieftainship no longer has this same power since we gained our political independence in 1966. The fact of the matter is that the chiefs are still the same chiefs belonging to the eight main tribes. They have every power, except that they do not make the laws for their subject tribes. They are still jealous of their position. Policy making in Botswana starts from the kgotla where the chiefs of the supposed senior tribes are the heads of the whole administration. They approve appointments of clerks, police and messengers. They select the three specially elected members who sit with them in the House of Chiefs. They determine who will be their chief's representatives, that is those who will supervise the headmen of the subject tribes. If these representatives happen to be members of a subject tribe, they must be completely and mentally subservient persons who cannot speak for their tribes but will dance to the tune of their supposed senior tribal chiefs.

The formation of the Botswana Democratic Party by Sir Seretse Khama, who was groomed into that idea by the colonial masters in 1962, changed the meaning of freedom of expression. Under his rule, true expression of one's opinion is absent from the minds of the peaceful uncounted majority tribes. This point has been demonstrated in the past five general elections, where the majority of subject tribes openly declared that they were going to vote for their *chief's* political party and not for political parties led by people whose parents never ruled. If a member of one of the subject tribes was a member of the BDP and was elected a councillor or an MP, people voted for him not as their representative, but as the servant of their chiefs. Many of the members of the subject tribes even thought that when Sir Seretse Khama said everybody was free to vote as he or she wished, he was laying a trap for them. They believed that Sir Seretse would use the chief's magic powers against them. Surely, the votes of such persons were not their free expression of their true opinion.

If this point is understood, then, one should ask oneself, whether it is true to say that minorities have fair representation in the policy making process. It is the master who is represented.

18.5 CONCLUSION

Tracing back, the past history of the peaceful majority (now called the minorities) as subject tribes under the previously war-mongering minority, or senior tribes as they are known, one cannot fail to come to the conclusion that in today's Botswana like in the old Bechuanaland Protectorate, culture, democracy, freedom and independence are only for the eight main or senior tribes of Botswana. The status of the various tribes in Botswana has been frozen at what it was in 1895. The subject tribes are still suffering from mental bondage or an inferiority complex. They are not mentally free.

I have already said that in Botswana freedom, independence and democracy are first and foremost for the eight so-called main tribes. These people have long been independent even before the birth of the Bechuanaland Protectorate. The danger in our supposed democratic practice in Botswana with regard to minorities is that the true majority has been and are still ruled by the minority, unlike in many countries in the world where the government is expected to honour Article 25 of United Nations Civil and Political Rights Covenant, which prohibits denial of the rights of any group because of religion, language or other aspects of their culture.

As long as the seniority of the eight Setswana speaking tribes is constitutional and enforced by the government in writing, cultural minorities will never have fair representation in Botswana's policy making process. The Botswana Democratic Party government must see my reasoning and immediately start amending sections 77 and 78 of the constitution, if they wish to see the true fruits of the democracy prevail in Botswana. It is my sincere belief that if sections 77 and 78 of the Constitution of Botswana are amended, this will guarantee the equality of all the peoples of Botswana. Who knows how long the true peaceful and patient uncounted majority tribes of Botswana will remain silent, peaceful and patient before they realize that in fact they are born as free as their so-called masters.

The time is long overdue for the ruling BDP to tell the truth about the true majority tribes of Botswana, tribe by tribe. Democracy is indivisible. Unity is indivisible. Democracy has no first, second, and third class citizens. It has only one class, first class citizens.

ENDNOTES

1   See Morton, F. and Ramsay, J. eds., *The Birth of Botswana: A History of the Bechuanaland Protectorate from 1910 to 1966* (Gaborone: Longman Botswana, 1987) pp. 52, 111.

2   Government of Botswana, *Botswana: A Review of Commerce and Industry* (Gaborone: Government Printer, 1987) p. 11. The italics are mine.

3   See Khama, T. *Bechuanaland Protectorate* (Johannesburg: South African Institute of Race Relations, 1957) p. 3.

4   Quoted in Campbell, A. *The Guide to Botswana* (Johannesburg: Winchester Press, 1980) p. 53.

19 What should be the role of trade unions?

I. Mbonini

19.1 INTRODUCTION

Democracy is an institutional arrangement for reaching political, administrative and legislative decisions. It is not an end in itself but a means to ends, which may take any number of forms including social and economic benefits or improvements in governmental processes. The important thing is that the interests being served are those desired by the people and not their rulers.

There are two main theories of democracy. In the classical one, the people themselves acting as a group make the decisions on important issues. The selection of top government officials to carry out the people's decisions is a secondary issue. In the modern theory of democracy, the people select representatives to make decisions for them. Leaders compete for the votes of citizens. Those who win become the representatives. The people end up with two main functions: choosing their rulers and recalling these rulers if they act against the people's interest.

In this modern system of democracy, trade unions have two important roles. First, we talk about what we in the labour movement think government should be doing to improve our members' lives. Second, we must make clear the changes which are required for organized labour to be effective in representing our members. I shall address both briefly.

19.2 A GOVERNMENT POLICY FOR THE WORKERS

We in the trade unions want more schools and less prisons, more jobs and less crime, more leisure and less greed, more justice and less revenge. We also want better housing and less squatters, good labour legislation and less exploitation, free collective bargaining and less restrictions.

A mistake made by many in our society is to think that these goals can be achieved by only concentrating on economic growth. We in the trade union movement want a broader goal of 'economic development'. Both economic and social concerns are involved.

On the economic side there must be increases in the gross national product and growth of productivity, consumption and investment. But development must also lead to social changes like greater literacy, longer life expectancy, reduced infant mortality, and *greater access of ordinary people* to a variety of basic government services. In a nutshell, development must entail the increased satisfaction of basic needs, both material and non- material. The benefits of development cannot be confined to the better off minority in the society. Real development must ensure a fairer distribution of income in favour of the poorer sections of society.

That is why we say development is a comprehensive process because it embraces all sections of the people − rural and urban, agriculture and industry, employed and self-employed, men and women, adults and children. Increased social justice, therefore is at the centre of our understanding of development rather than being an accidental product of economic growth. This can only be achieved if the 'top-down' strategies which have characterized development up to this point in Botswana are abandoned. Ordinary people must be involved in decisions affecting their lives; otherwise government leaders will not be pressed to respond to their needs.

19.3 THE ROLE OF LABOUR IN BOTSWANA'S DEMOCRACY

The state embodies and magnifies the frailties of man and his capacity for good or ill. The state unchecked and unopposed is a deadly engine of oppression in the extreme. It is therefore important to hold the state within bounds which allow for citizens to be free. In addition, we as citizens must tell those in government the constructive ends which they should seek. The trade union movement is committed to both these activities, to the protection of our rights as free citizens and to telling the government the ends it should pursue.

Our role in government policy making involves a number of important activities. We must participate in all decisions related to the development of our country. At the enterprise level, this means workers should participate with management in major decisions. Each economic sector should have councils including capital, labour and government which set general policies. Labour should even make its views know on all aspects of development plans. To insure that these goals are achieved, we should build coalitions with other movements and groups whose aims converge with our own. Finally, we must attack the theoretical underpinnings which allow academics, businessmen and ordinary people to mount anti-union rhetoric for seemingly altruistic motives. We are the liberation movement of mankind, and this has to be firmly anchored in the minds of workers, the people and government.

A number of specific changes are required in the present relations between government and the labour movement if a truly democratic situation is to exist:

1 The unions must sit on such bodies as the National Employment, Manpower and Incomes Council and the Labour Advisory Boards not as advisers but as participants in the decisions which establish policy.
2. Government should ratify International Labour Organization conventions dealing with human rights and labour relations.
3. Government and the Botswana Federation of Trade Unions should revise the National Policy on Incomes, Employment, Prices and Profits in a way which is mutually acceptable, rather than unilaterally imposed as is currently the case.

4. Government must repeal those provisions of the Trade Union and Employers'
   Act which unfairly restrict the ability of unions to represent their members
   including the following:

a) the right of the Registrar of Trade Unions and Employers' Organizations to
   cancel the registration of a trade union for any act violating the law or the union's own constitution;

b) the requirement that any dismissed employee ceases to be a member of his
   union, thus preventing the union from representing the affected individual in
   disputes related to the dismissal; and

c) the prohibition of officers of unions from being full-time employees of the union, which means that these officers can only represent their organizations on
   a part-time basis.

The changes we desire are not extreme. They are necessary if trade unions are
to be free to stand up for their members in political disputes with government and
employer groups. They are necessary if trade unions in Botswana are to exist in
a fully democratic climate.

19.4 CONCLUSION

Government in seeking the cooperation of trade unions to carry out their economic
and social policies should recognize that the value of this cooperation rests to a large
extent on the trade union movement being free to promote social advancement. The
government should not attempt to transform the trade union movement into an instrument for pursuance of particular political aims, nor should it attempt to interfere with the normal functions of a trade union movement.

We can reach our grass-roots level quickly and effectively. Our members know
and understand us better than government officials. Thus we can provide critical
two-way communication between the government and its citizens. In the planning
for a new National Development Plan such communication should be particularly
beneficial to all concerned in that it is the members of our trade unions who will
be providing most of the manpower for the increases in production which we all
want to take place. If the workers are to participate enthusiastically in these developments, thus assuring success, they must also be involved in the planning. We
as trade union leaders are ready to be the frank intermediaries in this process.

SECTION IX
HOW EFFECTIVE ARE INTEREST GROUPS?

20 How effective are interest groups in representing their members?

John D. Holm

20.1 INTRODUCTION

Economic development requires increasing intensification of the division of labour. A plethora of separate and often competing economic interests are thereby created. A liberal democracy must provide some form of access to government for these groups if it is not only to respond to public problems but to shape the course of economic change.

Elections cannot help much in this regard since representatives are selected on the basis of geography. Most economic groups are small minorities within one or more districts, and may easily be overlooked by whoever wins the election. Only a few economic groups, such as farmers in rural areas or wage earners in urban centers, are large enough in number to be assured recognition because of their voting power.

This paper is concerned with the development of organized economic interest groups in Botswana since independence. It focuses on two concerns: a) How have Botswana's political structures incorporated the array of economic interests which are emerging with economic development? b) Are these interests incorporated in a way which facilitates democratic practice?

In focusing on economic interest groups, a number of other types of organized groups are overlooked which are active in today's Botswana, including women's associations, youth groups, churches, and sports organizations. These latter groups are important, especially if Botswana's government is to respond effectively to society as a whole. However, rapidly expanding economic interests present the most direct challenge to Botswana as a democracy. If the problems of these groups are not addressed in the long run, there is a good chance that at a minimum the continued health of the economy will be threatened and possibly the very legitimacy of the state may be questioned.

The rate of interest group development varies greatly with the culture of a country. The politics of United States has long focused around group conflict.[1] West African states today, while having their problems establishing representative government, are already notable for the degree of economic interest group activity which exists.[2] On the other hand, countries like Italy, Spain and Mexico have a relatively low level of group politics given their level of development.[3]

The focus of democratic theory with regard to interest groups is on the extent to which politically active groups originate and function relatively independent of the state and political parties. It is presumed that the more pluralistic or autonomous groups are relative to the state, the more economic and other concerns of citizens will be recognized and attended to by policy makers.[4]

This paper evaluates the Botswana interest group structure from this perspective; that is in terms of the extent to which Botswana has developed a structure of autonomous economic interests groups which negotiate with government officials relative to the important policy concerns of these groups. The thesis developed is that in Botswana the growth of politically active economic interest groups has been retarded relative to other aspects of democratic practice, and particularly relative to the development of political parties. This underdevelopment stems from the traditional political culture, the partisan domination of politics in Botswana, and the state's monopoly over economic decision making.

The discussion which follows is organized around four aspects of Botswana politics: a) cultural norms relative to group politics, b) the relation of interest groups and political parties, c) the relation of interest groups and the civil service, and d) the organizational effectiveness of Botswana's major economic interest groups.

20.2 THE CLIMATE OF GROUP POLITICS

Tswana traditional political culture did not give much recognition to the organization of interest groups along economic lines. The primary social groups with which chiefs and headmen worked were families, age regiments, geographic communities, and ethnic groups. Even these groups were heavily dependent on the chief regarding when and under what conditions they could participate in the politics of the community. The chief commissioned a new regiment, decided when the regiments would undertake projects for themselves or the community, recognized and demarcated the area for a new ward or village, determined which ethnic groups could associate with the community, and had a substantial say over the appointment and removal of leaders of these various groups. For political purposes, groups existed primarily to serve the state, and their legitimacy derived from the state.

Modern Botswana now has a growing number of economic interest groups. However, the climate in which they exist limits in many ways their autonomy from the state. In the vast majority of cases government officials initiate the formation of economic groups. In the agricultural sector, it is the officers of the Ministry of Agriculture who promote the formation of marketing cooperatives, dip groups, and farmers associations. Community development officers from the Ministry of Local

Government and Lands organize and supervise at the village level a whole series groups concerned with development, health, schools, and public safety. The degree of government involvement in such groups even goes to the extent of imposing a standard constitution on each type of group, regardless of whether the group itself might like to generate its own.

In the urban areas, non-governmental organizations are often initiated by group members; however these groups, ranging from women to trade unions, often end up looking to government or foreign donors for much of their funding. This financial dependence means they must define their activities in terms of government priorities and not ends their membership might prefer.

Particularly limiting of group initiatives designed to influence government is the general belief that it is preferable if organized groups of all kinds including economic ones do not participate in 'politics'. This means that they are not to ask politicians to promote their goals in exchange for campaign support in the form of money and votes. When we asked the councilors we interviewed whether they had to worry about organized groups in their communities when they ran for election, only 20% said this was a concern. Among the MPs the figure was virtually the same(18%).[5]

The leaders of organized groups for the most part prefer to contact civil servants if they have proposals for either changes in existing programmes or the establishment of new ones. Such contacts are generally not perceived as political either by the group leaders or by the civil servants involved.[6] Rather the discussions are seen solely as relating to issues of economic development. It is only as a last resort that interest group leaders will approach politicians.

When we asked our sample of ten ministers, whether interest groups had contacted them since the last election to propose a policy or complain about a particular programme, only three could remember that they were so contacted. To be sure a number of others acknowledged that they had informal discussions with the leaders of organized groups after addressing a national meeting of these groups. The figure was somewhat higher among government backbenchers and opposition MPs. Half had been contacted by an interest group, but almost all mentioned only one group, and then it appears to have been on one issue usually having to do with farming.

Government officials have much more extensive contacts. For instance, out of the 14 officers of permanent secretary status we interviewed, only four said that they were not approached by leaders of voluntary groups.[7] Many of them talked about interactions with group leaders as being on a regular basis. One of the most influential of the permanent secretaries called such contacts 'a daily occurrence.'

Developing a healthy group politics in Botswana probably requires that the citizenry itself rethink the means by which it makes contact with political leaders. Basically, two approaches took place traditionally. A person contacted influential persons such as the headman, an elder in the family or a regimental leader and asked him to intervene with the chief. Or, if an issue was brought to kgotla, adult males at least could speak their peace and hope to gain general support in the community. If people are to join groups to seek political objectives, they must see such groups as the preferred method of influencing their politicians rather than these traditional approaches.

To evaluate citizen attitudes toward taking a group approach to politics, we asked our respondents in the Democracy Project's mass survey which of the three approaches — the kgotla, having an important person intervene, or using a community group — would be most effective with regard to both the local MP and councilor.[8] For both types of politicians the results were similar: Two-fifths chose groups, a similar proportion liked the kgotla, and the remainder preferred an important person. In short, well over a majority of the population have not come to see groups as a useful way to communicate with their elected officials.

The one factor we were able to identify which induced our respondents to move to the group approach was formal education. Only a quarter of those who had a primary education or less saw groups as effective. The proportion inclined toward using groups increased to half among those who had attended secondary school. For those attending college, the figure rose even further to 70%. One factor we thought would enhance citizen preference for a group approach to politics was the degree to which the person was already involved in group activity.[9] Our data showed no such effect.

Our survey data thus indicate that the swing to a group oriented political culture is beginning at the mass level and that it seems to be particularly a function of formal education. The fact that group membership itself does not bring any greater inclination to see the group approach as effective could compound the problem of Batswana becoming more group oriented. The citizenry appears to not be learning by doing, probably because groups thus far have been hesitant to be involved in politics or have not been very effective in so doing.

20.3 LINKAGES OF ORGANIZED GROUPS TO POLITICS

In most industrial democracies, interest groups become directly involved with political parties. Sometimes, these groups have formal associations with political parties, as is the case with labour unions linked with the socialist and communist parties in a number of European countries. In other cases, interest groups contribute money and manpower to political campaigns or at least urge their members to vote for specific candidates or parties.[10]

In Botswana no interest group even contemplates either course of action. In part this is because political parties have not to this point organized their political activity to mobilize economic interests. Ethnic identification is the primary focus of organizational activity. As a result any given interest group is likely to have members and leaders in both the government and the opposition parties. The Chamber of Commerce is a classic example. The Francistown president is the BDP mayor of the town council. The Gaborone president is a member of the BNF central committee. In another interest organization, the executive secretary is active in the BDP, and his deputy is a member of the BNF.

Given this reality of a strong attachment of their members to several parties, interest group leaders reject out of hand the idea that their organizations endorse or otherwise support a particular party in an election campaign. They feel this approach would add unnecessary internal conflict. In addition, interest group leaders inclined to support the opposition believe that being non-political protects them from arbitrary action by ministers and civil servants.

The political parties do not encourage interest groups to become involved in political campaigns. Rather, party elites view their own organizations as capable of making the necessary contacts with the voters through house-to-house campaigns and speeches in freedom squares. One BNF leader, for instance, told us that their party did not need to enlist the support of trade unions in political campaigns because the party's programme was clearly the one which most appealed to the workers economic interests. The BDP gains most of its votes in the rural areas where few interest groups exist. Thus from their point of view, interest groups are not even a possible alternative in terms of reaching the voters.

If anything, political parties view interest group organizations as institutions which they seek to penetrate to give added prominence to the party. They want their leaders to be seen in these organizations so that their party will be perceived as composed of people who are serving the community. A BDP organizer told us that he looked upon the Red Cross and the Botswana Council of Women as demonstrating service by wives of party leaders, and thus enhancing the image of the party. A BNF leader said that his party urged its members to participate in church organizations, women's groups and the chambers of commerce for the same purpose.

The political parties also encourage their members to raise issues within interest group organizations that will benefit their party. The BNF has found the Gaborone Chamber of Commerce very useful in articulating issues regarding the need to protect Batswana businessmen from foreign competition, thus forcing the BDP government into the embarrassing position of supporting foreign corporations. The BDP politicians in turn have relished exposing the financial and organizational problems of several Ngwaketse community groups led by BNF leaders as part of their general campaign against the BNF in the region.

In sum, it often seems that rather than interest groups manipulating the parties, it is the parties which exploit interest groups for their purposes. Dr Koma at the most recent BNF Congress proposed the establishment within the party organization of groupings representing various interests, most of which would be economic, e.g. workers, lawyers, journalists, and youth. It would not be surprising to see the BDP do the same. This move would seem to be a formalization of an ongoing attempt by the parties to make interest groups an instrument of partisan campaigning and their preference not to deal with autonomous interest groups.

In so far as interest groups make contact with politicians, it is on an individual rather than organizational basis. For the most part their target has been back bench MPs. Cabinet members generally resist contact because they perceive themselves as remaining impartial between interest groups and the bureaucracy, as well as defenders of government policy.[11] On the other hand, backbenchers are free to speak their peace and see themselves as representing the people against the injustices of government. Government backbenchers are preferred to the opposition MPs in that the former are much more likely to be taken seriously by the front bench, especially when they are able to provoke divisions within the party parliamentary caucus.

Some of the more prominent examples of individual MPs taking up the cause of interest groups are Ronald Sebego who pushed hard for Botswana Civil Service Association's (BCSA) ideas on the tenant purchase scheme,[12] and David Magang who has spoken generally for business interests including a number of ideas put forward by the Botswana Employers Federation (BEF). Several MPs keep in contact with the teachers and have presented their case in parliament. Recently, Minister Kwelegobe has been speaking out in favour of wage-workers and against private employers on a number of issues.[13]

The effectiveness of such individual efforts should not be overestimated. Not much leverage is involved except the fact that the MP speaking out receives some publicity. Sebego's motion on the tenant purchase scheme was overwhelmingly defeated. Magang has yet to come up with a set of proposals that the cabinet is willing to support. Also, it should be noted that no MP mentioned to us interest groups as a source of information for questions asked in parliament. A BFTU leader stated that to his knowledge no MPs had come to his organization to ask for help in formulating questions or motions related to labour matters. The main utility which an MP provides to interest groups is publicity relative to government programmes these groups would like to see developed or changed. Interest groups themselves are often hesitant to use an MP for this purpose because they believe none of the MPs are sufficiently competent to present their case.[14]

20.4 LINKAGES OF ORGANIZED GROUPS TO THE BUREAUCRACY

If politicians have little interaction with economic interest groups, the civil servants are constantly in contact with these groups. The government bureaucracy prefers, however, to establish formalized contacts in which it has the upper hand. These involve councils or boards which meet three or four times a year to discuss and negotiate issues between government and particular sectors of society relative to a specific policy domain. Examples are Central Bursaries, Rural Development Council, State Land Allocation Advisory Committee, and the National Manpower and Incomes Council.

Each is constituted in a way that assures government officials of a dominant position. As the leader of one interest group told us, 'We can make all the proposals we want, but if the permanent secretaries (on the commission) oppose, there is really nothing we can do.' Moreover, these councils make only advisory decisions. The final authority rests with the permanent secretary and minister who are responsible for taking action, though in most cases they follow the recommendations they receive.

In some cases the representatives on an advisory council do not even receive a report from the permanent secretary or the minister stating the reasons a certain recommendation was accepted or rejected. The result is a lack of enthusiasm, especially on the part of employee groups, about participation in a council's or board's deliberations. In the case of the trade unions, their enthusiasm to attend the advisory board meetings has been further reduced by the fact that some employers will not pay employees while they are absent from work for such a purpose.

Interest groups also find themselves hampered by legislation governing their activities, particularly if they are representing employees. Most important, the principal elected officers of labour organizations cannot be full-time paid employees of the organization. They thus must serve as the leaders of the group while working in another capacity to earn their living. Employee organizations can only have part-time elected leaders. In addition, government has interpreted the Public Service Act as not allowing the officers of BCSA to speak to the press without obtaining the approval of their individual superiors on the job.

The maze of consultative bodies that are associated with the various ministries are the main means of formal access to government. Unless a group is recognized for participation in these bodies, it is likely to have great difficulty influencing government policy making. Thus this power of recognition becomes vitally important if any interest group is to become effective. The Botswana Federation of Secondary School Teachers (BOFESETE) has struggled for one and a half years, just to force the Ministry of Education to consider recognizing it. It was recognized as a society in February of 1987, held one strike in December of 1987 relative to marking results, and still has not been able to move the Ministry of Education to include it in any policy making bodies. Until it is admitted to the consultative process, its influence on government will be minimal.

This power of the civil service to control interest group contacts with government is reinforced by the ministers. Most prefer not to meet with interest group representatives until these representatives have first tried to settle the matter with the appropriate civil servants. If a meeting is deemed necessary, permanent secretaries brief the minister beforehand and sometimes participate in the discussion in order to uphold the staff position. In most cases the best a petitioning group can hope for is that the minister will ask civil servants in the ministry to reconsider their position, not that he will actively mediate, let alone suggest a solution.

Most interest groups find that the only way to succeed in this environment is to keep hammering away at consultative council meetings and in meetings with the minister, if they take place, over a long period of time. Most agree that if they do this they will eventually obtain some of their objectives.

Interest group organization

A limited number of economic sectors are represented by organized interest groups. The agricultural sector for instance is very weakly organized. The areas with white farmers, like Ghanzi and the Tuli Block, are organized but do not seem to have much influence. The former is more effective than the latter, which was a few years back involved in an incident with the Minister of Agriculture which caused very bad feelings. Batswana arable farmers in Barolong and Ngwaketse pushed the government hard in 1984 to write off their loans. Again, last year they launched a protest against the National Development Bank's repossessing of tractors of those who had not paid their loans. The Pandamatenge Farmers Association has succeeded in obtaining considerable support from the Ministry of Agriculture and the National Development Bank. Cattle farmers in spite of their significance for the economy have no national association representing them and only a few local ones that occasionally are mobilized to protest a particular government policy.

Much more influential organizations exist in other major sectors of the economy. For purposes of the discussion which follows attention will be focused on seven organizations: Botswana Civil Servants Association (BCSA), the Botswana Employers Federation (BEF), Botswana Federation of Secondary School Teachers (BOFESETE), Botswana Federation of Trade Unions (BFTU), Botswana Teachers Union (BTU), the Botswana Chamber of Commerce and the Kalahari Conservation Society (KCS). We were both able to interview at least one of the leaders and to obtain some written information relative to the activities of these groups.

Success in pressuring government is very dependent on a group having an effective organization. This means at a minimum:

a) a full-time office staff consisting of trained professionals who can formulate proposals, organize the lobbying effort, and partially implement actions required;

b) a small cadre of elected leaders organized and available for contacting politicians and top civil servants;

c) permanent cooperation with related interest groups on matters of common concern; and

d) a publicity programme designed to inform members and the public as to organization programmes.

Full-time staff

Only three of the above groups of which we have studied have their own office: BFTU, BEF, and KCS. BTU, BCSA, BOFESETE, the Chambers of Commerce of Gaborone and Francistown and the various farmers association among others have no permanent office or staff. These latter groups end up moving at a snail's pace, if at all, in persuading government to take some action on their concerns.

The reason so few groups have a full-time organization is a lack of adequate funds. The dues charged members are for the most part extremely low. The BFTU levy is 30 thebe per month for a member; that of the BTU, BCSA and BOFESETE is P1 per month per member.

Only two organizations we interviewed charged their members a substantial amount. The BEF has a base fee of P66 per year and works up to P7 000, depending on the number of employees. The KCS charges individual members P20 per year and corporate ones P500. Both these latter organizations have effectively decided to limit their membership to those who are committed sufficiently to the group's goals to be willing to pay a significant amount in dues. In addition, both have been able to use the device of corporate membership to expand their coffers.

While the BFTU has obtained grants to compensate for its low income from dues, the other three organizations without an office staff have not been able to find such an alternative source of income.[15] The result is that the leadership must take on the responsibilities of an office staff. In their spare time these individuals must analyse their members plight and come up with proposals, plus keep the basic records on the organization, plan for the annual conference, and send out intermittent circulars on matters of particular import. Committee work often requires that the members come together from various parts of the country. Then if contacts are to be made with ministry officials, the members must also travel to Gaborone. The benefits of doubling dues could be substantial.

Leadership contacts

The second aspect of effective organization is a board or central committee composed of people who can undertake critical contacts with ministers and top civil servants. These are usually persons who are already personal friends with the government officials they need to contact. Particularly effective in this regard have been the BEF and the KCS. When their staff runs into a roadblock with the civil service, the elected leaders of these two organizations can go right to top if necessary. Having done so on several issues over the last few years, some crucial civil servants have become much more flexible.

The trade unions on the other hand find themselves with only occasional help in terms of such contacting activities. Not only are their leaders spread around the country but they do not have many personal connections with leading politicians. The result is that they cannot put very effective political pressure on the civil service. As one union leader put it, 'We are on our own' against the civil service. BOFESETE has been in a similar situation, though is has been able to keep informed on some government discussions relative to their plight through middle ranking civil servants in the Ministry of Education. BTU and and BCSA are somewhere in between. Some of their leaders have fairly good contacts in the civil service, but both lack much ability to activate top political connections.

Building alliances

The third basis for organized interest group influence is coordination of the activities of various groups with common interest on a particular policy. Very few such alliances have been formed thus far in Botswana. In the environmental area, five groups – the Forestry Association of Botswana, the Kalahari Conservation Society, Thusano Lefatsheng, Botswana Bird Club, and the Botswana – have set up a coordinating committee to obtain funds from the donor community and to lobby on matters of common concern.[16] BTU, BCSA, and the Unified Local Government Service Association in 1985 coordinated their campaign for a pay increase. A number of ministers were sharply critical of this endeavour, and it has not been repeated subsequently. The BFTU has not worked with any group, in part because its members are looked down upon in status terms by other employee groups.

It is very possible that a coalition of all employee groups on the annual pay increment recommended by government could produce the most sizeable gains for employees in the formal sector. Thus far, however, each group seems to be concentrating on improving its own position and protecting its status. The University's Academic Staff Association, for instance, in 1988 was most intent that their members be excluded from the government's job evaluation process in order to protect their status as academics rather than seeking to obtain maximum gains through inclusion with other employee groups. Such actions only serve to balkanize the efforts of employee groups regarding wages and salaries.

Local interest groups can also coordinate their activities with various foreign organizations with similar concerns. There is no doubt that international influence can at a minimum cause serious debate in government and often lead to changes in government policy. The KCS has probably been the most effective in this regard. In part, this is because many environmental groups in the West are very willing to use their influence on their own governments to see that foreign aid to Botswana promotes conservation. In addition, KCS's foreign allies have produced a number of films focusing fairly critical attention of Botswana's conservation record.[17] Recently these international groups were instrumental in stalling the expansion of TGLP ranches into wildlife areas and in promoting the commitment of the government to a more conservation oriented management of national parks, particularly the Central Kalahari Game Reserve and some wildlife areas.

The BEF sometimes coordinates its actions with multi-nationals which are involved in Botswana, particularly in relation to work permits and other barriers which face foreign investors. The recent Budget Speech indicates that they have had an impact.[18] The BFTU has enlisted the support of foreign trade unions and the International Labour Organization to pressure government to adopt a whole series of ILO conventions.[19] It seems likely that the government will take some positive action on a number of the conventions involved.

Public relations

Communication of an interest group's position to its membership and to the public in general can sometimes be an effective means of influencing government policy. As far as internal membership is concerned only two organizations, the KCS and the BEF, have a regular newsletter for members. The others rely on occasional circulars, annual conferences and various types of seminars to inform their members. This low level of communication means that the membership remains relatively uninformed on what the leaders are attempting to achieve.

Most interest groups in Botswana do little to attract general public attention for their cause. BCSA did attempt to generate some public support for their ideas on the tenant purchase scheme. The KCS has at a minimum worked with foreign journalists to inform its overseas audience. Internally, the most effective in generating publicity for itself has been BOFESETE which has received a mixture of favourable and unfavourable press regarding its effort to receive recognition from the Ministry of Education. For the most part, however, interest groups in Botswana are hesitant to take their case to the public because they fear that such publicity would anger the government and thus only hurt their cause.[20] The consequence is that the public remains relatively uninformed about interest group politics.

Summary

From the review of interest group activity presented in this section, it can be seen that only two groups, BEF and KCS, out of the seven considered, have established an effective lobbying effort to promote the interests of their members. Several reasons for their success should be noted. First, they have more income than the others and thus can afford an effective office staff. Second, they are serving largely expatriate constituencies which are experienced in lobbying from their home countries. Third, they have influential board members who have both the status and knowledge to deal very effectively with both civil servants and politicians. Finally, they experience little hindrance from the laws governing their political activities, in part probably because they have insured this through their lobbying.

20.5 CONCLUSION

The development of economic interest groups as effective political actors is in its initial stages in Botswana. The public is only beginning to see the value of such an influence strategy. Most interest groups have emerged under heavy government tutelage. The main political parties have shown little inclination to deal with interest groups as autonomous political actors, preferring for the most part to make their own direct contacts with the publics involved.

Given the strong institutional presence of political parties, it is possible that citizens will look directly to the parties to represent their interests. The experience of KCS and BEF, however, indicates that those groups which promote their own interest are likely to obtain much more in the long run.

ENDNOTES

1   De Tocqueville, A. *Democracy in America,* translated by Henry Reeve (New York: The Colonial Press, 1900).
2   Chazan, N. 'The New Politics of Participation in Tropical Africa,' *Comparative Politics,* 14, 2 (1982).
3   Almond G. and Verba, S. *The Civic Culture* (Boston: Little Brown, 1965).
4   See for a comprehensive statement of this position, Dahl, R. A. *Dilemmas of Pluralist Democracy: Autonomy vs. Control* (New Haven CN: Yale University Press, 1982).

5   This and other data in this paper relating to elites comes from interviews the Democracy Project faculty conducted with various elite groups participating in the politics of Botswana. The interviews took place between October of 1987 and August of 1988.

6   This is not to say that such leaders will not acknowledge when pressed that they are in fact engaging in political activity. Rather, the common assumption unless pressed is that only technical matters are discussed.

7   Three of the four not contacted were not surprising, e.g. the head of the police, the military and foreign affairs. The fourth did meet with interest groups on various advisory bodies.

8   For a discussion of the character of the sample and the methodology used in this survey see G. Somolekae's paper in this volume.

9   Huntington S. and Nelson, J. *No Easy Choice: Political Participation in Developing Countries* (Cambridge, MA: Harvard University Press, 1976).

10 Truman, D. *The Governmental Process: Political Interests and Public Opinion* (New York: Alfred A. Knopf, 1971).

11 There are some exceptions to this tendency, most notably Daniel Kwelegobe, Minister of Agriculture, who often intervenes in the ministry on behalf of farmers' interests. The general mentality of the ministers interviewed by Democracy Project staff was not in this direction.

12 Since becoming an assistant minister in the Ministry of Local Government and Lands Mr Sebego has had to defend the government's policy on this issue.

13 See 'Minister still unhappy about Metro wage increase,' *Mmegi wa Dikgang*, 2-8 July 1988, pp. 1, 4.

14 This may well be a function of the fact that interest group leaders have so little contact with the politicians. Some MPs clearly can understand and present complex issues.

15 The Chamber of Commerce is currently soliciting a foreign grant which would fund the activities of a permanent staff for several years.

16 Interview with the Executive Director of the KCS, 28 June 1988.

17 This is not to say that KCS agrees with all the adverse conservation publicity Botswana has received. The most biased probably was one produced by National Geographic Society in the United States about the research and propaganda of the Owens in the Central Kalahari Game Reserve.

18 Delivered to the National Assembly on 22 February 1988.

19 That the government is very concerned about these international pressures is indicated by the 32 page analysis of the extent to which Botswana is in compliance with the various ILO Conventions and Recommendations which are to be found in the *Annual Report* for 1985/6 of the Department of Labour and Social Security (Gaborone, n.d.).

20 In part this reasoning stems from the fact that in the political culture of Botswana the belief is that organized interest groups are not supposed to participate in politics.

DISCUSSION

Mr R. Molomo (BDP) started the discussion by raising questions on all three papers. According to him, Holm's paper does not raise questions or provide solutions to problems of interest groups. He said interest groups needed funds and full-time staff, though care should always be taken not to overdevelop these groups. Interest groups in his view should not be allowed to identify with any political group. He said the fact that politicians currently have less ties with these groups was healthy for both sides.

On Mbonini's paper, Molomo said it perhaps criticized government legislation out of context. At the end of the paper, Molomo felt it showed the usual trade union militancy against the state. In Molomo's view there was no need for parliamentary representation of trade unions as a special group.

Mr Mpho's paper according to Molomo was controversial. He said the author's emphasis on minority interests was devisive rather than promoting national unity which should be everyone's concern.

Mr Hudson (Bank of Botswana) said Mr Mbonini's paper would have been more helpful if he made recommendations on the changes to be made on existing legislation. He said that legislation such as that creating an arbitrary cut-off point on who can join trade unions and who cannot is harsh and needed amending.

Mr P. Matlou (University of Botswana) asked Holm whether the interest groups being discussed were similar to Molutsi's ruling elites. He also wanted a definition of an interest group.

Professor Crick stood to support Molutsi's call for lifting the restrictions on trade unions but said this should only be done in the context of international laws relating to the role of trade unions.

Mr Tlhomelang (MP, BNF) said Mpho's paper was an accurate statement of the reality and called for a constitutional amendment. On Holm's paper he said the author was not correct when characterizing interest groups as generally ineffective. He said the Employers Federation was effectively influencing government policy.

Dr Maripe stood to support Mr Mpho and said we must create a nation of equals, and Mr Molomo is wrong to suggest that by talking about minority rights we are promoting disunity. Mr Rantao strongly agreed with both Mr Mpho and Dr Maripe on the matter of minorities.

Professor Tordoff agreed with Mr Molomo that close relations between interest groups and political parties may lead to undesirable developments as the Tanzania experience demonstrates. He said in Tanzania trade unions are controlled by the state.

He said advisory boards were potentially useful. On foreign assistance of interest groups, he said care should be taken otherwise they can be run from outside.

Mr Malila (Student, University of Botswana) said integration and not disintegration of ethnic groups was what was essential at the moment.

Mr Sethantsho (BNF) complained of the disadvantages faced by the minority groups living in state-lands such as those in the Kalahari.

Summing up Mr Mhpo regreted Mr Molomo's support of the status quo and described him as the enemy of the nation. Mr Mbonini said that the strike is the only weapon available to trade unions.

Holm said the House of Chiefs was a symbolic body with no power. He said Mr Molomo's insistence on de-politicisation of issues was a characteristic way of talking about political issues in Botswana.

SECTION X
POLITICAL RIGHTS

21 Group rights in Botswana

M. D. Mokama

21.1 INTRODUCTION

When Bechuanaland's chiefs sailed for England to seek protection against the Boers, they sought the protection of not only the country's political system but also its traditions and customs. They succeeded in this regard.

The form of government was called indirect rule. The chiefs were left in charge to rule as they had in the past, while a few British officials monitored their actions and only interfered in very special circumstances. The chiefs represented wider tribal groupings under various alliances which were acceptable to the people as a whole. It is true that a large number of these tribal groupings consisted of various tribal clans. However, the various clans considered themselves unified under a senior chief whom they regarded as paramount ruler in their geographic area.

The result of indirect rule was that at independence tribal customary law with some modernization remained the law of the land, just as it was in 1885 at the time of the declaration of the protectorate. Territorial government for the most part afforded almost total protection of the group rights of the various tribal groupings whose chiefs were recognized as paramount rulers by the British.

21.2 GROUP RIGHTS AFTER INDEPENDENCE

At independence two schools of thought emerged. One wanted to perpetuate the past system of separate tribal governments with a federation. The majority view was that a unitary state was preferable. This meant that all power would reside in the central government instead of dividing governmental authority between a central government and the various tribal groupings. Some people were worried that such a unitary system of government would allow certain tribes to dominate others unduly, and that it would be necessary to establish some form of group rights. These arguments were dismissed as it was felt that with a population under a million (about 700 000) it was unnecessary to create any special group rights which needed protection. The view that carried a lot of weight was to the effect that in a small coun-

156

try like Botswana, the best protection of any group rights is far better served by the entrenched protection of individual human rights.

Article 3 of the Constitution thus makes clear that 'every person in Botswana is entitled' regardless of 'race, place of origin, political opinions, colour, creed or sex' to the following basic rights:

a) life, liberty, security of the person and the protection of the law;
b) freedom of conscience, expression, assembly and association; and
c) protection for the privacy of his home and other property from deprivation without compensation.

Members of various groups within the nation are also protected by Section 15 of the Constitution which prohibits discrimination on the basis of 'race, tribe, place of origin, political opinions, colour or creed' by any law or any public officer in the performance of his duties. There are several exceptions to this law, e.g. non-citizens are not included and matters related to family law are exempted, but otherwise a member of a specific group has a right to petition the courts for redress if he feels the government is treating him differently than other citizens because he is a member of any of the above mentioned types of groups.

The decision our country made at the time of independence not to afford special rights to groups was a good one. History and experience have shown that in Africa, tribal affiliations and groupings have an extremely powerful impact on popular thinking and are consequently readily manipulated to undermine national unity. Throughout the continent it is tribal hostility and suspicion which creates political instability. I need not elaborate or name countries where this is happening. For this reason most African leaders have opted for a one-party state to prevent a whole series of tribal political factions from being formed under the banner of a political party name.

Even the African Charter on Human and People's Rights reflects this concern with national unity. Article 29 provides that the individual has a duty in all aspects of his life, e.g. family, work and his relations with other members of society, to preserve and strengthen social and national solidarity. Fostering national solidarity must be the paramount government objective for the foreseeable future in Africa. Our boundaries are artificial and various tribal groupings have been divided up and displaced in different regions indiscriminately by the colonial powers. Unfortunately some politicians may not realize that by agitating for group rights or the minority rights of different tribal clans within the national state, they are contributing to the future destabilization of their own country.

Critical to building national unity is a common language or languages by which all citizens can communicate with each other and their government. We cannot afford to recognize for legal and commercial transactions all the various languages which are spoken in our country. This would only foster tribal disunity. For the most part in Africa, English, Portuguese or French are the languages of government, depending on which colonial power previously ruled. In Botswana we are very lucky that prior to colonial rule only one language, Setswana, was universally spoken. We are thus able to use it as a recognized means of communication along with English. I am aware that there are some citizens who still do not speak Setswana. But, it is reasonable to conclude that it is commonly spoken within our boundaries. Our country thus has the basic element of a unifying language and it would be unwise to undermine this unity by recognizing additional languages.

In the past 22 years, Botswana has reaped enormous dividends from being a united nation. Our country has been stable and prosperous; there are no racial clashes; and the six political parties are based so far, on national rather than tribal lines. No foreign power has been able to destabilize us by exploiting internal conflicts. We therefore have reason to be grateful. Anyone who intends raising an ugly tribal monster must be aware that enemies of Botswana would be wishing him the best of luck and that the future generations of Batswana would remember his infamous mistake.

A young nation like ours cannot afford to imagine or create group differences. It is imperative that we focus our attention and effort on building the common features that unify us. At any rate we are too few to start dividing ourselves into groups. After all, if individual fundamental rights are entrenched and protected by the supreme law of the land, is there any need to create or protect group rights?

Recently some persons have complained about the constitutional provisions governing the composition of the House of Chiefs.[1] These sections (77, 78, and 79) provide that the chiefs of the eight Tswana tribes will automatically be members of the House of Chiefs. There is a perception that this discriminates against the other ethnic groups residing in Botswana. The argument seems to be that each ethnic group has a right to have its paramount traditional authority in the House of Chiefs.

In 1966, when the constitution was drafted, the founding fathers sought to frame a government structure which conformed with the political realities of the country at the time. Sections 77, 78 and 79 reflect their judgement with respect to the chieftaincy. There is no doubt in my mind that those sections represented an accurate picture of the critical divisions of the country at that time. If it causes anybody offence today, it certainly did not then. A constitution must be flexible and adaptable. If the majority view is that these sections should be amended, it is certainly within the power of parliament to do so and to reconstitute the House of Chiefs in any shape that may be acceptable to the majority of the people.

21.3 GENDER RIGHTS

Another group rights issue that has received attention lately is the matter of gender discrimination. Our constitution outlaws such discrimination. Before 1966 women used to receive three-quarters of the salary received by men. The new constitution repealed that. Now women receive the same salaries as men for the same job throughout the country. Our marriage laws have been repeatedly amended to enable parties to marry either in community of property, thereby retaining the traditional marital power of the husband over his wife, or out of community, and ensure the removal of such marital power. It is all a question of choice. Some women prefer the old concepts. Each taste is catered for under our marriage laws.

The Law Reform Committee has recently gone throughout the country seeking the views of the public on the laws of inheritance, particularly under customary law. The opinion of the public is that parliament should enact the new law of inheritance to ensure that children are treated equally irrespective of whether they are sons or daughters, and in the case of the daughters whether they are married or not. If the recommendations of the forthcoming Law Reform Committee report are accepted, such legislation will be in the statute book by the beginning of 1989.

A few women have also complained that the Citizenship Act of 1982 discriminates against their sex. The 1980 Law Reform Committee recommended this act to parliament only after it had previously sought the views of the public. Its opinion was unanimous and was accurately recorded in the 1982 act, namely that children born in wedlock become citizens of Botswana if their father holds Botswana citizenship. If their father is not a citizen of Botswana, they do not become citizens, regardless of the status of the mother. This is as it has always been under Tswana custom.

Those opposed to the act contend that this provision is unfair, particularly in those cases where the father is a non- citizen and the children are made stateless, even though their mothers are citizens of Botswana. In the recent Law Reform Committee, 1986, the views of these dissatisfied women were put across to the public throughout Botswana. The people's views were again unanimous and that is, that the current Citizenship Act should remain as it stands.

21.4 CONCLUSION

The Botswana government does not seek to protect group rights. Instead we have placed a very heavy premium on the protection of the individual fundamental rights so that individuals as members of groups do not face discrimination. With a small population of just over a million it is understandable that Botswana is loathe to create group rights which could promote tribalism and thus undermine national solidarity.

On the separate issue of women's rights, various forms of discrimination against women in Botswana have been progressively eliminated since independence. Those which remain are ones which run counter to deeply held customs and traditions. In these cases the public will probably resist any change for some time to come.

ENDNOTES

1   See the essay in this volume by Motsimai Mpho.

22 The role of Botswana Police Force in democratic Botswana

The hon. P.H.K. Kedikilwe, MP*

22.1 INTRODUCTION

According to Lord Baldwin, democracy is the most difficult form of government because it requires the participation of all people in the country for its realization. It cannot function well unless everyone, men and women alike, feel their responsibility to the state. It is not a matter of party; it is common to all of us because democracy requires constant guarding.

The relationship that exists between the majority and the minority is one of the best tests of democracy; each must play a constructive part. Although the majority governs, differences are talked over, not fought over. Issues that divide the people deeply are settled by open debates. Violence is not tolerated.

For democracy to produce a legitimate government, the top officials must be voluntarily elected by the majority of the people. This is the reality of present day Botswana. After every period of five years Batswana go to the polls to elect a government of their choice. Our government goes further in that it holds regular consultations with the people, both those who are opponents and supporters, on a regular basis when there are issues of local or national concern.

The primary duty of the Botswana Police in this context is to uphold this system and the laws which the National Assembly enacts. In so doing the police seek to work with and through the people, rather than being an authoritarian presence opposed to the people. It is to the ways and means by which the police functions to achieve these ends that this essay is directed.

22.2 THE POLICE AS SERVANTS OF THE PEOPLE

In upholding the law, the police must respect the rights of citizens. This involves the protection of such basic political freedoms as those related to speech and association, the right to silence, and the various procedural requirements involved in protecting the innocent from arbitrary and unreasonable action in criminal cases.

In enforcing the law, the main emphasis of policing is on prevention of crime. In this way, the security of person and property, and the preservation of the public tranquility will be better effected than by detection and punishment of the offender

* This paper was prepared by the Police Department and has been cleared for publication by the Minister.

after he has committed the crime. To be sure the detection of offences is also important in deterring offenders and in protecting life and property.

The people must also help the police. There is now abundant evidence that police action alone is insufficient to reduce crime. The aim of gaining the cooperation of others, therefore, goes beyond earning respect and approval for policing and extends to invoking the active assistance of the public in preventing crime and helping to preserve peace.

There is a need for an organized framework for promoting positive cooperation between the police and the public. The continuing aim of the Botswana Police is to work with others to develop collaborative strategies against crime and disorder. In pursuance of this aim the police work closely with local communities with a view to:

a)   sharing information and jointly analysing crime and public order problems;
b)   anticipating trends of crime and disorder;
c)   identifying and discussing alternative means of reducing crime and disorder;
d)   recognizing community interests and helping to coordinate the activities of formal or informal groups; and
e)   implementing and monitoring specific courses of action.

In brief, the aims of the Botswana Police are to be the leaders in the community in terms of law enforcement, but at the same time they are requesting a constructive contribution by the members of the community to the solution of the problems they encounter.

22.3 THE POLICE AS ENFORCERS OF THE LAW

While the police fully support co-operation and consultation, they are also conscious of the fact that they enforce the law. They are not subject to political control in operational matters nor in individual prosecutions. Politicians, regardless of party affiliation, are subject to prosecution as well as ordinary citizens. In addition, politicians cannot seek special favours for those they represent when it comes to decisions regarding the enforcement of the law. The job of elected officials is to make the law, not to decide when it is to be enforced.

From time to time, the police must deal with political demonstrations which threaten to become or actually do turn into a riot or another form of public disorder. In such situations, it is the duty of the police to think first in terms of finding a peaceful means to mediate the conflict. Their intervention should be as short-term as possible, but they must make every effort to prevent physical conflict. If despite these efforts, disorder erupts, the police must act firmly and decisively, meeting force with force, as is necessary and reasonable in the circumstances. The police must make every effort to develop professional skills with a view to containing disorder with the least possible injury to all the people involved. The safety of the people is paramount.

It is the duty of the police to strive to be brave and selfless in the face of danger and to serve the people, if need be, to the limit of their capacity. They are required to act always for the general public good, as helpful and reasonable public servants. They are required to be, and must be seen to be, unfettered by any other obligation, deciding each issue without fear or favour, malice or ill-will.

This is not an easy task. Throughout the country, scores of arrests are made each day, many of them involving violent and drunken people. Though there may be an initial struggle, the vast majority of arrests are accomplished peacefully. This is a credit to society and to the police, whose restraint and skill, strategies and tactics, have often received acclaim.

The police must be sure that when they are threatened by violence that they protect the people as well as themselves. In its various ugly forms, violence is all too prevalent in some areas of the country, particularly in places like Naledi, Botshabelo and the residential areas of Francistown. All these incidents are hurtful and unpleasant, and occasionally some are very serious indeed, leading to grave incapacity and even to death. Rightly, there is always public concern about these assaults. Much is said, particularly in crime prevention seminars, in the House of Chiefs, in parliament, and other places.

The police force is putting much effort into fulfilling its obligation to perform professionally in the face of violence. It is developing the training methods, tactics and policies which will help. Hand in hand with this, there has been considerable progress in the way the force selects, equips, trains and assesses those officers who are authorized to use firearms. The tactics and strategies which might be employed by senior officers directing incidents where firearms may need to be used are the subject of constant review and refinement.

22.4 CONCLUSION

With public help and through our consultative machinery, our police force must perform better the primary duties as prescribed in the law. They should be able to maintain a state of civilized tranquility which facilitates the enjoyment of individual rights and which allows the unfettered attainment of lawful aspirations.

Police officers number only two thousand or so in Botswana. They are charged with policing, helping and guiding over a million people of widely different backgrounds, skills, religions, aspirations, cultures and habits. This is a marvelous mix of interesting folk. This means that the pursuit by police of public acceptance and cooperation has now become a matter of urgent need. The police is the only part of government which, as a matter of duty, is required and empowered to lay hands on citizens. In so doing, it must be firm but respectful of those it serves, those who are the ultimate rulers of this country.

23 Political rights in Botswana: regression or development?

Athaliah Molokomme

23.1 INTRODUCTION

In recent years Botswana has come to enjoy a reputation as one of the few Third World countries which has successfully protected civil and political rights. Prominent scholars have gone so far as to call it 'the shining example of human rights protection in Africa'[1] and 'the regional symbol of liberal democracy'.[2] This recognition is substantiated by the uninterrupted retention of the constitution adopted at independence and the fact that the constitution has a comprehensive bill of rights guaranteeing fundamental rights and freedoms.

In addition, the existence of several political parties which freely compete at periodic elections, an independent judiciary, free speech, the existence of trade unions, the absence of political prisoners and preventive detention - all bear testimony to the very special position which Botswana occupies as a model of democracy and human rights on the continent of Africa. The authors of one study on human rights in Africa thought all the praises for Botswana might have been 'overdone' but they concluded that 'surprisingly, a close examination does little to refute these laudatory images'.[3]

This paper focuses on the state of political rights in Botswana since independence. While recognizing that most African states probably have a worse record than Botswana with regard to political rights, the thesis developed below is that the maintenance and improvement of Botswana's record is by no means insured and in fact could be threatened. The criteria of judgement employed are those presented in various international human rights covenants. On this basis, it is argued that while the Botswana Constitution provides a reasonably firm basis for the enjoyment of political rights, two factors inhibit their full realization: a) the constitution has a number of provisions which allow for the extensive derogation of almost all political rights; and b) Government has chosen to take advantage of these loopholes in recent years to pass legislation impinging on the political rights provided in the constitution.

Four aspects of citizen political rights are considered in this paper: a) the right of citizenship, b) freedom of assembly and association, c) freedom of opinion and expression, and d) freedom of movement. Under each topic, the analysis is based on relevant provisions in the constitution, pertinent legislation, legal cases and other types of public decision making indicating both the *de jure* and *de facto* state of the political right being considered.

23.2 THE RIGHT TO CITIZENSHIP

Citizenship must be the starting point of any discussion of political rights because it is the key to the enjoyment of most other political rights. Prior to 1982, the rules applying to the acquisition of Botswana citizenship were mainly enshrined in the constitution. Any person born in Botswana could become a citizen by birth, except in a couple of specified cases. Provision was also made for the acquisition of citizenship by registration and naturalization. Each mode of acquiring citizenship conferred the same rights. There was no discrimination.

In 1982 the National Assembly repealed the citizenship sections in the constitution and adopted new and more restrictive provisions under the Citizenship Act. This Act and its subsequent amendment in 1984 effectively abolished citizenship by birth, providing that a person born in Botswana must also qualify by descent to become a citizen. In the case of a child born within marriage, descent is traced through the father; while in the case of a child born out of wedlock, it is traced through the mother. Excluded are children of Batswana women who marry non-citizens. These women cannot pass their citizenship to their offspring. Such children are not entitled to Botswana citizenship, even when they are born in Botswana and their parents reside in Botswana continuously thereafter. The children of these women must obtain residence permits like any other alien, and must wait until they are twenty-one years of age to apply for naturalization, which most probably will require ten additional years of residence. Thus they effectively cannot become citizens until they are thirty-one years of age.

Similarly, the alien husbands of Batswana female citizens are not given any special rights of residence or citizenship. This is in sharp contrast to the special provision made for the alien wives of Batswana men and their children to acquire Botswana citizenship irrespective of where they are born or live. The misguided assumption underlying this 1982-84 change in Botswana's law of citizenship is that women always follow their husbands to the latters' countries and obtain citizenship there for themselves and their progeny.[5] The effect of the change is to interfere with these women's rights to remain in their country of citizenship, as some are left with no alternative but live in the place where their children can have a nationality. By denying such women capacity to pass Botswana citizenship to their children, the law is indirectly but effectively interfering with a woman's political right to reside in her pre-marital country of citizenship. Where the citizenship of the husband is not available to the woman he marries and their children by reason, perhaps, of his being a refugee, the children end up without a nationality. This act therefore has the effect of rendering the children of Botswana women who marry a stateless foreigner stateless themselves, a situation which is contrary to international norms. Moreover, it is a shame for a country that calls itself democratic to deny individuals its citizenship simply on the basis of the sex of their mother.

Another category of citizens who are discriminated against by the Citizenship Act are naturalized citizens. Having complied with the ten year period of residence and other requirements, naturalized citizens may be deprived of their citizenship on various grounds which are not applied to other categories of citizen.[6] Among these grounds are failure to renounce a previous citizenship within a specified time, assisting enemies of Botswana during hostilities, being sentenced to a term of imprisonment, and residing in other countries for seven continuous years without giving notice of intention to retain Botswana citizenship. The section containing the most drastic implications for political rights is that which provides that where a naturalized citizen 'has shown himself by act or speech to be disloyal or disaffected towards Botswana,' such naturalized citizen may be deprived of Botswana citizenship. The terms 'disloyal and disaffected' are not defined by the act, a situation which leaves the door wide open for arbitrary decision making. In view of the requirement that persons who acquire Botswana citizenship must renounce their previous citizenship, naturalized citizens deprived of their Botswana citizenship will most probably become stateless.

The Constitution Amendment Act of 1987 provides for an additional form of discrimination against naturalized citizens. It requires that to qualify for election as President of Botswana, a person must, among other things, be a citizen of Botswana by birth or descent. The effect of this is that mature naturalized citizens who were neither born in Botswana nor had Batswana parents - but may have spent many years of their lives in the service of Botswana - are second class citizens who do not qualify to occupy the country's highest office. The provision is effective *ex post facto*, in that takes away the right to run for president from persons naturalized prior to 1987. Thus, the law in this regard violates the very idea of rule of law.

23.3 FREEDOM OF ASSEMBLY AND ASSOCIATION

Section 6 of the Botswana Constitution specifically guarantees freedom of assembly and association. This same provision allows for the passing of laws restricting this right on a number of grounds so long as the infringements are 'reasonably justifiable in a democratic society'. This loophole has been most grossly utilized by the Government in the Trade Unions and Employer's Organizations Act.[7]

The act restricts the right of certain classes of persons to join unions. Those under fifteen years of age cannot under any conditions obtain membership. Youth between fifteen and eighteen years are excluded by a union's constitution.[8] The result is that young people, who in large numbers drop out of the school system after finishing Standard Seven or their JC and seek formal employment, do not automatically obtain the right to union representation. There seems no reason why such young persons should be excluded from exercising their freedom of association except perhaps for their own protection, which in our view can be done in more empowering ways than to exclude them from trade union membership.

A second group of persons whose freedom of association is interfered with are those whom the act calls 'members of management'. These persons are excluded from being members of trade unions or other bodies which deal with matters affecting relations between the employees and the employer or industry in which they are employed, unless such a body represents only members of management.[9] This provision would not be a serious infringement on the right of association except for the fact that the act defines members of management rather widely, seemingly including very junior employees who may not have the monetary benefits of top level management, but who have access to confidential information and exercise supervisory and other powers listed by the act. Such employees' interests may be in jeopardy if they cannot become trade union members, and they may find themselves in an organization which is not sufficiently representative of their interests.

A third group of employees whose trade union rights are violated are workers whose employment has been terminated. The act provides that upon a person ceasing (voluntarily or involuntarily) to be an employee, his or her union membership terminates.[10] This provision effectively denies an employee who has been dismissed (even if unfairly) the assistance of his union at a time when he needs it most.

Still another way in which the act interferes with workers' freedom of association is by permitting direct state surveillance of trade unions. One of the most drastic provisions allows a representative of the minister to attend (but not vote) certain types of trade union meetings. Another allows the appointment of a 'minister's commissioner' to take charge of the affairs of a trade union following its dissolution by the minister. Such dissolution may occur, among other possible conditions, if the minister is satisfied that the affairs of a trade union are being conducted in a manner oppressive to one or more of its members, or are not in accordance with sound financial management.

All the above provisions have adverse implications for the rights of workers to form and belong to trade unions and, more importantly, their activities within these organizations. It is rather far fetched to say these various restrictions are 'reasonably justifiable in a democratic society,' or that they are reasonably required in the interests of defence, public order, public morality or public health, or for protecting the rights or freedoms of others - the exceptions specifically mentioned in the constitution.

A new series of restrictions on freedom of association are to be found in the National Security Act,[11] especially section 10, which deals with the matter of communication with foreign agents. According to this section, if someone is proved to have communicated with, or attempted to communicate with a foreign agent, it shall be presumed that such a person has, 'for a purpose prejudicial to the interests of Botswana, obtained or attempted to obtain or passed or attempted to pass information which might be, or intended to be directly or indirectly useful to a foreign power'. The section further provides that a person shall, unless *he* proves the contrary, be deemed to have been in communication with a foreign agent if he has visited the address of such an agent, or addressed communication to such agent's address, or consorted or *associated* with the latter. The possession of the address or other information of a foreign agent may be sufficient, unless the accused proves the contrary, to lead to a conclusion that the possessor is in communication with such foreign agent. The prosecution under this act need not show that the accused person is guilty of any particular act tending to show a purpose prejudicial to the safety or interests of Botswana. Such a person may be convicted on evidence of the circumstances of the case, his conduct, or his known character as proved.

These provisions in a more restricted form may be justifiable for reasons of national security, especially in view of the very difficult position in which Botswana finds herself in Southern Africa. As it is now, however, the law casts the net far too widely. This is particularly the case in the act's definition of communication with foreign agents, which is potentially unfair to those who may associate with foreign agents without knowing that they are foreign agents, and who may be used by the latter without being aware, as is sometimes the case in these matters. The reversal of the well established presumption of innocence guaranteed by the Botswana Constitution is also very disturbing. So far these provisions of the act have not been used to prosecute anyone, although a case which is still *sub judicie* uses certain of the act's provisions to charge two alleged South African agents.

As earlier mentioned, restrictive measures sometimes need to be taken even in a democratic society, in a situation as politically volatile as Southern Africa. But the response should be proportional to the problem. Sweeping restrictions may end up catching innocent persons, who may be used by others to further the interests of a foreign power without being aware of this. Without the protection of well established procedures such as the presumption of innocence, such persons are left without the protections of the constitution, and their freedom of association is thereby abridged.

23.4 FREEDOM OF OPINION AND EXPRESSION

Although guaranteed by all international human rights documents, the freedom of opinion and expression are the most controversial rights worldwide. This is due to lack of general agreement about its scope as well as the legitimate restrictions which may be placed upon such freedom. The provisions of international covenants and related documents have set out certain basic requirements intended to ensure the protection of this freedom. Central to this is the right to hold opinions without interference and to seek, receive and impart information and ideas through any media and regardless of frontiers.[12] However, this freedom carries with it special duties and responsibilities and may be subject to restrictions which are provided in law and necessary for respect of the rights and reputations of others, or for the protection of national security, public order or public morals.[13]

In providing for freedom of opinion and expression, the Botswana Constitution incorporates the forgoing limitations on the excercise of such freedom but also specifies additional justifications for state interference. These additional justifications for abridging freedom of opinion and expression include state action required to prevent the disclosure of information received in confidence, maintenance of the authority and independence of the courts, regulation of educational institutions in the interests of persons receiving instruction therein, regulation of the technical operation of telephony, telegraphy, posts, wireless, broadcasting or television, or discipline of public officers, employees of local government bodies, or teachers.

These exceptions to freedom of opinion and expression are rather comprehensive and have far reaching implications especially for students, teachers and public servants. The recent requirement by the University Council that students sign a document undertaking to desist from taking part in demonstrations and related incidents unless approved by the University Administration, was a good test case for the scope of this limitation. That the Students Representative Council was unsuccessful in having this regulation declared unconstitutional in the High Court shows the limited nature of Botswana's constitutional protection of freedom of opinion and expression[14]. One may ask what remains of a right if such comprehensive exceptions are placed upon its enjoyment? Particularly regrettable is that the constitution or the courts have provided no guidelines to assist in the definition of such concepts as public morals, national security, public safety and health. In the absence of such guidelines, the last word on this may be left to the state through its control of the legislative branch of government. This is a situation which one would have thought is to be avoided in a democratic society, as a guarantee against arbitrary state action.

A strong and independent judiciary is the only check in this situation against excessive infringement by the legislative and executive branches. Apart from a few cases involving racial slurs between employers and their employees however,[15] the courts have only decided a few landmark cases in which the content of the right to freedom of speech and its limitations have been seriously tested. Even in the few cases to come before the courts, the judges have rarely entered into a comprehensive general discussion of the scope and limits of the right to freedom of expression. They rather have tended to base their decisions on narrow legalistic considerations.

We can, however, learn some lessons from these cases about the record of the courts in dealing with the freedom of opinion and expression. Most of these cases involve speeches given by politicians at rallies. In *The State v Lebuku 1975 1 BLR 46*, the accused was charged with using abusive language contrary to section 89 (1) of the Botswana Penal Code. The accused was within the property of a private house. He spoke into a loudspeaker insulting the members of a political party which he opposed and which was holding a rally on adjoining property. A witness stated that he was 'annoyed and provoked by what he had heard'. The magistrate found that the offence as charged was not established as it had not happened in a public place, but he convicted the accused under another section of the penal code which prohibits the use of insulting language. On appeal, Chief Justice Aguda stated that it was the duty of the courts jealously to guard the fundamental right of freedom of expression. He went on to say that the relevant section of the penal code was not intended to deny freedom of expression to prevent the use of vulgar expressions which might be likely to provoke a breach of the peace. The appellant's conviction was set aside for the reason that it was not such as to provoke a breach of the peace. In sun, the court in no way sought to limit the potential scope of the application of the law, except to say that it did not apply to the case in question.

In *Gaborekwe Molake v The State*,[16] the magistrate's court at Selebi-Phikwe held that the accused uttered words with a seditious intention to excite disaffection against the person of the President of Botswana at a political meeting. He had allegedly said that President Masire had stopped a cattle auction in order to buy all the cattle himself. On appeal, counsel for the accused referred the court to the protection of fundamental rights and freedoms contained in the constitution, especially freedom of conscience, expression and assembly. He argued that this provision of the constitution must be construed as widely as possible, and the law of sedition with corresponding strictness. He urged the court to adopt the standards of freedom of expression applied by the Supreme Court of the United States of America, where 'the citizen and the press have an absolute, unconditional, constitutional privilege to criticise official conduct'.[17]

The judge rejected this standard for Botswana, although he agreed that the provisions of the penal code dealing with sedition must be read together with the constitutional freedom of expression. The accused's conviction was quashed on the grounds that seditious intention 'is one of effect and consequence, actual or potential'. The accused's words were found to be neither defamatory nor self-evidently seditious. Again, the judge avoided dealing with the issue of the scope of the constitutional protection of freedom of opinion and expression.

In a third case, *The State v Frank Marumo*,[18] the accused was charged with attempting to incite mutiny, contrary to section 42 (b) of the Botswana Penal Code and with sedition as in the above case. The charges arose out of a speech made by the accused, a member of the opposition BNF, at a political rally in Serowe. In his speech, Marumo referred to a recent military coup in Nigeria and asked for the reaction of the president, the ruling party and members of the Botswana Defence Force to the situation. The State's case was that in his speech, the accused attempted to incite members of the Botswana Defence Force, in particular the BDF commander and his deputy, to commit a mutinous act by urging them to overthrow the government of Botswana as lawfully constituted. Alternatively, it was said that the accused had uttered seditious words intended to excite the inhabitants of Botswana to attempt to change their government by unlawful means. One of the state witnesses said that he disapproved of the accused's speech, but the magistrate rejected him as an example of those who felt agitated. The fact that the witness was a member of the ruling party, and that he was at a meeting convened by the opposition — reasoned the magistrate — meant that his observations should be treated with caution before accepting him as a representative of an impartial and objective view. The accused was resultantly acquitted on both counts, the magistrate relying on the authority of *Molake* to find him not guilty of sedition.

One of the most important aspects of freedom of expression is press freedom. Post-colonial African governments have been particularly unconcerned about this freedom.[19] In Botswana, while the independent press is of relatively recent origin, the government's record is much better than almost any other African country. Several recent events do indicate that press freedom is by no means firmly entrenched.

Most chilling has been the case of *The State v Mbaiwa and others*,[20] in which Mbaiwa, a government journalist, was charged with a series of penal code offences including publishing false statements likely to disturb the peace and uttering words with a subversive intention.

During the 1987 Bontleng disturbance in Gaborone, residents of Bontleng stoned and set on fire the house of a woman they alleged had kidnapped a child. The accused journalist conducted an interview with the second accused, a man who alleged that the facts as the residents perceived them were true and that he himself had removed the child from the woman's house. This interview was later broadcast on Radio Botswana, which broadcast is alleged to have fuelled the violence on the woman's property, hence the prosecution of the journalist. The magistrate's court in Gaborone acquitted Mbaiwa on the grounds that there was no evidence to indicate that he had acted unprofessionally. The state recently lost an appeal against the decision of the magistrate. This case would seem to indicate that if a journalist acts according to generally accepted professional standards he will be covered by the constitution's protection of freedom of press.

Also related to freedom of press has been the deportation of two foreign journalists in recent years. Both journalists had written numerous articles in the private press critical of the government. Some fear that such treatment of journalists indicates that Botswana may be joining the ranks of other African countries where deportation of foreign journalists is common.[21] It should be noted that the specific reasons for the deportation of the journalists has not been made clear since the law utilized does not require the president to give reasons for his action.[22] The general issues raised by the declaration of aliens resident in Botswana prohibited immigrants and its implications for freedom of movement are discussed in more detail in the next section of this paper.

Any definitive judgement on the state of the political right of freedom of opinion and expression is impossible to make at this stage in Botswana's constitutional history. The government has on a number of occasions sought to prosecute persons on grounds involving serious encroachments on freedom of speech and press. In almost every instance, the courts have rejected the government's argument, either in magistrate's court or upon appeal. Except in the Mbaiwa case, however, the courts have chosen to avoid making a strong statement in defence of the constitutional protection of freedom of opinion and expression.

23.5 FREEDOM OF MOVEMENT

The Botswana Constitution grants 'the right to move freely within Botswana, the right to reside in any part of Botswana, the right to enter Botswana and immunity from expulsion from Botswana'.[23] The normal exceptions are made permitting the deprivation of this right in cases of lawful detention, and in the interests of defence, public order, safety, health and morality. The most significant and one which has been exercised on numerous occasions permits the imposition of restrictions on the freedom of movement of persons who are not citizens of Botswana.

This last restriction is provided for in the Immigration Act which empowers the president on information deemed by him to be reliable to declare a foreign visitor or resident a prohibited immigrant. The act further provides that a person thereby declared prohibited has no right to be heard before or after the president's decision. Nor does such a person have the right to demand information as to the grounds of such a decision, nor shall any such information be disclosed in any court. Chief Justice Hayfron-Benjamin observed,

These are indeed wide and sweeping powers, but as the saying goes, extreme maladies require extreme remedies. The republic of Botswana is a landlocked island set on a sea of racial bigotry and political injustice . . . Tight security cannot be regarded as an expendable luxury in Botswana.[24]

The learned Chief Justice was not willing to grant that this power was completely unlimited. He pointed out, 'Political justification however does not connote legal vindication. The law in Botswana recognizes the possibility of an overzealous exercise of legislative power . . .'[25] He contended that every written law must be read and construed subject to the constitution, which guarantees everyone freedom of movement. The learned Chief Justice made these remarks in a case in which the Attorney General, on behalf of the government of Botswana, claimed that the defendant, Frank Modise, was not a citizen of Botswana, and also that he was a prohibited immigrant. The defendant, who had been born in South Africa, had lived in the former Bechuanaland Protectorate for ten years and had strong tribal ties through his family with Botswana. He was declared a prohibited immigrant in 1969 but claimed that he was a citizen of Botswana by descent, having been born in South Africa to parents who were citizens of Botswana. The court found on the evidence however that he was not a citizen of Botswana and thus Modise could be declared a prohibited immigrant.

The judgment was not unreserved with respect to the government's authority to declare a foreigner a prohibited immigrant. The Chief Justice stated:

> Section 33 of the Immigration Act purports to clothe the information on which the president relies in declaring a person a prohibited immigrant with absolute confidentiality, and precludes its disclosure in any court . . . In a proper case, the court would no doubt consider the effect of these provisions against the background of the constitutional commitment to the rule of law.[26]

The opportunity to test the constitutionality of the above-mentioned section almost arose in 1978, when another Modise case came before the High Court. Unfortunately, the issues in *John Kealeboga Modise v The State*[27] were rather narrow, and the point was not raised. The accused was charged with entering Botswana unlawfully whilst being a prohibited immigrant. One of the grounds of his appeal was that the letter declaring him a prohibited immigrant was signed by the Permanent Secretary to the President and not by the President himself. Although he did not succeed on this argument, the case shows the desperate lengths to which persons affected by the provisions of the Immigration Act are forced to go, because they cannot attack the decision itself on any other ground.

The provisions of the Immigration Act even visit the 'sins of the father' on his wife, children (under 18) and other dependents. All must leave with the father, even though they may not be living with that person and have no means of knowing that he has been declared a prohibited immigrant.[28] The above-mentioned Frank Modise's wife had been subjected to the order declaring her husband a prohibited immigrant. She challenged her order in *Modise v The State*.[29] She asserted that since she had previously been married to a Botswana citizen, she therefore was entitled to be registered as a Botswana citizen. The High Court decided that this was no defence to the declaration that she was a prohibited immigrant, if she had in fact not registered. However, it was further held that following such declaration and after deportation, she had the right to apply for registration and, having been registered, the order declaring her a prohibited immigrant could be set aside.

The Modise cases are exceptional because orders declaring a person a prohibited immigrant do not normally end up in the courts. Two of these cases, however, ended up in court because the issue of citizenship was also involved. In almost all other cases, there is no way to challenge the order in court. Given the lack of cases involving deportation and since no reasons are ever given publicly for the action against them, it is impossible to assess the extent to which the right to freedom of movement is protected in Botswana, especially for non-citizens.

It can be observed that these sweeping powers require restraint on the part of those who possess them, and especially those who provide the latter with information. Even then, they should only be exercised in genuine cases where national security or other public interests are threatened, and not to persecute certain aliens who may have displeased the state or certain powerful individuals on other grounds.

23.6 CONCLUSION

We began by observing that Botswana has fairly solid democratic foundations, as she possesses most of the attributes of a liberal democracy, a situation which is rare on the African continent. This has earned the country much praise, especially abroad. In the preceding discussion, we have taken a closer look at the Botswana experience and discovered that certain flaws exist in the area of political rights. A significant finding has been that the constitutional guarantees are themselves inadequate, because of the constitutional derogations from various political rights in the name of national security and public health, safety, and morals. As a result, much legislation which unduly restricts the enjoyment of rights such as freedom of association and movement cannot be challenged on the basis of its unconstitutionality.

While the courts have in the few cases before them performed admirably in upholding fundamental rights and freedoms, very little jurisprudence has developed in our higher courts elaborating the scope and content of these rights. Compounding the problem in the case of declaration of aliens as prohibited immigrants, parliament excludes the courts as the final arbiters between the state and the individual. This in our view is not desirable. In a democratic society the established role of the courts to pronounce on the constitutional excercise of state power must exist, unless the issues involve sensitive and genuine issues of national security.

A human rights author has correctly pointed out:

> Constitutional provisions are, in any case, a mere guide to statements of principle, to which adherence can be assumed only when the political culture en-

genders respect for the constitution, and when there are institutionalised means for forcing the government to respect it.[30]

In the case of Botswana, there is reason to believe, as Somolekae's paper in this volume points out, that there is a lack of awareness on the part of the population as to the nature of its rights. In addition, many lack the resources to litigate for protection of these rights. Thus while the country started off with a Westminster type constitution emphasizing individual rights and freedoms, the political culture does not provide strong extra-political reinforcement. The combination of social, political and economic changes, which are bound to bring domestic discontent especially in the cities, with the worsening racial crisis in South Africa has brought about a resurgence of traditional Tswana authoritarianism which is not conducive to the enjoyment of political rights.

In recent years, there have been signals indicating a general attitude in favour of restricting political rights. This is borne out by the comments of some politicians when citizens complain about the restriction of political activity. They remind us that we are better off than the citizens of other African countries, some of whom are denied the most basic human rights, such as the right to vote for a party or candidate of their choice. In the Democracy Project interviews with members of parliament and other decision makers, the tone of some suggested that standards relating to the observance of political rights may be dropping. One, for instance, remarked that he favoured the flogging of those involved in political demonstrations instead of using preventive detention because the latter attracted international criticism. Such a remark seems to suggest that its author is more concerned with the reaction of the outside world to the state of our democracy than with promoting it to benefit those living within our borders.

The eighties may well mark the beginning of major restraints on the political liberty of Batswana citizens. It can only be hoped that this is not the case. If the public becomes more aware of their rights, it may well bring the required pressure on government to respect them.

An ideal democracy in which everyone enjoys unlimited rights does not exist anywhere in the world. However, it is our view that we should continue to consider it a desirable goal. To do otherwise is to sacrifice the emergence of Botswana as beacon of democracy on the African subcontinent.

ENDNOTES

1 Amoah, P. K. A. *The independence of the judiciary in Botswana Lesotho and Swaziland*. CIJL Bulletin, nos. 19 and 20 (April-October 1987) p. 16.
2 Morgan, E.P. *Botswana: Development, Demography and Vulnerability* in Carter, G. & O'Meara, P. (eds): *Southern Africa, the Continuing Crisis* (Bloomington, IN: Indiana University Press, 1982) p. 237.
3 Welch, C. and Metzer, W. *Human Rights and Development in Africa* (Albany, NY: State University of New York Press, 1984).

4   See especially the *Universal Declaration of Human Rights* and the *International Covenant on Civil and Human Rights*, both of which Botswana has not signed or ratified. Also relevant to this discussion is the *African Charter on Human and Peoples Rights*, which Botswana has ratified.

5   See interview with the Attorney General in *Botswana Guardian* of 11 October 1985; also his remarks in this volume.

6   See Section 15 (c), *Citizenship Act* act no. 25 of 1982.

7   Act no. 26 of 1983.

8   Section 20.

9   Section 61.

10 Section 21.

11 Act. no. 11 of 1986.

12 *Universal Declaration of Human Rights*, Article 19.

13 *International Covenant on Civil and Political Rights*, Article 19.

14 (Eds) In August 1989, the Appeals Court unanimously decided that the University had exceeded its powers, in forcing the students to sign such an undertaking.

15 See for example *State v. O'Connel 1972 BLR 29*; and *State v. Dunkerley 1971 BLR 27*.

16 Criminal Appeal 185 of 1983, HC (unreported).

17 Page 10 of the judgement, per Corduff J., quoting the case of *New York Times co. v. L.B. Sullivan 376 45 Sct 254*, p. 257.

18 CRB G678/1984, Gaborone Magistrates Court.

19 Takirambudde, P. N. 'The Press and the Law: Past, Present and Future,' a paper delivered at a convention of the Uganda Journalists Association, March 1988.

20 CA 275/87.

21 See Howard, R. *Human Rights in Commonwealth Africa* (Totowa, NJ: Rowman and Littlefield, 1986); and the Grant and Egner chapter in this volume.

22 Section 7 (f) *Immigration Act*.

23 Constitution, Section 14.

24 Chief Justice Hayfron Benjamin in *Attorney General of Botswana v. Frank Modise Civil Trial 231/1977* (unreported), p. 24.

25 Ibid.

26 Hayfron Benjamin, C. J. in *Modise* (supra) p. 28.

27 Criminal Appeal 26 of 1979.

28 Hayfron Benjamin, C. J. In *Modise* (supra) pp. 22-23.

29 1970 BLR 288.

30 Howard, *Human Rights*.

DISCUSSION

Mr Mothobi (BNF, Lawyer) started the discussion by pointing out that group discrimination is a fact of life to ethnic groups such as Basarwa. He said Basarwa could not be found in the army, civil service, or at the university. He said Basarwa were moved out of their habitat with little consideration for their rights. He said their absence in these institutions was not by accident. He therefore asked Mr Mokama (Attorney General) to seriously reconsider his dislike of group rights being enshrined in the constitution.

Commenting on Mr Kedikilwe's paper Mr Mothobi said Mr Kedikilwe was talking theory and not practice. He said in practice the police force was not a reflection of what it is supposed to be. He also said while he agreed that Botswana respected human rights, there were certain limitations in the law which hampered the realization of some of these rights. For example, many people go to court without legal representation because of their poverty. The use of a foreign language in courts was also an impediment to those who cannot speak that language, especially as Botswana does not have professionally trained interpreters.

Finally Mr Mothobi felt discussing human rights outside social and economic rights was a serious limitation to the whole issue of rights and democracy.

Reacting to accusations of discriminating against minority groups Chief Linchwe angrily said the majority were not responsible for the existence of minorities. He claimed the so-called majorities worked hard to be what they are and should not be held at ransom by the minority groups.

Replying to Chief Linchwe Dr Maripe (BPP, Leader) said what the chief said was a typical reaction of the Tswana dominant group to minority issues. To Mr Mokama, Dr Maripe said despite claims in sections 15.2 and 15.3 of the constitution, there was discrimination when minority children are forced to learn a language that is not their mother tongue.

Mr Mokobi (BIP) asked the Attorney General to define what he meant by 'group'. He asked if the AG was not aware that Basarwa were treated as serfs by many Tswana groups.

Dr Molutsi (University of Botswana) asked the AG to explain his use of the pronoun 'we', which he referred to in his presentation. He also said the claim by the AG that denying group rights led to national unity was not absolutely correct as in the long term suppression may lead to disunity, as those suppressed organize themselves to resist further suppression.

Mr Mongwa (BPP) wanted to know how clear the laws of Botswana were to ordinary citizens. He also asked if these laws were flexible enough for changes which were taking place in society.

Professor Nsibambi said individuals join groups to be better protected and to realize their goals better. Thus the need to recognize group rights. He wanted to know from Ms Molokomme how political rights affected duties.

Answering questions and comments Mr Mokama said that asking the Basarwa to move from Central Kalahari Game Reserve was nothing new. Many non-Basarwa groups have in the past been asked to move from areas which had some potential for economic development, e.g the areas where the diamond mines are now located. He agreed that trials were not totally fair and called on lawyers who understood customary courts to participate in kgotla trials. He insisted that affording each group its right will create the impossibility of teaching in many languages available in Botswana.

Ms Molokomme said there was reciprocity between rights and duties. She said the newness of Botswana's judicial system excludes any history of activism, and it will be difficult for judges to be activists at present. She asked the AG to reconcile his statement that he is a traditionalist on gender issues with his rejection of group rights which is traditional in Botswana.

Mr Mokama said Botswana's constitution enshrines a Bill of Rights. He said the constitution can be changed any time politicians feel it is necessary. He said his position is in the interest of nation building, whereas those who insisted on group rights wanted to 'rock the boat of the nation'. His traditionalism refers to the fact that his wife must adopt his name with marriage to him, otherwise he would not marry her.

SECTION XI
ELECTIONS AND DEMOCRACY

24 Elections and democracy: how democratic is the process?

L. E. Serema

24.1 INTRODUCTION

It is generally accepted that in a democracy people should choose their representatives. To have citizens actually making policy decisions on a daily basis would be highly inefficient and time consuming. For the election process to be democratic, every qualified person must have access to participate as a voter and/or candidate. In Botswana, the 'Electoral Act' specifies how elections are to be conducted. I argue in this paper that this law is consistent with accepted standards of democracy.* I will consider the role of the Supervisor of Elections, franchise, qualification for election to the National Assembly, polling procedures, and possible reforms.

24.2 SUPERVISOR OF ELECTIONS

The chief election officer is the Supervisor of Elections. His duties, set out in the Electoral Act (Part I Section 3), are to see that the registration of voters and the election process itself are carried out fairly, impartially and in conformity with the law. In accomplishing this objective he must establish the polling districts within constituencies and appoint officers to conduct both the registration and election process.

---

* My understanding of Symposium organizers' instructions for this topic was that I was only to deal with matters covered by the Electoral Law. Thus I will not discuss other aspects of Botswana's elections.

In the constitution framed at the time of independence, the Office of Supervisor of Elections was directly under the President. Some argued that this arrangement must render the Supervisor partial to the President's party, thus undermining the fairness of the elections. Debate on this issue culminated in the nation deciding by referendum that the Office of Supervisor of Elections should be removed from the Office of the President and enjoy an independent status like the courts and the Auditor General.

Some in the opposition still question the impartiality of the supervisor because he is appointed by the president. This is wrong in that like a High Court judge, once the supervisor is appointed he is no longer subject to direction by the president. A similar appointment process is used for other statutory offices such as auditor general, and this does not interfere with their impartiality. Thus the administration of the elections clearly takes place in a non-partisan manner, as is expected in a democracy.

24.3 THE FRANCHISE

The Botswana Constitution (Chapter V Section 67) specifies that any motswana aged 21 years or above is entitled to vote unless disqualified by law. The Electoral Act (Section 6) disqualifies any person who owes allegiance to a foreign power, is imprisoned for over six months, is legally certified of unsound mind, or has been convicted of violating certain provisions of the Electoral Act. There is certainly nothing unreasonable about such disqualifications. They are standard in all democracies.

Some would propose that persons under twenty-one be allowed to vote. Such young people are however not capable of exercising sound judgement, like those certified of unsound mind. Voting is a heavy responsibility that requires mature judgement. Those below the age of twenty-one years are immature. Advocates of lowering the voting age to eighteen years have advanced several arguments to support their view.

First, they say that eighteen year olds can join the armed forces in Botswana and are given responsibility for defending our country. If we expect them to be mature enough to perform this task, such young people are mature enough to exercise sound judgement at voting. Superficially this argument seems plausible, but upon closer examination there is a basic flaw. Members of the armed forces act on command. The nature of their duties is such that they carry out orders. Military service thus is not evidence of maturity of judgement.

Another argument used by proponents of lowering the voting age to eighteen is that persons of this age can marry, and therefore they should have sufficient judgement to vote. However, to marry at an age below twenty-one requires parental or guardian permission. I have not heard any calls for removing this provision. I can only suggest that this is an admission that children under twenty-one are immature and therefore need parental guidance when it comes to making serious decisions.

The real question is whether eighteen year olds are mature enough to be given the responsibility to elect a member of parliament. To answer this question we must consider the educational system in Botswana. Children start formal school at the age of seven years. Primary and secondary education take twelve years, and tertiary education takes a minimum of three years. Altogether this is fifteen years of education at the end of which the student will be twenty-one or twenty-two years old and ready to take up his responsibilities in society, including voting in general elections. Education is a process of molding the mind to give student sound judgement; it is also a process of giving the student the skills necessary to enter the world of work as mature citizens.

It is not by accident that a student completes his education at the age of twenty-one or twenty-two. Those better qualified than myself in this area tell us that an average child reaches mental and indeed physical maturity at this time. Those opposed to my view will argue that most children enter the world of work right after secondary education, or indeed after primary education, and they should therefore qualify to vote. My submission is that those below the age of twenty-one are immature and therefore must not be expected to share with adults the heavy responsibility of voting at general elections.

24.4 QUALIFICATION FOR ELECTION TO THE NATIONAL ASSEMBLY

The constitution (sections 61 and 62) sets out the qualifications for election to the National Assembly. An MP must be a citizen, twenty-one years of age, registered as a voter, able to speak and read English well enough to take an active part in the proceedings of the National Assembly, and not a chief, civil servant, election official or person convicted of violating certain aspects of the election law.

Most of these requirements are self-evident; however, a word is required about the exclusion of chiefs and public servants. In our tradition, chiefs should stand above electioneering and politics. They have special responsibilities to the nation. They will continue to be chiefs regardless of change in government. To allow chiefs to run for the National Assembly would erode their power and compromise their ability to carry out their duties as chiefs. The position of public officers is similar. We expect our public officers to serve regardless of which party is in power. Therefore, it is not wise that they become involved in partisan politics including elections.

24.5 POLLING PROCEDURES

Current political debate in Botswana has not included much mention of polling procedures. While this is not proof, it may be an indication that citizens and other interested parties find this aspect of the Electoral Act satisfactory and democratic. The act requires that after a general or special registration, the Supervisor of Elections should prepare a roll of voters in each constituency containing the names and addresses of those registered together with serial numbers of their registration cards. The Supervisor of Elections makes copies of the role available for public inspection.

After reviewing any objections, the final roll is presented for public scrutiny at the Office of the Supervisor of Elections. Copies of each constituency roll are also available for review at government offices within the area. The public may, without charge, make copies of a roll or take extracts therefrom. A registered voter may object to the final decision of the supervisor. The appropriate magistrates court hears these appeals and may overturn the supervisor's decision.

Overall, it is evident that great care is taken to ensure that only those qualified to vote are allowed to vote without making it unduly difficult for the average qualified voter to vote. This is a *sine qua non* if the process is to be seen to be democratic.

According to the Electoral Act, the President determines when an election is to take place and sets the day on which it will be held. After this announcement, there must be at least 14 days for nomination of candidates and another 21 before the poll is held. This insures that all parties have adequate time to prepare their slates of candidates and to campaign. After nominations, the local election officer publishes at various points around the constituency a notice stating the day and hours for the poll, the nearest polling stations, and the candidates and their symbols and voting colours.

Before the polling station is opened, the candidate or his officially appointed agent ensures that each ballot box is empty, then the presiding officer closes it and places 'his seal upon it in such a manner as to prevent it being opened without breaking the seal'. Each voter is provided with a serially numbered and authenticated ballot envelope and different coloured counters for each of the candidates for a given office. In a great majority of cases a candidate's voting colour and symbol will be that of his political party and will have been so registered.

Voting is done by having the voter select the coloured counter which represents the candidate of his choice and placing it in his ballot envelop, which he then places in the ballot box. The counters of the other candidates are deposited in the discard box. All this is done in the secrecy of the polling booth.

Care has been taken to ensure that the presiding officer checks the authenticity of each registered voter presenting himself to vote. This is done against the roll as described earlier and against the voter's registration card which he must produce. The qualification/disqualification clause specifies that even on polling day if a candidate, his agent or a voter makes before the presiding officer a written declaration under oath stating that he believes and will prove that a person presenting himself to vote has done so illegally, the presiding officer must not allow the accused to vote unless the person so accused challenges the allegation, in which case he or she votes.

The presiding officer at a polling station must account for all ballots in his possession to the chief election officer in the constituency as soon as the polls close. This latter officer supervises the counting of ballots for the entire constituency, in the presence of the candidates, their wives or husbands, and/or their agents. The chief election officer in the constituency publicly announces the outcome and dispatches the certified results to the supervisor of elections, who in turn notifies the clerk of the National Assembly for publication in the Gazette. All documents (including counters) relating to the conduct of the election are stored at the High Court for six months unless the court decides otherwise, or legal proceedings are pending. The act allows for a recount if a candidate or his agent so requests.

180

24.6 CONCLUSION

We of the Botswana Democratic Party believe that the Election Act and its implementation live up to the basic democratic tenants. Our law provides for an impartial supervisor of elections, permits almost all citizens over twenty to vote; allows all who are qualified to stand for elections; and insures a fair registration and voting process. We admit the process is by no means perfect and have from time to time urged improvements.

There is a growing body of opinion within the party which feels that the use of coloured counters may not be the best method of polling. The feeling is that a voter either deliberately or through ignorance has an opportunity to leave the polling booth with unused counters on his person rather than putting them into the discard box. It is felt that if this were to happen, the element of secrecy may be violated as a voter could present his discard counters to someone as evidence of his choice. Proponents of this view suggest that the use of a ballot paper with printed colours on it for the various candidates would be a better way of ensuring secrecy. Any problems of this new system must be studied before final proposals are put forward. Care will be taken so that voting is not made difficult for large sections of qualified voters.

The requirement for proficiency in English as a qualification for nomination for membership to the National Assembly has also been questioned. The constitution (section 61) requires that candidates for election to the National Assembly read and write English well enough to take an 'active part in the proceedings of the assembly'. If the language of the National Assembly continues to be English, it is only right that members of this Assembly should be proficient in this language.

The real question is whether English should continue to be the sole language of the assembly. This question is currently being debated actively in different fora and I believe, in true Setswana tradition, it will be resolved in the public interest. My heart tells me Setswana must be used in the Assembly as one of the two official languages. My brain however tells me it is not a decision that can be taken hastily. Concern must be given to the fact that the language of the executive, the courts, our laws, and much of our education system is English. All these and many other issues will have to be taken into consideration before my heart has its way.

25 Elections and democracy in Botswana

M. T. Motswagole

25.1 INTRODUCTION

This paper attempts to do two things. The first part places the electoral process in Botswana within the wider context of the social class structure. The second explores the specific aspects of the Botswana electoral process to determine the extent to which it conforms with bourgeois democratic norms.

25.2 THE ECONOMIC BASIS OF BOURGEOIS DEMOCRACY

The emergence of capitalism within feudalism involved two important processes, the dispossession of the peasants of their property and the peasants' release from feudal restrictions. The result was that the labourer was not restricted to one master but could move about selling his labour to any willing capitalist.

This seeming equality between capitalist and worker was very deceptive. The labourer during his work day henceforth not only produced his own wages, but also surplus-value, which was distributed among various categories of the capitalist class - from the industrial bourgeoisie to the commercial and agricultural bourgeoisie.

On the basis of this economic structure, the distinction between formal and substantive democracy is very important in understanding the limitations of the bourgeois conception of political rights. Effectively political rights and particularly elections become a means by which the exploited classes are given the illusion of participating in politics while in the economic realm they are being robbed of the product which is rightfully theirs. Having only limited economic resources the exploited classes cannot compete effectively in campaigns or otherwise take advantage of their rights. The capitalists can with all their money dominate the system.

The task of the socialist is to make use of the bourgeois democracy to force the democratization of all aspects of society, and most importantly the economy. The working classes in all countries are waging a struggle to attain the freedom and equality which is proclaimed by the bourgeoisie. To do so they must capture political power, hence the intensified struggle for control of state machinery. Such struggle is multifarious and is fought on various platforms, one such being parliamentarianism. The forms of the struggle are not an end in themselves but a means to an end, advancement of the social and economic interests of each of the contending classes.

The current class structure in Botswana arises from the colonial period. Colonialism undermined peasant production and turned Bechuanaland into a reservoir of cheap labour for monopoly capital in the mines and farms of South Africa. The colonial government won the cooperation of various chiefs of the Tswana kingdoms in the exploitation of the peasantry. In addition, the colonists took the best land, thereby putting pressure on some tribes because of the resultant shortage of land. Faced with this shortage of land, able bodied men had to seek employment in South Africa. The colonial government also promoted labour migration to the South African mines and farms through various taxes. This exodus of much of the working age population meant that peasant production declined and no economic development was possible.

Within the territory, those with larger holdings of cattle gained control over land and water and the benefits of government extension schemes. These upper classes enhanced their dominance through access to European education. There was thus a feudal aristocracy dominating a majority of peasants who were reduced to serfs. In between was a small middle class of small traders and teachers.

With the advent of nationalism in Africa, Botswana's feudal aristocracy and middle class allied with the colonial government to avoid a radical takeover. The result was the formation of Bechuanaland Democratic Party in 1962. It dominated the colonial structures such as the Executive and Legislative Council, where it controlled 10 out of the 12 seats. Right from the start the BDP became a party of order. The economic boom in the 1970s due to the discovery and exploitation of mineral resources brought a ray of hope among the landless peasants. However, on reaching the towns in search of employment they met the realities of capitalism: unemployment and lack of housing. We thus see today a society of poverty amidst wealth; of shanty towns and big houses in the city, and of landless peasants and cattle barons in the rural areas.

25.3 THE ELECTORAL PROCESS IN BOTSWANA

The irony of the electoral process in our country is that the BDP has continued to dominate the scene in spite of the fact that it has created a nearly explosive situation both in the urban areas and the countryside. To understand why this is possible, it is necessary in part to study the electoral process. The following aspects of this subject will be considered: a) the type of electoral system employed in Botswana, b) the process for drawing electoral boundaries, c) electoral procedures, d) restrictions on voting rights, e) regulations governing candidature, f) campaign irregularities, and g) problems in reporting election results.

The electoral system

Botswana has a single-member constituency system, where the candidate with the most votes (a plurality rather than a majority is sufficient) wins. The problem is that a candidate receiving a minority of the votes can win. For instance during the last elections the votes cast for the opposition parties in Francistown far exceeded those for the BDP, but the latter won the constituency. It is such 'minority' victories that allowed the BDP to win 85% of the seats in the current parliament while only taking 68% of the vote, and relegated the BNF 12 per cent of the seats while obtaining 24 per cent of the vote.[1]

A second discomforting feature of our electoral system is that once a candidate is elected the voters have no power over him. A winner can even change party affiliation without consulting his followers. The BNF's position is that the right to elect must include the right to recall the candidate. In Botswana, many citizens support, both morally and materially, a candidate because he belongs to a particular political party and espouses a programme in line with the party's interests. If supporters cannot recall a representative when he changes parties, this is a fraud upon the electorate.

The electoral constituencies

The establishment of electoral boundaries (constituencies) may have a direct bearing on the outcome of elections, and it is very important that the way demarcation is effected must be seen to be fair and practical for the purpose of elections. In some countries manipulation of the system has been minimized by establishing a set of rules providing for a non-partisan approach. The body doing the delimitation is independent of government and its proceedings are open to the public.

Theoretically Botswana has such rules; however, the practice is that the Delimitation Commission has for one or other reasons been under the influence of the ruling party. For instance in the case of Lobatse-Barolong constituency, Lobatse which supports the BNF and could be a constituency on its own is combined with the Barolong, which is overwhelming in its sympathy for the BDP. The result is the BDP candidate has always been the winner. The other area that could be cited is Francistown where the BDP has resisted the removal of Matsiloje from the Francistown constituency, even though this village is geographically located in the North East District.

Another problem is that areas which are different in terms of needs and perspectives, and located far apart have been lumped together into one constituency in order to make it extremely difficult to canvas for elections. The ruling party has at its disposal massive material support from both local and foreign capital; besides, they control the state machinery and they can reach any part of the country any time under the pretext that they are informing the people about government policies.

The BNF has always stated that considerations in determining constituencies must be spelt out and the exercise should be done well before elections and should not be subject to political manipulation. The following factors should be considered: a) community of interest, i.e. people of common interests and identity should as far as possible fall within one constituency; b) population numbers (an upper limit should be set); and c) ease of communication and transportation.

Electoral procedures

Administrative procedures for elections must be clear and those charged with the responsibility of running elections must be seen to be impartial. The method of selecting the supervisor of elections and his assistants is very crucial in ensuring fairness. Under this section we consider the control over the calling of elections, how people exercise their voting rights and the counting of votes. All these factors may determine the winner and therefore must be clear to the participants.

One of the most important aspects of administering elections is the preparation of the electoral lists and the registration of electors. The two essentials of this process are that only those qualified are allowed to register and that there is no double voting.

One of the sad features of the electoral process in Botswana is that the process has been dominated by the ruling party alone, and it has resisted any calls for collective responsibility over the process. Instances quoted by the opposition as revealing a closely knitted cheating mechanism involve registration of BDP supporters even after the registration process has been concluded and making use of state resources in determining the people who had died or left the country since registration and then issuing voting cards of these people to BDP supporters.

In an attempt to tackle the problem of double voting, the opposition parties, among other things, suggested that the finger of a voter be stained with some ink. However, the ink used proved to be easily removable. A computerized system may be more practical and efficient in that it could check multiple registration and voting within seconds. The introduction of identity cards should ease the problem but it is better to computerize the system as well.

Restrictions on voting rights

Voter eligibility in Botswana involves restrictions with regard to age, residence, property, citizenship, language, mental status and criminal record. Two of these restrictions are particularly unfair, age and residence. In Botswana one is entitled to vote at the age of majority (twenty-one years) — an arbitrary figure copied from the days of the Roman Empire. The opposition parties have consistently called for the reduction of the voting age to eighteen years but the government has equally resisted that possibility because it fears the young generation. In our view, political expediency aside, there are insurmountable reasons for the reduction of the voting age.

The rate of population growth in Botswana is put at 3% per annum which results in a very youthful nation. If we take the age group from fifteen to sixty-five to be constituting the work force of our country and subtract the age group 15-20 (those working but not eligible to vote) we come to the conclusion that a mere 36.4% of the population under 65 are eligible to vote. (Source: 1981 Population Projections, Central Statistics Office).

In their attempt to defend the indefensible the BDP ideologues have argued that the people under twenty-one are immature and therefore not capable of exercising their discretion properly, an argument transparently false. It is now common knowledge in most of the Commonwealth countries that voting age has been reduced to 18 or even 16. In Botswana the police and the armed forced recruit persons aged 18 to 25 years. The jobs are highly sensitive and involve a very difficult exercise of discretion, including in some instances when to take the life of an individual.

The other factor that can be considered is that non-residents do not vote even if registered. Studies show that a number of people are registered to vote but they do not vote because on the voting day they are either somewhere else in Botswana or outside the country, i.e. migrant labourers in South Africa or students. The percentage is put at 8.9% of the eligible voters in 1984. If we add to this a large number of people who are in prisons during election then it becomes clear that only a minority do take part in the electoral process.

Restrictions on candidature

The electoral process in Botswana favours the property-owning classes. In the case of parliament, a candidate is required to be fluent in the English language. This requirement excludes a large number of people who would otherwise contest elections. The acquisition of academic qualification is tied to, and determined by, the control of property or put in proper terms, the social relations of production determine an individual's access to formal education. The BDP has always opposed any move to introduce Setswana language as a medium of communication in parliament.

Elections in Botswana are contested mainly by political parties and individual participants have so far been marginalised. People seem to prefer political party candidates as opposed to individuals who are seen as opportunists. Thus knowledgeable persons without party affiliation have little chance of reaching the voters.

Requiring deposits also deters many Batswana from seriously considering running for office. Instead of this approach to countering frivolous candidates, a better way would be to require a large number of sponsors for a candidate.

In the past there were some problems regarding the issue of sponsors. The accusation levelled against the BDP was that it purchased sponsors for a candidate who would be disqualified when the sponsors withdrew their names. As a result, the BDP candidate ran unopposed. To safeguard against this abuse, it should be required that once one appends his signature on the relevant form he cannot withdraw.

Campaign irregularities

Election campaigns are grossly one-sided affairs favouring the ruling BDP. This is particularly apparent with regard to mass communication, campaign financing, use of government powers for campaign purposes, and publication of utter falsehoods.

In some countries candidates are given equal opportunity to use government mass media. In Botswana, mass media are mostly government controlled and have largely been used by BDP functionaries to promote their party and give a negative picture of the opposition, e.g. reporting internal disputes or political mistakes. The BDP totally controls the kgotla, which plays a predominant role in the mobilization of the peasants. It has been contended that the kgotla is not a place for talking politics but only for development issues. It is an absurdity to try to draw a distinction between political and development issues. All development choices are political. The reality is that all kgotlas addressed by ministers at the kgotla are occasions to attack the opposition. In the past some chiefs even denied the opposition the right to hold political meetings in their villages.

The bias in terms of campaign funding is also weighted heavily in favour of the BDP. The rules in this regard are meant to ensure that no candidate gets an advantage over the others by purchasing electorates and/or obtaining other means of manipulating the electorate. In Botswana, breaching these requirements may result in the disqualification of a candidate. However, in practice the provisions have never been enforced. The BDP has boasted of using thousands of Pula during an election, well in excess of the permitted limit. Right from the 1965 elections the BDP has received massive financial backing not only from the local businessmen but also from foreign powers.

The BDP has also not hesitated to use its position as the governing party to manipulate government policy for pure partisan purpose. Five months before the elections in 1974 the government made major salary increases for the public service as the civil servants had previously shown sympathy for the opposition. The projects which had already been started in rural areas were hastily finished to be ready for opening by incumbent BDP candidates. This was done under the label Accelerated Rural Development Programme. The other tactic used by the BDP is the co-option of opposition sympathisers and of recent development, outright purchasing of elements within the opposition camp to cause inner party fighting.

Sometimes the BDP functionaries engage in utter falsification and insinuations of criminal nature merely to discredit opponents. During the 1984 elections Comrade Koma was accused of plotting to topple the government with the assistance of the Boers. If this was true, obviously he could have been charged with treason. However, a fearless journalist took the story seriously and embarked on investigative journalism (which is very uncommon here) and exposed the allegation as false. A few months later the same journalist had to find another country of asylum — an arbitrary exercise of unquestionable power came into action.

In order to facilitate popular participation and to ensure that economic disability does not debar the majority from participating in elections, government should subsidize election expenses, allow free mailing of campaign materials, provide regular subsidies to political parties and institute fair and impartial execution of the existing rules. In addition, a cadre of civil servants specializing in the administration of elections should be developed and adequately staffed.

Reporting election results

The Election Act seeks to provide for a fair and honest counting, recording and reporting of the results. In order to avoid another Tshiamo scandal some changes need to be made. It would be better that the ballot boxes are checked and counted by ward instead of lumping them together as is presently the case. By reconciling the number of ballot discs with the number of those who voted as reflected in the electoral list a lot of possibilities of cheating could be eliminated.

The decisions of those in charge of counting should be subject to automatic review by an impartial body. The use of counting machines could speed up the process and minimize human errors, and above all save money. In our view the whole process of counting should be open to the public so that public scrutiny should be felt by officials. The people must gain confidence in the system of counting.

25.4 CONCLUSION

Our agitation both in Parliament and freedom squares must make it clear that bourgeois democracy while an advance over feudalism must remain an instrument of the rich against the poor. Over-indulgence in self-congratulation and romantic excitement about the 'uniqueness' of Botswana should not deceive anyone. In a country where the majority live in extreme conditions of poverty whilst a minority is wallowing in wealth, democracy will always be class-based and partial.

In their account on Botswana, both the local and foreign bourgeois scholars and propagandists develop a common theme, which is a hodgepodge of sentimental good wishes, nationalistic aspirations and populist verbiage. We are made to believe that Botswana is an 'island of sanity' in a region embroiled in political upheavals. It is an attempt to legitimate a regime which has lost touch with the realities of life in our country - homeless and workless masses of our people.

The task of the socialists and progressive forces in our country is to link the socialist struggle with the struggle for democracy such that there is no dichotomy between the two. We should fight against any attempt to turn parliamentarianism into a career whereby we have people whose only task is specialization in the art of oratory. It is a step in the right direction that the BNF intends to establish a House of Representatives where all nationalities, trade unions and churches will be represented.

As long as the mass of our people entertain illusions about bourgeois democracy, we will endeavour to work within bourgeois institutions in order to make our way out and by propaganda and agitation to rally the oppressed classes towards the realization of truth and meaningful democracy, a democracy whereby one's ability and desire to work will dictate one's vote in the political life of the country. The working masses must have direct influence on the state structure and administration. The whole electoral process must be transformed to allow for reelection and the recall of deputies. The system of specially elected councillors and MPs must be renounced as treacherous and a rape on democracy. The BDP has used this procedure to defeat and frustrate the will of the people.

ENDNOTES

1   There are other unfair consequences which will not be dealt with here. For
     instance, the smaller ethnic groups in Botswana have little chance of being
     represented.

26 Elections and democracy in Botswana

John D. Holm

26.1 INTRODUCTION

The essence of democracy is that all citizens have equal political power. In an ideal
world, this would mean that all citizens would vote to determine government policies, and government would execute those policies supported by a majority. Except in very small communities where citizens are willing to give much time to public
debate, such direct democracy is not feasible.

Most modern states seeking to be democratic have adopted a system where citizens
choose representatives through elections. However, the rules under which such regimes conduct elections, and the conditions under which their elected officials serve
differ greatly. These differences can significantly affect the extent to which the citizenry enjoys equality of influence − the ideal of democracy − through their choice
of representatives.

Over time existing liberal democracies have changed their rules to enhance political equality for their citizens. In most cases groups experiencing some form of
discrimination force those in power to grant them one or another forms of equality.
Sometimes courts have declared certain practices undemocratic, or political leaders have seen the granting of greater equality as expedient to gaining or retaining
power.

Many analysts of democratic development argue that the expansion of political
equality by these various processes must occur gradually if government is to remain stable. The reasoning is that a slow expansion of citizen participation insures
that elected officials are not overwhelmed by too many demands at one time, and
that only a minority of the population can effectively be trained in the appropriate
norms and behaviour of democracy in one historical period.[1]

From this perspective, the critical question which Botswana needs to address is:
What aspects of democratization ought to be considered under the present conditions of social and economic development? This means that the costs and benefits

189

of enhancing equality in any particular manner must be assessed. The debate will obviously be political; however, hopefully consideration will also be given to other costs and benefits, such as whether a given group has certain needs which can best be attained through political participation.

This paper is concerned primarily with outlining potential inequalities which should or could be assessed within contemporary Botswana.[2] In this sense it is concerned with raising issues for discussion. Some possible costs and benefits are suggested, but ultimately assessing the merit of a particular change is a matter which must be left to the citizens of Botswana, and particularly their political leaders.

Political equality in a representative democracy can be addressed from a number of perspectives. We have chosen three principles which are recognized in most such democracies as generally worthy of recognition. These principles are:

a)   every citizen should have equal influence in the selection of public officials;
b)   persons representing different points of view should have the opportunity to take political action including running for office; and
c)   elected officials should determine the basic direction of public policy.

Each will be considered in the discussion which follows.

26.2 EQUALITY IN VOTING

Every person in Botswana twenty-one and over theoretically can vote in elections. There is no discrimination with regard to sex, race or ethnic group as there was in traditional government. Since independence the number of polling stations has been increased so that most voters are within an acceptable distance. The vote is conducted on Saturday, so that most people are free from work to go to the polls. Coloured disks are used in voting so that illiterates are not disadvantaged because they cannot read. In sum, Botswana has gone far toward achieving equality in voting.

There are some problem areas which remain in terms of every person having equal opportunity to influence the outcome of elections. These are malapportionment of districts, the disenfranchisement of migrants, the need for permanent registration, retention of twenty-one as the minimum voting age, and primary rules which heavily favour incumbents. We shall consider each briefly.

Malapportionment

Malapportionment means that the districts[3] from which representatives are elected are of significantly different size in terms of population. We are not talking here of differences of ten, twenty or even a hundred persons, but rather of situations where one district may be two, three or even four times that of others.

This inequality has several consequences. First, in the districts with the larger population, each voter has less influence in selecting a candidate than another voter in a smaller district. In effect, a citizen in the large district is not equal to another in the small district.

Second, and more important, if areas of the country where certain social groups live are systematically overpopulated, these groups end up having less influence in the legislature than the rest of the population. In most industrialized democracies, rural areas have been over represented in contrast to the cities. Thus, farmers have more representatives relative to their total number than wage-earners.

This same situation is becoming increasingly apparent in Botswana. According to a recent report, the four urban parliamentary constituencies (Lobatse, Francistown, Selebi-Phikwe, and Gaborone) in 1986 ranged from almost two times to two and half times larger than the smallest rural constituencies.[4] This situation will not be remedied until after the 1991 census, that means for the 1994 elections.

This malapportionment is mostly a consequence of rapid population growth in the cities during the current decade. The last delimitation committee, which is the body which draws constituency boundaries, was well aware that there would be such a population explosion. Nevertheless, it made these four urban districts one and a half times the smallest rural ones as of the time of the 1981 census. Thus in parliament the cities of Botswana started out under represented at the beginning of this decade and have become worse since.

In overall terms the four urban constituencies together had an average 23 % more voters per district than did their rural counterparts in 1981. By 1986 the difference was 50 %.[5] By the next election it will be close to 70 %. If urban areas were to have equal representation to the rural areas, they would probably need three more seats in 1989 assuming that population growth continues at the present rates.

The more serious problem of malapportionment has to do with council wards. In 1981 the disparity in the sizes of wards in terms of registered voters varied from as high as 17 to 1 in Lobatse and 12 to 1 in Ghanzi to a low of 2.5 to 1 in Gaborone.

Some of the distortions have significant partisan effect. In Lobatse one BNF ward, Woodhall, has almost as many registered voters as in all the BDP represented wards (5) combined. In Gaborone, population growth has served to distort the situation considerably. A whole new section of town, Gaborone West, has been included in Sekgwa ward.[6]

There are several reasons for this malapportionment at the council level. First, there are no rules governing the drawing of ward boundaries except that the Supervisor of Elections is responsible for gazetting polling districts. Council ward boundaries are based on polling districts. The supervisor's main concern is to establish polling districts which are convenient for voters when they vote on election day. Since his office's knowledge of the various localities for these purposes is poor, the supervisor prior to 1984 authorized the district commissioners to chair committees of five government officials to draw the boundaries of the polling stations.

In the districts we have studied it appears that the politicians on these committees were the dominant influence because of their knowledge of the community was superior to that of the civil servants. As a result, the politicians drew boundaries which effectively insured their persistence in power, especially since they were 'not instructed to apply a population quota', but to consider 'natural community of interest, means of communication, geographical features, density of population, and boundaries of Tribal Territories and administrative districts'.[7]

A second reason for ward malapportionment is a tendency among Batswana to think of representation as a communal concern, namely that each community has a right to be heard. That each community should have a number of representatives proportional to its population has not been significant. For instance, when the chief meets with his headmen, each represents a ward or village regardless of population size. There is no sense that a large community in population terms should have more than one representative.

Migrants

A considerable number of Batswana are engaged in migratory labour, either within or outside the country. They are disadvantaged in several senses. First, they may not be at home when it is time to register. Second, even if they are registered, they may not be able to vote unless they travel home at election time. The reason is that there is no provision for an absentee ballot.

The proportion of the migratory population is quite substantial. The National Migration Study estimated that 8 per cent of the working age population was out of the country, mostly in South Africa.[8] Such persons are effectively excluded from having a vote unless they can come home both during the registration period and at elections.

Another 21 per cent of the population are migratory within the country in the sense that they are absent from their place of residence for more than one year. They either must go home at election time, or during the registration period declare that their temporary residence is their 'principal' residence.[9]

These various problems for the migrant population are probably a major factor explaining why no more than 56% of the total voting age population has ever turned out in an election.[10] While this figure is higher than in the United State where turnout has recently been just over 50% at best, it is much below Europe where 80% figures are not uncommon.

Registration

The registration process itself works to exclude citizens from voting. The present policy effectively is that before every general election there is a registration of the entire electorate. The old rolls are destroyed and new ones are created.[11] This means that at every election a citizen must first take time to register and then come back again to vote. Where people are underemployed and not too far distant from the polling station, this may not create a big problem. Otherwise, the extent of registration will depend on the efforts made by government and party officials to mobilize the people to take the time to register.

There needs to be some form of permanent registration. In the long run the government's attempt to provide all citizens with national identification cards could be used in establishing that the person is eligible to vote. Unfortunately, this will not help in the 1989 election since the distribution of the identification cards has proceeded so slowly.[12]

Voting age

Another issue related to political equality is the matter of voting age. Within democratic theory, all adults should be given the right to vote unless they can be justifiably excluded, e.g. because of crimes, not being a citizen, or being mentally incompetent. Most western democracies have lowered the voting age to eighteen.

As has been indicated in Somolekae's paper,[13] the explicit reason given in Botswana for not allowing those between eighteen and twenty to vote is that they are not sufficiently mature. This is simply a prejudice carried over from traditional society which cannot be justified in fact. Persons in this excluded age group earn a living, have a much higher education level than any older age group, and are taken into the military to defend the country. In the final analysis this issue seems to be largely a partisan one with the BDP opposing the reduction because it perceives it would be hurt, and the opposition supporting the change because it believes it would benefit.

Primaries

The inequalities discussed so far, to varying degrees, benefit the ruling party. This is not surprising. It occurs in all democratic systems. Only with the alternation of parties in office is there a chance of change toward democratization. In some cases, abuses of franchise equality are likely to continue even with an alteration of parties, if only redone to benefit the new ruling party or coalition.

One issue of franchise equality is internal to the parties themselves. It relates to the operation of primaries wherein members of a party vote on who is to be the party's candidate in the forthcoming election. Primaries are a part of the overall election process. The rules governing the primaries can enhance or reduce equality of the voters by including or excluding them from participating in selecting their party's candidate. Of primary concern is a) who participates in the primaries, and b) what is the role of the primary relative to the party leadership in the final choice of candidates?

The BNF has no written primary rules which the Democracy Project was able to obtain. The custom seems to be that every member of the Party in a given district is eligible to vote.[14] The decision to hold a primary, the way the members are informed, and the extent to which members are assisted to attend meetings varies. The result is that incumbents tend to have an unfair advantage. For instance, the incumbent sometimes seems only to inform his relatives and friends who unanimously vote for him.

The BNF central leadership sometimes preempts the primary process at the parliamentary level by backing certain candidates as its choice unless a party member in a particular constituency decides to challenge the decision in a primary. If a contest then takes place, it may not be a fair one in that the party leadership has already given its nominee the benefit of an endorsement.

The BDP primary system is more open than that of the BNF. The BDP has a published set of rules, and there are no endorsements preceding the primaries. The party organization also sends an official observer to the primary meeting to ensure that the rules are followed. In a number of places the party supplies transportation to bring persons from the various sections of the ward or constituency to the meeting, thus facilitating a representative grouping.

There are several ways, however, in which party leaders do limit the influence of grass-roots members. As in the case of BNF the incumbent may selectively inform his friends and relatives about the date of the primary, and it is unlikely that the outside observer will know.

For MP primaries, the ward members choose delegates (six) to a constituency caucus. The only role of the average member is to select his delegates. All district leaders, i.e. the committee of 18 and the elected officials in the area (possibly as many as 22 or 23), automatically have a vote in the caucus. The end result, particularly if there is not a good turnout is that the local party leaders dominate the primary.

Finally, the Central Committee both counts the vote and decides whether to accept the winner of a primary as the nominee. For the most part the committee goes along with the results of the primary. In 1984 there were three reversals. In quite a number of cases, at the council level, incumbents were thrown out.

While both party primary systems have their limitations, of which the leadership is well aware, the fact remains that rank and file party members have used the primaries to check the power of their leaders to impose themselves or their favourites as candidates. Recently attempts by at least some in the BNF party leadership to oust Dabutha were foiled by a party primary in the Gaborone North constituency. The BDP leadership is currently very concerned that several of its cabinet members may not be able to win in the 1989 primaries. As a result the organization is making every effort to ensure that these persons make contact with the appropriate constituency members. If nothing else the primaries have made the leadership very sensitive to concerns of the local party organization.

Possibilities for change

The problem areas we have just discussed are normal in developing democracies. The fact that Botswana is facing them is to be expected. While it is understandable that the BDP is hesitant to democratize when the opposition parties would benefit, there is something to be said for the BDP allowing the opposition some opportunity to grow. The resulting increase in opposition MPs and councillors would not be sufficient to threaten BDP rule but would give the ruling party a more representative set of critics.

The procedures in the primaries probably will improve. The BNF wants to have some formal rules. The BDP and the BNF would like to ensure that all members have an opportunity to attend.

26.3 FREEDOM OF POLITICAL ACTIVITY[15]

In a democracy all citizens should not only have the right to choose their leaders but the right to take part in political activities, including running for office. The result of this right is that the citizenry is offered a variety of points of view in the political debate that leads up to elections. In Botswana, legal, cultural and economic factors function to constrain this right.

Legal limits

In terms of legal limitations, the following are excluded from actively participating in politics: permanent and pensionable public servants, teachers, police, soldiers, chiefs, and employees of some parastatals.[16] This is a significant group in political terms. Together these groups form at least two-thirds of the population which can be considered politically sophisticated, that is those who are able to read and discuss public policy in any sort of meaningful way. The only way a person in this group can take an active role in politics is to resign his or her position. This resignation is permanent unless a particular individual has skills which government requires and he or she is subsequently rehired. In effect, members of these excluded groups must decide to leave the security of the civil service and take the risk that they must look for another career if they lose the election.

The rationale for this exclusion is that public employees are supposed to remain politically neutral so that they can serve 'whatever political party may be elected'.[17] There is a lot to be said for this argument in that Botswana government employees have shown an apolitical quality not evident in many African states.

But the fact remains that in many respects this civil service has created a facade behind which politics are freely practised. The top civil servants formulate much of the policy of this country after debate internally, placing the finished result before the ministers so that they can convince the pubic. Such policy making is in many respects kept secret from the public.[18]

Some in the civil service, probably not a large number, actively assist the political parties. In public party meetings they can be seen participating in discussions.[19] Many of the civil servants who have become politicians were, while in government employment, part of a partisan underground which in various ways covertly assisted their party. Even several of the ministers who now worry about opposition influence in the civil service were previously active in the BDP civil service underground.

In economic affairs, civil servants are now able to invest in private firms as long as they do not take part in the management of the firms. This is to insure that since civil servants, who constitute the bulk of the economically sophisticated population, are available to the private economy to counter the overwhelming foreign influence. The only requirement is that civil servants make their investments public. A similar argument could be made with respect to political participation by government employees: To insure that an adequate pool of sophisticated activists, if not candidates, is available to the political parties, such employees should be allowed to undertake certain forms of political activity as long as specific conditions are observed.

Such an opening was potentially involved in the Sesinyi incident. Mr Sesinyi was town clerk in Selebi-Phikwe and decided to stand in the BDP primary in 1984 in Mmadinare. He never resigned as a civil servant. He simply attended the primary meeting. Since he did not win, he never entered an active campaign in which he sided with one political party. The Unified Local Government Service took no formal action against him. Other civil servants running in the 1984 BDP primaries resigned before standing. The general opinion seems to be that participation of government employees in primaries is not to be permitted in the future.[20]

Participation at the higher levels of Botswana's politics is further limited by a constitutional provision which requires that members of the National Assembly must 'speak . . . and read English well enough to take an active part in the proceedings of the Assembly'.[21] The consequence is that the MP, Cabinet and Presidential roles must be held by those from the literate minority of the population. In effect, a Motswana need not contemplate, let alone attempt, a career in politics above the local level unless he or she has attained the literacy of a Standard VII. When Setswana is accepted for debate in parliament in the near future, the rationale for this limitation will be less plausible.

Social discrimination

Participation in Botswana politics is also limited by a number of other cultural factors, which are nowhere a part of the law but are nevertheless very powerful. First, more and more politicians must come from the dominant ethnic groups in a ward or constituency. Persons from minorities have little chance in garnering votes.

Second, Batswana traditionally did not permit women to participate in most political activities. These days this cultural barrier is still present. The Democracy Project survey showed that close to a majority of the public in the rural areas said that a woman should not run for president. Even for lower political office, women face serious prejudice in terms of running for office, and politicians are not likely to risk supporting them. The consequence is that many very capable women do not even contemplate politics as a career. So far there have only been three women in parliament.

Financial limits

A final limitation on citizen political activity is financial. The fact of the matter is that very few persons in Botswana have sufficient income to afford to make contributions to the political parties. Moreover, many corporations are foreign based and do not have much interest in funding political activity in Botswana. The result is that Botswana political parties are severely restricted in their income from domestic sources.

One option in this situation is look to foreign sources. The ruling party has been most successful in this regard. Some indication of this subsidy was demonstrated in a recent court case where a BDP employee was convicted of diverting P50,000 from a Friedrich Ebert Foundation grant to the BDP for his own use. More is obviously involved. There is reason to believe that the BDP may receive something like half its donations from foreign sources. The BDP says the money is used for educational seminars for party members. If this is true, and there is no reason to believe otherwise, then the opposition parties should have equal opportunity to obtain such funds when they are engaging in similar educational activities.

Possibilities for change

Botswana's political class is drawn from a small pool. Expansion of this pool will be very difficult. Cultural and economic barriers will only change for the better slowly. The rules on political participation by the civil service will probably not be liberalized at all, especially because of the significant support within this group for the BNF. Thus, the political class will largely come from retired civil servants, businessmen and farmers, not a broad base from which to develop a competitive and capable elite structure.

26.4 ELECTED REPRESENTATIVES CONTROL POLICY MAKING

If elections are to have any significance, those elected must determine the policy direction of government. To the extent that this does not occur we can say that democracy has not been achieved in a liberal democratic form. Three factors limit the policy effectiveness of representatives in Botswana: a) 'specially' elected councillors, b) civil service domination of policy making, and c) crossover politics.

Specially elected representatives

In the parlance of Botswana politics there are two types of representatives, those elected by the people and those who are 'specially' elected. The latter term is technically correct in regard to Parliament in that such persons are selected by a vote of elected MPs.[22] In the case of councils, those claiming to be 'specially' elected are 'nominated' by the Minister of Local Government and Lands.[23]

For the National Assembly the specially elected MPs have little significance in that the party gaining the most seats through the elections determines who is selected. These extra seats simply serve to bring a few individuals into the assembly to help the majority party rule.

In councils, the effect is not as benign. The rationale for these nominated councillors is that the skill level of elected ones is not sufficient to guarantee that the councils can effectively make policy. Many elected councillors are not sufficiently literate to read and understand policy documents, let alone analyse the contents. The nominated councillors are intended to improve the policy sophistication of councillors.

To some extent this has happened. In the areas the Democracy Project studied, nominated councillors have 10.8 years of education compared to 7.8 for those who are elected.

The fact is however that the ruling party uses the nomination process for other purposes as well. It has prevented opposition parties from coming to power at the local level in the past. In the last election the opposition was allowed to rule in four councils where it won; however, so many BDP members were nominated that the opposition was able to rule, except in Gaborone, with only a majority of one or two. Subsequently in Jwaneng and Francistown, desertions of one or two from the council majority party brought the BDP to power, thus reversing the decision of the electorate as to which party should govern.

In other cases where the BDP has won a majority, nominated councillors are used to provide leadership for the council.[24] The individuals so selected often seem more responsive to national party interests than their colleagues who were elected. Some might argue that the national ruling party must do whatever is necessary to insure its control of local councils so that it is able to carry out its policies at the local level. If such reasoning is accepted, then the real question is why have an elected local government at all. The idea of such councils is to provide some limitation on the ruling national majority. Nomination of councillors renders realization of this goal much less likely.

Civil service domination

Equally devastating for rule by elected representatives is the tendency of civil servants to emasculate the representative role of politicians. At the national level this posture is starting to break down with MPs and cabinet members taking an active role in some policy formulation.[25]

The councils have very little freedom. Central government determines the amount of income their budget is based on and vetoes any legislation it does not find acceptable. In addition, council civil servants formulate appropriations with no more input than pleadings from various councillors that projects in their wards be included in the budget. The net result is that councillors have a marginal say in the determination of most policies.

Crossing the floor

A final problem related to the democratic character of representation is the movement of councillors from one party to another. In spite of the fact that the public seems to vote largely for party labels, a number of councillors have seen fit to change parties, mostly going from the opposition parties to the BDP. Since the last election at least nine have done so. The public is effectively denied the party orientation for which it indicated a preference at the last election.

If such switches were rare and relatively balanced between government and opposition, they would not be of any significance. In the present circumstances, however, it might be best to make those who cross the floor test their decision in a by-election.

Possibility of change

As we noted at the beginning of this section, elected officials should provide overall direction to public policy making in a liberal democracy. Much remains to be accomplished in Botswana. At the national level elected representatives are starting to take an active role in policy making. At the council level, there are considerable barriers to effective representation.

The chances that this situation will be rectified is not good. There is little awareness of the constraints which exist even among the elected councillors. Only one-third told us in the Democracy Project survey of elites that they disapproved of nominated councillors, and two-thirds said they thought that national government officials did give local councils a chance to make their own policies. It was only on the question of whether local councils had enough power relative to central government that the elected representatives seemed to recognize their plight. Three-fifths said they did not have sufficient power, while the same proportion of the nominated councillors said their council's power was adequate.[26]

26.5 CONCLUSION

Willingness to address the problems we have identified in the foregoing paper requires first that the politically attentive public perceive each problem as a matter of concern. Our discussions with politicians of the various parties provided us with the distinct impression that not many were seriously worried about the inequalities existing in the present system.

The opposition parties have been particularly unconcerned about ways in which the rules might be reshaped to benefit those who are excluded. Many seem happy simply to reject the whole idea of representative elections as bourgeois. Such a perspective misses the point that election, can be molded to benefit various groups which are not bourgeois.

The ruling party has shown some inclination to listen to criticism of the present system, but for the most part the problems which it has addressed are minor ones, such as the current attention to the idea of moving from counters to a ballot. Matters related to the expansion of the electorate have not been given serious consideration. Given their present impressive majorities, the BDP could afford to make some significant extensions of the franchise without jeopardizing its dominant position.

ENDNOTES

1   See for instance Dahl, R. *Polyarchy: Participation and Opposition* (New Haven, Conn: Yale University Press, 1971).

2   For an excellent description of how elections operate in Botswana, see Polhemus, J. H. 'Elections as Administrative Process: A Survey of the 1984 Botswana Elections', a paper presented at the University of Botswana Election Study Workshop, Gaborone, May 1985.

3   In the lexicon of Botswana politics, MPs are elected from 'constituencies' and councilors are elected from 'wards'. Reference to both in this paper will be made with the word 'district'.

4   Government of Botswana, *Report of Constituency Grading Committee* (Gaborone: Government Printer, 1987).

5   This calculation is based on 1986 population estimates for the constituencies provided in *Report of Constituency Grading Committee.* The one for 1981 was derived from Holm, J. D. 'Elections in Botswana: Institutionalization of a New System of Legitimacy', in Hayward, F. ed. *Elections in Africa* (Boulder, CO: Westview Press, 1987).

6   This situation is likely to be corrected for the next election by the addition of a polling district for Gaborone West. Interview, Mr Mmono, Supervisor of Elections, July 12, 1988.

7   See Polhemus, 'Elections as Administrative Process', p. 14.

8   On migration patterns in Botswana, see *Migration in Botswana: Patterns, Causes and Consequences* (Gaborone: Government Printer, 1982), pp. 107-120 and 213-220.

9   In practice, definition of the principal residence is completely left up to the voter.

10 Holm, 'Elections in Botswana', p. 124. This percentage was achieved in 1965 and 1984.

11 Interview, Mr Mmono, op cit.

12 Ibid.

13 See her paper earlier in this volume as well as Mr Serema's defence of the BDP position in this section.

14 Interview with P. Rantao, May 25, 1988.

15 This discussion concerns absolute exclusion from political activity and cultural and economic limitations specifically related to running for office. The political freedoms of assembly, speech, press, and organization are dealt with in A. Molokomme's paper.

16 See the conditions of service for these various groups. Each parastatal has its own policies, some of which allow participation of some or all of their employees. Thus at the BMC employees are free to participate in politics including being elected as councilors; however, an employee must resign if he decides to run for parliament. In the case of the Bank of Botswana, an employee cannot run for elected office. Some employees of private corporations have also been in doubt about whether they could participate in politics. For example the BNF in Jwaneng was hesitant to put up employees of Debswana in the

1984 elections for fear that they would be dismissed. Subsequently, the BDP nominated a councilor who worked at the mine. The BNF is therefore planning to nominate mine employees in 1989. Also, after the 1984 election, a private bank proposed to transfer a newly elected councilor to another town. He was able to oppose the move successfully.

17 Government of Botswana *General Orders Governing the Conditions of Service of the Public Service* (Gaborone: Government Printer, 1987) p. 15.

18 See M. G. Molomo's paper in this volume.

19 Public employees are sometimes asked to remove themselves from one side of the meeting room so that they will not appear in news photographs.

20 The BNF alleges that Soblan Mayane did not resign before the 1987 primary in Ghanzi. It appears that Mayane did resign about two weeks before the primary. He did not however give the civil service the requisite 3 months notice. Therefore, he had to pay back to the government a month's salary.

21 Constitution, Section 61.

22 Constitution, Section 58.

23 These nominations are provided for under the Townships Act and the Local Government Act.

24 This was most evident in the Southern District where the Council Chairman and most of the committee chairpersons are nominated members.

25 See P. P. Molutsi's paper on representation in this volume.

26 These results come from a survey of 67 elected councilors and 19 nominated ones.

DISCUSSION

Mr David Magang (MP) said both Mr Motswagole's and Professor Holm's papers showed that the authors were out of touch with the political reality of Botswana. He said the newly introduced amendment to the Electoral Act which requires observers to be 200 metres away from voters referred to the voting process and did not apply to vote counting.

Regarding constituency size and delimitation he said this was based on the decennial population census and the delimitation was carried out by an independent commission.

On the lowering of the voting age from twenty-one to eighteen, he said all parties were consulted and many people preferred it to remain at twenty-one years of age. He said Mr Motswagole's accusations levelled against the BDP were unwarranted.

Mr Tlhomelang (BNF, MP) said many of his supporters wanted the voting age to be lowered to eighteen years. After all, the eighteen year olds held important positions of responsibility. He suggested that in order to avoid cheating during voting, an impartial judge of some sort could be appointed to monitor the process.

Mr T. Mongwa (BPP, Councillor) said there is a need to lower the voting age and also to encourage young people to participate in politics. He said most MPs were less informed because they do no research.

Mr Mogwe (MP, Minister of Mineral Resources and Water Affairs) said the Electoral Law needed no amendment as it was fine as it is.

Mr K. Maripe (Leader, BPP) said it was agreed in 1987 by the all-party meeting that floor crossing should be prevented by law. He said legislation should be developed to stop this. On the issue of nominated councillors he said that an all-party meeting requested that the nominations should be left to the council and not to the Minister of Local Government and Lands, as is currently the case.

Mr Mpho (Leader, BIP) felt that the problem of cheating during voting did not come from the inefficiency of the act, but from cheating done by the BDP and the BNF. He said therefore that changing the law will not solve the problem of cheating.

Mr Giddie (BNF) felt both the nomination process and crossing of the floor by politicians was a corrupt practice. He also expressed concern that after dissolution of parliament, ministers and the president continued to use their official positions to hold meetings in the kgotla, thereby disadvantaging other parties.

Mr D. Kwele (Leader, BPU) said he could not understand why after the all-party meeting resolved that the Supervisor of Elections be appointed after consultation with all parties, the President decided to do it alone.

Mr B. Otlhogile (Law, University of Botswana) said that in the past candidates were permitted to stand in the constituencies where they did not register and that this was against the law. He said while talking about voting age the conference should consider not only the lower but the upper limit as well. He said some MPs were far too old to speak for their constituencies effectively.

Professor Holm (Democracy Project) replying to reactions to his paper said if constituents were happy with candidates crossing floor then there was no need to question it. He said introducing the upper age limit as Mr Otlhogile suggested was tantamount to asking the BDP to cut its support. He said making the election rules to benefit the ruling party was a universal problem in democracies.

Mr Motswagole (Lawyer, BNF) said the angry reactions to his paper were indicative of bourgeois behaviour, especially when this class wanted to avoid real issues. He said a significant number of active people in Botswana were below the age of twenty- one and that is why eighteen year olds should vote. He said he saw no point in setting the upper age limit for voting since all citizens should have the right to vote.

Mr Serema (Lawyer, BDP) said he made no claim that the law is perfect. Imperfections will always be in any law. He agreed with the point on the absentee vote raised by Professor Holm. He said perhaps the law should be amended to cover this important point.

SECTION XII
POLITICAL PARTIES

27 Political parties as facilitators of democracy in Botswana

Rwendezi Nengwekhulu

27.1 INTRODUCTION

This paper assesses the role political parties play in Botswana to facilitate the development of democracy. The analysis focuses on two considerations. One is the extent to which the system of multiparty competition helps to realize mass control of public officials. The other is whether the internal organization of the parties enhances the empowerment of the masses.

Some of the data employed in the analysis below are the preliminary results of a survey of party elites which the Democracy Project conducted during 1987 and 1988. It is hoped that the paper will provoke discussion and comments which will be valuable later when a more comprehensive analysis of these data are undertaken.

27.2 A BRIEF HISTORY OF POLITICAL PARTIES IN BOTSWANA

Unlike most African states, political parties in Botswana are of recent origin. Their history only extends to the 1950s with most of them actually only coming into existence in the early 1960s. Some have emerged after independence, most notably the Botswana National Front (BNF) which has become the most important opposition party in recent times.

But any analysis of the origins of political parties in Botswana can only be properly understood within the wider framework of the political history of Southern Africa and the African continent in general. This does not mean that one can ignore the influence of the internal or local conditions in the shaping of the complexion of political parties in Botswana. If anything this approach recognizes the historical specificity of the origins of political parties in Botswana and the uneven socio-economic and political developments in Southern Africa in particular and Africa in general resulting in part from colonialism and imperialism.

The emergence nationalist movements in Botswana was slow, only beginning on a sustained basis in the 1960s. There were intermittent signs of national conscious-ness as early as the 1920s when individuals such as Simon Ratshosa began to criti-cize British colonialism in Botswana and the corrupt and despotic rule of the chiefs. It is common knowledge that the cause of the liberation struggle and quest for in-dependence in Africa developed as a response to colonialism. The intensity of colonial administration and exploitation determined, to a large extent, the complexion and the rate of national formation and maturation. In Botswana the process of colonial domination and exploitation was 'milder' than in the other parts of Africa. This was manifested in the absence of large scale land alienation policies and the small-ness of the white settler community. The result was that landlessness never emerged as a political rallying point as was the case with Kenya, Zimbabwe and South Afri-ca. Another consequence was a delay in the birth of a working class, which in other African colonies served as a catalyst for the formation of the nationalist movements.

The reason the 1960s brought the emergence of national consciousness and na-tionalist movements in Botswana is connected with the fact that this period saw the massive wave of decolonisation and the granting of independence to a number of colonies in Africa. In Southern Africa 1960 is one of the crucial years in the strug-gle for national liberation. For it was a year in which nationalist movements pitted their strength against the forces of oppression and exploitation culminating in the massacres at Sharpville. As a result both the Africa National Congress and the Pan African Congress were outlawed in South Africa, forcing most of their leaders to flee the country into neighbouring territories, especially Botswana, Swaziland and Lesotho. Some of these leaders were the nationals of these territories who because of the clamp down on ANC and PAC decided to return home. These were the peo-ple who later formed the nucleus of nationalist movements in three territories.

In Botswana the outcome of the influx of these exiles from South Africa was the formation of nationalist movements. This was especially so with regard to the for-mation of the Bechuanaland People's Party,(now Botswana People's Party, BPP) where two of the three founders, Matante and Mpho were former active members of the PAC and ANC respectively.

Other factors promoted the spread of nationalism in Botswana in the 1960s. One was the granting of independence to most of the colonies in West and East Africa during the early sixties. Batswana began to see their independence as inevitable. As important were the migrant workers employed in South Africa. These workers were active in black nationalist politics in South Africa, and some rose to high po-sitions. When they returned to Botswana, they formed the nucleus of budding working class which was the major driving force behind the formation of political parties, especially the BPP.

Finally, the decision by the colonial administration to initiate policies designed to lead the territory towards independence also contributed to the formation of po-litical parties in Botswana.

27.3 THE TWO-PARTY SYSTEM AND DEMOCRACY IN BOTSWANA

The multiparty systems which arose at the time of political independence in Africa have all but disappeared. In their place is the 'popular' one-party system. There are a number of reasons for this change. First, a multiparty system is a threat to national unity because opposition parties are believed to encourage tribalism and other forms of internal conflict.

Second, political parties in Africa compete for scarce human and material resources. These resources must be concentrated on development of the economy, the state and other more basic social organizations. The result is that countries can only afford one party. Only a few states in the Third World allow a multiparty system to continue to exist. And in Africa the number of states which can be so classified is less than five.

Botswana is one of this small group. Indications are that liberal democracy will grow from strength to strength here for the foreseeable future. The existence of a multiparty system is said by some to be vital to this process. This type of party system is supposed to provide voters with a wide variety of choices, unlike a two party system where the voter's choice may be determined by the principle of the better or lesser of the two evils. In a situation in which no single party obtains absolute majority a coalition government becomes an alternative. The voter does not consider his or her vote wasted in backing a party that best represents and expresses his or her views concerning desirable policies and ideologies.

Whilst in theory the multiparty system may have the potential to facilitate the development of democracy in society, in Botswana the system has serious limitations. The most obvious is that there is one dominant party, the ruling Botswana Democratic Party (BDP). This has been the situation since independence in 1966. Opposition parties both individually and collectively, are extremely weak. In the current parliament the total strength of the opposition parties is a mere 6 seats as opposed to the 38 for BDP. The story is the same at district and town council level with the BDP commanding an overwhelming majority of 195 seats while the opposition parties collectively have 59.

This dominance of the BDP has almost effectively negated the claimed value of the multiparty system by making unnecessary the liberal notion of politics as a process of bargaining and accommodation between political parties. Botswana is de facto a one-party state.

27.4 THE PARTY ORGANIZATIONS AND DEMOCRACY IN BOTSWANA

In a democracy parties are supposed to discharge a variety of functions which facilitate popular control. This is supposed to be especially so in a liberal democracy such as practised in Botswana. The following functions will be considered below: a) political education, b) leadership training and c) eradication of social discrimination.

Political education

Political parties should provide political education to their supporters in order to sharpen their understanding of political events and their appreciation of democracy. The best means for achieving this goal is through seminars, workshops, and study groups.

Political parties in Botswana hardly hold any education programmes. The ones that are held are sporadic and are held only for party activists. There is no evidence that any of the six parties has ever sought to reach ordinary members by this means. Nor is there any evidence that party activists who attend political education programmes convey whatever knowledge they have gained to their supporters.

The inherent significance of political education in this regard cannot therefore be over emphasized for it helps to extend the political horizons of the masses. This in turn facilitates mass participation in politics. The result is that relatively few people actually engage in political activities of any kind beyond voting, and those who do are generally those who belong to the dominant class. This is especially so with regard to the rural population.

The fact that so few participate casts some doubt on political parties as vehicles for the extension of democracy in Botswana. In addition, one can question whether this low level of participation serves to check the power of those in control of the state and its apparatus. Without a concerted programme of political education and mobilization, the masses cannot comprehend the processes by which they can undertake the various activities required to check their leaders.

Where only a few take meaningful part in the electoral process, decision-making and general political activities in the society, there is little democracy. Political parties in Botswana have a huge task to make democracy a reality. This can only be achieved if there is active political education and mobilization of the masses. Such political education and mobilization must be directed towards sharpening the masses' political intellect and making them aware of their aspirations and the structural arrangements which frustrate these aspirations. This education requires much more than freedom square demagoguery.

Training of political leadership

Political parties are supposed to provide training for political leadership. The parties in Botswana cannot be said to be fulfilling this expectation for there is very little circulation of party leaders. Those at the top of the various political parties have been there for almost twenty years. Most of them have become so institutionalized that their presence is synonymous with the party.

As a result an aura of indispensability has developed around them making the survival of the party appear to depend on them. Effectively, the party leadership is inaccessible to the masses. In addition, most party leaders are members of the petty bourgeois class. Thus despite the rhetoric of equal access to party leadership, the petty bourgeoisie has retained an iron grip on the top positions, even in the parties which proclaim themselves to be supporting Marxism-Leninism.

The system of primaries introduced in some parties such as the BDP has not succeeded in opening the party leadership to the lower classes. The primaries have not even succeeded in introducing processes of leadership circulation among the members of the petty bourgeois class.

It is therefore difficult to conclude that parties in Botswana are breeding grounds in any sense for national political leaders, especially for the unacessesible working class and poor peasants.

Class and gender discrimination

Political parties in a liberal democracy are also supposed to facilitate social and economic equality. In practice political parties do discriminate against members who are from the lower classes and are female.

As far as discrimination on the basis of class is concerned, the parties exclude workers and peasants from any meaningful political participation. The number of these groups in senior party positions is very small, constituting less than 2% of the leadership. Even this 2% is a very generous estimate.

Denis Cohen aptly remarks, '. . . the political elite in Botswana is, in comparison with the people of Botswana, also an elite of wealth.'[1] Although his study was carried out in 1974, its calculations are still valid even today, for our study has also found this to be the situation. It is therefore clear that although the membership of political parties in Botswana cuts across class divisions, their leadership comes almost exclusively from petty bourgeois class. The democracy they promote is thus the democracy for the petty bourgeois class. This is certainly reflected in the legislation passed by the National Assembly in the last twenty-two years or so. It has promoted the class interests of the petty bourgeoisie and permitted this class to consolidate its political hold on the economy and the state apparatus.

It is therefore not surprising that income distribution is highly skewed and social inequalities are still highly conspicuous in Botswana. This was eloquently confined by the 1974/1975 National Income distribution survey which showed that cattle ownership in Botswana is highly skewed. While 5% of the rural population owned more than 75% of the national cattle herd, 45% owned nothing nor cultivated any crops. Income disparities are also highly skewed in the urban areas. These inequalities exist in spite of the growing wealth resulting from mining and cattle.

Political parties in Botswana also discriminate on the basis of gender. The parties exclude women from senior party positions as well as from nomination for parliamentary and council positions. Only one woman was nominated for a parliamentary seat in the 1984 general elections out of 81 candidates nominated by all parties. There are two women in the parliament out of 38 members. One of these two fills a nominated seat. Thus parliament is almost exclusively a male political preserve.

At the council level, the situation is somewhat better, although it still leaves very much to be desired. In the 1984 elections only 25 women were nominated by all the parties to compete for a total of 264 seats.

There has been some improvement. No party nominated a women for parliament in the 1965 and 1969 elections. In 1974 only 2 women were nominated. In the local council elections of 1966 only about 8 women were nominated out of a total of 165 candidates. This figure rose to about 22 out of 176 candidates in the 1969. In 1974 there was a slight regression to 19 women nominated.

Of the 22 female candidates for council in 1969, 15 were BDP, 7 were BNF. In 1974 the BDP nominated 14 women. BNF 5. These figures indicate very clearly that political parties in Botswana discriminate against women and this devalues their role as facilitators of democracy.

Women's representation in the decision making organs of the parties is no better. In fact it is almost non-existent. In the Central Committee of the BDP there are only 2 women out of the total of 16. In the BNF before the 1988 national congress, there were two women out of the total membership of about 40 on the Central Committee. The story is the same in the other parties.

The world of party politics is therefore exclusively a man's preserve in Botswana. The irony is that more than a majority of grass-roots activists are women. Their absence from top leadership positions has nothing to do with the myth that women in Botswana have traditionally shied away from politics. That they are not included has something to do with male prejudice. It is also a reflection of induced feelings of political inadequacy stemming from a socio-economic and political environment structured and dominated by males.

There is no evidence that male domination of Botswana's political parties will change in the future. Perhaps the women's movement in Botswana, especially *Emang Basadi*, will accelerate the process for recognition and acceptance of the political rights of women in Botswana. But considering the degree of opposition to giving women political leadership positions within the parties and the organs of government, this is likely to be a prolonged and arduous struggle. This has been, to a certain extent, confirmed by our mass survey results. For instance most male party members are reluctant to consider women for the position of head of state. And even those who are willing to consider women do so conditionally, i.e provided women have adequate education.

This resistance to female participation takes on a more sophisticated complexion among male party leaders. They say there is no barrier to women seeking offices in government or politics. It is just that they are not inclined to do so up to this point. Most elected official see no need to make special provision for an increase in the number of women in politics. They seem unable to comprehend that gender discrimination might be the reason so few women are political leaders.

27.5 CONCLUSION

It is very clear from the above analysis that there are fundamental weaknesses regarding the role of political parties in Botswana as facilitators of democracy. The existence of political parties does not necessarily guarantee the extension of democracy to the masses. However, to say that political parties in Botswana do not insure democracy is not to imply that they have not been assisting in the extension of democracy. Their impact has been minimal thus far.

Ample room does exist for the parties to become real facilitators of democracy in the future since there are no significant restrictions on them in this regard. To do so, the parties must undergo a fundamental ideological re-orientation in order to become parties of the masses, by the masses and for the masses. This will allow the masses to become active participants in the decision making process. As they are presently constituted political parties in Botswana promote and defend democracy for the petty bourgeois class. The extension of some aspects of democracy to the working class, poor peasants and women is incidental rather than central to their existence and operations.

In practice the multiparty system becomes merely a sophisticated way of guaranteeing the circulation of the political leadership amongst the members of the petty bourgeois class. As Karl Marx put it, 'The oligarchy does not perpetuate itself by retaining power permanently in the same hand, but by dropping it with one hand, in order to catch it again in the other . . .'[2]

Viewed from this perspective, it is perhaps expecting too much to expect Botswana's petty bourgeois political parties operating within a liberal democracy to facilitate the extension of democracy to the masses in Botswana. For the liberal notion of democracy only extends as far as the legal fiction in which the masses' participation in politics involves the right to vote without the possibility of them being voted into power. Liberal democracy thus does not mean and cannot mean government by the people, of the people and for the people. But rather it means government for the bourgeois and of the bourgeois.

ENDNOTES

1   Cohen, D. L. 'A Profile of Political Leadership: Characteristics of Candidates for Election in the 1974 Botswana General Elections,' in Young. H. *Voters and Candidates in the 1974 Botswana General Elections* (Gaborone: University of Botswana, 1974) p. 124.

2   Marx, K. *Collected Works*, Vol. 14 (Moscow: Progress Publishers, 1980) p. 338.

DISCUSSION

Mr Mogome of the Botswana People's Party (BPP) expressed concern that Botswana's political system is still geared toward and controlled by the former colonial master, Great Britain. He alleged that this was a major block to popular participation in Botswana's democracy. He also said that Britain agreed to Botswana's independence in 1966 only because she did not know of Botswana's mineral wealth.

Commenting on Negwekhulu's paper, Mr Mogome felt it was too broad. He said contrary to Negwekhulu's assertion, unity but not ideology was a major consideration during the early days of political party activities in Botswana. He was greatful to our leaders such as Messrs Matante and Seretse Khama who were determined to unite Batswana and not to divide them. On ideology he claimed there was no Marxist party in Botswana — 'not even the BNF'.

Mr Mokobi of the Botswana Independence Party (BIP) said central to the BIP manifesto is peace and stability, because without these there can be no democracy and development. He however noted that as an ordinary man's party BIP had suffered, especially in the early days, from discrimination by some chiefs. Its leaders were often confronted with questions such as: 'Whose son are you? On whose soil are you standing? These questions were intended to stop the BIP from opposing BDP and others supposed to be led by royal citizens.

Mr Mokobi said that it should always be noted that liberal democracy has some limitations relating to freedoms of speech, movement, assembly, and participation. He said in Botswana liberal democracy was influenced by tradition and that women in particular have been victims of limited participation. He however noted that even in developed democracies such as Britain, it was only recently that women have begun taking an active role in politics.

On education of the population Mr Mokobi said BIP has within the limits of meagre resources at its disposal conducted workshops and seminars for its cadre, youth and women's organizations. He said his party cannot at present afford to educate the general population using the above methods.

Mr Kwele of the Botswana Progressive Union (BPU) said that political parties are the consciousness of the people. Political parties should therefore be assisted with resources to help them mobilize and educate the population, especially because many people are reluctant to attend freedom square rallies.

Mr Kwele expressed concern that the ruling BDP has sufficient resources at its disposal to frustrate efforts of other political parties. He said the problem of lack of resources, especially for newly formed parties such as BPU, was insurmountable. He reiterated concerns of the other discussants that the lack of resources was a major stumbling block to the effectiveness and competitiveness of opposition parties in Botswana. He observed that not long ago the National Democratic Institute (NDI) of the USA wanted to help all parties by establishing a training institute in Botswana. He claimed that the NDI's offer was refused by the BDP government, which does not want to see opposition parties develop to a stage where they can compete with it effectively.

Mr Giddie of the Botswana National Front (BNF) said when discussing liberal democracy one should always ask the question: Whose freedom does the constitution enshire? He said in essence these are freedoms of the ruling, propertied classes — 'the bourgeoisie of our society'. These freedoms are projected as if they could be realized by all citizens, and yet in a class society such as Botswana's this is impossible.

He further claimed that Botswana's tradition was partly responsible for poor political activity by women. This tradition raises men to the level of dominance.

He said BNF was encouraging participation by all sections of the population. He however noted that lack of resources was frustrating political activities of political parties in Botswana.

Mr Mayane of the Botswana Democratic Party (BDP) summarized the BDP manifesto since 1965 and emphasized that BDP has carried out education of the nation and party cadre. He claimed that the party has structures starting from committees of 18 at the ward level to similar committees at the constituency, regional and national levels. These structures, said Mr Mayane, encouraged participation by all.

The Honourable K. Morake (Minister of Education) complained that members of opposition were turning the symposium into a court of appeal, pleading for this and that. He said that BDP did not start off as a government party but worked hard to build itself to that level. He agreed that women's participation in politics was limited, but noted that over the 20 years (a short period for political transformation) Botswana has achieved a lot.

Mr Mpho (BIP) agreed with Negwekhulu that there has been no change or very little change in the leadership of most political parties since independence. He agreed that more should be done to develop young and active people to lead.

On the issue of education of the population he felt the freedom square should be more effectively used and political language controlled.

Dr Wallace (University of Birmingham) wondered whether BDP was going to reply to allegations that Friedrich Ebert Foundation (FEF) may be subsidising it.

Mr Modise (BPP) noted that Botswana's multiparty democracy is important and should be retained but wondered whether it makes any sense if opposition parties remain as underdeveloped as they are at present. He said while opposition parties lack resources, the BDP was on the other hand being supported financially by the FEF.

Mr Sethantsho (BNF) said foreign finance of one political party amounted to interference in Botswana's internal affairs.

Reacting to the issue of external financing of the BDP, the Honourable Minister Kwelagobe (Secretary General of BDP) said that if they had to declare their sources of funding then all the other parties should do the same.

In summarizing their comments both Mr Negwekhulu and the party activists on the panel emphasized that political parties, especially those in the opposition, have a lot still to do to make them effective and alternative government paties. Lack of resources and organizational skills by activists were underlined as two major problems facing most political parties.

SECTION XIII
THE KGOTLA AND FREEDOM SQUARE

28 The kgotla and the freedom square: one-way or two-way communication?

Kgosi Seepapitso IV

28.1 INTRODUCTION

The kgotla and ʀeedom square are two very different types of community institutions. The kgotla is traditionally accepted as a meeting place for tribesmen and women for the purpose of discussing developmental issues, tribal affairs or anything of interest or concern to the tribe. Our forefathers created this institution many years ago, before recorded history. Kgosi, or one of the senior tribesmen, appointed by kgosi, presides as chairman during deliberations. The task of the chairman is to insure that all discussion is respectful. There should be no heckling or emotional outbursts. Partisan speeches are not allowed. In sum, the kgotla is a place where all the members of a local community meet to hear about and discuss matters of mutual concern in a non-partisan but frank manner.

Besides community discussion, the kgotla has other functions. Dikgosi use it as a place to hold their customary court. Ministers, civil servants, members of parliament and councilors ask dikgosi to call kgotlas so that they can disseminate information on development plans and assistance programmes to the people. All such presentations, however, must be conducted in a non-partisan manner.

Political parties introduced the freedom square to Botswana in the years before independence as they campaigned for an end to colonial rule and for their election to office. Any person can attend freedom square meetings, though the majority of those attending are the followers of the party which organizes the event. While development programmes related to the local community are sometimes discussed, the meetings are dominated by the concern of each party's leaders to enhance the image of their party. This means that the speakers are basically preaching their current political doctrines in a dogmatic manner.

In the discussion which follows, I will make two points: a) the freedom square is an undemocratic place in which party leaders are intent on lecturing their followers, and b) the kgotla is a means of two-way communication which government often neglects to the community's peril.

28.2 COMMUNICATION IN FREEDOM SQUARES

The problem of communication in freedom squares arises from the fact they are dominated by party leaders without being challenged by their followers in any sort of critical fashion. The reason for this submissiveness is that each party's supporters fear that if they ask searching questions of their representatives they will be exposing the weaknesses of their party and be accused of disloyalty. The resultant conclusion one must draw is that only one-way communication takes place in a freedom square.

Compounding the problem is the fact that freedom square meetings are open to disruption by followers of opposing parties. This often comes about by way of questions which wildly distort information supplied by speakers. This leads to heckling which further undermines the chances for a serious dialogue between the politicians and their audience. There is no possibility of feedback to party leaders from those who have serious questions to ask.

The political party leaders are primarily concerned with mobilizing their followers at freedom squares. Experience has shown that the majority of people who attend any political meeting are the followers or those affiliated to the party which convenes the meeting. At best discussions at these assemblies revolve around the achievements of the party convening the meeting and the weaknesses of other parties, with little concern for objectivity.

In so far as politicians do talk about policies, they seem to be solely concerned with promoting their own, leading one to believe that public concerns come second to their wishes. Two cases in point are the issues relating to *matimela* cattle and the tribal land administration. As a result of public complaint a commission was appointed some two or three years back to look into the administration of matimela to see how it could best be changed to suit the wishes of the majority of Batswana farmers. The commissioners travelled extensively throughout the country addressing the people on the subject and seeking their opinions. The findings were compiled and presented to government, but up till now there has been no feedback. As a result, the people continue to complain.

Again some two or three years back our political government launched a review of tribal land administration because Batswana were not happy at all with changes which have been made since the 1968 law. Up to date we have not heard anything from government, and the people are still complaining. This is why I say politicians tend to stick strictly to their policies in freedom squares without listening to and meeting public concerns.[1]

Batswana are still not politically educated. This is why the majority only attend assemblies of parties to which they are affiliated. They often expect to get what their representatives promise, forgetting that they as voters must impress upon their representatives the programmes which ought to be undertaken and the manner in which government ought to behave. In many cases the electorate does not even appear to know the contents of the manifestos of the parties they support. They expect to be told by word of mouth, which unfortunately does not usually happen at freedom squares.

Many Batswana, particularly those who are elders, do not even attend freedom squares. They are disgusted by the insults which are hurled at the speakers and the gross lack of respect for age. The majority who attend are young voters and those who are still not of age to vote. These young people seem to see nothing wrong with disrupting the meetings with abusive language. I do not see how the politicians can begin to believe that they are getting feedback about the concerns of the voters.

In summary, my argument with regard to the freedom square is that at best they are fora of one-way communication in which the politicians preach the virtues of their party and tear down the reputations of the others. Any possibility of the people speaking back is prevented by the fact that politicians do not want to listen, that Batswana do not understand that they must instruct their politicians as to what government should do, and that vulgar behaviour reduces attendance to only the youth of the community.

28.3 COMMUNICATION IN THE KGOTLA

As I said in my introduction, the kgotla as an institution is well understood by Batswana and used by both politicians and civil servants whenever they have a need to communicate with the public. Most members of a village feel free when attending kgotla meetings to speak their minds on whatever is being discussed. The ministers are free to address people on government policies and programmes everywhere in the country. To this end there is no doubt that through the kgotla people are being consulted.

Particularly important is the atmosphere for discussion which prevails. People attend kgotla meetings as their traditional right without fear of victimization. They express their opinions freely. The atmosphere is completely different from that at freedom squares. Discussions are held in a calm atmosphere, with those present showing dignity and respect for each speaker.

This is not to say that the kgotla is immune from exchange of strongly held and widely varied ideas. In some cases, a minority or a majority may actually voice total rejection of a proposal being presented. Unlike at the freedom square, should such a situation arise, people are given the opportunity to speak freely without harassment. In addition they are always guided by those who are informed on the topic so that the issues are fully clarified before a decision is made.

There is thus two-way communication in the kgotla. The only problem is that politicians often fail to respond to the complaints which the people voice in kgotla. A classic example of this failure to listen is that nothing has been done to alleviate the problems which have arisen from the implementation of the Tribal Land and Matimela Acts. Before these laws were enacted, these two aspects of community governance were administered by dikgosi. The operation in each case was very smooth because everything was done and agreed upon by the tribe in kgotla. The national government has transferred both functions to political institutions. Specifically, the land boards allocate tribal lands and the district councils control matimela cattle. Since both the land boards and the councils are run by and for partisan political advantage, there is bound to be much confusion and discontent over the results.

This problem of a lack of response to community concerns expressed in kgotla also occurs with civil servants, who are supposed to be the non-partisan implementors of government policies. They primarily use the kgotla to tell the members of local communities about development and assistance programmes to be implemented in a particular area. They also seek to mobilize the people to provide free labour for self-help projects. They do not, however, come for the most part to hear the community's problems and talk about potential solutions. That is done in government offices. The duty of civil servants in kgotla is just to follow directions of their superiors, which includes giving the appearance of listening to the people.

28.4 CONCLUSION

At first glance one might think that the kgotla and freedom square promote democracy. The facts of the situation are quite different. The kgotla in tradition does allow for dialogue between the people and their rulers; however, the politicians and civil servants for the most part do not listen to what they are told when it comes to implementing policy. The freedom square has not yet developed into a medium of two-way communication; rather it functions merely as an outlet for partisan propaganda. If our democracy is to survive, both the politicians and civil servants must begin to learn from the dikgosi the importance of listening and responding to the people's concerns expressed in community assemblies.

ENDNOTES

1   By editors. The Report of the Commission on Land Tenure referred to was released in December of 1983 and was considered by Cabinet in January 1984. Probably the local authorities were not given copies of both the report and subsequent white paper.

29 The kgotla and the freedom square: one-way or two-way communication?

Mogopodi H. Lekorwe

29.1 INTRODUCTION

In a representative democracy candidates compete in regular elections for constituent votes. Critical to the development of popular control through this process is the presence of communication structures whereby politicians and government officials, on the one hand, and the public on the other discuss community problems and potential solutions. In industrialized countries there is an array of mass media such as television, radio, newspapers and magazines which perform this political communication function.[1] In developing countries both the availability of these mass media and their effectiveness in providing for dialogue between rulers and ruled is limited. Therefore, in such countries the effective operation of a liberal democracy requires that alternative means of communication be utilized.

In Botswana the need for this alternative communication strategy has been particularly pressing. The conditions of low literacy rates, dispersed population and limited penetration of both official and private press beyond the major urban centres have meant that face-to-face interaction remains the most effective way for political and governmental elites to communicate with citizens.

The persistence of a representative form of democratic government in this country requires the grass-roots communication processes be monitored for their effectiveness. The discussion which follows is an attempt to provide at least a partial picture of the present situation.

The kgotla and the freedom square have emerged as the two most predominant means for direct interaction between the public and political and government leaders. The kgotla is a traditional form of gathering where the chief until recently discussed issues of public concern with the community. Now politicians and civil servants use it to discuss community issues in an allegedly non-partisan manner. The freedom square on the other hand was developed in the 1960s by the politicians as a means of mobilizing the public outside the control of the chiefs and colonial authorities for electoral purposes.

In small villages both types of meeting are held for the whole village. In urban centres and large villages each is usually held for a subsection of the community.

This paper evaluates the kgotla and freedom square with regard to two concerns. First, to what extent can each form of public discussion provide a means by which information flows between the public and their governors? Second, to what extent does each enable the electorate to influence both politicians and civil servants? The first part of our discussion will concentrate on the overall structure of the two types of community meeting. Each will be considered separately. Then attention will focus on public perceptions and evaluations of the functioning of both types of public meeting with regard to the twin concerns of information exchange and citizen political influence.

The argument presented is that while elites make some attempt to listen to specific community concerns in both the kgotla and freedom square, the effectiveness of politicians and civil servants at manipulating their audience has limited public influence over their rulers. The two institutions do complement each other in terms of their strengths in that the kgotla focuses on local issues while the freedom square induces the public to think about and react to matters of national importance.

29.2 THE KGOTLA: ITS STRUCTURE

The kgotla in general terms is a place where the community meets to discuss openly issues of common interest with the chief. The power of the kgotla stems from its multifaceted weaving together of various aspect of community life.

At least four functions have been identified.[2] Most important is that the kgotla provides the people with a means by which they come to agreement as to what ought to be done with respect to a particular government programme in the community. On some occasions, the chiefs use the kgotla to discuss publicly and gather views on matters affecting their communities before government makes policy decisions. Government officials, including members of parliament and councillors, often see the kgotla as a means of informing the various tribal communities about new legislation and other developments or inquiring into local disputes.[3] Finally, the kgotla is a judicial institution in which cases relating to traditional and modern law are heard by the chief and his advisers.

The chief together with his advisers is still in total control of the functioning of a kgotla meeting. Through this control an effective chief can be both the moral and legal head of his community. He can also use kgotla to set agendas for community discussion, to organize collective community action and to intimidate councillors, government officials and other local influentials to seek his support. The means by which this is possible can be seen by examining the aspects of the kgotla's operation.

Formality: The kgotla follows strict forms of address and behaviour. The tribe is referred to by its totem, e.g the monkey (kgabo) if one is addressing a Bakgatla community or the kudu (tholo) if one is addressing Barolong. A male speaker always shows respect for the kgotla by taking off his hat. Every effort must be made to avoid harsh or abusive language which might be regarded as disrespectful, e.g. instead of saying a person has lied, one says that another is mistaken. Members of the assembly are always addressed by their surnames even in the case of a close friend.

Seating arrangement: Traditional status plays an important role in determining where people sit in kgotla. Closest to the chief are his uncles and his immediate advisers. The older members of the tribe come next.[4] The middle aged and the young are expected to sit at the back. Women sometimes stay away from the front, especially at the large kgotlas. Visitors including government officials are given a prominent position, normally sitting at the centre. The audience remains seated except when a person stands to speak.

Scheduling and announcing the meeting: Kgotla meetings are given priority over any other community meetings. Any conflicting community events must be rescheduled. In terms of custom, the whole community is expected to attend. The public is informed of the time and place of the meeting by kgotla police telling headmen who in turn announce the specifics to members of their wards. Also, teachers pass the message to students to relay to their parents. Radio Botswana often announces kgotla meetings, particularly when they are held in big villages and an important issue is involved. This is to ensure that persons from others parts of the country can return for the event.

In the past a kgotla could be called any time, though it usually took place early in the morning during the week so that daily village activities would not be interrupted. In small villages, kgotla meetings are still called during the week. In large villages, on the other hand, the ideal time to call a kgotla is over the weekend when most people including workers are present.

The only problem is that because of the existence in recent times of mortuaries, funerals are held on Saturdays when relatives from out of town can return. A funeral, particularly that of a prominent person, will almost certainly greatly reduce attendance, and may force the cancelation of a kgotla. It is difficult to call kgotla meetings on a Sunday because many attend church.

Personal behaviour: The kgotla is considered sacred and the preserve of the tribe. As a result, people who attend are expected to be sober. Only during ceremonies can beer be served. Once the meeting has started people are not expected to leave before the meeting is finished. Although heckling may be observed at the kgotla when henchmen of the chief shut down a person, it is uncommon, and discussions are conducted in an orderly manner. In case of misconduct discipline is enforced immediately.

Music: Kgotla meetings do not normally include music. Choirs are used at ceremonial events to praise the chief and glorify the tribe. Occasionally the singers warn the chief of discontent. When there is a guest speaker, particularly a government minister or the president, a choir will sing patriotic tunes or praise poems concerning the guest speaker.

Freedom of speech: Theoretically discussions are conducted in a free atmosphere where those who are entitled to attend have the right to speak their mind.[5] In some instances even the chief is heavily criticized.[6] To be sure, negative remarks about the chief often take a highly stylized form of songs or poems.

In practice, tribal status determines who speaks, when and for how long. Those with status, like the chief's uncles are likely to make extended speeches and may even speak several times. Ngcongco rightly observes that the lower status groups like the Bakgalagadi, although allowed to attend meetings, were not expected to speak in pre-colonial kgotlas.[7] The same is true today in many areas.

Women while recognized as having the right to attend kgotla still feel that they do not have the right to speak. Thus in our Democracy Project survey, while women come in larger numbers to the kgotla than men (probably because men are seldom in the village either taking up employment in the cities or away in South African mines), only about 25% mentioned having spoken up at all. In most of the kgotlas we observed, women's participation was even less than this percentage. The longer and repeating speakers were almost all men.

The Basarwa are in a still worse category in many cases. Many Batswana still do not recognize the right, granted by government, for Basarwa to attend kgotla,[8] let alone to speak up if they do attend. The perception of many as Murray notes above is that they are not part of the morafe and thus should not be included.

Decisions: Kgotla meetings are sometimes called to make a decision on a issue. After the chief decides there has been sufficient discussion, he summarizes the points of view and announces the decision. Where opinion is sharply split, the chief in most cases will often attempt to present a consensus position, but the concept of status plays a role in his assessment.[9] The opinion of wealthy royals and chief's uncles carries more weight than that of ordinary tribesmen. If the chief still feels that a consensus has not been reached, he may call for another meeting.

In the post independence period a number of kgotlas reported that they occasionally take a vote if a consensus could not be reached on an issue. But generally, the only voting that is accepted in kgotla is when a community selects members to development, health and education committees or the land board.

Agenda: The chief in consultation with his headmen and his personal advisers sets the agenda for kgotla discussions. Since independence civil servants often suggest to the chief items for the agenda that relate to their areas of responsibility. The head of the council water department may want to talk about the siting of new boreholes or the director of community development may request time to explain a new programme.

Most chiefs insist that persons wanting to hold a kgotla inform them of the substance of the issue to be discuss and decide on their own when the meeting should be held.[10] A politically astute chief can insure that persons promoting projects he favours and who show him sufficient respect are given particularly good position on the agenda.

In the past discussions revolved only around the issue for which the meeting was called. The right to public to place issues on the agenda in the form of new business has not until recently been recognized. While some kgotlas are now permitting this practice, it is not yet a common event.

Partisan politics: The kgotla is supposed to be non-partisan in the sense that the participants are not to identify themselves as members of a party or present issues in a partisan manner. People are expected to focus on issues and discuss them with reference to community concerns. Even elected officials avoid partisan attacks in the kgotla. Positions must be presented without reference to a party.

This is not to say that the kgotla has not been used as a forum for partisan politics. In fact, there seems to be an increasing tendency in this direction. The Minister of Agriculture and the Secretary General of the BDP has shown an uncanny inclination in the last two years to hold kgotlas on agricultural policy questions in areas where the opposition Botswana National Front has been engaging in intensive membership recruiting. The election of committees such as the village development committee and school board of governors are also examples of partisan politics in kgotla in the sense that different political parties present their own candidates and seek to mobilize support for them.

Attendance: In the past, all adult males were expected to attend kgotla meetings. Those who absented themselves without valid reasons were located and persuaded to attend, sometimes with force. In these circumstances, attendance was high.[11] Today things are different in several respects. As noted above, women, youth and minorities are now permitted to attend.[12]

Attendance is no longer required. The size of the crowd tends to vary depending on the topic and the size of village. In the Kgatleng, the biggest attendance is for discussions and events related to the initiation school. During the drought, women came out in large numbers for kgotlas dealing with drought relief labour. Issues relating to development projects often draw little more than those who are community activists of one type or another. Remoteness of the village is also a factor. Generally, the more remote ones with less employment available nearby will have a larger number attending.

29.3 THE FREEDOM SQUARE: ITS STRUCTURE

The concept of the 'freedom square' is not an easy one to define as it is known by different names in different countries. However, for the purpose of this paper, by freedom square we mean a political gathering where politicians and members of the public meet to discuss politics without constraint or fear of victimization. The terms freedom square and political rally may be used synonymously. Political parties usually sanction and organize freedom square meetings, but this need not be the case. Intra-party conflicts often surface publicly when a group of dissidents hold a series of freedom squares.

The freedom square meeting is not as old as that of the kgotla. It dates back to the 1960s where it originated as part of the anti-colonial struggle. Freedom squares were first organized by members of the Bechuanaland People's Party (BPP) [13] who had participated in freedom square meetings held by the South African liberation movements such as the African National Congress (ANC) and the Pan African Congress (PAC) in the 1950s. When they arrived in Bechuanaland they found that neither the colonial government nor the chiefs would allow them to use the kgotla. As a result, they had their meetings in beer halls and football grounds, which locations came to be called a freedom squares.[13]

The freedom involved was not just freedom from colonial rule but also the right to hold discussions not bound by the norms of the kgotla. In the view of the politicians they were communicating a message which involved rejection of the authority of the head of the kgotla, the chief. Thus they were not about to bound by his rules.

The Botswana Democratic Party (BDP) was not an exception to this generalization when it was formed in 1962. It was opposed to the chiefs and to promoting feelings of tribal solidarity. In some areas like Mochudi, the party did attempt to address kgotla meetings but the tribal authority refused to allow them to do so. The establishment of the freedom squares thus also became a means of reducing the influence of the chief on partisan politics. Surprisingly, the BDP on gaining control of the government in 1966 did not attempt to abolish the kgotla as an institution which had been used to thwart its rise to power. Instead they retained it side by side with the freedom square.

The freedom square has evolved as a distinctly different institution from the kgotla. This is not surprising given its anti-kgotla origins. On many dimensions the two types of community meeting are almost complete opposites of one another.

Formality: Unlike in the kgotla, there are no particular formalities that need to be observed in the freedom square. People are often addressed by first names. Members of the audience may speak with each other rather than listening to the speaker. Although originally harsh and abusive language was not common, these have become common features of freedom square in the 1980s. Perhaps this is due to intensification of party competition in the current decade.

This development has been of major concern to many in the public. The leaders of all the political parties will readily admit things are out of hand; however, they seem unwilling to discipline their followers. The general feeling is that the other party is the one which provokes the intemperance. All sides seem to feel that the practice of police tape recording political rallies, especially in the cities and big villages, is a good thing in that the speakers can thus be called upon later to defend what they have said.

Seating Arrangement: People sit or stand wherever they feel comfortable. Some just sit in their cars or on a bicycle. Some even perch in a tree. There is no 'pecking' order relative to age as in the kgotla.

Scheduling and announcing the meeting: Scheduling of political meetings has no priority in competition with other community meetings. Politicians hold their rallies where and when they think they can obtain a crowd. They do have to obtain a permit from the police in urban areas, and party leaders usually inform the headman in the rural areas. There can be as many political meetings as political parties want on a given day. This means it is possible to have more than one meeting in a village as long as each observes the specified distance apart required by law. It is not unusual for citizens and even politicians to move from one party meeting to another when two or more are held at the same time. There is no particular area in a village which is designated as a freedom square. It is an institution and not a place.

The parties inform citizens about meetings by sending trucks with loudspeakers around the community on the day of the rally. The only advance announcements come over the radio. The meetings often begin as much as an hour late and people in the audience come when it is convenient. Speakers and even the police who are assigned to the rally may arrive late.[14]

In the cities and large towns freedom squares are usually held on Saturday morning or Sunday afternoons. The Saturday morning sessions can be hurt by a funeral.

In the more remote rural areas political rallies are often held during the week. Members of parliament when they are on tours of kgotlas after a session of parliament will often hold a kgotla in the morning and then follow it in the afternoon with a freedom square.

Personal behaviour: Heckling is the order of the day. In many cases it is the member of an opposing party (to the one addressing the rally) who interferes and shouts at speakers. As early as 1969 the late P.G. Matante wrote a letter to the District Commissioner complaining that a police officer, Sergeant Nyepi heckled in the Northeast and disturbed a meeting addressed by the BPP. However, the ruling of both the District Commissioner and the Office of the President was that he was provoked into heckling.[15]

It is possible for the organizers of a rally to ask a person to stop excessive heckling and, if he refuses, they can ask the police to intervene by taking the culprit away. The party holding a rally is not, however, responsible for the behaviour of those attending. Anyone may tell a person to be quiet. Those who cannot tolerate criticisms to their parties may register their protest by walking away while the meeting is on. Although drinking of beer at these meetings is not encouraged, it is not uncommon for some people to come to the meeting drunk, and a few people may be seen drinking.

Music: Organizers of freedom squares consider choirs to be an important device for drawing a crowd. Whenever possible they like to have one or even several choirs which perform in between speakers. Although choirs have come to play an important role in the 1980s, there is evidence to suggest that even in the 1960s rallies began and ended with political songs often composed for the occasion.[16]

The lyrics of the songs praise the leader, tell of party victories and discredit other parties and individuals. They are set to traditional or religious tunes. At large rallies a number of party choirs may actually compete to give the best performance. It is not unusual for a choir from Gaborone to go to Francistown to boost the quality of a rally. Prominent politicians will sometimes even pay the bill for transport and food of a good choir to come to their freedom square.

In the BNF some party ideologues have voiced concern that the prominence given to choirs at party meetings is impeding the dissemination of the party programme.

Freedom of Speech: Generally, there are no limits on what can be said; however, this freedom can be limited by the fact that one can be convicted of using abusive language. A case in point is where, the Secretary General of Botswana National Front (BNF) was in 1980 charged for contravening section 93(i) of the Penal Code. The charge was that he had used abusive language against the Head of State when addressing a political rally in Serowe.[17]

The primary objective of every speaker is to build up ones own party and criticize the opposition. As a result, there is little in the way of an impartial presentation of the facts. Party slogans are echoed from time to time especially when it is felt that one has made a good point. Party leaders rue the absence of policy discussion in freedom squares, but for the most part audiences clearly prefer speakers who heap abuse on the opposition and glorify their own party.

Decisions: There is no group decision making in the sense that people are not expected to take a decision on a particular issue either through a consensus or a vote at the end of the rally. The party simply seeks to persuade individual listeners to decide to associate with it.

There have been occasions, however, where the opposition parties have proposed programmes in their freedom square meetings which have gained widespread popularity, forcing the BDP to decide to implement the idea. The most prominent was the BNF's call for free secondary education. When the top BDP leaders decided to act because of the gains the BNF was making, they did not even take time to consult the Ministry of Education about the feasibility of the change. They just announced the date of implementation. There is thus a sense in which popularity of a proposal in freedom squares can force government to make a decision it might otherwise resist.

Agenda: The only fixed agenda in freedom squares is the list of speakers, and even it may change depending on the mood of the audience. Speakers are sometimes assigned a topic, but this means little.

A favourite type of speaker for all parties is a recent convert from another party. They usually provide a ponderous chronicle of the devious intentions of the their former party colleagues that strains the imagination of even the loyal members of their new party.

Most freedom squares focus much of their attention on personal attacks on what opposing politicians have said and done. At best the purpose of the speeches is to give information supportive of the speaker's party. A lot of issues are covered during a rally, but most in no significant depth.

Partisan politics: Those who attend rallies do so out of an interest in political parties. Some of the top politicians make an attempt to rise above brutally partisan speeches, but this is only after a partisan tenor has been set by earlier speeches.

Attendance: Attendance at freedom squares tends to be greatest on the weekends before elections, particularly in the cities and larger towns.

Young people are much more likely to attend freedom squares than the kgotla. Persons over sixty are few in number and generally do not speak up as they find the behaviour of the speakers and the audience to be unacceptable.

There is a general sense that people come to be amused. Some politicians are crowd pleasers who can produce a good turnout. Hard hitting speakers like Lenyeletse Koma, Ray Molomo and Danial Kwelegobe are almost certain to draw a good crowd. Party dissidents generally bring out a crowd because their attacks on the party leaders are certain to be titillating. Needless to say the party leaders like President Masire and Kenneth Koma draw a crowd when their presence is advertised.

The significance of this amusement factor is reflected in the fact that there is no correlation between size of crowd and the number of votes a candidate receives. Willie Seboni for instance attracted more people at some of his rallies in 1984 when he ran as an independent than the total number of votes he received. People came because they knew Seboni would provide plenty of entertainment with his attacks on top BDP leaders.

29.4 PUBLIC PERCEPTIONS OF THE KGOTLA AND FREEDOM SQUARE

In the Democracy Project mass survey several questions were asked concerning public perceptions of the kgotla and freedom square as mechanisms of political communication. In this section an evaluation is made of the responses from this survey. In particular we are concerned with whether the public considers these institutions to be effective sources of information and the extent to which it looks to either as a means to influence politicians.

Political information

Politicians and civil servants like to believe that the whole process of decision-making related to village development operates with reference to the people's discussion in the kgotla. Initiation of policies and projects comes as the result of discussions in which councillors and the members of parliament solicit their constituents views relative to the problems and needs of the village. These elected politicians then report back to the villagers on what their respective bodies decide to do. When it comes time for policy decisions to be implemented, civil servants hold meetings to discuss with the community how a project will be carried out. This means that the community is constantly informed throughout the decision making process. If this process is carried out properly and effectively, there will be two-way communication.

The politicians also see the freedom square as a place of two-way communication. They inform the public about their programmes and their candidates and attack those of other parties. They also believe they learn much about what the people are really thinking from the often heated debates in freedom squares.[18]

There are, however, other forms of communication which the government and politicians use to inform the public. The government radio and the various newspapers summarize the debates and decisions in parliament and local councils. Development projects usually are also announced through these media as are the activities of political parties.

In our mass survey we sought to find out how the public assessed the kgotla and the freedom square as sources of information relative to the mass media. Despite some claims from the politicians that they always report back on their legislative activities, Table 1 demonstrates that the radio and newspapers are much more important sources of political information than the kgotla. We assume that the responses of 'politicians', 'public meetings', and 'civil servants' were most likely indicating that the respondent received his or her information in kgotla, though some may have received it through some other means. The last response 'neighbour', would appear to be derivative from either the mass media or the kgotla.

From the survey we see that the radio is by far the most important (51% to 59%) on all three information dimensions. The kgotla at maximum on the other hand is relied on by about ten per cent of the community. It is interesting that newspapers, which can only be used by those who are literate, are almost as important as the kgotla as sources of information.

Table 1: Primary source of information (percentage)*

	Parliament	Council	Development programmes
Radio	58,8	51,3	57,2
Newspaper	8,6	9,0	9,8
Politician	7,4	8,2	5,2
Public meeting	2,7	4,1	3,2
Civil servants	0,8	2,2	3,7
Neighbour	7,3	8,1	8,0

$$N = 1279 \qquad N = 1275 \qquad N = 1275$$

It would thus appear that the mass public does not consider the kgotla a place in which information on government decisions is passed down to it. Since there is not much reporting of council decisions on the radio, this means that councillors are not perceived as performing their role of reporting back on the activities of their bodies or of development projects affecting the local community through local kgotla meetings.

Freedom squares on the other hand do appear to have a significant information function for the mass public. As indicated in Table 2, the public uses them more than the radio and newspaper when it comes learning about party issue positions and party activities. Sub-group analysis of this data shows that political rallies were particularly useful for those with a Standard VII education or less and for those in medium size villages, like Moshupa and Gabane. In short, those with less access to the mass media find freedom squares particularly useful. In the case of freedom squares we can say that face-to-face communication is performing an important function.

Table 2: Primary source of information (percentage)*

	Party issue positions	Party activities
Newspaper	10,9	9,2
Radio	11,1	10,5
Rallies	30,8	27,7
Politicians	3,8	3,9
Neighbours	8,9	15,2
Other	1.0	0.3

$$N = 1205 \qquad\qquad N = 1203$$

* The table does not include persons indicating no source.

The above data would seem to suggest that the freedom square is much more effective from the public's point of view in conveying the information it is supposed to convey than the kgotla. On the other hand, people have an alternative source to the kgotla in the form of the radio which they both trust and does provide the information they desire. It may well be that the kgotla is only useful for informing the people who are actually involved in development projects (particularly drought relief) about what is going to happen. If this is so, the kgotla may not so much provide information which informs citizens as it serves as a means of bureaucratic supervision and control.

Political influence

Another way to look at the kgotla and the freedom square is in terms of the extent to which the public influences the politicians through these two types of public meetings. By influence we mean the ability of a person or a group to induce another to do what he, she or it otherwise would not do.[19]

In this instance, the public either through the kgotla or freedom square should be able to affect the intentions of politicians. In an attempt to determine how citizens used their influence on politicians, we asked politicians whether the kgotla and the freedom square were helpful in gaining information from the public about their needs. Their overwhelming response was that they (politicians) took the information they received from both the kgotla and freedom square to their legislative bodies and sought to take action on the matters their constituents brought up. The matters they reported working on were, however, for the most part at the level of registering complaints with the bureaucracy.[20]

To see whether the public had a similar perception, namely that politicians were following up on their needs, we asked our respondents if they see the kgotla or the freedom square as useful in communicating their opinions to the politicians. The survey showed that slightly over seventy-five per cent of the population do not consider either the kgotla or freedom square helpful in this regard. Most of the public thus seems to be fairly cynical that stating their opinions in these two public fora has an impact on the politicians.

Why this difference between the perception of the public and the politicians? With regard to the kgotla several factors may offer some explanation. First, the public demands are often for things that the councillors or members of parliament can do very little about, say to provide jobs in the rural areas. Second, councillors and members of parliament submit their requests for specific action to their respective bodies in the form of questions or advisory motions, only to be told in most cases that nothing can be done until the next development plan. Thus a number of years can transpire before a response is given to the village. In the meantime, the villagers may become so frustrated that they are not prepared to see the connection between their request and the government action.

In the case of the freedom square, the politicians are simply interested in hearing what the public thinks about their parties. Therefore they feel they have done their job if they listen and respond to the rally audience. On the other hand, many of the public tend to see freedom square meetings as at best a time of abusive language and entertainment. Most do not see their attendance as offering an opportunity to communicate with their political leaders.

In preparing our mass survey, we had suspected that the kgotla would be among the more likely mechanisms in the public mind for influencing politicians. Therefore we included it in a list with two other forms of grass-roots influence on politicians, namely working with a group to contact politicians or asking an influential person in the community like a chief to help. We asked which of these was most likely to be effective. For the sample as a whole around thirty-five per cent chose the kgotla. The one area where the kgotla is still favoured by a slight majority (51%) of the population is in the cattle-post areas where minority populations, i.e. the Bakgalagadi and the Basarwa predominate.

29.5 THE KGOTLA AND FREEDOM SQUARE COMPARED

Both the kgotla and the freedom square offer settings in which the local communities engage in discussion of political issues with their leaders. Each however only performs the communication function with respect to particular groups and particular concerns. Neither conforms to the classic idea of a town or village meeting in which all members of the community participate with an equal voice. They are not evidence of direct democracy. Rather each type of meeting performs a specific political communication function.

The kgotla is more for people who are older in age, particularly those above forty, and males. Interestingly, while many Batswana do not think minority groups have a right to speak up in tribal kgotlas, the minorities look to kgotla meetings, probably those in their local villages, as places where they are most likely to have an influence on civil servants and politicians.

The issues discussed in kgotla tend to relate to the implementation of government programmes in the community in which the discussion is taking place. The kgotla, however, is not a place where the public is informed about significant policy decisions. Only about a quarter of the rural population perceives the kgotla as a means by which they can influence politicians. Overall then it would seem that the kgotla is a place dominated by civil servants and hence represents downward communication. Effective chiefs can to some extent use it to limit central government control of local affairs. The one place where the local population can use the kgotla to influence policy is during the implementation process.

The freedom square is a forum in which the youth predominate, that is those under forty. There is a highly visceral tone to much of the speech and political opponents are treated in a very derogatory manner. Many come to the freedom square for entertainment; however, the people do look to the freedom square as a place where they can find out about the positions and activities of the various parties.

While the public does not see the freedom square as a means of influencing politicians, there is some evidence that the BDP does pay close attention to positive grass-roots reactions to opposition party policy proposals. Some at least are adopted as policy to undercut potential electoral challenges. Also, freedom squares are the only forum in which those without radios and lacking in literacy have a chance to be exposed to political conflict on national policy issues. In short, while the freedom square has many defects, particularly in the eyes of the older population, it does function more as a two-way communication process than the kgotla.

29.6 CONCLUSION

With much of the population having little or no literacy and the mass media only beginning to develop, the kgotla and freedom square serve as critical means of communication in Botswana's democracy. They also provide for a face-to-face contact between politicians and citizens which is missing in many Third World countries. There is no doubt that for the foreseeable future these community meetings will remain important for political communication, particularly in the rural areas.

We must admit, however, that the overall picture that emerges from this analysis is of the kgotla and freedom square as institutions where a limited segment of the public actually becomes involved in two-way communication which has some utility to both participants and their rulers. In the kgotla community activists can inform themselves about government programmes and they may be able to stop programmes which they dislike. In the freedom square, attentive members of the public can gain some perception of what the parties are thinking about political issues. It is also a forum where politicians find out about basic community feelings. We can cautiously argue that these two institutions have some upward communication.

Both institutions could become more effective instruments for informing the public and for permitting the public to communicate with their leaders. Three problems areas need to be considered:

a)   In the case of the kgotla, there is a real problem of the lack of education of most of the participants. According to our survey, 80% of those attending kgotlas have less than Standard VII and 50% have had no formal education at all. The problem in this context is that those addressing the meeting speak over the people's heads. We need to ask ourselves just exactly what kinds of information can be presented and how must it be presented so that the people will understand? Is it really possible for most of the people in the kgotla to understand and react to the policy proposals suggested for such programmes as the National Conservation Strategy?

b)   In the freedom square, many in the public find the rough and tumble language to be offensive. In addition, the personalistic character of much of the discussion, leaves the audience with little idea of what are the differences between the parties on policy issues. However, our survey of politicians indicated that they were not prepared to accept any further legal limitations placed on their freedom to speak. About all that they would accept is that the parties themselves should try to school their public speakers on the need to clean up their

228

language and to speak more to the issues than to personalities.

c) A problem in both the freedom square and the kgotla is that politicians and civil servants make very long speeches that leave little time for citizens to ask questions. In both types of community meeting, it is not unusual for the audience to be only given time to ask a very few questions. Or, if adequate time is provided, it is only after the audience is exhausted by several long speeches. There is a need to think about means by which the public's question periods can be extended. The politicians can only know the public mind if they give people in kgotla and the freedom square ample opportunity to ventilate their grievances. A more effective two-way communication system can be set in motion through extending the question time.

ENDNOTES

1   Ball, A. *Modern Politics and Government* (London: The Macmillan Press Limited, 1979) pp. 132-135; Noppen, D. *Consultation and Non-Commitment: Planning with the People in Botswana* (Leiden: African Studies Centre, 1982).

2   Among the recent works on the importance of the kgotla, see Odell, M. 'Local Government: Tradition and Modern Role of the Village Kgotlas,' in Picard, L. (ed) *The Evolution of Modern Botswana: Politics and Modern Development in Southern Africa* (London: Rex Collings, 1985); Tordoff, W. 'Local Administration in Botswana,' *Public Administration and Development*, Vol. 8, No. 2, 1988; Noppen, D. *Consultation and Non-Commitment*, p. 130.

3   Rural Sociology Unit, 'Local Government and the Institution of the Kgotla,' Gaborone: Government Printer, 1979 p. 4.

4   See L.D. Ngcongco's paper in this volume.

5   Ibid.

6   Rural Sociology Unit, 'Local Government,' p. 4.

7   See Ngcongco's paper above in this volume.

8   Odell, 'Local Government,' p. 65.

9   Murray, A. Nengwekhulu, H. and Ramsay, J. 'The Formation of Political Parties' in *The Birth of Botswana*, edited by Morton, F. and Ramsay, J. (Gaborone: Longman Botswana, 1987) p. 172.

10 One respondent refused to call a kgotla meeting for the Minister of Local Government and Lands because the Minister would not disclose what he wanted to talk about.

11 It is not very clear as to whether before independence all adults were forced or persuaded to attend kgotla meetings. However, a male adult at Kopong complained during the kgotla meeting that attendance was very low since independence because the meetings are no longer compulsory.

12 Morton and Ramsay, *The Birth of Botswana*, p. 175.

13 Ibid., p. 175.

14 During our research we attended political rallies where members of the police arrived late and delayed the proceedings. Amongst them were rallies held on 25 and 26 June 1988 at Maru-a-pula and Jinja respectively.

15 Picard, L. A. 'Bureaucrats, Elections and Political Control: National Politics,

the District Administration and the Multiparty System in Botswana' in *The Evolution of Modern Botswana*, p. 185.

16 Morton and Ramsay, *The Birth of Botswana*, p. 175.
17 *Daily News*, September 2 1980, No. 168.
18 Personal observation from attending several freedom squares in 1988.
19 Dahl, R. *Modern Political Analysis* (Englewood Cliffs, NJ: Prentice Hall, 1976) p. 30.
20 See *Daily News*, October 19, 1987, No. 198, and October 26, 1987, No. 203.

DISCUSSION

Chief Seepapitso disagreed with Mr Lekorwe's claims that:
a) kgotla administers flogging instead of corporal punishment.
b) the attendants of the kgotla cannot change or add to the agenda; and
c) there are restrictions on women and minorities participating in kgotla discussions.

With regard to Linchwe's idea, mentioned earlier, of recording kgotla meetings, Seepaptiso said in his area recording of kgotla proceedings started as far back as 1901. He agreed with Lekorwe that the freedom square atmosphere is generally rough when contrasted with the kgotla.

Mr Mongwa (BPP) said Tswana tradition was similar to that of many peoples in Africa. He said the impediment to the present chief and kgotla traditions is government interference. He complained that chiefs have been turned into civil servants but need to be made independent.

Mr K. Sebele (Permanent Secretary, MLGL) agreed that the kgotla was central to rural development programmes in Botswana and that it is better than the freedom square.

Professor Sharma (Politics, University of Botswana) said since independence the kgotla has been used by politicians and government officials to pass information but not to receive it from the people. He said it is important not to use the kgotla for partisan activities.

Mr K. Morake (MP, Minister of Education) said the kgotla is and has always been a political forum. He said this is one important traditional institution which should be retained.

Mr R. Molomo (BDP) said all parties are permitted to use or address the kgotla but on matters of development and not for purposes of campaigning in a partisan way.

Mr Matsheng (Politics, University of Botswana) said the kgotla was unaccommodating for the inexperienced youth and women who are often shouted down when they make mistakes. He however agreed that the freedom square was even more limited in its usefulness.

Mr Magang (BDP) said as an MP he uses the kgotla for two-way communication.

SECTION XIV
THE BUREAUCRACY

30 Civil service consultation: an examination of three cases

Seeiso D. Liphuko[1]

> Elections should not be the only time for dialogue between Government and people. Hence when Government formulated its proposals for changing the traditional system of land-use and tenure, an issue of concern to every Motswana, Government decided to consult the people. (Minister L. Makgekgenene, foreword for the Consultation report on TGLP).

30.1 INTRODUCTION

An evaluation of consultation exercises would basically entail an examination of their nature and whether their objectives were in fact achieved. A broader and more relevant question is: Were the consultation exercises, which have been carried out from time to time, genuine attempts by government through the civil service to enhance the nation's democratic principles? This latter concern will be the focus of this paper. In my view successful consultation means that public views, even those which are fundamentally different from government, are considered for incorporation in the policy, projects or programmes being formulated. Such a process of consultation is a genuine reflection of the principles of democracy at work.

Before addressing this subject a word needs to be said on the role of the civil service in the policy making process. The civil service is neither monolithic nor homogenous. It is constituted of a plethora of different individuals with different social, political, economic and educational backgrounds and beliefs. They however all function in a hierarchical structure which operates and thrives upon initiating policies and carrying them out with enthusiasm, drive, originality and circumspection. The result is a rich variety of different ideas and approaches by the various ministries and their subdivisions.

It goes without saying that the consultative process initiated by one ministry or department will differ in many respects from that used by another. However, all consider consultation to be necessary not only because it is democratic but because it is a critical part of our culture with respect to how those in government are to behave.

231

30.2 THE CONSULTATION PROCESS

Consultation with the public almost always begins with consultations within the confines of government. These initial dialogues serve to coordinate the concerns of the various ministries which will be involved in implementing the policy being developed. Thus in carrying out the consultations relative to the Tribal Grazing Land Policy (TGLP), various sections of the Ministry of Agriculture worked with a number of divisions of the Ministry of Local Government and Lands as well as the Department of Water Affairs in the Ministry of Mineral Resources.

These intra-governmental discussions are a regular part of any policy formulation. When it is determined that the programme is likely to affect people's lives fundamentally, the civil service invariably moves to conduct some form of grassroots consultation.

Government's consultation processes neither originated with TGLP nor will they cease with the National Conservation Strategy (NCS). This aspect of decision making is basic to Botswana's development policy. For instance, there is a long standing commitment to a comprehensive consultation in preparation for national development plans. This process begins with the Ministry of Finance first consulting all ministries and departments including the local authorities, which in turn solicit the views of village leaders through district conferences. Based on the resulting information, which details the public's concerns, plus relevant data on the state of the economy, government sets general goals.

A second set of consultations are then conducted throughout all institutions based on these specific goals. Only then do ministries and departments prepare their sector chapters for the national plan. Thus, except in so far as there are economic constraints, the final contents of each plan arise from a comprehensive consultation structure.

In order to understand the specifics of the consultation process three specific consultations will be examined in the discussion which follows. They are the Self Help Housing Agency (SHHA), TGLP, and NCS.

30.3 THE SELF-HELP HOUSING AGENCY

SHHA seeks to provide inexpensive housing to low income groups in urban areas. Out-migration by people from the rural into the urban areas in expectation of non-existent job opportunities has resulted in a constant and ever-increasing tide of people into squatter areas of Botswana's four major towns. As a result of government's concern for the shelter of these people, it adopted the self-help approach as a major element of its housing policy in the early seventies. Programmes were established in four cities — Gaborone, Francistown, Lobatse and Selebi-Phikwe. The Agency provides serviced plots for new houses and upgrades existing residences in squatter areas.

To improve the operational efficiency of the scheme, SHHA staff hold meetings, often over weekends, with their clients. Discussions deal with the Certificate of

Rights of SHHA participants and the rights and duties which derive from it. Such discussions have been essential for the establishment of a climate of opinion in which plot holders can claim services and local SHHA officials in return can collect the service levy and exercise their right to repossession on failure to build a house. These meetings are also used by local authority staff to consult on a wide range of subjects, often not directly related to the responsibilities of the agency.

In 1983 the Ministry of Local Government and Lands undertook a more extensive consultation in connection with a general evaluation of SHHA. The evaluation report states that attendance of the communities at these meetings was often below expectations. In Woodhall (Lobatse), Monarch (Francistown), Botshabelo (Selebi-Phikwe) less than 60% of the intended beneficiaries attended. At all the Gaborone settlements (Naledi, Bontleng, Ext. 14 and Broadhurst) in excess of 75% were present.

The report does not indicate any specific reason for this difference. What can be learnt from these figures is that people, even when directly affected, do not always view particular government initiatives with the same concern as officials. This may be because government does not always explain its intentions very clearly, and as a result people concern themselves with more pressing issues at hand.

The evaluation exercise explored views of respondents regarding the problems facing their households. The main problems mentioned were related not to housing but the respondent's condition of poverty. Only 3% mentioned poor plot services; 6%, poor housing; and 3%, the physical condition of the area.

That problems remain can be seen by the fact that more than 76% of those responding felt that improvements were necessary. And more than two-thirds of the plot holders in all areas, except Old Naledi (Gaborone) said they would be prepared to pay more than they do now if they were given the improvements they wanted. This clearly shows some confidence and attachment to the SHHA areas. This consultation also indicates the overall success of the policy from the point of view of the beneficiaries.

30.4 TGLP CONSULTATION

The TGLP consultation was, until the consultation on the National Conservation Strategy, the most comprehensive of its kind. The objective of the exercise focused on improving specific aspects of implementation rather than development of the policy itself.

Beginning in 1971 the government became particularly concerned about the severity of the overgrazing problem. This was also emphasized in a symposium of the Botswana Society in that year. In the years that followed civil servants and consultants evolved TGLP to stop overgrazing, promote greater equality of income in the rural areas and facilitate growth and commercialization of the livestock industry on a sustained basis. Government Paper No. 2 of 1975, which laid out TGLP, called for a consultation process which would inform the public of the policy, encourage discussion, provide feedback of this discussion to the implementing organs of government, and instruct citizens on how they could benefit from the policy.

In recognition of the comprehensive nature of this consultation exercise and the fact that government was aware that the implications of this policy would be wide ranging, affecting the lives of almost every Motswana in some way or another, it mounted its national consultation exercise. The body which was set up to coordinate this exercise included the relevant ministries (Local Government and Lands, Agriculture, and Finance), the University of Botswana, the then Botswana Extension College and other institutions.

The process itself included four phases:

a) Kgotla meetings led by cabinet ministers which took place in August of 1975.

b) Workshops, seminars and briefings for government officers which were conducted between August 1975 and February 1976.

c) A series of ten radio programmes were listened to for 5 weeks in June and July of 1976 by local village groups, organized and monitored by civil servants residing in the area.

d) Subsequent analysis of responses from the campaign were directed to the land use planning process.

The Radio Learning Groups, (RLG) were the primary source of information obtained from the consultation process. RLG leaders were trained to fill and return report forms at the end of each of the study sessions, reporting on the responses of group members to various aspects of the subject discussed in the evening's radio programme. The campaign set a target figure of 4000 RLG's across the country. Although this target was not achieved, the consultation was by all standards a very comprehensive one. A total of 3510 leaders were trained; about 90.5% sent in one or more report forms; 49.5% sent in at least 9 report forms. The exercise reached 85,300 people equally divided between men and women. About 47% of the participants were small farmers; about 46% claimed not to have any cattle.

The campaign was not without its problems. The process would have gone better had the nation been informed of the problems that the lack of a rural land policy created. There should also have been a consultation as to the need for a policy once there was recognition that a problem existed. It is interesting to note that the primary cause for the formulation of the policy, that is the conservation of grass resources, was not regarded by most respondents during the campaign as a problem. In spite of these weaknesses, the campaign did influence subsequent implementation of the policy. Two illustrations will suffice. With regard to conservation, the report on the consultation concluded 'they (RLGs) seemed more worried about making a living now than about trying to conserve the grazing for future use'. It was therefore recommended that the Ministry of Agriculture should develop 'teachable methods of conservation'. This education process has been a major activity of the Agricultural Resources Board and the Extension Staff.

Three quarters of RLGs supported exclusive grazing rights in commercial and communal areas. There was, however, concern about the implication of exclusive rights. It was therefore recommended that, 'the granting of exclusive leasehold rights is in general acceptable but will likely require further refinement in detail and should be proceeded on with care in the communal areas'. The final implementation of the policy granted exclusive rights in the commercial ranches but not in communal areas. Because these latter areas, which include most rural grazing, were not affected, the policy itself could not reverse much of the degradation of land that was occurring.

While the policy itself could have been more effective, there was real consultation on the part of government. This process undoubtedly enhanced democratic principles. It could be argued, however, that consultation exercises on issues of such major national importance should first determine if the public shares government's concerns relative to a particular problem. If it does, the next stage could then be consultation on feasible policy options. If little recognition of the problem exists, the primary policy thrust should be to educate citizens prior to formulation of appropriate policies.

30.5 THE NCS CONSULTATION

The NCS consultation sought to overcome the limitations of the TGLP exercise. It covered about 24 months and included a wide range of institutions and persons across the nation. Its purpose was to consult all the strata of the nation on the problems, solutions and the policy to be formulated. Government was determined to achieve this very ambitious goal. The primary foci of the consultation were various government organizations, the private sector including NGO's, and the public at large.

The consultation within government was carried out through the normal inter-ministerial committee structures which concern themselves with matters relating to natural resources conservation or the environment in general, i.e. the Inter-Ministerial Environment Sub-Group, the Natural Resources Technical Committee and the Rural Development Council. Outside of central government, those consulted included churches, journalists, local governments, NGOs, district conservation boards, and the trade unions. Representatives of these groups were invited to seminars and workshops organized by the Botswana Society on behalf of government or by the Department of Town and Regional Planning itself. Some of these groups then held conferences and meetings which NCS staff members addressed.

Members of the public were invited to a series of kgotla meetings where following explanations of the purpose of the consultation by government staff, they were asked about their concerns for the environment.

The Department of Town and Regional Planning also initiated a more scientific public opinion poll which covered 3000 households in villages, cattle posts and crop areas. Respondents expressed particular concern about overgrazing, deforestation, soil erosion, fuel wood shortage, pollution, wildlife and veld products. As a result, these problems became the main focus of the Conservation Strategy. Policy makers then built possible solution packages for these various concerns, and a Public Discussion Campaign was undertaken to seek citizen reactions to each package.

What was evident in this consultation process was that the objectives of the process were met and the public's understanding and awareness of the implications of natural resources exploitation and of government concerns were enhanced.

As a result of the consultation of NGOs, the government became aware that while those concerned with natural resources are making a significant contribution to the conservation effort, they lacked an institution which could mobilize them into the mainstream of the conservation effort. These groups at the village level were numerous, including village development committees, farmers committees, parent teachers associations, youth clubs, Boy Scouts, Girl Guides, churches, burial societies. To mobilize all these groups, government has take the rather bold step of promoting the establishment of an appropriate non-governmental institution. The new NGO, provisionally (until National Assembly ratification) called the Natural Resources Trust of Botswana, will assist village NGOs in seeking funding and manpower, enhancing conservation awareness, implementing village originated projects, and promoting applied research at village level.

30.6 CONCLUSION

Certain aspects of the consultations we have discussed should be noted. First, the dichotomy between government and the civil service is somewhat academic in terms of policy formulation. The political establishment and the civil service are very closely interrelated. Both participate in the formulation of the policies with regard to which consultation takes place. The decision to consult can come from either. In the case of TGLP it was the politicians in cabinet who made the decision to consult, while civil servants for the most part formulated the policy. On the other hand, with the NCS the civil service decided to initiate the consultation but then obtained political approval to do so from the cabinet.

Second, consultation exercises are not consciously intended to enhance the democratic process. The SHHA consultation was specifically intended to educate beneficiaries as to their rights and obligations; the TGLP exercise was intended to provide the public the opportunity to have an input into the implementation of that policy; and the NCS discussions were intended to influence problem identification, policy formulation and successful implementation. All these efforts have enhanced, however, the principles of democracy in Botswana. People have become aware that part of policy development and implementation is the solicitation of their views.

Third, the consultations provide effective guidance to government on how to proceed with specific issues of policy formulation and/or implementation. The result is a policy which is tailored to public needs. Some caution should be exercised in interpreting the opinions reported. They are representative of the respondents actually surveyed. In many cases only a small portion of the citizenry actually attends the meetings which are called.

Fourth, every consultation is directed at a selected part of the entire population. For instance, only the low-income groups in the urban areas were consulted on matters related to SHHA. That some or even the majority of people are not interested, and thus not consulted, on a particular policy does not mean the objective of the relevant consultation exercise has not been achieved. The objective is to improve policy implementation, not to tell the politicians which policies to adopt.

Fifth, on the part of the people who are consulted and respond either positively or negatively, there is generally the feeling that government is more sympathetic to their involvement. It could be suggested that consultation in this context enhances the feeling that democracy is being seen to be done. Conversely, where such consultation is desired and does not occur, sections of the public may conclude that the government is not being sufficiently democratic.

ENDNOTES

1   This paper in no way presents the views of civil service. Rather it is a personal statement based on my experience in the Ministry of Local Government and Lands.

31 The bureaucracy and democracy in Botswana

Mpho G. Molomo

31.1 INTRODUCTION

Regular elections in Botswana have convinced many commentators that the country is a promising example of a political system committed to an orderly and rational political process, a regard for fundamental human rights, and democratic participation. The aim of this paper is not to underscore the eulogy the country has received, but to put our democracy under scrutiny. The essential concern of this paper is to outline the importance of the bureaucracy in facilitating the realization of democracy in Botswana.

Most commentators regardless of perspective see bureaucracy as an essentially undemocratic institution. Weber for instance labels bureaucracy a 'steel-hard cage' which is not easily accessible for the vast majority of the population.[1] Marx sees it as 'undemocratic because bureaucrats are not accountable to the mass of the population affected by their decisions'.[2] The aim of this paper is to examine the impact of this quality of bureaucracy on Botswana's practice of democracy.

This analysis will concentrate on citizen participation in the decision making process. Such participation is important in our democracy, more so that our government is based on puso ya batho ka batho (government of the people by the people).

While there are various forms of citizen participation in politics, attention will be directed at three forms:

a)   participation in the decision making processes which provide control over economic resources and political institutions;

b)   consultation in which the views of the population are aggregated and then shaped into constituent elements of public policy; and

c)   informing the people about decisions taken in their behalf.[3]

For purposes of this paper the bureaucracy consists of senior officers in the civil service (including police and military personnel), parastatals and the private sector. These are the persons who direct the formulation and implementation of public policy.

31.2 THE BUREAUCRACY AND THE COLONIAL STATE

An understanding of bureaucratic institutions in post-colonial Botswana is rooted in the developments which took place during the colonial period. The British Protectorate in Botswana began as 'dual rule', a process in which the colonial administration operated alongside traditional political institutions. In a short time, this system was overturned for 'indirect rule' wherein the British sought to control the local population through the chiefs. Under indirect rule the colonial government made little attempt to develop local administration and institutions. The result was that 'independent kingdoms became bureaucratic extensions of imperial rule'.[4]

British colonial rule characteristically developed elaborate bureaucratic structures, particularly where there were white settler populations. The bureaucracy involved the creation of a civil service, police and military. These institutions were designed to take care of the daily administration of the colonies as well as maintaining law and order. At independence they were inherited by the newly independent states of Africa and Asia.

As Alavi and Saul note, the 'bureaucratic-military oligarchies'[5] created a problem for the newly independent countries of Africa and Asia. They had an 'overdeveloped' state apparatus. Propagated during the colonial period, these institutions were tailored for metropolitan interests of subordinating their colonies to the dictates of their imperial rule. At political independence the weak and less articulated local ruling classes were unable to cope with these complex structures.[6]

More often than not, Alavi argues, when the new post-colonial leaders tried to govern through these structures developed for colonial subordination, tension and conflicting interests often emerged. The tension and conflict was said to result in political instability and military coups. In fact the real problem was the persistence of institutions developed in the colonial period.

Alavi's formulation of the 'overdeveloped' state has been critiqued by both Leys, and Ziemann and Lanzendorfer. Leys argues that the colonial bureaucracy did not subordinate the indigenous ruling classes but rather 'pre-capitalist social formations to the imperatives of colonial capitalism'.[7]

Ziemann and Lanzendorfer question the validity of the 'over-developed' state.

They contend that Alavi's argument is wrongly conceived 'when he maintains that, with independence, the colonial structure is separated from the metropolitan' influence and control.[8] Their position is that the end of colonial rule brought indigenous political leaders while the economic institutions of colonialism remained intact. In sum, there was neo-colonialism.

In Botswana no developed, let alone overdeveloped, bureaucracy existed at political independence.[9] The colonial state was characterized by administrative neglect in that little was done to foster local institutions. Most important was the absolute neglect of the educational system. The consequence was that Batswana did not possess the requisite skills to take over their public service. Despite pressures by Batswana for localization, the bureaucracy up until the end of the colonial period remained predominantly white. Picard writes;

> Within the civil service in 1962 there were only four Batswana (out of a total of 155) in the administrative and professional grades, fifteen (out of 260) at the technical grade, and only twenty-two (out of 182) at the middle level executive grade. Even at the clerical level the government continued the widespread use of European stenographers and typists . . .'[10]

Strong demands for localization made as early as the 1950s were turned down on the grounds that it would 'result in the lowering of the efficiency of the service'.[11] This emphasis on efficiency became the key word in the development of the Botswana bureaucracy. It assured selective recruitment as well as keeping most of the people in society out of the policy making process. Picard comments;

> Until the eve of independence gradualism remained official colonial policy, and the maintenance of standards became a code for the continued expatriate dominance in the civil service. By the end of 1964, expatriates filled 27 per cent of the total civil service establishment of 2 575 positions, occupying 82 per cent of the executive-level positions and above.[12]

After the attainment of political independence, state structures expanded rapidly. A full-fledged bureaucracy began to develop. The dominance of the civil service by expatriates continued, especially in the technical professional ranks where the educational neglect of the colonial period had its most profound impact.

31.3 BUREAUCRACY AND PARTICIPATION IN POST-COLONIAL BOTSWANA

The central bureaucracy has sought to control participation of the public in decision making since independence.[13] The result is that there is little meaningful interaction between civil servants and the public. Thus the Democracy Project survey indicated that a minuscule 3.8 per cent of the sample hear about development projects through meetings with civil servants. The predominant means is the radio (58.2 per cent).

In order to document this lack of public involvement with the government policy making process, the experience of several well publicised consultations will be briefly considered. They are the ones which took place as part of the development of the Tribal Grazing Land Policy (TGLP) and the Self Help Housing Agency (SHHA).

TGLP

Notwithstanding the fact that TGLP was conceived in an expatriate written report, it is one of the most cited examples in Botswana of public consultation and popular participation in the shaping of government policy. The underlying assumption of TGLP is that traditional forms of tenure are not consistent with modern husbandry. To correct the problem government decided to introduce a leasehold system where individuals or syndicates could fence their land and exercise private control. The expectation was that private control would result in the protection of land from over-grazing and that land would be used productively. Since this policy change involved traditional farming practices, it was bound to affect the majority of Batswana. Therefore, a nationwide campaign was mounted in which citizen participation was solicited through radio listening groups and addresses of public officials in kgotla.

For this analysis the critical consideration is the quality and the type of participation which took place. TGLP was originated from the top of the bureaucracy and filtered down to the bottom of society. The participation of the public was merely token in quality. Some minor changes were made as result of the consultation process. These changes should have been incorporated at the beginning. For instance, the programme was not implemented in the Kgatleng and North East District because there was no available land.

The massive consultation that was mounted did not address the most basic issue of TGLP: Should Botswana privatize part of its heretofore communally held lands? This is where the consultation process should have begun. Other issues were also not addressed.[14] Government was asked to spell out clearly the benefits which the poor farmers would receive. The only response of public officials was that this matter would be considered later. The issue of dual rights was raised, that is, whether TGLP leaseholders could still graze their cattle in the communal areas. Government has yet to decide on a policy. There was concern about the danger of dispossessing some people of their land. Again, no policy direction was forthcoming.

In sum, the TGLP consultation did not give the people a chance to say whether they wanted the policy, nor did the government feel obliged to answer the questions many communities raised. The changes which were made could for the most part have been made without the consultation. Effectively government was attempting to obtain symbolic approval for programmes it had already decided to adopt.

SHHA

Consultation has also played an important role in policy making related to the Self Help Housing Agency (SHHA). The process of urbanization has resulted in a growing concentration of low income persons in Botswana's cities. Government restricted most of its housing responsibilities to providing housing for public sector employees.

The unemployed and wage earning parts of the community had little alternative but to erect squatter camps. SHHA was instituted in 1973 out of recognition that something had to be done about this growing squatter population. SHHA, apart from the fact that it is run by the town councils, represents one of the most centralized programmes in this country.

While government has provided some of the funding for this programme, much of the financing has come from foreign donors. United States Aid for International Development has generously contributed infrastructure, technical assistance, and building material loans; the Canadian International Development Agency generously covered infrastructure and supervisory costs of Old Naledi squatter upgrading; the United Nations Overseas Development Administration also took care of part of the infrastructure and supervisory costs; and the European Development Fund funded the reticulation of the water system. These agencies concentrated their aid on infrastructure and technical expertise which families and communities did not have the resources to provide for themselves. The participation of donor agencies in Botswana's housing project has been phenomenal.

While SHHA has scored a notable success in providing low income housing, it is open to criticism for being overly influenced by donor agencies and reflecting limited local participation in its formulation. Public meetings which SHHA holds are basically on the operational efficiency of the scheme rather than the formulation of the programme. The meetings are designed to educate the people on the rights, privileges and duties of a new form of tenure that has been introduced - the Certificate of Rights.[15]

31.4 THE BUREAUCRACY AND ELECTED OFFICIALS

Democracy as it is practised in the modern world is based on representation where political leaders are elected into office for a constitutionally specified term on the strength of policies they sell to the electorate. Once in power politicians are supposed to formulate policies and the rest of the state apparatus, namely the civil service, police and military, implement these policies as formulated. This does not happen in Botswana. Public policy is instead formulated by the bureaucracy.

Bureaucratic dominance in the state of Botswana has its origins in the colonial period. As mentioned above, the relative neglect of the territory led to very little development of education and management skills which would be necessary to direct the commanding heights of the politics and economy once political independence was attained.

It is very possible that this lack of development of the local institutions and personnel underlies Botswana's internationally acclaimed stability. Alavi and Saul have pointed out that most post-colonial societies which inherited 'overdeveloped' state institutions were subjected to political instability as a result of the lack of congruence between the structures designed to uphold imperial rule and the interests of the new post-colonial ruling class.

In Botswana on the other hand the lack of education and emergence of only a very small bourgeoisie meant that no such strong ruling class emerged. Those who have assumed political positions have felt unprepared to cope with the much better prepared civil service. Moreover, the rapid growth of the economy under state supervision has meant that the technical and professional cadres have had to be staffed with large numbers of expatriates who have little interest in promoting the involvement of politicians. The intrusion of extensive foreign aid organizations has further exacerbated this expatriate influence. The result is that policy making initiatives come from the bureaucracy and their allies in the foreign aid organizations.

In effect, Botswana came to political independence without a ruling class which was prepared to contest the colonially developed bureaucracy for power, and foreign aid has served to perpetuate this bureaucratic suffocation of the emergence of a local ruling class. The result is political stability and an absence of political input into the policy making process. The bureaucracy covers up its domination of government decision making by contending that it is simply planning and coordinating policies. The fact of the matter is that in the process it is also making policy.

31.5 CONCLUSION

The foregoing discussion of the post-colonial state of Botswana shows that the dominance of bureaucratic institutions undermines the realization of both participatory and representative democracy. This paper has shown that with TGLP and SHHA there was a measure of public participation, but that the centralized bureaucracy relying on its expertise compromised any meaningful influence on the important questions involved in these policies.

The dominant trend has been that government officials only address people to inform them of the range of programmes and to encourage them to participate in development efforts. With respect to elected officials, even they have not been able to excercise their constitionally granted power of giving basic direction to the policy making process.

The future of democracy in Botswana very much depends on the ability of politicians and the people to challenge bureaucratic domination. When and if this occurs, the result may be an increase in political instability.

ENDNOTES

1   Held, D. *Models of Democracy,* (Stanford, CA: Stanford University Press, 1987) p. 152.

242

2   Ibid.
3   Tsiane, B. D. and Youngman, F. 'The Theory and Practice of Peoples Partic-
    ipation in Rural Development', *Proceedings of the RECC Workshop* (Kanye,
    1985) p. vi.
4   Picard, L. *The Politics of Development in Botswana: A Model for Success?*
    (Boulder CO: Lynne Rienner Publishers, 1987) p. 42.
5   Alavi, H. 'The State in Post-Colonial Societies: Pakistan and Bangladesh', *New
    Left Review*, No. 74 (July-August 1972) p. 63.
6   Ibid., p. 60.
7   Leys, C. 'The "Overdeveloped" Post-Colonial State: A Re-Evaluation'. *Review
    of African Political Economy* No. 5 (1976) p. 42.
8   Ziemann, W. and Lanzendorfer, M. 'The State in Peripheral Societies', *The
    Socialist Register*, ed. Miliband, R. and Soville, J. (London: Merlin Press,
    1977) p. 145.
9   A detailed analysis of the overdeveloped bureaucracy can be found in Alavi,
    H. 'Pakistan and Bangladesh'; Block, F. 'The Ruling Class Does Not Rule:
    Notes on the Marxist Theory of the State', *Socialist Revolution*, Vol. 7:3 (1977);
    Saul, J. 'The State in Post-colonial Societies: Tanzania', eds. Miliband, R.
    and Soville, J. *The Socialist Register* (London: The Merlin Press, 1974); Von
    Freyhold, M. 'The Post-Colonial State and its Tanzanian Version', *Review
    of African Political Economy*, No. 74 (1977); and Ziemann, W. and Lanzen-
    dorfer, M. 1977, 'The State in Peripheral Societies', in Miliband, R. and Soville,
    J. eds., *The Socialist Register* (London: The Merlin Press, 1977).
10 Picard, *Botswana*, p. 85.
11 Ibid., p. 83.
12 Ibid., p. 88.
13 Inger, D. 'Constraints to Popular Participation in Rural Development', in Tsiane
    and Youngman, eds., *Theory and Practice of Participation*, p. 31.
14 Peters, P. 'Struggles over Water, struggles over Meaning: Cattle Water and
    the State in Botswana', *Africa: Journal of International African Institute*, vol.
    53, no. 3 (1984) p. 44.
15 See the paper by Seeiso D. Liphuko in this volume.

DISCUSSION

Ms Moremi (Ministry of Finance and Development Planning - MFDP) as a discussant noted that the two papers have both strong and weak points. She said Molomo's paper made useful theoretical and practical comments on the issues of participation, consultation and information communication. She also noted that the paper
correctly observed problems in Botswana's civil service in terms of its conduct of
consultation and flow of public information.

The paper however suffers from a narrow definition of what constitutes a
bureaucracy in Botswana's case. Its definition excludes public and local officers
at district levels, parastatal and private sector organizations. The paper also failed

to address the machinery involved in the process of popular consultation. She criticized Molomo's paper for treating the bureaucracy as if it were a homogeneous unit.

Reacting to Liphuko's paper Ms Moremi observed that it tried unsuccessfully to use a case study method to show existance of consultation by the civil service. She said the two policies of Self Help Housing Agency (SHHA) and Tribal Grazing Land Policy (TGLP) were a mockery of consultation.

Expressing her views Ms Moremi said government has encouraged consultation and democracy through policies such as the one on decentralization. She saw a number of problems in realising these policies. There is a shortage of trained personnel to implement them; a lack of coordination between central government, councils and non-governmental organizations; and a lack of experience on the part of civil servants as to how to implement policies more effectively.

Professor Nsibambi asked whether Botswana did not, as is the case in many African countries, have a Commission on Inspectorate of Government? He said this commission could control excessive power by the civil service.

The Honourable Kedikilwe (Minister of Presidential Affairs and of Public Service) said Botswana does not have such a commission but does have ministerial consultative committees which deal with all problems relating to the civil service.

Mr Mathangwane (civil servant) expressed concern that there were a lot of ills within the civil service. He complained for example of victimization of junior officers including women by their seniors.

Mr Mpho (BIP) complained of harassment and intimidation which he had personally received from junior members of the civil service.

Mr Matambo (Director of Financial Affairs, MFDP) saw nothing wrong in a powerful dominating civil service. He said this was necessary for it to be able to implement decisions.

Mr Amisi (civil servant) felt that Mr Molomo's paper failed to make the necessary distinction between traditional and modern bureaucracies. He also wondered whether there was no consultation at certain levels of the bureaucratic hierarchy.

Mrs Venson (senior civil servant) said that civil servants should be ready to accept complaints and public criticism and should not always be on the defensive. She agreed that there is at the moment not enough consultation with the general public.

Summarizing their positions the panelists emphasized the need for more civil service consultation with active political decision makers. Concluding the session the chairman, Mr Gaolatlhe (PS, MFDP) said he was worried by some unfounded criticisms made relative to the bureaucracy by both politicians and some paper authors in the symposium. He said the relationship between the civil service and politicians was healthy, although there was room for improvement. He also said donor agencies do not set any agenda for government as the paper on the ruling class appeared to suggest.

SECTION XV
THE MEDIA

32 Government media as promoters of democracy: an examination of three cases

L. M. Mpotokwane

32.1 INTRODUCTION

Most governments run official mass media. The use to which these media are put varies. Some strictly propagate official positions on issues of national or international interest, with little or no room for coverage of anything else. Others both propagate official views and enable citizens to express their opinions on all manner of subjects, including questions of national policy.

The government of Botswana takes the latter approach. It believes in the free flow of information and the free exchange of ideas between itself and the people. The Department of Information and Broadcasting was specifically created to provide a channel for this two-way communication. The question is whether the department in fact fulfils this function. Since it is generally agreed that the government media promotes government views, I shall concentrate on upward communication, that is showing that the government media facilitates distribution of opinions of those outside of government.

32.2 GOVERNMENT MEDIA AS DISTRIBUTORS OF PUBLIC OPINION

If a government media is to effectively promote democracy, it must be concerned with promoting two concerns:
a) the right of the electorate to be fully informed about the policies of competing political parties or individuals before exercising its vote, and
b) the right of citizens to have freedom of speech, consultation and debate.

Election time in Botswana is busy and exciting. Politicians travel to every corner of the country to woo voters. Journalists must follow to report on what the candidates are saying. This is no small task in a country the size of Botswana. Because the private press is so small, most of the burden of covering campaigns has inevitably fallen on the official media.

The latter has taken its job very seriously, providing extensive coverage without any comment on the part of the journalists. The electorate is left to make its own judgement as to the best candidates. There is also no discrimination in favour of any political party, either in news coverage or in the announcement of politicians' itineraries on Radio Botswana. This latter service is provided strictly on a first-come-first-serve basis.

In the heat of electioneering, the official press is often accused of all kinds of bias in its news coverage. Such accusations usually relate to things like the allocation of air-time for interviews, the publication of stories on the front page of *The Daily News*, and the quality of the pictures of politicians which appear in the official media. The interesting thing about such complaints is that they come from all the political parties, without exception. The fact that all sides complain shows the official press is covering both government and opposition fairly and thus assisting the electorate in deciding whom to elect as their representatives.

The official media also contribute significantly to the promotion of freedom of speech, consultation and debate in this country. Again, this role is thrust upon the official media partly by the present stage of development of the private press in Botswana. Our main concern is to allow persons from all points of view to have an opportunity to present their ideas to the public. In the case of Radio Botswana this objective is realized by audience participation in a number of programmes.

In the weekly show *Matshelo a Batho kwa Dikgaolong*, for instance, rural people air their views about what they think the government is or is not doing for them. The topics discussed are not pre-determined but are decided on the spot by the people themselves. The participants are frank and forthright in their comments.

Similarly, when the president tours the country, his audiences are free to ask questions or comment on his speeches. Such contributions are always given ample coverage by Radio Botswana and are followed with keen interest by the rest of the nation.

Another example of audience participation on Radio Botswana is *Maokaneng*, a popular twice weekly phone-in programme which discusses issues of concern to the nation. The programme is broadcast live and so cannot be edited. The same is true of *Round Table*, a discussion programme which allows invited participants to air their views on the subject under discussion.

Finally, readers are free to write to *The Daily News* or other government publications on any subject. Such audience and reader participation in the official media not only expands the range of public debate but also promotes an awareness among the electorate of their right to such freedom and in so doing facilitates the understanding of what democracy means in the public mind.

The ability of the Department of Information and Broadcasting to function as a two-way communication channel is protected by the fact that it alone decides what is published in its various publications or broadcast on Radio Botswana. No other government department can give it instructions on the content of Radio Botswana programmes or *The Daily News* articles. This is not generally known. Many people think that the Office of the President, under which the Department of Information and Broadcasting falls, vets the stories before they appear in *The Daily News* and the commentaries and other programmes which are broadcast on Radio Botswana. This is not the case.

32.3 CONCLUSION

I do not want to paint too rosy a picture of the government media. They have their share of problems. As a government department, they suffer from the same financial and manpower constraints which afflict other departments. In addition, the emergence of the private press has led to the loss of competent staff by the Department of Information and Broadcasting to the private newspapers.

It is however obvious from the preceding analysis that the government media have played a major part in facilitating and strengthening our democracy over the past years. Although the private press is already making a significant contribution in this regard, there is no intention whatsoever that the role of the official media should diminish in any way in the future.

33 The private press and democracy

Sandy Grant and Brian Egner

33.1 THE LEGAL BACKGROUND

The rights of the public, and by extension those of the private press, stem from those freedoms set out in the constitution of Botswana. Of these, the most important are the freedoms of conscience, of expression, assembly and association (section 3(b)). These rights are subject to respect for the rights and freedoms of others and for the public interest (section 3).[1] The Penal Code enjoins expressions of hatred and ridicule on racial grounds, obscenity (section 92) and criminal defamation (section 197). Further limits are set by the widespread and somewhat vague provisions of the National Security Act of 1986.[2]

33.2 THE POLITICAL BACKGROUND

If government policy regarding freedom of information is reflected in the specific provisions of the law, the intentions and thinking of those in power are also made plain in their public utterances. In November 1982, the Hon. D.K. Kwelagobe, then Minister for Public Service, Information and Broadcasting, in a major policy address, stated:

> We believe that freedom of the press is one of the cornerstones of democracy. For democracy to thrive there must be adequate public debate on issues of importance to the nation . . . I wish to assure them (the press) that they have nothing to fear from the government. It has always been our policy to encourage the development of a responsible, independent press in this country . . . We recognize that such a press will not necessarily be sympathetic towards everything that government says or does, but we shall always uphold its right to express an independent view of any issues of concern. And we hope of course, that it will always be done in a responsible and constructive manner.

These liberal sentiments have not been reflected in the pronouncements of the Hon. P.H.K. Kedikilwe, who succeeded Mr Kwelagobe in 1984 and is still the Minister of Presidential Affairs, Public Service, Information and Broadcasting. In September 1985, a few months after the first South African Defence Force raid on Botswana, Mr Kedikilwe began to develop the theme of subjection of freedom of information and the rule of the law to the needs of security. In the context of increasing regional instability and the struggle for freedom in Southern Africa, the minister in September 1985 referred in parliament to 'a very sensitive question of people deliberately misunderstanding what we understand by the freedom of the press' and observed that 'whatever that freedom of the press, it cannot and it should not be at the expense of the security of this nation.'[3]

The minister added that the security of the country would not be determined in a court of law 'as those champions who write some of the editorial letters in their papers think'.[4] The minister's view appeared to be that he has a right, acting on behalf of the president, to decide what is a security matter, and that this right overrides the rights of both the judiciary and the press in their traditional constitutional roles. This attitude comes dangerously close to declaring that, even when there is ample time for judicial review and public debate, both the judiciary and the press have an automatic duty to back all decisions of the executive branch of government whenever the word 'security' is invoked.[5]

33.3 POLITICIANS VERSUS JOURNALISTS

The minister's pronouncements on national security, the law and the press did not go unchallenged. In *The Botswana Guardian* for 26 February 1986, Rampholo Molefhe, under the heading 'A Closer Look at the Pres's Right Hand Man' considered Mr Kedikilwe's view that the press must not 'attempt to cross the line between freedom of expression and the protected state domain'. Molefhe suggested that the authors of the 'editorial letters' which the minister had found so objectionable were merely exercising their constitutional rights. The columnist wrote that 'the minister would be well advised, in consultation with the press, to explain the dimensions of the restricted "state domain".'

Although there may have been lingering grievances in some quarters about the way the press had covered the October 1984 election, the increased tension between government and the media in the second half of 1985 was also the result of the September 1985 decision to deport a refugee journalist, Mr Mxolisi 'Ace' Mxgashe of *The Botswana Guardian*.[6] All three independent newspapers carried editorial protests, letters to the editor and requests for explanation or review of the decision.[7] They elicited only the philosophising about security and the 'state domain' which we have already noted. Meanwhile, Mr Mxgashe remains in a stateless limbo between the United States and Ghana.

Further controversy arose in February 1986 when the Minister of Presidential Affairs showed no concern at the fact that the editor of *The Gazette*, a Malawian, had been threatened with both physical violence and deportation in a series of anonymous phone calls (The callers wanted an end to further stories about alleged abuse of governmental powers in connection with the land deals of a company called Leno). According to *The Daily News* of 5 February 1986, the minister said 'if the press felt frightened by the alleged phone calls made to them they should also be aware that government was equally concerned about the way in which the press printed pseudonymous letters attacking the government.'[8]

The rifts between press and government over Mxgashe in 1985 and the Leno affair in 1986 remained open. By March 1987, two other political figures had begun calling for 'controls' to be applied to the press. Mr Chapson Butale, MP, asked parliament to 'come up with legislation that will control these people. They never cross-check their information. They just damage anybody, anyhow, anywhere. The question is how long we should tolerate this.' He was followed later in the same month by the Vice-President , the Hon. P. S. Mmusi, who told a political rally in Gaborone, 'I wish to say I do not deal with the press. I deal with other politicians. But let the press be warned lest they be engulfed in a storm. Beware, the storm is coming your way.'

The speeches by Messrs Butale and Mmusi drew a storm of protest from the press.[9] No action was taken to give effect to their threats. It would be unwise, however, to assume that the government and the press have now reached a permanent truce.

33.4 GOVERNMENTAL PRESS RELATIONS

Some of the friction between government and the private press arises from the way they relate to each other on a routine level. The three newspapers, *The Botswana Guardian, The Gazette* and *Mmegi wa Dikgang*, have been asked by the government to respect the need for state security and for obvious reasons of patriotism have variously indicated their willingness to do so. This cooperative stance has not been reciprocated, for example by affording to senior journalists the opportunity of confidential background briefings on matters of public concern. At best, the three editors may, with the rest of the world, receive handouts and attend official press conferences; at worst, they may be denied the opportunity of in-depth interviews which, even today, are more readily granted to external reporters, even those from South Africa, than to any local, non-governmental reporter. The result is that the best and quickest source of news about major events in Botswana is often the BBC and occasionally even Boputhatswana television.

Newspaper editors complain that they cannot extract even routine facts from government departments or ministries. Failure to answer questions from the press is so common as to amount to normal practice. Treating the private press as a problem which will have to be solved and in the meantime should either be ignored or controlled is merely to reject an opportunity which could be exploited for the benefit of all. The government has the power to contribute to both the achievements and failings of the private press. A press relations policy which treats all those who work for newspapers as mischief makers and gossips who cannot keep a confidence is bound to produce some bizarre results.

33.5 THE WAR MENTALITY

The government's unwillingness to communicate regularly with the private press on major issues may well arise from a feeling that the press is a political adversary and an ally of the opposition parties and even of the country's external enemies. The central question is whether a state of war really exists between Botswana and South Africa. The Botswana paradox is that normality reigns in the country's day-to-day material relations with South Africa; the cross-border traffic of visitors travelling from one country to the other continues unimpeded on the day before and after the South African army conducts its brief and intermittent raids on 'selected' targets in Botswana, murdering innocent people at will. As far as the economy is concerned, no state of war exists. But when freedom of information is at issue, the authorities are inclined at times to act as though the country is in the middle of a continuous shooting war.

33.6 THE ARMY AND THE PRESS

All news about the Botswana Defence Force (BDF) appears to be treated by senior officers as falling under the heading of state security. The details of the BDF's budgetary requirements are not publicly available and are only sketchily considered by the National Assembly. Yet parliament's duty, on behalf of the public, is to scrutinize the financial detail, even of arms, uniform and ration purchases, and to find out exactly what it is that the army is doing about guarding the nation. The right of the people to closely control those who bear arms on their behalf is regarded as fundamental to the democratic process in all countries with a parliamentary form of government. The details of how the military conduct their affairs are openly discussed in many countries with much larger armed forces and much greater security problems than Botswana. Such countries conduct searching and independent enquiries into the reasons for military failures; their reports are both essential reading matter for the informed public and useful guidance for the military themselves in how to avoid repeating the same mistakes in the future.

Reflecting mounting public concern over the lack of information on defence and security matters, *Mmegi wa Dikgang*, in common with such public figures as Kgosi Linchwe of the Bakgatla, has frequently argued that as an essential element of the struggle for freedom in Southern Africa, the general public needs to be fully informed about the security situation and to as great an extent as possible to be involved in its own defence. In practice, the BDF and the police have retained the sole authority over protecting the lives of Botswana's inhabitants.

From some of the very rare and brief utterances of the BDF spokesmen, and from their many refusals to speak at all, it appears that BDF personnel have the impression that the army is entitled to a degree of immunity from the norms and controls under which the rest of the society lives. In particular they take it for granted that the army is in no way obliged to release information on any matter whatsoever. This attitude is explained by reference to the dangerous regional security situation. The danger which is overlooked, however, is that excessive secrecy over regional security could lead to an emergence within Botswana of a privileged sector of society which is armed to the teeth and protected from criticism in the media as well as exempted from the normal processes of public scrutiny and accountability to parliament in financial matters.

33.7 SEEING JUSTICE DONE

Only recently has the press begun to articulate this concern, albeit with a most delicate touch. Before then, unarmed people had been killed by BDF soldiers without comment from the press. In the crisis atmosphere caused by South African terrorism, the press apparently assumed that criticism of the security forces would be seen as unpatriotic. For example a British citizen was shot dead at a BDF road block in Francistown in 1987. There was no public outcry, no charges were laid, and rumour was left to run riot, with only the sketchiest of reports in the local press.

The private press would have done a service to the concerned public and to the rule of law if it had reported in full the circumstances of this particular death, including eye-witness versions of what happened and (in due course) the details of the inquest proceedings. The press failed in its duty to the public in this instance, either because of self-censorship or because it allowed itself to be warned off.

A similar failure was evident when *The Gazette* of 27 January 1988, reported without comment at the end of a story about elephant poaching that 'over the last two months, the Botswana Defence Force patrolling the area (Linyanti-Chobe) have shot dead at least four armed poachers.' These dead people were human beings. Should it not be the press's routine role, assisted in every possible way by the public service, to report the circumstance of death, the names of the dead, their ages, sex, dependents, parents, places of abode and nationality? Did they simply disappear? With what weapons were they armed and did they attack the BDF? Where were they buried and by whom? What injuries were sustained by the BDF and when will the inquest verdict become available? Have their relatives been notified?

In these two instances, the proper concern of the press is the same as that of the public and the judiciary — that justice must be seen to be done. National security would in no way have been compromised by detailed and accurate reporting of what actually happened. The public must be assured that its security forces are competent, well-led and disciplined and that they are not exceeding their authority.

This same concern over the arbitrary use of authority led to the furore over the deportation of Mxgashe. It came up again more recently when the BDF found means to persuade reporters to surrender their notebooks at the court martial of a BDF corporal who was convicted and sentenced to 15 years imprisonment on charges of cowardice. Little can be said about this incident because Cpl. Kgantlepe's appeal is still to be heard in the High Court. Sufficient to note therefore that reporters were prevented from reporting the evidence and the court martial was in effect turned into a secret trial even though no order had been either granted or requested to allow the trial to be held *in camera*. The Minister of Presidential Affairs replied to the press criticisms of this incident in July 1988 without waiting for the corporal's appeal to be heard, or even mentioning that an appeal was pending. He told a passing out parade of the BDP that 'I am sure any reasonable thinking person can see that . . . cowardice cannot be allowed to be left unpunished.' He went on to describe the press as ignorant, malicious, insensitive, naive, irresponsible, abusive, misguided, sensational and (by implication) unpatriotic and anti-BDF. He asserted that he was 'exercising restraint' and expressed the hope that the press would 'do the same.'[10]

33.8 PRIVATELY VERSUS PUBLICLY OWNED MEDIA

Not least of the private press's achievements since 1982 is that it has succeeded in bringing about a major improvement in both the quality and quantity of news in the government's official organ, *The Daily News*. Even self-censorship has its limits, and the mere existence of independent papers has persuaded the government press officers who produce *The Daily News* to censor themselves less than they used to do and to print many of the stories they used to leave out.

The Daily News is today a credit to those who produce it; the competition from the private press has clearly brought out the best in its staff. Yet the Office of the President has for years refused to allow private entrepreneurs to open commercial radio and television stations, which would surely by now have led to an equally badly needed improvement in the quality and quantity of Radio Botswana's output.

33.9 OWNERSHIP, CIRCULATION AND READERSHIP OF THE PRIVATE PRESS

The Gazette company is owned by a citizen consortium whose interest is avowedly to make profits. The owners support the ruling party but do not 'push' any particular political line. *The Botswana Guardian* has similar profit-making aims and is similarly eclectic in its politics. It is foreign-owned and has a British General Manager. *Mmegi wa Dikgang* is owned by a non-profit trust which represents all shades of political opinion.

The combined weekly print order of the three private newspapers is some 33 000 copies (15 000 for *The Botswana Guardian*, 10 000 for *The Gazette* and 8 000 for *Mmegi wa Dikgang*). Unfortunately little information exists about the nature of the buying public and how many people read each copy, but certain assumptions can be made about the readers from the content of the papers themselves:-

a)   Most of the papers are sold in Gaborone and the major urban centers and all three newspapers give most of their coverage to the interests of Gaborone readers.

b)   All three are written in English. Only *Mmegi wa Dikgang* provides any coverage in Setswana.

c)   Each provides regular coverage of sports, especially football; of African popular music; and in the case of *Mmegi wa Dikgang* of other forms of art as well.

d)   A few specific attempts are made to provide for the interests of women, with advice to the lovelorn in *The Botswana Guardian* and a more upmarket women's column in *The Gazette* being the most obvious examples.

33.10 CONTENT OF THE PAPERS

The Gazette, has been under the same editor since it was founded three years ago and *Mmegi wa Dikgang* recently changed its editor for the first time recently since the paper's revival on 31 August 1984. *The Botswana Guardian*, however, has in its six year life had four editors.

The inconsistency which sometimes appears in the content of the papers is due less to the turnover of editors than that of their staff, whose transition from one paper to another and indeed into and out of the profession of journalism occurs with such frequency as to reflect the lack of basic job security, to say nothing of a career structure, which is one of the press's greatest problems.

As for content, the oldest and largest circulation private paper is *The Botswana Guardian*, which has a reputation for spot news coverage and which covered the 1984 elections, particularly for the Gaborone seats, with a flair it has shown only rarely since then. *Mmegi wa Dikgang* has a more intellectual tone and has adopted its own style of political analysis; it also covers major elements of public policy such as housing and the wider issues of national development planning. *The Gazette* has taken the popular tabloid approach; it has dramatised the seamier side of life, drawing public attention to those issues that public policy has so far failed to reach - the limbless child Kabo, the 'bo-bashi' beggar children of the Gaborone Mall, the scavengers who survive on pickings from the Gaborone refuse dump; most recently *The Gazette* has taken a lone stand against proposals to change the laws to allow flogging of women.

All three newspapers have done the best that their limited resources allowed to cover such major events and issues as terrorist raids by the South African Defence Force, the Kgantlepe court martial, a mystery visit by South African foreign minister Pik Botha to President Masire's brother in Jwaneng, the Bontleng witchcraft disturbances and the subsequent hearings, and the 'Leno affair,' a long running story which first appeared in *The Gazette* and was later picked up by the other papers, which ran 33 stories on this theme between January and March 1986.[11] 'Leno' raised questions about property speculation, enrichment and the extent of the influence of high ranking officials and politicians over the urban land allocation process.[12]

A fair proportion of independent newspaper coverage since 1982 has been of outstanding quality, e.g. Mxgashe's political reporting in *The Botswana Guardian* before he was deported and Rampholo Molefhe's since then; *The Gazette's* coverage of the Leno affair; and *Mmegi wa Dikgang's* handling of such economic issues as water development, conservation, and the national shortage of housing. There have been some errors of judgement and taste as well, and *The Botswana Guardian* in April 1988 moved into a class of its own when it carried an editorial calling upon the government to ban the importation of the South African newspaper *The Citizen* − a demonstration, if one was needed, of how the 'state of war' mentality can cause some of those working for the private press to forget what newspapers are supposed to stand for in an open society.[13]

33.11 WHAT HAS BEEN ACHIEVED?

Has corruption been exposed where it was previously hidden? Has Botswana become more or less an open society? Has abuse of power and office been denounced and have the weak been defended? Has national unity been enhanced at a time of external threat? The achievement is hard to define but the record, self evidently, has been uneven. Nevertheless, it must be quickly stated that since its emergence in 1982 the private press has revolutionalised society by breaking the government's monopoly of information and allowing the public a choice of interpretations of events which before 1982 was simply not available. The existence of such a choice enhances of the power of the people at the expense of a bureaucracy which previously had virtual control over the release of information.

33.12 COULD MORE HAVE BEEN ACHIEVED?

Local distributors estimate that some 7 500 Zimbabwean, overseas and South African daily and a further 10 000 Sunday papers are bought by people who want to keep up with the world and regional news. The private press still carries a good deal of agency material about the outside world, whereas some areas of local news have been neglected − the House of Chiefs, the proceedings of the High Court, the Court of Appeal and Magistrates Courts could all use better coverage; divorces, affiliation cases and civil cases in general are rarely reported at all. New laws which will be debated in parliament at its next session are published in the official gazette but never reported, analysed and explained in the press, thereby depriving voters of a chance to lobby their MPs and mobilize to support or opposition to the proposals.

Routine reporting, straightforward interviewing, legwork and combing through public records for court or business news are the normal training areas for aspirant journalists. These mundane activities appear to be neglected by editors who accept banal think-pieces and world news rehashes by local pundits as substitutes for hard news. There is a distressing tendency to take a fact (e.g that a political party meeting is about to take place) and to surround and embellish it with 'political analysis' consisting of the opinions of unnamed political commentators, sources, observers, insiders, etc. who all appear to have axes to grind and whose reasons for requiring anonymity are never explained.[14]

All such strictures as these have to be seen in the light of the financial constraints on newspaper publication in a small market — world news, think-pieces, endlessly long letters to the editor, rehashes and thumb-sucking political analysis come cheap; hard news and in-depth reporting require more time and money than are available to the private press.

33.13 COSTS AND REVENUES OF *THE DAILY NEWS*

A disquieting development from the viewpoint of the private press is the strength of journalistic and business competition from the government, which is spending increasing amounts of money on ensuring that its own organ, *The Daily News*, reaches every corner of the country.

The Daily News is printed by the Government Printer, who produces 45 000 copies a day, compared with the 33 000 weekly output of the three private papers combined. The Government Printer has no cost-estimating procedures and keeps no separate figures covering the cost of paper and printing *The Daily News* (on a P1 million web offset machine which is under-utilized and which the Office of the President will not allow the private papers to use). It is therefore not easy to estimate the cost of producing *The Daily News*. If, however, the rates charged by local printing firms to the private newspapers are taken as a guide, it would cost at least P9,000 a day or P2.2 million a year to print *The Daily News*. Add to this a further P2.15 million a year to cover half the 1988/89 recurrent budget cost of staffing and running the Department of Information and Broadcasting Services. This yields an estimated annual recurrent cost of producing *The Daily News* of P4.35 million. After deducting the P200 000 of advertising revenue budgeted for 1988/89 (and achieved by selling advertising at below the cost-covering rate), the estimated net cash loss incurred by the taxpayers in producing and distributing *The Daily News* works out at P4.15 million a year. Interest charges and depreciation on the approximately P10 million of capital (housing, offices, factory space, machinery, equipment, furniture, vehicles, etc.) employed in producing *The Daily News* should also be taken into account. The estimated loss to the taxpayer attributable to the production costs of *The Daily News* is then increased by approximately 25 per cent, to around P5 million a year, P20,000 a day, or 57 thebe for each copy given away.

33.14 COSTS AND REVENUES OF THE PRIVATE PRESS

By comparison, the total estimated revenues of the three private newspapers from advertising are around P1.5 million and from newspaper sales P250.000. Net profits before tax on this turnover of P1.75 million are unlikely to have reached as high as five per cent in the year ended 30 June 1988. (*The Gazette* states it barely broke even, *Mmegi wa Dikgang* made losses, and only *The Botswana Guardian* could possibly have made a profit). While criticism of the contents and poor distribution of the private newspapers is certainly justified, money counts in this as in any other business. The total annual cost of producing the three private newspapers is less than one third of what the government spends each year on producing and giving away *The Daily News*. *The Daily News* is served by more than 40 full-time pensionable journalists and photographers, whereas the three private newspapers together could muster only 18 ill-paid and insecure full-time journalists and photographers between them in July 1988.

33.15 *THE DAILY NEWS* VERSUS THE REST

The Daily News began life in 1964 as a two-page roneoed internal government newsletter. Its circulation was expanded to about 5000 a day after independence, avowedly to fill the gap left by the lack of a private press. It has now, however, taken on a life of its own as a fully-fledged eight-page printed newspaper; its staff, capital equipment and budgetary allocations have all expanded each year since the inception of the private press in 1982. It seems that the intention of the government is no longer to fill a gap and to retire from the market as soon as a private press appears. It has now embarked upon a process of competition with the press which has already appeared.

The unequal nature of the struggle for readership between a loss-making state-owned newspaper and the independent press is obvious. On the one hand the government employs its political power to denigrate and threaten the existence of the press; on the other it uses its financial power to maintain its dominant position as the main source of information to the public. In doing so, it has not driven the private papers out of the market, but it has undermined their financial viability and created conditions of uncertainty and stringency in which they cannot improve the quality and quantity of their coverage. *The Gazette* in February 1986 reverted to weekly publication after four months as a daily. *The Botswana Guardian* fell back at the same time from twice-weekly to weekly publication. The combined sales of the three private papers remained fixed from 1986 to 1988 at less than 33,000 copies a week; during the same period, the number of *The Daily News* being given away went up by 46%, from 24 000 to 45 000 (as in September 1989).

33.16 IS THIS THE GOVERNMENT'S MEDIA POLICY?

With 175 000 copies of the official *The Daily News* (5 days X 35 000) being given away and 33 000 copies of the independent papers being sold each week, five-sixths of the local newspapers reaching the public are provided by the government and one-sixth by the private press. A crucial barrier to the further development of the private press as an informant of the public is the governments's increasing use of public funds in a bid to expand the readership and influence of the government-owned *The Daily News*. The undeclared public information and media policy of the government appears to be that it intends to retain 100% control of Radio Botswana and (say) 80% control of the print media, always provided that those who control the private sector 20% do not intrude into the 'state domain'.

33.17 IS IT ALL A SHAM?

A Marxist might at this stage suggest that the so-called independent press, no matter how independent it seems, will be allowed to exist only for so long as it serves, or at least does not significantly threaten, the interests of the dominant class.

Louis A. Picard, an astute and prolific writer on Botswana politics,[15] has referred to the Botswana tendency to indulge in 'symbolic politics' or 'pictures in the mind'. According to Picard, our rulers include those senior bureaucrats who later move into ready-made cabinet positions without significantly changing their attitudes and practices. This elite is prepared to tolerate and even encourage all kinds of ineffective and well-publicized opposition in a bid to convince the masses that we have the kind of genuinely free and open society that they know the masses want. Only when their opponents who by definition include the independent press, show signs of becoming truly effective and damaging the interests of the elite will the rulers intervene and give a tug on the chain.

33.18 THE BOTSWANA COMPROMISE

All such theses about the attitudes of Botswana's political leaders remain to be proved. The situation we have to deal with in 1988 is a uniquely Botswana compromise. For those who like to look on the dark side, the public is being deluged with a constant flow of selected information from the state-owned and controlled radio station and daily newspaper. But on Wednesdays and Fridays the weekly independent newspapers appear. They print the really embarrassing ('sensitive') stories that are in such bad taste that the official media ignore them; they focus on the kind of 'sensitive' issues the government, the department, the bishop or the management of the company would prefer not to discuss just yet; they needle, complain and pontificate about matters they cannot possibly understand, display bad manners, insensitivity and lack of respect, and generally carry on like the press in any multi-party pluralistic democracy anywhere in the world.

There is nothing sham or 'symbolic' about the way the private press of Botswana goes about its business, nor is there anything bogus about the annoyance the press causes to leading politicians. The only surprising factor is that in Botswana some senior politicians appear to find difficulty in accepting that annoyance is part of the normal relationship which exists in a democratic society between politicians and the press.[16]

33.19 THE PROPOSED NATIONAL PRESS COUNCIL

Reference has been made above to the uneasy relationship and lack of understanding which has persisted between government and press since 1985. Although such a relationship is normal in any free society, democracy will be facilitated if ways can be found of both preserving the freedom of the press and improving the distrustful atmosphere which has prevailed since 1985. An initiative has been taken by the 17 member Newspaper Trust of Botswana (NTB), a private non-profit body set up in 1982 to foster the development of the independent press. The NTB in June 1988 appointed a steering group to take whatever steps are necessary to secure the formation of a voluntary National Press Council on the lines of those which exist in democratic countries throughout the world.[17]

Detailed proposals as to how the Press Council should operate are still being discussed. What is needed is a trustworthy, independent, voluntary body which will be capable of arbitrating between the various interested parties and more especially between the press and those who from time to time consider they have been damaged by the actions of newspapers or journalists. The voluntary press council should help to ensure that a law-abiding and competent independent press continues to serve the public without undue intrusion into the private lives of individuals, and without provoking the government of the day into taking measures aimed at limiting press freedom and thereby restricting the access of the public to information. It is particularly important that the government should be prepared to encourage the press to regulate itself in this way. His Excellency the President on 2 July 1988 in Francistown called upon the private sector to 'increasingly assume general functions specific to business and economic activities and entities in regulation and control, promotion and advertisement, social standards and ethics and in arbitration of disputes.' He went on, 'Government is now burdened by all these functions and has had to assume them because there was and continues to be a vacuum.'

33.20 LEGAL SUPPORT FOR THE PRESS

The police and Attorney General have since 1982 prosecuted several journalists; searched newspaper offices, seized property, and detained and interrogated other journalists who were alleged to have broken the law. At least four non-citizen journalists have been deported. The journalists were generally unable to afford to pay lawyers to represent them, and at the time of writing at least one is in deep financial

258

trouble over legal fees despite the fact that he was acquitted in court and again on appeal.

There is a need for some agency to appeal for funds to pay for the legal representation of accused journalists. Such an agency could also and to undertake legal research into those provisions of such laws as the National Security Act which may be inimical to the right to freedom of information. Another NTB steering group has been set up for this purpose. If funds allow, a draft of a Botswana Freedom of Information Act will be prepared; all-party political sponsorship will be sought to enable the law to be brought before the National Assembly.

33.21 TRAINING AND LOGISTICAL SUPPORT

Some criticisms of the quality of reporting and even of the business management of the private press could be met or deflected if more training opportunities and equipment were made available. The NTB disbursed or committed in 1987-88 some P200 000 of training and logistical support funds which it obtained from Dutch, American and British donors; cash prizes for an annual merit awards scheme for best stories in the private press came from local businesses with an interest in media development. Some funds went to cover training costs, some to strengthen business and advertising management and expand the distribution network of *Mmegi wa Dikgang*, and some to provide *Mmegi wa Dikgang* with two vehicles, desk-top publishing equipment and a proof copying machine. A further P25 000 went to *Mmegi wa Dikgang* as working capital in early 1988.

33.22 FINANCIAL ASSISTANCE

In seeking financial assistance for the press, the Newspaper Trust has encountered some paradoxical limitations and definitions governing the disbursement of donor funds to the different private papers. In brief, grant funds can go freely to an unprofitable non-profit newspaper like *Mmegi wa Dikgang*, but donors are nervous about helping such allegedly profit-making papers as *The Botswana Guardian* and *The Gazette*, where their funds could be used to top up the profits of the owners. Thus a bankrupt non-profit newspaper or a privately owned paper under poor management and obviously not making profits will attract grant assistance, whereas a moderately profitable publication under good management will be unable to find finance either to expand or to cope with periodic crises. The grant funds in question all come from western capitalist and mixed economies and the irony implicit in having to comply with donor criteria which reinforce failure and fail to support success is obvious.

Diplomats and the governments they represent are also wary of providing financial aid to private newspapers lest they be accused of interfering in Botswana's internal affairs. The NTB will continue to seek sources of funding which are flexible enough to enable all three newspapers to improve the quality of their coverage as well as to survive their periodic cash flow crises until such time as they become financially viable. This time may not be too far off: *The Botswana Guardian* is believed now to be producing reasonable returns for its owners; *The Gazette* is said by its management to have broken even last year; and *Mmegi wa Dikgang*, which had major increases in advertising and sales revenues in the first half of the year, has high hopes of reaching a break-even point by the end of 1989.

33.23 GOVERNMENT SUPPORT?

Newspapers do not presently qualify for any form of government subsidy. They are denied the Financial Assistance Policy grants which go to many of the businesses which advertise their wares in the press. The Ministry of Commerce and Industry has not accepted the view that newspapers are linking industries which assist in the dissemination of business and economic information and in the marketing of other goods.

The Office of the President, which controls the Government Printing Department, not only sells advertising in *The Daily News* at far below its real cost; it also turns a blind eye to the possibility of sharing with the private press a lucrative source of revenue in the form of fees for publication of trade licensing advertisements and tender notices. The law states the adverts must appear on two occasions both in the official gazette and in 'a newspaper which circulates in Botswana.' The Government Printer, however, collects a single P40 fee covering the cost of insertion of the advertisements in both the official gazette and the official *The Daily News*. No refund is made to those who might prefer their advertisements to appear in a private newspaper, and the law is thereby circumvented. In other countries both central and local government support the press by making it compulsory for all trade licensing advertisements, tender notices, legal announcements, etc. to appear in the private newspapers.

33.24 CONCLUSIONS AND RECOMMENDATIONS

At the time of writing, Botswana provides a fairly secure environment for the kind of private press that can only exist in an open democratic society which does not believe in imposing controls on the press or in abridging the right of freedom of information. Despite some hectoring by leading politicians, a form of co-existence has been achieved. Freedom of the press seems, after the six year existence of private newspapers, to be fairly well established. The main constraints on the private press are not political but financial. These constraints have been made worse by a governmental media policy which ignores the existence of a private press and encourages civil servants to spend ever increasing amounts of public money on flooding the newspaper market with free copies of the government-owned *The Daily News*.

As for what could be done by the government to remove barriers and make the private press a more effective democratic institution, abolition of *The Daily News* (perhaps on condition that the private press agreed to publish all governmental press releases), or at least its privatization as a cost covering parastatal should be considered as part of the rethinking of media policy that is long overdue. Other alternatives include reducing the numbers printed; turning *The Daily News* back into the internal civil service newsletter it used to be selling instead of giving it away; and ceasing to sell advertising at below cost in competition with a private press which needs advertising revenue to survive.

The government continually complains about the inaccuracy of stories which appear in the press. It does not, however, have a single press liaison officer, let alone one whose function is to serve the local media, so it cannot be said at present to have established any press relations policy or any working relationship with the press at all; it should do so, particularly with a general election coming up in 1989.

As for what can be done outside the governmental framework to remove barriers and make the private press more effective, certain initiatives are being pursued by the Newspaper Trust of Botswana. These envisage setting up a voluntary National Press Council and a legal defence and research fund; raising funds for training and logistical support of the press; and lobbying for changes in government policy. The attainment of these objectives will call for practical, moral and financial support from all parts of the society as well as continuation and expansion of the generous assistance the private press has received in the past from interested bodies outside Botswana's borders.

ENDNOTES

1   The right of freedom of expression is defined in section 12 of the constitution: 'no person shall be hindered in the enjoyment of his freedom of expression, that is to say freedom to hold opinions without interference, freedom to communicate ideas and information without interference whether the communication is to the public generally or to any person or class of persons', — such freedom being limited only to the extent that the laws may make reasonable provision for defence, public safety, public order, public morality or public health (section 12a), the rights of others (section 12b) and 'impose restrictions upon public officers, employees of local government bodies, or teachers' (section 12c).

2   The act was introduced as a response to the destabilizing terrorist attacks of the South African regime against Botswana. It contains features of the British Official Secrets Act plus other provisions resembling South African security legislation. The burden of proof is on accused persons to prove their innocence rather than on the state. No journalists have been prosecuted under the Act, but it has occasionally been invoked either as a threat or as an excuse by public officers and soldiers who were unwilling to answer questions from reporters.

3   *The Botswana Guardian*, 20 September 1985. 'Kedikilwe Lashes Out at Press.'

4   Ibid.

5   In a recent example where neither the judiciary nor the press lived up to the minister's expectations, the Office of the President took exception to a senior magistrate's verdict that a Radio Botswana reporter was not guilty of inciting a riot; The Attorney General appealed to the High Court for a conviction; the High Court upheld the magistrate's verdict. The Senior State Counsel was then reported as saying he would now take the matter to the High Court of Appeals.

6   Mr Mxgashe was declared a prohibited immigrant by Presidential decree and held in prison until another country could be found to take him; the action was taken in terms of a law which says that the authorities do not need to give reasons for their decision and that no appeal may be made to any court of law. Some local journalists believe that 'Ace' was deported because of his reporting of the 1984 elections as well as such 'sensitive' (i.e. embarrassing) matters as the Botswana Defence Force's slow reaction time after the June 14 1985 South African raid and certain aspects of the treatment of Zimbabwean refugees. Mr Mxgashe had lived in Botswana for 15 years at the time he was deported. He is married to a Motswana and they have children.

7   See *The Gazette*, 4 September 1985, 'Govt Official Refuses to Comment on Alleged Crackdown on Press'; *The Gazette*, 11 September 1985, 'No Press Crackdown, Journalists Assured'; *The Gazette* 25 September 1985, 'The Press and Authority'; *Mmegi wa Dikgang*, 28 September 1985, 'Our Own House in Order', 'Not Guilty Mr Kedikilwe'; *The Guardian*, 4 October 1985, 'Champion Replies to Kedikilwe'.

8   See *The Gazette*, 5 February 1986, 'Our Press is Free', and 'The Kedikilwe Parallel'; *The Gazette*, 14 April 1986, 'Comment on Leno'.

9   See *The Guardian*, 6 March 1987, 'Comment' and 'The Press — Familiar Polecat'; *The Gazette*, 11 March 1987, 'Alarm over Butale Call'; *The Guardian*, 13 March 1987, 'What was that about the Press Mr Butale?'; *The Guardian*, 20 March 1987, 'Watch Says Mmusi'; *The Guardian*, 27 March 1987; 'Look about Yourselves'.

10 See 'Army to Counter Terrorism Acts', *The Daily News*, 21 July 1988.

11 'The Press and Evolution of Political Opposition in an African Democracy: The Case of Botswana' by James Zaffiro, Department of Political Science, Central College, Pella, Iowa. Mimeo, October 1986, p. 48.

12 For examples of press coverage, see *The Gazette*, 20 January 1986, 13 February 1986; *Mmegi wa Dikgang*, 15 February 1986, 'Leno: the Deafening Silence' and 'The BNF and Leno': *The Botswana Daily News*, 4 February 1986, 'Press Threatened by Callers to Stop Investigating Leno'; *The Guardian*, 14 February 1986, 'Kedikilwe Lays it Down for Press'.

13 *The Botswana Guardian*, 15 April 1988. 'Comment'.

14 See for instance 'BNF's Options Narrow . . . An Insider's View' in *Mmegi wa Dikgang*, 9 July 1988.

15 See for instance, Picard, L. A. *The Politics of Development in Botswana: A Model for Success?* (Boulder, CO: Lynne Rienner Publishers, Boulder, 1987), p. 298.

16   Their attitude is far from that of Lord Jacobson who opened a debate in the House of Lords on the state of the press with a warning that 'Relations between politicians and the press have deteriorated, are deteriorating . . . and should on no account be allowed to improve.' Quoted in 'A view from Abroad: The Experience of Voluntary Press Council' by Kenneth Morgan. Mimeographed. Paper presented to the Conference on Media Freedom and Accountability, Columbia University, 4 April 1986, pp. 4, 38. Kenneth Morgan's view is that 'The relationship between a country's press and its politicans should be distant and reserved rather than easy; and critical, even abrasive, on both sides rather than fawning or adulatory.' Ibid, p.4. We suspect that some Botswana politicians would prefer the tone of British Conservative Prime Minister Stanley Baldwin's celebrated criticism of two Conservative newspaper proprietors when he said:

> Their methods are direct falsehood, misrepresentation, half-truths, the alteration of a speaker's meaning by putting sentences apart from the context, suppression and editorial criticism of speeches which are not reported in the paper. What the proprietorship of these papers is aiming at is power, but power without responsibility — the prerogative of the harlot through the ages. Ibid, p. 3.

17   Ibid, passim. Norway has had a press council since 1912, Sweden, 1916, Britain, 1953. Other countries with press councils include India, Portugal, Israel, West Germany, Australia, and New Zealand.

DISCUSSION

Mr Ephraim Setshwaelo (Institute of Development Management -IDM) set off the discussion by expressing disappointment in the fact that government media still has basic problems that he personally experienced when he was working there ten years ago. He suggested that the Office of the President consider:

a)   Upgrading the position of the Director of Information to that of a permanent secretary. He said this will facilitate information flow between the director and the minister responsible and ease a lot of problems of communication which currently exist.

b)   That government media should consider printing fact sheets for public consumption on regular basis as many government media do.

c)   Government media should be strengthened to fill the gaps left by the infant private press.

Turning to private press Mr Setshwaelo agreed with the authors that its main problems were not political or government restriction as often alleged but financial. He encouraged young journalists to work much harder, be creative and produce substantive stories, e.g. on government loans to farmers and how much of these have been written off.

Mr Kgosinkwe Moesi (Botswana Development Corporation — BDC) was generally pleased with the two papers but personally suggested that:

a) Government media should play the role of public relations rather than pretending to be journalistic. He said public relations and journalism were two different professions and should not be confused.
b) That the media should consider writing in Setswana since English is spoken by only 30% of the country's population.
c) He also recommended that the Newspaper Trust and other government departments, e.g. Judiciary, should play an important role in democratising the media and protecting it against abuse.

Chief Seepapitso (Chairman House of Chiefs) was concerned about the lack of media coverage of the debates of the House of Chiefs and also that Setswana was not the language in the media, in spite of the fact that many people including MPs could hardly express themselves well in English.

Mr Lebang Mpotokwane (Office of the President) replying to Chief Seepapitso said government does not interfere or determine what goes or does not go into the government *The Daily News* and the radio. He said all decisions as to content of the government media are left to the Department of Information to decide. He however said with regard to coverage of debates in the House of Chiefs, government was still considering the matter.

Professor Crick (Edinburgh University) was concerned that governments often underdeveloped the media by flooding it with adverts and at the same time denying it enough resources for development. He said a democracy should avoid the dangers of using media as a propaganda tool which no one ever believes anyway.

Mrs Margaret Nasha (Director, Department of Information) said she disagreed with the current approach to covering parliamentary debates. The programme on which MPs are interviewed is too long. She agreed with the Egner and Grant paper that part of the solution to problems of the media is the introduction of a Press and Broadcasting Act. She also agreed that government media in Botswana as elsewhere is controlled but still felt it has an important role to play in development.

The Honourable Kedikilwe (Minister of Presidential Affairs and Public Service) expressed regrets on both the Egner and Grant paper and Professor Crick's comments. He said despite concerns by both the authors and commentators, government still felt that the media can be controlled without falling into the trap of countries like South Africa. He said in news writing like in football, someone must be a referee and raise the yellow card when need arises.

Mr Mothobi (BNF) felt that the private media was too fearful and self-censoring. He suggested that private media could test the legality of the National Security Act in court. He said as a lawyer he was prepared to defend a journalist arrested under this act.

Ms Mpho Makgema (National Assembly staff) asked whether it was possible for the private press to use government printing facilities.

Mr Metlhaetsile Leepile (Editor *Mmegi wa Dikgang*) said the current problems between the private press and the politicians arose from the fact that neither side has experience in dealing with each other.

Professor Nsibambi (Makerere University) said that coverage of news by both government and private media was essential since the international community needs to be informed of Botswana's special security problems.

Ms Athalia Molokomme (Law, University of Botswana) wanted to know why some journalists have over the past few years been declared prohibited immigrants in Botswana and who did it? She said this was a practical concern of the private press.

Ms G. Kgathi expressed concern that private press was concerned with profit-making news at the expense of the country's pride and cultural identity.

Dr B. Mguni (Statistics, University of Botswana) wanted to know if private radio stations were allowed in Botswana.

Mr L. Mpotokwane said the policy is still that private radio stations should not be allowed in Botswana. He also said there was no government hostility toward the private press. It is just a problem of learning to cope with each other.

The Honourable Kedikilwe said government has considered giving the private press access to government printing facilities but the problem was that of dealing with political parties which will demand the same right. Replying to Ms Molokomme's question he said it is not only journalists who have been thrown out of the country under the Immigration Act.

SECTION XVI

ROUNDTABLE OF OUTSIDE OBSERVERS

34 Democracy in Botswana: A Pan-African perspective

Okwudiba Nnoli

34.1 INTRODUCTION

The condition of democracy in Botswana and its prospects for the future must be understood within the context of the present crisis of democracy in Africa, the history of this crisis, and its causes. Africa is experiencing a severe crisis of democracy. This is reflected in the crisis of legitimacy of the African state, the ubiquitous one-party state, the life presidents, detention without trial of political opponents, the physical liquidation of dissenters, equation of the criticism of government policies with sabotage and subversion, absence of the rule of law, the muzzling of the press and popular organizations, obsession with the desire to control all centres of power in the society, and the personalization of political power.

This crisis is symbolized in its crudest form by the phenomenon of Idi Amin, Jean Bedel Bokassa and Mobutu Sese Seko. Nevertheless, singly and in various combinations, these anti-democratic traits exist in most African societies. Ideologically, the crisis is expressed by various concoctions such as African socialism, negritude, authenticity and Afrocracy. The content of all these ideologies is the same: service to the leader and his clique.

Even where democratic forms persist, as in Senegal and periodically Nigeria, they are emptied of all content. Their objective seems to be to prevent the people from coming to a true consciousness of their interests as men and women and of the moral essence of their humanity. The leaders seem bent on banishing the people from history. Through mass bribery, intimidation, thuggery, and the outright rigging of elections, they turn the electoral process into a farce. The political campaign has become irrelevant for taking positions of a moral nature.

34.2 THE MEANING OF DEMOCRACY

One wonders at the ability of Botswana, so far, to be immune to this anti-democratic malaise. This ability is most clearly demonstrated by its perseverance with the conduct of free and fair elections, including those by-elections that are ordered by the courts.

Elections epitomize democracy. The equality of the individual to vote or seek political office goes side-by-side with freedom of speech and association, as well as with fairness in the machinery of the electoral process. In addition, elections provide the individual with an opportunity to influence national life by enabling him to put into government those groups that espouse policies that will benefit him, and to replace those in office if they fail to implement acceptable policies.

It is important for the democratic process that two or more political parties vie for the people's support. Parties aggregate the various demands in the society and formulate alternative policies, the choice of which enables the people to influence political decision-making. In trying to fashion a common policy, the party necessarily brings together the socio-economic and political interests of a large number of people, thereby giving weight to each of the separate views or interests the party represents.

Once the party has evolved a common programme on the basis of the interests of its members, it mounts a campaign of education to sell its programme to the electorate at large. Through the use of various media, the party helps to give expression to political and social interests that would otherwise have been dormant or remained the private ideas, views or interests of specific individuals.

This political education function of the party is one of the most direct results of the contest of political parties to secure the mandate of the population to control the government. Parties achieve political education by highlighting the problems of society, outlining their own approaches to a solution such as the construction of housing or the introduction of free education. There cannot be a truly democratic system without a plurality of political parties. Mere consultation of the people is not enough.

The democratic polity of Botswana permits a plurality of political parties, and they vie periodically for the electoral support of the people. Outside the electoral framework, Botswana has promoted the articulation of the interests of the vast majority of the population and their political education through the kgotla system and freedom squares. The country has permitted the existence of popular organizations such as the Student Representative Council and the trade unions. The press is largely unrestricted in the pursuit of its functions, and basic political freedoms can still be enjoyed by various fractions of the ruling class as well as segments of the underprivileged classes. The oppressed populations of the rest of Africa are envious of this democratic condition of Botswana and wonder when their countries can attain it.

Democracy does not convey much meaning and will not last under a pervasive condition of hunger, ignorance and disease. There cannot be a question of freedom, equality or justice for people eternally oppressed by hunger, ignorance and disease. Thus, the people must struggle for the democratization of access to ownership of the means of production and wealth in order to ensure full political equality. They must struggle for the universalization of the systems of education and medical services in order to abolish the political inequality, discrimination and injustice that arise from large differentials in educational attainments and medical fitness. Absence of democracy tends to suspend these struggles. Therefore, it stultifies the further advancement toward the ideals of democracy, such as the expansion of democratic gains from the political to the economic and social realms of life, and from the bourgeoisie to all the other classes and strata in society.

34.3 THE CRISIS OF DEMOCRACY IN AFRICA: ITS CAUSES

The present agreeable democratic condition of Botswana must not give rise in the population to euphoria or arrogance in comparison with the rest of Africa. There is a lesson to be learned from the political histories of many African countries when the ruling class faced serious challenges. Between 1960 and 1965 Nigeria was presented as a show case of democracy in Africa. Nigerians revelled in this image. For most of this period, the interests of the ruling parties, the Northern People's Congress (NPC) and the National Council of Nigerian Citizens (NCNC), were compatible. In 1964 these interest became divergent as each jockeyed for overall supremacy. At this point, respect for democratic norms and values began to wane. The end result was the military coup of January 1966. Ever since, democracy has fluttered and foundered on the rocks of petite bourgeois interests. The same pattern has been repeated in numerous other African countries including Uganda and Zambia. Recently in Senegal, the growth of the electoral influence of the opposition parties has caused the ruling party to rely on fraud and other undemocratic means to win elections and maintain its hold on political power.

Some recent trends in Botswana is not salutary. As the opposition parties have grown in electoral strength, the ruling Botswana Democratic Party (BDP) has turned to undemocratic means to deal with the problem. For example the government has manipulated the financial allocations to the local government councils in such a way as to dominate the policy process. It has also gerrymandered electoral constituencies in its favour. As the press has become more critical, the government has become more impatient with it. There is an obsessive desire to control popular organizations such as the trade unions and the student association. In other words the signs, while not yet ominous, are nevertheless disturbing. The increasing salience of the ethnic question and the parochial emotions it is raising make the situation even more disturbing.

How do we explain the African crisis of democracy? The view point that associates a breakdown of democracy with cultural heterogeneity cannot be sustained. Empirical evidence indicates that the democratic crisis of Africa afflicts both culturally homogenous and heterogenous societies. Somalia, Morocco, Tunisia, Libya, Mali and Niger which are culturally homogenous are not democratic societies.

One explanation for the crisis of democracy in Africa may be found in the degree of commoditisation of the African economy. An enduring characteristic of democracies from Athens to the modern bourgeois and people's democracies is a high level of commoditisation of the economy. The consequence is a high level of atomization and individualization of social relations. Under these conditions, the mediating instrument of the law can be impersonal. The state as a legal entity is above and beyond all the personal and group interest of the competing factions of the ruling class. This relative autonomy of the state permits the rule of law to be practised and, therefore, democratic values and norms to be sustained.

In African, on the other hand, the limited penetration of capitalism and commodity relations has led to a low level of commoditisation of the economy and the consequent lack of autonomy of the state in intra-class and inter-class relations. Many people are still locked into natural economies in which loyalty and commitment are to an individual, family grouping or ethnic group. Politics becomes a zero-sum game in which the stakes are very high. The high stakes arise from the very crucial role of the state in the accumulation process. Through its control and manipulation, individuals can radically transform their economic and social circumstances. Thus, politics is conceived as warfare in which the winner takes all, and all is fair that brings victory.

Under the circumstances, democratic values and institutions become luxuries which the ruling circle cannot afford. The leader must trust only himself and his blood relatives. Others become objects of control. The search for legitimacy soon gives way to reliance on naked force. Dissenters are imprisoned or liquidated. Inevitably, the society becomes polarized into a small clique of rulers intolerant of criticism, even from within its own class, and utterly selfish and ruthless in its political and economic activities.

The petite bourgeois character of the African ruling class also accounts for the crisis of democracy on the continent. The petite bourgeoisie play an essentially dependent role in production. They do not create products and do not benefit from the discipline that derives from creativity in the production process. Their task is that of an intermediary, shifting resources from one part of the society to another. During the struggle for independence, they paid attention only to superstructural activities such as matters of political relations, social discrimination and national unity. As a result, they produced an elaborate programme of political action and principles. But they paid no attention to problems of production. The struggle for economic independence was postponed to a future which is yet to come. Therefore, such achievements as were realized proved to be ephemeral in character. At the slightest excuse or pretext, they are willing to discard democratic practice.

Imperialism must also be recognized as a significant causal factor of the African crisis of democracy. Imperialism adversely affects democracy in various ways. The politics of imperialism is first and foremost the politics of economic exploitation and domination of the African populations and economies by the process of accumulation in the advanced capitalist countries. The heartbeat of this politics is the minimization of wages, the maximization of prices and monopoly profits, and the subordination of the economy to the influence of market forces which ensure the attainment of these objectives by the imperialist powers. The search for these objectives is intense and urgent in the present conjuncture because of the worldwide competition between capitalism and socialism, the stirring of the oppressed peoples against foreign economic exploitation and domination, and the emancipation of the erstwhile colonies from the political domination of imperialism.

In this context, imperialism promotes or opposes democracy in African as it deems opportune. However, it has been difficult for the petite bourgeois regimes to practise democracy while at the same time subduing labour and the peasantry in the interest of the accumulation process of imperialism. For instance the various structural adjustment programmes of the International Monetary Fund reverse the social and economic gains of the African populations that had been accumulated over the years. They call for job retrenchment, removal of subsidies on staple food and the end to various social welfare services.

The people become more hungry, miserable and discontented. Their discontent must be held down with an iron hand by governments that are heavily supported politically and militarily by the imperialist powers of Wester Europe and North America. The result is a crisis of democracy. The imperialists portray industrialization as a process which must entail severe sacrifices. Development is like warfare in which casualties must be sustained and democratic freedoms curtailed.

34.4 THE FUTURE OF DEMOCRACY IN BOTSWANA

The historical experience of the African states suggests that Botswana faces a difficult future in its desire to sustain and advance its present democratic condition. As in all the other African societies, the level of commoditisation of the economy is very low. Colonial economic penetration of Botswana emphasized mining in South Africa and later in Botswana itself. The penetration of commodity relations was confined to these mines and to urban enclaves that serve them and the colonial administration. The vast majority of the population carried on their pre-colonial forms of existence as if nothing had changed.

This low level of penetration of commodity relations into the countryside is correlated with the colonial administrative policy of indirect rule which left the chiefly system of pre-colonial administration very much intact. The economy, culture, tradition and customary laws of the people were not tampered with in the rural areas. The vast majority of the population were directly governed by chiefs who were only subject to monitoring by the colonial government.

Some of the consequences of this low commoditisation are just beginning to emerge. The most disturbing is the increasing tension along cultural community lines. It is reflected in the question of cultural minorities, their equality in the spheres of language, and access to social and economic resources of the country. Often the minority demands are articulated by members of the privileged classes in their intraclass competition and in their search for privileges. They exploit and manipulate parochial sentiments of the rural populace that persist because of the low level of commoditisation and consequent low individualism. If not properly handled, such ethnic contradictions will intensify and pose a serious threat to the pursuit of human rights. Also, in Africa escalating ethnic tension has always provided an excuse to wind down the democratic process.

Another threat to Botswana's democracy comes from petite bourgeois character of the ruling class and its anti-democratic propensity. With the exception of the leading livestock and crop farmers, the members of the Botswana ruling class are not directly associated with the creation of a product. They are involved in tertiary economic activities such as administration, commerce and the professions where they shift resources between one sector and another. Sometimes they are absentee farmers as in the case of bureaucrats who also own farms.

Within this class, the bureaucrats seem to be the preeminent section. They are inclined toward a rationalist mentality, deference to authority, use of force, and technical rather than political solutions to social problems. Under these conditions, persuasion gives way to coercion, discussion to command, freedom to regimentation, and social justice to law and order. The inevitable consequence is a crisis of democracy.

Imperialism is at present flattering Botswana as a country enjoying an economic boom. One remembers similar flatteries of Ghana in the 1950s, Zambia in the 1960s and Nigeria in the 1970s. Like these others, Botswana has a single product economy. Its major export, diamonds, is dependent on world market prices determined essentially by the whims and caprices of monopoly capital. The dynamics of imperialism and its regional surrogate, South Africa, does not permit the country to diversify its export products or to create enough jobs to absorb its ever rising army of unemployed.

Even before the bubble of the favourable world market price for diamonds bursts, a myriad of social problems are severely taxing the patience of the country's rulers. The country's foreign reserves are growing, but the people continue to live in very severe social and economic conditions. Unable to plough these reserves into employment and growth generating industrial enterprises, the country is not preparing itself for the very harsh economic realities of a post-boom economic depression and crisis of the type which has been and is being experienced by Ghana, Nigeria and Zambia when prices for their single export product tumbled. The inevitable consequence of such a crash will be economic depression followed by political repression and the abandonment of democracy. All these would take place to the applause of imperialism.

To make matters worse, imperialism has created a hotbed of tension and social crisis in apartheid South Africa. The signs of this regional threat are increased sabotage, subversion and even outright raids and invasion of Botswana by racist South Africa. The pretence, as usual, is the search by racists for ANC freedom fighters alleged to reside in the country. Increased destabilization by South Africa will lead to increased militarisation of Botswana. The military establishment will come to the fore of national life. Democracy will recede. Political leaders will rely more and more on para-military institutions and the army. The latter may even take over the government. The result will be a military which sees itself as indispensable not only for the defence of the country but for the governance of the society as well. The democratic tradition will be destroyed.

34.5 HOW TO SUSTAIN THE DEMOCRATIC CONDITION OF BOTSWANA

The struggle for the sustenance of democracy in Botswana must be seen as part and parcel of the overall struggle against imperialism and its surrogate in South Africa. In this struggle, democracy is a potent instrument that unites the people behind their leaders. It must never be seen as a luxury which the leaders cannot afford. The truth is that the country cannot be pulled out of its problems of development, lack of discipline of the petite bourgeoisie, and the exploitation and domination of imperialism without the active participation of the masses in the politics of their country.

The task of the leaders is to continually raise the consciousness of the masses to new heights and to respect their electoral wishes at every turn. Otherwise, their enthusiasm for the democratic process will wane and they will abandon the struggle. The political education of the masses comes from their close interaction with their leaders as they fight their battles for existence, in which the one teaches and learns from the other. Through such an interaction, the masses generate forces which supply the leaders with their dynamic and make it possible for them to forge ahead politically, socially and economically. It also teaches the masses that the leaders are essential for the coherence of the society. The time taken up in explaining policies to the people and the time 'lost' in treating them as human beings by participating in their daily struggles with nature and social forces of exploitation and domination is usually made up in their political support and determination to make the necessary sacrifice for the success of the leaders.

The enthusiasm of the masses for democracy will wane unless there is associated with it, an economic programme concerning an equitable and fair division of national wealth. Although the masses are usually willing to sacrifice everything for the nation, they have to be encouraged especially in the sphere of the distribution of material welfare. A fair system of distribution according to work done, coupled with an enormous increase in the funds for the social forms of personal consumption such as state welfare services will stimulate an upsurge in the peoples labour and political enthusiasm. Such a policy is possible if legislation is used to limit nonproductive incomes.

In the political sphere, the incentive the masses need in order to realize their potential for democracy and progress is relief from the monstrous oppression arising from bureaucratic arrogance of both the public and private institutions. The people are treated with disdain as ignorant, incapable of appreciating the technical requirements of policy in a modern state. The government assumes the task of supervising the masses. It becomes an administration relying on the police and the army to control the people.

Unless the people are politically involved in an organized form, their involvement will not last and democracy cannot be sustained. Their unorganized efforts can only be a temporary dynamic. A leadership that is committed to democracy must devote a significant proportion of national resources to the creation of viable and independent organizations of the masses in the social, political and economic fields. In this regard, the present government control of trade unions and other popular organizations is unhealthy.

Finally democracy cannot be sustained if the leadership does not cultivate consistent democracy. This means consideration of all national and sub-national issues from the point of view of no inequality, no privilege and no exclusiveness. More particularly, in view of the growing problem of ethnic minorities, consistent democracy must appraise each concrete ethnic question from the point of view of removing all inequality, all privileges and exclusiveness. Constant democracy also demands strict adherence to the rule of law, especially in relations between the ruling party and the opposition parties. Neither must use its power to procure unlawful advantages and privileges over the other. There can be no detention without trial, retrospective legislation, gerrymandering of constituencies or unfair treatment of institutions controlled by the opposition parties. Only such a policy is capable of uniting the various ethnic groups in a manner that sweeps away all pre-capitalist, caste, parochial, religious and other particularistic barriers to progress.

35 On democracy and development in Botswana

Richard L. Sklar

35.1 INTRODUCTION

I have been asked to assess the effectiveness of democracy in Botswana with reference to comparative cases. Other contributors to this volume have pondered the scope and practical limits of democracy in Botswana today. My contribution will focus on the impact of democracy on development. Does the practice of democracy in Botswana effectively promote economic and social development? Does it help Botswana cope with the restrictive circumstance of its geographical and economic dependence on South Africa; with its harsh physical environment, including recurrent drought; and with economic underdevelopment in general?

35.2 THE DANGER OF RENT-SEEKING

A remarkable contrast exists between Botswana's economic performance and that of other African states which have an important economic characteristic in common with Botswana. The common characteristic is this: substantial reliance on mineral exports — up to 10% of gross domestic product (GDP) or 40% of merchandise export trade. There are twelve such countries in Africa, not including the Republic of South Africa. On the basis of several standard indicators of national development, these countries as a group have not fared better than most of the African countries which are less well-endowed with natural resources. Overall the mineral-rich countries display relatively low rates of growth for both agricultural and industrial production, relatively poor records of economic diversification, relatively high rates of unemployment, and a tendency toward the accumulation of staggering foreign debts.[1] By way of comparison, Cote d'Ivoire and Kenya, which have comparatively modest endowments of natural-resource wealth, have maintained far higher annual rates of growth in GDP — 6% and 6.5% respectively — than mineral-rich Guinea, Liberia, Niger, Zambia, or Zaire. Among those African economies which are mainly dependent on mineral exports, other than oil, the sole exception to this surprising rule of relatively poor performance — the lone-star state — is Botswana. (See Table 1.) As Geoffrey Bergen has observed:

> While the rates of growth in GDP for most of the mineral-exporting countries in Africa have been relatively stagnant, Botswana's rate of growth for the period 1965-1980 was 14.3%; for the period 1980-1985 it was 12.1%. During the decade 1975-1985, Botswana's annual per capita income increased from $290 to $1 690. The key to Botswana's performance lies not in the character of diamonds as a commodity — like any mineral, diamonds are subject to slumps and upswings in world markets; the key is prudent and well-implemented economic management. Whereas other states with mineral-based economies have dispersed sudden windfalls of income from mineral price booms as if there were no tomorrows, Botswana has established a workable policy of running up cash balances in good years for use in bad, and this has kept the economy on a stable course. As a result, Botswana has been able to hold its debt to a comfortably low margin of national income.[2]

What is the secret of Botswana's remarkable success? Except for Botswana, each state listed in Table 1 is characterized by a kind of behaviour known to political economists as 'rent-seeking'.[3] A rent-seeking state extracts wealth from its population in return for economic and political services. In Africa today, this means that the state transfers wealth from farmers, workers, merchants, and industrialists to state officials and related sectors of the urban intelligentsia. Symptomatically, the average earnings of governmental employees in Africa (measured as a multiple of per capita GDP) are twice that recorded for Asia.[4]

Typical rent-seeking practices include deflation of agricultural prices and overvaluation of the currency. Such policies hurt the farmer and the entrepreneur in that they receive a depressed price for their goods and services. This reduces the motivation of these producers and cuts the amount of products which are exported. On the other hand, the overvalued currency makes imports, many of which do not contribute to development like automobiles, relatively cheap. The result is that the more well-to-do consumers, many of whom are civil servants, end up obtaining these imported goods at good prices.

Table 1: Development Indicators

Country	GDP Growth (avg. ann. rate) 1965-80	1980-85	Growth of Agricultural prod. per cap. (1970-82)	Index of Food Production (1969-71 = 100)	Growth of Ind. Manuf. avg. 1970-82
Non-fuel					
Botswana	14.3%	12.1%	−6.0%	89	na
Guinea	3.9	0.9	−0.6	89	na
Liberia	3.2	− 1.9	−1.4	88	4.5%
Mauritania	2.1	0.2	−1.0	73	5.2
Niger	0.3	− 3.6	0.7	88	na
Togo	4.4	− 1.8	−0.3	89	− 10.0
Zaire	1.4	1.0	−1.7	87	− 2.3
Zambia	1.8	0.1	−1.4	87	1.4
Petroleum					
Angola	na	na	−5.4	77	na
Congo P.R.	5.9	7.8	−2.0	81	3.3
Gabon	na	na	−0.8	93	na
Nigeria	7.9	− 3.4	−0.2	92	12.0

Sources: World Bank, *World Development Report,* 1987
World Bank, *Towards Sustained Development in Sub-Saharan Africa* (1981)

The rent-seeking hypothesis may furnish a satisfactory explanation for the difference between agricultural prosperity in Kenya and Zimbabwe, on the one hand, and agricultural decline in Tanzania and Zambia. Reversal of a rent-seeking tendency may also account for the remarkable turnabout and sustained economic recovery in Ghana, beginning in 1983. To be sure, states with extreme rent-seeking characteristics, such as Zambia and Zaire, are deeply in debt and forever after loans and grants.

By 1988, twenty-two sub-Saharan African countries were designated by the World Bank as 'debt distressed': their debt service obligations were in excess of 30 per cent of their foreign exchange earnings.[5] In Zambia, the debt service ratio verges on 70 per cent. It is hardly possible for the governments of these heavily indebted countries to meet the pressing needs of their people for public health, safety and sundry services. Potential critics abound, but they are muzzled; organized political opposition is prohibited; labour unions are regimented; the press is made to do the bidding of the regime. In short, the state itself becomes the enemy of society.

Botswana stands out among the twelve mineral-dependent states, listed in Table 1, as the only one which has not fallen into the rent-seeking trap. The revenue-stabilization fund, established in 1973, does not appear to have been used for the distribution of income to influential groups. No one appears to be draining the surplus, which is as admirable as it is remarkable for a mineral- rich Third World country.

Compare Botswana with Niger, two countries with common characteristics, including pastoralism and intractable problems of drought. When the bottom dropped out of the uranium market, following a uranium boom during the early and mid-1970s, Niger could not manage its financial crisis. By way of contrast, when the diamond price dipped in 1981-1982, Botswana had both the financial means and management capacity to cope with that challenge.[6] The earnings of boon times had been managed in a responsible manner. They were neither appropriated by rent-seeking interests nor distributed by the officials of a rent-seeking state.

35.3 GOVERNMENT ACCOUNTABILITY IN AFRICA

Botswana's economic achievement is not unrelated to its practice of democracy. Responsible economic management is directly attributable to the most fundamental principle of democratic government, namely the norm of accountability. By accountability, I mean that those who exercise power on a continuing basis are required to answer or account for their conduct to others who are entitled to judge it. There does appear to be a direct relationship between the lack of accountability and rent-seeking behaviour in numerous African countries. Thus, governments which have managed to minimize rent-seeking behaviour have also created confidence in the minds of agricultural producers and other entrepreneurs that such groups have been and will be able to assert their interests effectively.

The African governments which most reflect this approach are Cote d'Ivoire, Kenya, Zimbabwe, and Botswana. Obviously, these four countries do not constitute an ideological grouping. The critical distinction here is rent-seeking behaviour versus responsible economic management, not capitalism versus socialism.

Senegal, a country with genuinely democratic features in its system of government, has not avoided the rent-seeking trap because the Islamic holy men (marabouts) there are immensely influential and manipulate the state to obtain financial resources, which they both keep and distribute to their followers.[7] In Senegal, as in Nigeria, we find a vigorous tug-of-war between rent-seekers and responsible managers.[8] Struggles of this kind are facts of political life in all countries, everywhere. Typically, the pressures for rent-seeking forms of redistribution are so powerful that comparably efficient mechanisms for accountability are needed to hold them in check.

Two forms of accountability are basic to the practice of democratic government. First, there is a direct relationship between democracy and those procedures which render leaders accountable to their followers. Elections at regular intervals serve that purpose. Second, there is an indirect relationship between democracy and those procedures which render office-holders accountable to one another for the lawful performance of their duties. Such procedures underlie constitutional, as opposed to the despotic, forms of government. In the Western World, constitutional accountability preceded the introduction of democratic accountability by many years and, in a few cases, by a few centuries.

In most other cases, including Africa and most of Asia, the constitutional and democratic forms of accountability are being introduced at roughly the same time. As in the West, democrats in all countries learn and relearn the lesson that democracy cannot be gained or maintained without the safeguards of constitutional government. The fight for constitutional government and against extra-constitutional usurpations of power is always crucial to the movement for democracy.

35.4 GOVERNMENT ACCOUNTABILITY IN BOTSWANA

In Botswana, as in Senegal, The Gambia and Mauritius (these four African states have governments chosen by means of electoral competition between rival parties), the indirect (constitutional) form of accountability is more effective than the directly democratic form. No message was conveyed more clearly during this symposium than the political supremacy of the Botswana Democratic Party (BDP). The acid test of electoral democracy in Botswana, as in Senegal, would be materialization of a credible threat to the Democratic Party's majority in parliament. No such threat is yet visible on the political horizon.

The only potential threat to rule by the BDP is the growing power of the army, which has never yet threatened the civilian and constitutional order. Logically, those who regret the relative weakness of electoral competition in Botswana should be the foremost defenders of constitutional guarantees which secure the political rights of all citizens. However, this symposium produced an ambiguous, if not disquieting, expression of elite and intellectual opinion concerning the crucial relationship between constitutional government and democracy.

It would be difficult to imagine freer discussions of political issues than those afforded by this symposium. Criticisms and complaints were freely aired by citizens, always without fear and frequently without favour. Public officials, who participated in their personal capacities, defended public policies and were criticized in turn for both the content of their responses and their omissions. Various imperfections of democracy in Botswana and fears for its future were boldly exposed. Among the alleged shortcomings, I noted these: overly restrictive electoral practices, apparent interference with the mail, financial strangulation of the private press, inadequate protection for the rights of labour, differential incorporation of certain nationalities in the body politic, and various abuses of administrative authority. In Botswana, as in every liberal democracy, the constitutional form of government is flawed in practice and threatened, from time to time, with erosion by the imperatives of national security.

35.5 THE INTELLECTUALS AND MARXISM

I would like to dwell more extensively on one threat which was manifest but not mentioned in our discussions. I observed a familiar tendency by intellectuals to excoriate the association of constitutional government with the protection of private property. Some (certainly not all) Marxist critics of capitalism are inclined to use the term 'bourgeois democracy' as a disparaging synonym for liberal democracy. That verbal ruse involves ideological deceit. Liberal democracy connotes divided power in accordance with the rule of law, freedom of expression, freedom of association, and competition for office at regular intervals.

Since the onset of the industrial revolution, no class has had a greater stake in the defense of liberal democracy than the working class. In many countries today, liberalism is a more revolutionary idea than communism; think of the working-class struggle for liberty in Eastern Europe. Free trade unionism has always been the first casualty of dictatorships instituted for the supposed sake of national development. No one loses more when liberal democracy is eroded than the working man and woman. It is misleading to suggest that liberal democracy favours the wealthier, property-owning classes more than the working classes.

Ponder the thinking behind statements which suggest that it may be good for working people to forego liberal democracy in favour of an allegedly more revolutionary alternative. Such thinking almost always presumes the commonplace fallacy of class rule, an idea that featured prominently in the proceedings of this symposium. Few informed people today cling to the naive conviction that a working class has ever actually 'ruled' under a so-called dictatorship of the proletariat. It is no more plausible, or less mistaken, to contend that liberal democracy implies class rule by the bourgeoisie. When an entire nation, or even the greater part thereof, participates in public life on the basis of equal political rights for all citizens, no one class as such can possibly be a 'ruling class'.

The very conception of a 'ruling' class involves a confusion of thought because it melds the idea of government with that of social structure. The concept is one of the more imprecise ideas of nineteenth-century political sociology. Its use in debates about contemporary development can have far-reaching consequences. Just as doctrinaire intellectuals used the Russian word *kulak* to justify ill-conceived and disastrous agricultural policies in Tanzania, so might the mistaken idea of a ruling class be propagated to dampen the spirit of enterprise in Botswana. The more critical issue for Botswana to debate is not whether capitalism or a capitalist ruling class is good or bad, but how the private economy can be made accountable for its behaviour.

35.6 CONCLUSION

I do not, in the least, wish to discourage the application of class-analytic methods, from the Marxist or any other intellectual orientation, to the study of politics. My sole purpose is to dispel the spectral presence of a malign notion that social justice implies anything less than total dedication to liberal democracy. In Botswana, as elsewhere in the Third World, the pursuit of social justice apart from intensive economic development is unrealistic.

For the sake of rapid development, every productive group, or estate, of the economic realm − including business, labour, farming, management, and administration – must be free to make its essential contribution to the process. Freedom must also prevail in the marketplace of ideas, where intellectuals can promote the cause of development by combating the influence of doctrines and terminologies that either demean the contributions of productive groups or justify their liquidation, as in the lamentable case of Tanzanian 'kulaks'. This freedom, however, must be tempered by various forms of institutional accountability. A developing constitutional government must seek to insure that required means to achieve this end, which will obviously vary from country to country and over time, are in place.

Liberal democracy, like a delicate plant, should be carefully nurtured and protected by those who wish it to survive. Liberals should not be timid in their defence of democracy when it is buffeted by militarists, on one side, and illiberal intellectuals, on the other. Their principled support is needed to keep the autocrats and rent-seekers at bay.

ENDNOTES

1   Giraud, P. *Geopolitique des Ressources Minires* (Paris: Economica, 1983) pp. 652-653. Cited in Geoffrey Bergen and Richard L. Sklar, 'Mineral Industries and Development in Sub-Saharan Africa', prepared for a workshop on 'Soviet-U.S. Cooperation for Aflrica', Moscow, December 1987 p. 1.

2   Bergen, G. 'Minerals and Development in Africa', Department of Political Science, University of California, Los Angeles, 1988 p. 8, citing Lewis, S. 'Botswana: Diamonds, Drought, Development, and Democraci', *CSI Africa Notes* (Washington, D.C.), No. 47, September 11 1985.

3   See Buchanan, J. M. Tollison, R. D. and Tullock, G. eds., *Toward a Theory of the Rent-Seeking Society* (College Station: Texas A&M University Press, 1980).

4   The World Bank, *Financing Adjustment with Growth in Sub-Saharan Africa*, 1986-90 (Washington, D.C.: 1986) p. 21.

5   Callaghy, T. M. 'Debt and Structural Adjustment in Africa: Realities and Possibilities', *Issue*, XVI, 2 (1988) p. 11.

6   Lewis, 'Botswana', p. 3.

7   O'Brien, D. C. 'Wails and Whispers: the People's Voice in West African Muslim Politics', in Chabel, P. ed., *Political Domination in Africa: Reflections on the Limits of Power* (Cambridge University Press, 1986) pp. 71-83.

8   See Diamond, L. 'Nigeria: Pluralism, Statism, and the Struggle for Democracy', in Diamond, Linz, J. and Lipset, S. M. eds., *Democracy in Developing Countries*, Vol. II, *Africa* (Boulder, Colo.: Lynne Rienner, 1988) p. 33.

36 Democracy in Botswana: an external assessment

William Tordoff[1]

36.1 INTRODUCTION

Botswana's political system is different from other African political systems in a number of respects. Botswana did not share in the trend, in most of post-colonial Africa, away from political pluralism towards the centralization of power in the hands of a single party. She is one of a very small number of countries (the others being Gambia and Mauritius) which have retained a multiparty system throughout the post-independence period. Whereas nearby countries such as Tanzania and Zambia have allowed some competition within their single-party systems, Botswana is almost unique in having consistently allowed competition between parties. From the mid-1970s a number of African countries have sought to reverse the earlier, single-party trend, but with limited success: thus, the restoration, following military withdrawal, of multiparty politics in Ghana and Nigeria in 1979 proved short-lived.

A controlled experiment in multiparty democracy is being made in Senegal where beginning in 1976 opposition parties have been allowed to emerge, register and compete in both legislative and presidential elections. To date, however, the introduction of inter-party competition in Senegal has not seriously challenged the monopoly of the ruling party, the Parti Socialiste Sénégalais (PSS), any more than such competition has undermined the monopoly of the Botswana Democratic Party (BDP) in Botswana. In political science terms, each country can be characterized as having a one-party dominant political system.[2]

Like the great majority of African states, Botswana has an executive president. Unlike these states, however, presidential power in Botswana has not been personalized. Many (perhaps most) major decisions are still taken collectively by the cabinet, whose members are advised by a relatively strong bureaucracy.

36.2 IDEOLOGY AND POLITICS IN BOTSWANA

No attempt has been made to erect an official ideology in contrast to other parts of Africa. President Sir Seretse Khama did recognize the need for African countries to 'develop their own guiding ideologies, which are rooted in their own experience and responsive to their own needs'.[3] His most explicit effort in this regard was to put forward four national principles — of democracy, development, self-reliance and unity — to guide the party and nation.[4] The BDP has never been preoccupied with the further articulation of these or any other set of ideas into an ideology.

Crawford Young has identified three main streams of ideology in African politics: Afro-Marxism, populist-socialism, and African capitalism,[5] Botswana best fits the last category. But these are not discrete categories, and it is important to recognize the government's commitment to social justice, reflected in its concern to distribute equitably the benefits of the country's mineral wealth among all parts of the country.

The editors of a recent four-volume study of *Democracy in Developing Countries* argue that democracy as a system of government must be kept conceptually distinct from both capitalism and socialism; however, they maintain that to date, 'one does not find democracy in the absence of some form of capitalism'.[6] Botswana, 'a paternalistic democracy' and the subject of a case-study in the Africa volume, is one of the countries which is held to substantiate this argument. Despite the disclaimer that the empirical association between democracy and capitalism is not necessarily permanent, the authors give little attention to alternatives to capitalism that might be compatible with democracy. The thrust of their study is the need for economic liberalism and the adoption of market mechanisms and incentives.

This argument sidesteps the practical difficulty that at independence the African state became, and is mostly still, the main agent of economic development precisely because of limited indigenous private ownership and control of productive enterprises. Botswana's cattle industry, predominantly owned and controlled by citizens, made this Southern African country a partial exception to this pattern; however, within a few years of independence, the Botswana government felt the need to tackle the problems of overgrazing and the deterioration of communal land in the tribal communal areas. Moreover, from the outset the government sought to prescribe the terms under which multinational companies operated the state's growing mining industry.

The result is that state intervention and regulation of the economy has been hardly less substantial in Botswana than in African states like Kenya, Nigeria and Zambia which have mostly pursued a state capitalist strategy of development. In Botswana, as in African states generally, such state control has made power holding attractive. The fact that many of the country's leading politicians and bureaucrats have extended or acquired business interests while holding, or upon vacating, public office has given them a strong commitment to maintain the country's present system of government.

36.3 BOTSWANA'S DEMOCRACY

Certain elements of Botswana's democracy fit the democratic model: Cabinet decision making in most matters, with the bureaucrats carrying great weight on economic and technical issues, a multiparty system, and (despite opposition party criticism) substantially free and fair elections at both national and local levels resulting in the control by opposition parties of the Gaborone city council and one district council.[7] Other elements consistent with democratic practice are open debate in parliament and the local councils, an independent judiciary, new authorities ('land boards') to deal with land matters, a good human rights record, a public service substantially divorced from politics, and a substantially free if resource poor private press.

All these things are important, but do not by themselves guarantee the survival of democracy in Botswana. For example Ghana's government was very similar at independence in 1957. Indeed, there was a larger and more outspoken press, more and stronger modern interest groups, and a much broader educational base than exists in Botswana today.

One must look, then, for additional elements in Botswana's democracy. I think back to the time in 1970 when I first visited Botswana as a member of a Local Government Study Group. I found it much more difficult to understand the working of Botswana's political system than that of other African countries in which I had worked, notably Ghana, Tanzania and Zambia. The BDP had a weakly articulated structure with only one full-time party organizer outside Gaborone; it did not have strong youth and women's sections, and only limited party-government assimilation had taken place. Again, popular participation was partial and intermittent (for example, at election times) rather than high and constant. Nevertheless, the political system seemed to work remarkably well.

The critical factor, I think, is the persistence of what is sometimes called neopatrimonialism,[8] a form of organization in which government leaders in the capital are linked in a mutual support system with their rural subordinates. This system is not governed by bureaucratic rules. Though political parties – the BDP more obviously than the Botswana National Front (BNF), its main rival – have stronger up-country organizations than they had in 1970, elements of this patron-client relationship persist.

Examples of these rural-urban links are the remittances which the 'big men' in Gaborone (and other urban residents) send home to their kinsmen and the provision which they make for the education of close relatives.[9] These links are reinforced by what John Holm has aptly described as the 'suprafamily security system',[10] and the variety of social welfare programmes and new jobs which the rapidly growing national economy has been able to support. This combination of factors helps to explain why explosive consequences have not followed the trend whereby the national cattle herd is concentrated in the hands of fewer and bigger farmers who appropriate the communal grazing land for their individual (or syndicate) use.

36.4 THE CIVIL SERVICE: A NEW RULING CLASS!

Is this neopatrimonial form of organization under threat? This question is raised because Patrick Molutsi's paper in this volume, 'The ruling class and democracy in Botswana' challenges accepted orthodoxy in a number of respects. On the basis of the survey conducted by himself and other members of the University of Botswana's Democracy Project, he argues that the senior, decision making section of the bureaucracy rejects cattle ownership. Seventy per cent of permanent secretaries (he tells us) do not have cattle; instead, most of them hold shares in private companies and parastatals such as the Botswana Development Corporation (BDC), Sechaba Trust, and Sefalana. His findings deny that there is a coalition of interests between politicians and bureaucrats. Rather he asserts that senior bureaucrats have moved to various forms of urban investment including real estate companies and moved away from cattle.[11]

In contrast, Richard P. Werbner, following Ornulf Gulbrandsen, states that 'Botswana is exceptional among African countries in that its governing elites, both nationally and in most districts, are dominantly cattle keepers; they are tied to commercial production for the beef market'.[12] If Molutsi is to be believed, an important shift from this pattern of investment has occurred in the case of senior bureaucrats (though not politicians).

There are a number of points to be made. Dr Molutsi's survey raises the kind of issues that highlight the need for qualitative and in-depth research into the careers and mobility patterns of contemporary civil servants. We know that many of the first generation of senior bureaucrats (and politicians) invested in cattle and land. Some of them, like Duplaix Pilane, took early retirement in order to look after their farms and cattle posts. Others, like Richard Mannathoko, took advantage of the changing opportunities for upward mobility by crossing over into the private sector.

Since Botswana is a country where people are very conscious of the risks of investing in one direction only, it would be surprising if the new generation of senior bureaucrats did not act in the same way and if some of them, too, did not eventually leave the public service in order to join private companies that deal with government. It may well be that the long drought has made it less attractive for permanent secretaries to risk the possibility of heavy cattle losses through personal cattle ownership, though Molutsi does not assert that they and other senior bureaucrats have withdrawn from investment in the people of the countryside or in other rural businesses, such as bottle stores. It is certainly true that the towns grew rapidly in size in the post-colonial era. Gaborone's population, for example, has grown from under 20 000 in 1970 to over 100 000 today. These new urban centres are bound to offer many new opportunities for investment. As urban migration inflated the demand for and value of residential plots and housing, bureaucrats (and some politicians and private businessmen) invested in property.

The elite in Botswana is not monolithic and it may be that significant changes in the patterns of elite investment are in train. As was pointed out above, many members of the elite have long favoured having a portfolio of investments which will offset the high risk of cattle loss. Speculation in real estate, like share holding in private companies and parastatals, has to be appreciated in the context of a long term tendency towards diversification of investment.

If the time should come when there is a major shift away from rural investment on the part of most individual members of the ruling elite, the organic relationships which the latter maintain with the countryside would be seriously weakened. In all probability, Botswana's political system would be destabilized as a result. This has not yet happened. For most of the salariat, 'their home, in the most compelling sense of the word, is still in the countryside',[13] and they continue to be tied to the latter by patron-client linkages.

As a society and system of government, Botswana has blended the modern and the traditional, combining elements of continuity with elements of change. Patron-client networks exist within a modern party organization. The kgotla continues to play an important role along side the freedom square. The land boards continue to rely in their decision making process on statements by wardheads and local representatives.[14] This combination of the old and the new serves to reinforce Botswana's democracy.

36.5 THE FUTURE OF DEMOCRACY IN BOTSWANA

While Botswana's economy functions as free enterprise system, there is no reason to believe that democracy can only exist in a capitalist context. Indeed, it is precisely by emphasizing those elements of social justice which socialism holds dear that democracy in Botswana can be extended and strengthened. Holm correctly summarizes the present situation in Botswana when he writes that:

> . . . economic inequality, which certainly is considerable, does not automatically create intense feelings of alienation and political dissent in either the urban or rural areas.[15]

Nevertheless, the danger signs are there, for example, in the form of increased land shortage, rural poverty, a widening income gap between rich and poor, and rapid urban migration without corresponding employment opportunities. So far there has been relatively little landlessness in Botswana as against a sense of land shortage and pressure on the land.[16] It is vitally important that full dispossession should be avoided since landlessness leads to polarization and Latin American style 'revolutions.'

The development of a mining economy in Botswana could in time prove to be politically destabilizing. The country has been drawn much more into the world economy over which it has no control. In addition, the economic expansion resulting from mining has increased the number of urban wage earners who, already in the 1970s, expressed their discontent through strikes and wage demands. Much will depend on the international price of minerals[17] and perhaps also on the extent to which South Africa still recruits wage labour from Botswana.

Other facts will condition the political stability of Botswana's democracy. The political elite must continue to distribute mining earnings equitably among all parts of the country. At an individual level, neopatrimonialism must continue to transfer part of the urban income to the rural areas, and the government must mitigate the effects of the skewed distribution of the country's land and cattle wealth by maintaining and expanding its various programmes for the rural areas. In drawing attention to the significance of what he calls the 'urban and rural peasantariat' in the political economy of Botswana, Jack Parson writes that since the economy depends on its labour, it 'is the critical class in the country's politics' and is thus, 'the crucial element in maintaining the coherence and stability of the system'.[18]

In sum, the question is whether Botswana's ruling, cattle owning politicians will be persuaded, for reasons of political expediency if for no other, to pass a self-denying ordinance by introducing a cattle tax and by depriving themselves of the opportunity to establish commercial ranches under private leasehold tenure.

Turning to the local government system, I have argued elsewhere that Botswana's record of representative local government is impressive when compared with that of the great majority of other Commonwealth African states.[19] District councils had a good record of implementing projects under the Accelerated Rural Development Programme in the mid-1970s and would have achieved a better than 55 per cent rate of implementing National Development Plan (NDP) V targets in 1979-85 had it not been for organizational problems within the central government and the considerable diversion of effort into drought relief during the plan period.

This achievement must not be exaggerated. District councils do not at present have either the councillors or staff with the education and skills to justify conferring on them substantial additional powers or resources. Since independence the central government has taken the lion's share of available qualified manpower and subjected district and town councils to fairly tight scrutiny and control. Moreover, central government ministries account for approximately 80 per cent of development expenditure in the districts. In these circumstances, Holm's statement that 'the centrepiece of Botswana democracy is the local council system' is wide of the mark.[20]

Equally questionable is the argument, advanced by Picard and Morgan, that strong local government institutions controlled by local socio-economic elites and central government civil servants are 'an essential component to further capital accumulation in the rural areas.'[21] This idea would make sense if district councils and land boards were controlled by radical elements fundamentally opposed to the main thrust of the BDP's land and fiscal policy. This is not the case at present and seems unlikely to become so in the near future. The fact is that many district councillors, even in opposition dominated districts such as Southern, are themselves substantial cattle owners.[22] The same group is also strongly represented on the land boards.[23]

Research needs to be directed to the question: Why do poor rural voters in Botswana choose as their representatives people considerably better-off than themselves?[24] Presumably the explanation is the persistence of patron-client linkages at the local level.

36.6 SOME RECOMMENDATIONS ON DEMOCRACY IN LOCAL GOVERNMENT

There are a number of ways in which Botswana's local authorities could be made more democratic. The central government could strengthen them further if it had the political will to do so. An essential first step would be to implement the recommendation of the 1982 Presidential Commission on Economic Opportunities that able and experienced Batswana public officers should be allocated to the Unified Local Government Service (ULGS).[25] The question here is whether Gaborone based bureaucrats would be willing to erode their own power base in this manner.

An argument likely to be advanced against further decentralization is the indifferent quality of councillors. The onus is on the political parties to put forward more able and better educated candidates. The critical difficulty the parties face is that such candidates will not come forward unless there is a prospect that additional powers will be conferred on the councils.

It has been suggested that another way of enhancing the democratic element in Botswana's local government system would be formally to incorporate the kgotla, with its deep roots in the culture and history of the country, into the local government structure.[26] Against this it can be argued that there is an advantage in retaining the kgotla in an ambiguous position since the effect of incorporation would be to convert a locally authorized, semi-autonomous forum of the various tribes into an appendage of the state. The fact that government ministers and other servants of the state have to come to the kgotla gives the people a sense of some power rather than powerlessness.

36.7 CONCLUSION

Several speakers at the conference referred to 'the miracle of democracy' in Botswana. This is mistaken: There are good practical, as distinct from supernatural, reasons for the emergence of democracy in Botswana. Apart from those given above, the contribution made by 'founding fathers' such as Philip Matante of the Botswana People's Party, ex-Chief Bathoen of the BNF, and Tshekedi and Seretse Khama are important. The fact that Seretse's traditional legitimacy as the *de facto* chief of the Bamangwato was reinforced by his electoral legitimacy as the President of the Republic gave him unrivalled political ascendancy within the political system.[27] He was able to institute a system of government which was based on the Westminster model and which is still, by and large, maintained by Dr Quett Masire, who succeeded him as president in 1980.

Despite the importance of such democratic origins, democracy in Botswana will only be secure if the Batswana themselves are determined to uphold it. Grant and Egner express concern over certain incidents which they fear will endanger press freedom in Botswana.[28] These writers are not competent to say whether their concerns are real or exaggerated. Nevertheless, it should be remembered that any government which seeks to avoid public accountability in the name of national security ends up discrediting itself both nationally and internationally. Strong political parties, free and fair elections, a free press and autonomous interest groups are among the many agencies which can help to check such abuse.

ENDNOTES

1   I am indebted to Dr Richard P. Werbner of the Department of Social Anthropology, University of Manchester, for providing helpful comments on the draft of this article. I have incorporated several of his suggestions in the text.

2   See Tordoff, W. *Government and Politics in Africa* (London: Macmillan, 1984) pp. 280-284, and passim.

3   Statement at the Third Summit Conference of Non-Aligned Nations, Lusaka, 8-10 September 1970, in *Non-Aligned Conference: Lusaka, 1970 — Botswana's Policy of Non-Alignment* (Gaborone: Government Printer, n.d.) p. 3.

4   'Kagisano — A Policy for Harmony', Address delivered by President Khama to the 11th Annual Conference of the BDP at Francistown, 1 April 1972 (Gaborone: mimeo.), and 'Botswana: a Developing Democracy in Southern Africa', Address by President Khama at Uppsala, Sweden, on 11 November 1970 (Gaborone: Government Printer, n.d.) pp. 3-4.

5   Young, C. *Ideology and Development in Africa* (New Haven: Yale University Press, 1982) p. 12.

6   Diamond, L. Linz, J. J. and Lipset, S. M. (eds.), *Democracy in Developing Countries*, Vol. 2 *Africa*, (Boulder, Colorado: Lynne Rienner Publishers, 1988) p. xxi.

7   The opposition criticizes the present system of democracy on several grounds. One is its resistance to reducing the voting age from twenty-one to eighteen. Another is that the BDP appoints its supporters to local councils regardless of the fact that on some councils there is a majority of elected representatives from an opposition party. In the case of Jwaneng, the effect of using this power was to deprive the BNF of its (1984) electoral majority when one BNF member defected to the BDP.

8   For a good, succinct discussion of this concept see Clapham, C. *Third World Politics: An Introduction* (London: Croom Helm, 1985) pp. 48-50.

9   See especially Werbner, R. P. 'From Heartland to Hinterland: Elites and the Geo-Politics of Land in Botswana', a paper prepared for delivery at a Symposium on 'Land in African Agrarian Systems', 10-12 April 1988, at the Centre for African Studies, University of Illinois, Champaign-Urbana.

10 Holm, J. D. 'Botswana: A Paternalistic Democracy', in Diamond et al., *Democracy in Developing Countries*, Vol 2, p. 199.

11 Molutsi, P. P. 'The Ruling Class and Democracy in Botswana', in this volume.

12 Werbner, 'From Heartland to Hinterland', p. 2.

13 Ibid., p. 5.

14 Hitchcock, R. K. 'Water, Land and Livestock: The Evolution of Tenure and Administration Patterns in the Grazing Areas of Botswana', in Picard, L. A. (ed.), *The Evolution of Modern Botswana* (London: Rex Collings, 1985) p. 121.

15 Holm, 'Botswana: A Paternalistic Democracy', p. 199.

16 See Gulbrandsen, O. 'Access to Agricultural Land and Communal Land Management in Eastern Botswana', Research Paper No. 81, Land Tenure Centre, University of Wisconsin, Madison, March 1985, pp. 60-61.

17   See Professor Richard L. Sklar's comments in this section regarding Botswana's ability to deal with the temporary drop in mineral prices which occurred in the early 1980s.

18   Parson, J. *Botswana, Liberal Democracy and the Labour Reserve in Southern Africa* (Boulder, Colorado: Westview Press, 1984) p. 117.

19   See Tordoff, W. 'Local Administration in Botswana', *Public Administration and Development*, Vol. 8 (1988), pp. 183-202. For a penetrating assessment of the performance of district councils in Botswana, see Engner, B. *District Councils and Decentralization, 1978-1986* (Gaborone, Swedish International Development Agency, 1987).

20   Holm, 'Botswana: A Paternalistic Democracy', p. 187.

21   Picard, L. A. and Morgan, E. P. 'Policy, Implementation and Local Institutions in Botswana', in Picard, *The Evolution of Modern Botswana*, p. 133.

22   Holm recoreds that a survey of three southern districts in Botswana found that 62 percent of district councillors had more than 25 cattle, while 42 per cent had more than 50 cattle. Quoted by Picard and Morgan, ibid., p. 137. Supporting evidence is to be found in Molutsi, 'The Ruling Class in Botswana'.

23   The Central District Land Board has a former Deputy Permanent Secretry as its chairman and an ex-Senior District Commissioner among its members.

24   Cf. Zambia, where Bratton's study of ward development committees in Kasama revealed that 'subsistence peasants were not well represented; relatively well-to-do elements had grasped WDC membership'. See Bratton, M. *The Local Politics of Rural Development. Peasant and Party-State in Zambia* (Hanover, New Hampshire: University Press of New England, 1980) p. 93.

25   *Report of the Presidential Commission on Economic Opportunities* (Gaborone: Government Printer, 1982), recommendation 10.09.

26   Malcolm Odell argues that the kgotla is 'the *only* present-day local government institution which is not an artificial creation'; it is 'the one indispensable unit without which no viable local government structure can be built in Botswana'. He urges that kgotlas should be given 'meaningful decision-making powers'. See Odell, M. J. Jr., 'Local Government: Traditional and Modern Roles of the Village Kgotla', in Picard, *The Evolution jof Modern Botswana*, p. 63.

27   This point was made by Professor Apolo R. Nsibambi in one of his responses to a comment made on his paper.

28   Grant, S. and Egner, B. 'The Private Press and Democracy' in this volume.

37 Democracy in Botswana: an outsider's view

Bernhard Weimer

37.1 INTRODUCTION

Based on the papers and discussion presented thus far in this volume I will make a series of four observations. These observations deal with the meaning of democracy as an idea, the extent of success of democracy in Botswana, potential threats to Botswana's democracy, and improvements that should be considered in the present system.

37.2 ON THE MEANING OF DEMOCRACY

Unless we — maybe idealistically — define democracy as the quest for a decent living or a life of harmony, we would have to concede that democracy is not an all-embracing concept of order which can be equated with civilization *per se*. Too many a war has been fought in the name of democracy, and too many undemocratic and repressive regimes and movements have been supported by self-appointed guardians of democracy.

From its very beginning in Greece until today democracy has always entailed the periodic exclusion of larger or smaller sections of the population from participation. Democracy in ancient Athens does not differ substantially from democracy in contemporary South Africa in that both exclude the majority of their respective populations from political decision-making. In my own country, Germany, it is less than a hundred years ago that the Social Democratic Party succeeded in extending the franchise to women.

Having dealt with the structural limitations of democracy, I would, however, argue democracy in the broad sense and with the qualifications put forward by Professor Crick and other distinguished speakers is a worthwhile objective for any society to pursue. I agree with Ms Somolekae, who suggested that the democratic process is essentially the broadening of the franchise and the increasing participation of all sections of society in decentralized decision-making.

37.3 THE SUCCESS OF BOTSWANA'S DEMOCRACY

Botswana's democracy has been an exceptional success story, on four accounts. First, Botswana is one of the few African countries to sustain a prolonged period of political liberty. This freedom includes a genuine multiparty system, fair elections, a free private press in more or less peaceful 'coexistence' with the government media, and a good human rights record.

If the democratic spirit in this country had needed any additional proof, the frank dialogue of this symposium is clear evidence. It is exceptional in an African context that persons from government and opposition parties, the bureaucracy, the university, and the general public can openly discuss issues, which are sometimes highly contentious, but at the same time be respectful of each other. This is possible in only a few countries. I am afraid that even my own Bavaria caanot be so described.

Second, Botswana's democracy is eceptional in that its founders, namely Sir Seretse Khama, Motsamai Mpho, Philip Matante and the others had the courage to choose a 'maximalist perspective'. Such a perspective on democracy not only grants political liberty but sees the realization of such democratic ends as of equal importance with economic development. In contrast, the 'minimalist approach' means that growth of the economy comes first and then political liberty.

The courage of choosing a maximalist strategy needs to be underlined in view of the fact that the 'planting of a delicate seed of democracy' in Botswana during the sixties took place amidst an uncondusive if not outright hostile regional and international climate, both in economic and political terms.

Third, Botswana is exceptional in that unlike other British former colonies at independence, it neither had a developed state (in terms of bureaucracy and military) nor a developed economy. As Dr Molutsi states, it was 'a rather prosperous post-independence economy that has created the basis of the emergence of a government bureaucracy' which increasingly took charge of the policy-making process within the ruling class or the 'state-class-alliance', as I would prefer the ruling class to be labelled.

Fourth, Botswana's liberal democracy is exceptional in that it has been stable over the past 20 years. The reasons for this stability have been identified at various points in this volume.

One factor has been the inclusive character of Tswana political culture even before colonialism. As Drs Murray and Datta point out, the tribal government often accorded economic, social and political rights to foreigners who thus were able to become equal to Tswana commoners. I wish that such a process of adaption and integration could nowadays take place in some countries of Europe. Mention should also be made of the language of kgotla politics, which Kgosi Seepapitso identified in his paper, that is a language of competence, confidence, dignity and mutual respect which is still prevalent today. I would call it a 'language of continuity' rather than a 'language of disjunction'.

Aslo contributing to stability is the 'state-class alliance' which as Dr Molutsi points out has not changed much. In his own class analysis, the Honourable Minister Butale, suggested that 'the ruling class might be made up of cattle owners and foreign business interests'. This 'alliance of cattle and diamonds' bears some analogy to the 'alliance of maize and gold' in South Africa from the twenties to the forties, which despite racial segregation can be considered the most stable period in South Africa's recent history.

Another factor which has leant stability to Botswana's democracy is the political leadership's determination to maintain a pragmatic economic and political relationship with South Africa which has not jeopardized Botswana's relations with its black African neighbours. The result is that neither side in southern Africa's racial struggle has attempted to destabilize Botswana. I would like to refer to this phenomenon as 'the art of the possible'.

37.4 THREATS TO BOTSWANA'S DEMOCRACY

A number of factors of instability could undermine democratic success. They may operate individually or in combination. Most prominent is an exceedingly strong bureaucracy coupled with the overhwelming importance of planning in the economic life of the country. In this context I would like to recall the words of the Hon. Minister Butale, 'We run a planned economy; we cannot allow the politicians to disrupt the plan'. The general question which arises is: How do you handle failure of the plan or particular polices? In the case of the Soviet Union, where to this point bureaucracy and planning have dominated government decision-making, failures are not easily admitted or debated, and those responsible are often not taken to task. Glasnost and perestroika mean reassertion of the primacy of politics over bureaucracy and planning. They mean public discussion of policy failures, and choosing new policies, both in the domestic and foreign policy fields.

A related factor which threatens Botswana's democracy is the abuse of power by top officials. As Mr Moesi of BDC noted in discussing the papers on the press, this is a 'natural tendency of any government' and, I might add, particularly any government which has stayed in power for a very long time. If a democratically elected government deliberately and continuously infringes upon civil liberties of its citizens, such as the right to unhindered postal communications and freedom to travel, this would rightly be considered as a serious onslaught on democratic principles and rules.

Also potentially destabilizing could be a widening of the cleavage within the state-class alliance rather than conflicts between the rulers and the ruled. I am not saying that such rifts and conflict are imminent in Botswana. However, if I observe things correctly, then some shifts in the relative political and economic weight of some segments of the state-class alliance are identifiable. In this context I should also say that in many African countries it is the conflicts within the 'ruling class', which give rise to military coups. This is why in democratic Botswana the framework should be known within which the military operates and what its role is in furthering and strengthening democracy here. The organizers of this symposium would have been well advised to extend an invitation to the army − as well as the police force − to participate in our deliberations.

Democracy in Botswana could face a threat from a resurgence of tribal institutions and chiefs as leaders in both the political and social (i.e. visible) or the spiritual (i.e. invisible) hierarchy. Such a tendency can be observed in many African countries, notably Guinea (Conakry) and Mozambique, which have experienced serious economic, social, ecological and political crises. It also is possible that excessive attention to material wealth and material development and neglect of the emotional and spiritual costs of development may be contributing to a resurgence of the 'traditional' functions of the dikgosi and tribal institutions. What would happen, if the people preferred to rally behind their 'traditional' leaders rather than their elected representatives?

37.5 SOME RECOMMENDATIONS

Both parliament and extra-parliamentary democratic activity could and indeed should be strengthened. Both parliament and government need an independent research capacity for domestic and regional affairs. The findings from this research should appear not only in English, but also in Setswana. Alternatively, research structures especially within the University of Botswana might be better geared towards the needs of parliamentarians and parliament as a whole.

A basic problem that needs to be addressed is the infringement of government on the interests and rights of citizens. One way to deal with this would be the institutionalization of parliamentary commissions of inquiry. Such commissions could be composed of members of all parties. Along the same lines, parliament could appoint a prominent person or one of its own members to monitor and publicise abuses of state power within various policy areas. In my country for example both state and federal governments have these one-person commissions to monitor infringement by the state data and information networks on individual persons as well as on civil liberties. They report to parliament and the general public. Still another means of dealing with abuse of state power is establishment of the institution of ombudsman as an advocate for the causes of various minorities.

Relative to the extra-parliamentary sphere, I fully endorse the statement of Gobe Matenge who, when opening this conference said, that 'continuous and free public debate outside the political structures is necessary to promote democracy in Botswana'. This means that there is a need for the increasing empowerment of women's organizations, environmental groups, and civic associations at all levels of society from the local to the national. On the same score I would fully endorse the call made yesterday for the scaling down of the weight of government media in favour of the private press.

37.6 CONCLUSION

At the beginning of this conference, Professor Bernard Crick stressed the importance of communication for life in general and democratic life in particular. Breakdown of communication is synonymous in many societies with severe crises and conflict. In my own view, in Southern Africa, apartheid, by the very meaning of the word and by its history in terms of policies, is synonymous with separation, non-communication and hence is the cause of crisis and conflict in South Africa itself as well as the region as a whole. For the sake of an alternative to apartheid and the conflict it generates and for the sake of peace and democracy in Botswana and in Southern Africa, may I appeal to women and men in Botswana, to all political parties, to government and the bureaucracy to continue courageously with the good practice of communicating with each other in the democratic spirit and in the 'language of continuity' of kgotla politics, which we all have enjoyed during this symposium.

DISCUSSION

Dr Maripe (Leader BPP) agreed with the speakers in their cautious praise of Botswana's democracy and noted that four important developments were necessary to consolidate democracy in this country. These were:
a)   giving more freedom and liberty to the unions;
b)   encouragement of the formation of effective interest groups;
c)   a new and more accommodating policy on ethnic relations and activities; and
d)   development and use of indigenous languages in schools.

Mr P. Kedikilwe (Minister of Presidential Affairs) thanked the speakers and highlighted the challenges of the future as:
a)   External security resulting from regional instability created by South Africa;
b)   Internal jealousies and conflicts related to poverty, underemployment and rapid urban growth without adequate housing and proper education;
c)   Continued dependence on minerals as a major source of revenue; and
d)   Consolidation of the electoral system.

Mr Kedikilwe said Botswana's political parties should jointly work hard to come up with an unanimous electoral system and consolidated democratic institutions.
    Professor Nsibambi said Botswana is no doubt an island of democracy. The question however is for how long can this continue? He called on Botswana leaders to condemn other autocratic African regimes which he said were not different from South Africa. He also appreciated Botswana's commitment to the liberation struggle in Southern Africa and said that this must continue. He said he felt that in discussing Botswana's democracy not enough tribute was paid to the founding fathers of this nation.
    Mr Tlhomelang thanked the organizers of the symposium for providing the forum to discuss issues of critical importance to the future of the country and hoped that this will continue to be provided.
    Mr Mongwa (BPP) thanked presenters for discussing Botswana as a democracy but expressed concern that issues relating to internal security were not adequately treated in this symposium. He suggested that more legislation should be promulgated to protect the country against external and internal enemies.
    Professor Rubadiri (Education, University of Botswana) praised Botswana for her aptness. He said as an expatriate he felt at home living in Botswana. Botswana,

he said, opened her social and physical borders to outsiders and this has turned out to be her strength. He urged Botswana to export their kindness to all Africa.

Mr Kwele was grateful that Botswana has not allowed itself to be a victim of superpower politics out of which the greatest loser is an ordinary citizen.

Mr Sikwane (BNF) warned that unless the issue of ethnic or minority groups is seriously discussed in an all-party conference, then Botswana's democracy is in serious danger in the long term.

Summing up his contribution Professor Sklar said one encouraging point about Botswana is that the state is not an enemy of democracy as in many developing countries.

In his turn, Professor Nnoli said democracy is too important a human value to be left to politicians, academics or government alone. It must be discussed by all members of society. This point was stressed by both Dr Maripe and Professor Tordoff who called for representative, progressive interest groups, a free press and a strong labour movement. Dr Weimer on the other hand stressed the point made earlier by Mr Kedikilwe that political parties need to work together more closely in order to evolve political rules based on consensus.

SECTION XVII
HOW CAN BOTSWANA IMPROVE ITS DEMOCRACY?

A discussion of the symposium

In the last session of the symposium, participants made a series of suggestions for the improvement of Botswana's democracy. These suggestions are listed below with the name of the person presenting the idea in parentheses. The order of these various proposals in no way indicates their importance to members of the symposium. They are a listing of possible issues to place on the national agenda for further discussion. This list should not be taken as a complete agenda on the concerns of those at the symposium, since the time available was very short.

1   Government should develop a policy relative to which military affairs issues should fall within the public domain (including parliamentary accountability) and which should not (Enger).
2   The Trade Union and Employer's Organizations Act of 1983 should be reviewed so as to remove those restrictions which prevent the unions from being autonomous from government (Mbonini).
3   Government should ratify the covenants of the International Labour Organization (Mbonini).
4   The media should make a better attempt to cover activities of the labour movement (Mbonini).
5   The restrictions on demonstrations and boycotts on students at the University of Botswana should be unconditionally scrapped (Miller).
6   Politicians who are rejected at elections should not be subsequently nominated for councils or parliament (Somolekae).
7   Tswana women who marry foreign males should be allowed to pass Botswana citizenship to their children (Somolekae).
8   Parliament should entrench in the constitution the political rights elaborated therein (Molokomme).
9   Parliament should review the derogations on political rights in the constitution for the purpose of limiting the substance and number of such derogations (Molokomme).

10   Parliament should establish an independent law reform committee with the capacity to formulate a clear policy on law reform (Molokomme).
11   A legal aid system should be established for indigent citizens so that they can have equal access to the court system (Molokomme).
12   MPs should have a retirement age (Phorano).
13   Parliament should have the power to impeach the president (Phorano and Sethantsho).
14   There should be direct election of the president (Phorano).
15   Teachers organizations like the Botswana Federation of Secondary School Teachers Association should be recognized by the government (Phorano).
16   Government should abolish all reference to tribes in public discussions (Gontse).
17   Parliament should be an independent institution from the Office of President and should be provided with sufficient skilled personnel to undertake the necessary research on policy and legislative questions (Mokgema).
18   Local governments should be given more independence in appropriating funds for their budgets, especially with respect to development projects (Mokgema).
19   The Delimitation Committee should meet more often than every ten years because of the rapid growth of the population (Giddie).
20   Political parties should reveal all sources of funds (Grant).
21   A symposium on Democracy in Botswana should be held on a regular basis to review the extent of development that has taken place (Nasha).
22   An all-party caucus should be convened to review issues related to the rights of minority groups (Sethantsho).
23   International funding of political parties should be made on a non-partisan basis (Sethantsho).
24   Government should fund political campaigns (Sethantsho).
25   The President of Botswana should be subject to questioning in parliament (Sethantsho).
26   Radio Botswana should be made a parastatal so that it would have more freedom from government (Sethantsho).
27   The tenure of the president should be limited to two terms of five years each (Motlhabane).